Weird Europe

Also by Kristan Lawson and Anneli Rufus
Europe Off the Wall
America Off the Wall: The West Coast
Goddess Sites: Europe

Also by Kristan Lawson
The Rules of Speed Chess

Also by Anneli Rufus
The World Holiday Book

Weird Europe

A Guide to Bizarre, Macabre, and Just Plain Weird Sights

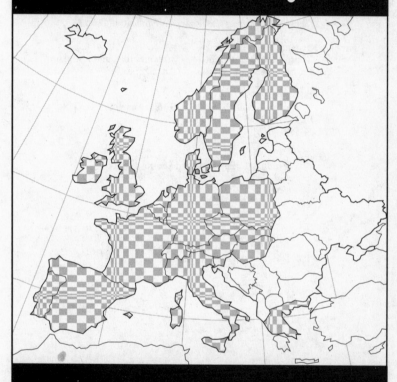

Kristan Lawson and Anneli Rufus

 St. Martin's Griffin New York

Library of Congress Cataloging-in-Publication Data

Lawson, Kristan.
    Weird Europe : a guide to bizarre, macabre, and just plain
weird sights / Kristan Lawson and Anneli S. Rufus.
      p. cm.
    ISBN 0-312-19873-6
    1. Europe—Guidebooks. I. Rufus, Anneli S. II. Title.
D909.L34 1999
914.04'559—dc21   99-10047
                                  CIP

Production Editor: David Stanford Burr

10 9 8 7 6 5

Acknowledgments

The authors would like to thank
Frank Key; Heidi, Sam and Edward
Byrne; Jenna and Chris Pascoe;
Fabian Hahn and Stefan for putting
us up and putting up with us;
Natalie Weinstein and David Kaim
for holding down the fort; and our
editor, Greg Cohn.

Photo Credits

Contents

Preface

Paris is what—the Eiffel Tower? It's also sewer tours, St. Catherine's corpse and the Museum of Counterfeits. Rome is the Trevi Fountain? Yeah. But it's also the Museum of the Souls of the Dead. Under Greece's ruined temples are miles and miles of spooky caves. And it could be argued that you haven't really *seen* Sweden if you've never slept in a hotel made entirely out of snow.

Frolic in a Pippi Longstocking theme park. Tour a chapel built entirely of human skulls. Play at being a Viking, a leper, a caveman, a Celt. Visit Peter Sellers' memorial rosebush. Then prospect for emeralds before lunch.

Another Europe reverberates just under the surface of all those cafés and cathedrals you've seen in pictures. It's *weird* Europe, a wonderland of the macabre, the shocking, the irresistible, the strangely gorgeous. This is where you'll see mummified monks, shin-kicking tournaments and the world's largest wallpaper collection. This is where you'll glide along underground lakes, get lost in mazes and watch mosquitoes play chess. It's where you'll see Bavarians impersonating cowboys.

These attractions weren't designed with you, the foreign tourist, in mind. Most of them sprang from someone's passion, some obsession, some spasm that couldn't be suppressed. How else to explain the Dutchman who covered the walls, ceilings, floors and furniture of his home in shiny cigarbands? Or the French cemetery worker who mosaicked *his* entire house with bits of shattered plates? Now their oeuvres await you. And how do you explain museums devoted to smuggling, to spying, to artworks so small they can only be seen through a microscope? You won't find Lund's Nose Collection in other books. You won't find the Undertakers' Museum in a picture postcard showing Vienna's grandeur.

This isn't the Europe you studied in school. It's the one where revelers in Renaissance garb pelt each other with oranges. It's the one where Siamese twins, if you know where to look, are preserved under glass. This Europe is minding its own business, waiting for you to match its obsessions with your own.

In this book you'll find pictorial keys guiding you to attractions in various categories—Underground Places, Outrageous Art, Vulgarities, and so on. But "weird" has so many meanings, from offbeat to hilarious to tragic. Medical exhibits showing what can go wrong with the human body and mind are definitely weird. But so are animatronic bears.

So go for it—scratch the surface.

Key to Symbols

 CEMETERIES, OSSUARIES AND CORPSES
Permanent lodgings for the bodies and bones of the dead

 CRIME AND PUNISHMENT
Bad guys, what they do, and where they end up

 ECCENTRIC ARCHITECTURE
Follies, castles, amazing homes and other crazily designed buildings

 EXTRAORDINARY EXHIBITS AND COLLECTIONS
Privately owned collections, or odd exhibits in otherwise ordinary museums

 FESTIVALS
Folkloric rites, revels and assorted merrymaking

 LIONS AND TIGERS AND BEARS
Animals of all sorts

 MEDICAL EXHIBITS
Anatomical oddities and medical marvels

 MINIATURES
Lilliputian creations

 MUSEUMS
Strange and unusual museums of every kind

 NATURAL WONDERS
Mother Nature's curiosities and conundrums

 ODD BUSINESSES
Hotels, restaurants and stores that defy expectations

 OUTRAGEOUS ART
Unconventional minds expressing themselves unconventionally

 QUIRKY GARDENS
Topiary, mazes and adventurous horticulture

 RELIGIOUS CURIOSITIES
Unusual churches, saintly relics and holy ephemera

 REMNANTS OF OPPRESSION
Vestiges of Europe's political nightmares, from Nazism to Communism

 STRANGE TOWNS
Cities and locales that are fundamentally unusual by their very nature

 THEME PARKS
From the extravagant to the ridiculous, amusement parks in all their glory

 TWISTED HISTORY
It's more fun the second time around

 UNCLASSIFIABLE
Sites and attractions so strange that they defy categorization

 UNDERGROUND PLACES
Caves, tunnels, catacombs, sewers and subterranean structures

 VULGARITIES
Kitschy decor and attempts at entertainment

How to Use This Book

The listings in each country are organized alphabetically by city name. France, Great Britain and Italy are so exceptionally weird that they have been divided up into regions; the entries appear in alphabetical order within each region.

Next to each listing you'll find one or two eye-catching icons that tell you at a glance what type of attraction it is—whether it's eccentric architecture, a religious curiosity or any of nineteen other categories. At the back of the book are special indexes that list all the attractions in each of these categories. Thus, if you're simply in love with quirky gardens or ossuaries, you can find a handy list of all your favorites without having to scan the entire book for the words "topiary" or "pelvis."

The Calendar of Weird Festivals that precedes the indexes makes it easy for you to schedule into your itinerary one or more of Europe's strangest celebrations.

Weird Europe won't tell you the train schedules or the address of the nearest cheap hotel: it's purely a guide to the strange and bizarre. So you should also consider bringing a standard guide to help with the nuts and bolts or where to eat and sleep.

All the information herein was correct at the time of this writing; be aware, however, that prices go up and opening hours change with alarming frequency. As with any guidebook, be prepared for the unexpected.

Comments or suggestions? Send them to:
Weird Europe
P.O. Box 295
Berkeley, CA 94701

ANDORRA

Don't miss:

★★★★ Ordino: Museum of
Miniatures   1

Engordany

2 km northeast of Andorra la Vella

ANDORRA MODEL MUSEUM
(Museu de Maquetes d'Andorra)

*Avinguda del Pessebre 16, near
the intersection of Avinguda de
les Escoles. Open Monday–
Saturday, 10am–1pm and
4–8pm. Admission: free.
Phone: 86 15 06.*

Proving once again this pocket-size country's passion for perpetual shrinkage, the museum houses immaculately detailed scale models of the principality's most notable buildings. Here are stark Romanesque churches, including Sant Miquel d'Engolasters and Sant Climent de Pal, no bigger than toaster ovens. Rendered in tiny brown stones and splinters of wood, all but a few are the work of Spanish painter and model-artist Josep Colomé, who died in 1995 and whose son now carries on the tradition.

Ordino

7 km north of Andorra la Vella

MUSEUM OF MINIATURES
(Museu de la Miniatura)

*In the Coma Building (Edifici
Coma). Open Monday–Saturday, 9:30am–1:30pm and
3:30–7pm. Admission: 400 ptas;
children 6–12, 200 ptas; children
under 6, free. Phone: 83 83 38.*

What better place than a teensy-weensy country for this collection of teensy-weensy artworks? Created by miniaturist Nicolaï Siadristy, they're hardly perceptible to the naked eye and can only be viewed through microscopes, which are conveniently arranged above each of the sculptures. These include not just one camel but a whole caravan's worth—complete with pyramid and palm trees—lodged inside the eye of a needle. Also here is a minuscule human figure walking on a coiled gold thread 400 times thinner than a human hair. An audiovisual program tells about the artist, who is normal-sized, and his fascination with the small.

Ordino

7 km north of Andorra la Vella

ST. GEORGE ICON MUSEUM
(Museu Iconogràfic Sant Jordi)

*In the Maragda Building (Edifici
Maragda). Open Monday–Saturday, 10am–2pm and 3–7pm. Admission: 400 ptas; children 6–12,
200 ptas; children under 6, free.
Phone: 83 83 76.*

The vicious-dragon-slaying patron saint of Catalonia lends his name to this collection spanning three centuries of Russian and Byzantine religious art. An entire room is dedicated to pictures of the Virgin Mary, another to George himself, who mercilessly gores beast after beast against lush golden skies. An audio-visual room screens images of monasteries, cathedrals and yet more icons, as well as Orthodox rituals— a surefire pick-me-up for anyone trapped in Andorra yet homesick for the Ukraine.

AUSTRIA

Don't miss:

Altaussee

Just east of Hallstatt

SALT MINE
(Salzbergwerk)

On the hillside west of town; signs point the way. Open April–October, daily, 10am–4pm; November–March, daily, 2pm by request. Admission: 135 AS; children, 65 AS. Phone: 03622/71 332-51.

Deep in the mine, a chapel dedicated to the miners' patron saint, Barbara, glows softly. In electric candlelight, the framed painting of the saint and tall golden statues flanking the altar stand in contrast to outcroppings of rough rock surrounding the shrine. The tour reveals how precious artworks were hidden in the salt mine's treasure vaults to keep them safe during WWII, and lets you explore the stage that flanks a silvery underground salt lake.

Bad Ischl

57 km east of Salzburg

THE SALT BARON'S MINE
(Das Bergwerk des Salzbarons)

Just southeast of town in the village of Perneck; buses run from the Bad Ischl train station. Open May–September; call for tour times. Admission: 135 AS; children, 65 AS. Phone: 06132/23 948-31.

With its little lamp shining, a mine train carries passengers far into the depths of the mountain, where narrow passageways are ribbed with beams and illuminated for a dramatic light-and-shadow effect. Shoot down wooden slides to see an underground salt lake and hear stories of how 19th-century nobles made themselves even richer with the help of humble salt.

Bärnbach

35 km west of Graz

CHURCH OF ST. BARBARA
(St. Barbara-Kirche)

 Bärnbach can be reached by train from Graz: from the Bärnbach train station, walk 20 minutes into the commercial center; follow the onion dome to find the church. Open daily. Admission: free. Phone: 03142/62581.

The eccentric artist Friedensreich Hundertwasser got inspired when a friend who lived in Bärnbach told him the old village church could use a facelift. Completed in 1988, the updated edifice sports a roof with huge turquoise polka dots on red tile; sinuous multicolored mosaics and tilework snaking up the clock tower; patchworky pastel paintwork on the walls; and freestanding structures surrounding it that look like stacks of gargantuan beads. It's topped off with Hundertwasser's trademark—an onion dome—and an obligatory cross, though a set of gateways in the garden honors other world religions. Tiled images on the gateways represent Taoism, Buddhism, Confucianism, Shinto, Judaism, Islam, and African and Oceanic spirituality. Inside, the church is deliberately dull by comparison. The designer decided the outside was to look at, but the inside was for prayer.

ST. BARBARA-KIRCHE—BÄRNBACH

Dorfgastein

85 km south of Salzburg

CHURCH INSIDE A CAVE
(Entrische Kirche)

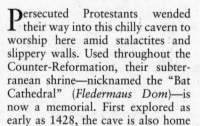 *In the Naturhöhle, off the B167 road at Klammstein, midway between Lend and Dorfgastein. Open April–June and September, Tuesday–Sunday, tours given at 11am, noon, 2 and 3pm; July–August, daily, tours at 10 and 11am, noon, 2, 3, 4 and 5pm. Admission: 90 AS; children, 50 AS. Phone: 06433/7695.*

Persecuted Protestants wended their way into this chilly cavern to worship here amid stalactites and slippery walls. Used throughout the Counter-Reformation, their subterranean shrine—nicknamed the "Bat Cathedral" (*Fledermaus Dom*)—is now a memorial. First explored as early as 1428, the cave is also home to underground lakes.

Gföhl

17 km northwest of Krems

WILD WEST PARK
(Winnetou-Spiel Gföhl)

  Just northeast of Gföhl off the road to the village of Mittelberg. Open Saturdays and Sundays in July and August; call for show-times. Admission: 200 AS, children 100 AS; for special shows 250 AS; children 150 AS. Phone: 02716/6401 or 0663/9208349.

The clatter of hoofbeats and the flap of fringed white buckskin transform the Austrian countryside into the Wild Western *Prärie* every summer, as Teutons and Apaches whoop it up together. Winnetou and Old Shatterhand are the stars among this cast of performers, who enthusiastically reenact rootin' tootin' adventures complete with bandits, feathered headbands, teepees, canoes and burning buildings.

6am–10pm; Saturday–Sunday, 9am–1pm and 4–8pm. Admission: free. Phone: 0316/ 48 24 82.

Arnold! The larger-than-life, super-human robot known as Arnold Schwarzenegger started here in Graz as a nerdy schoolboy. A few years ago he returned, and for pocket change built a state-of-the-art sports stadium and named it after himself. The gym at the back of the stadium features a petite but touching museum devoted to Arnold's early years in Graz. See the Terminator as a scrawny kid, then a budding young weightlifter, then winning the 1965 Mr. Austria championship, then launching on the path to world domination in his *Pumping Iron* phase. By the end he's chumming around with Gorbachev and other luminaries. Also artfully arranged here are positively antique weight sets and exercise equipment that Arnold himself once used to build those arms of steel, back in the early '60s. As you leave, say to the exercise addicts huffing away on the nearby *Stairmeisters,* "I'll be back."

Graz

ARNOLD SCHWARZENEGGER MUSEUM

 Located at Stadionplatz 1 in Arnold Schwarzenegger Stadium, inside the Fitness Paradies health club; enter stadium on Liebenauer Hauptstrasse, walk through parking lot and past a cafe to the health club. To reach the stadium, take Tram 14 from central Graz, south to the end of the line. Open Monday–Friday,

Hallein

15 km south of Salzburg

SALT MINES
(Salzbergwerk)

 At Bad Dürrnberg, in the mountains above Hallein. Open April–October, daily, 9am–5pm; November–March, daily, 11am–3pm. Admission: 180 AS; children, 90 AS; children under 4 not admitted. Phone: (0) 6245/85285-15 or 82121.

Yes, it's back to the salt mines—in this case the world's oldest. Ride a mine train through deep tunnels to the heart of the mountain, where miner-guides explain the science, lore and 3,000-year history of the "white gold" that lent its name to the Salzkammergut region. Glide across a mirror-still underground lake in a flat boat and explore a 3D exhibition in which mannequins demonstrate salt-mining methods used in Celtic times. Slide down slick wooden chutes on your derriere at top speed.

73 km southeast of Salzburg

BONEHOUSE
(Beinhaus)

Kircherweg 40, behind the Catholic church on the hill at the northern edge of town. Open daily, 10am–6pm. Admission: 10 AS; children, 5 AS. Phone: 06134/8279 or 06134/8208.

Because the graveyard has limited space, skeletons are traditionally unearthed to make room for the newly dead. So over 1,000 human skulls dating back hundreds of years are neatly stacked in a quaint little chapel. In keeping with charnel-house etiquette, each skull is carefully painted with floral designs, crosses, the name of its onetime occupant and the year of his or her demise, along with other details. You can trace the names and see whole families' skulls resting side by side, row by row, generation after generation. Leg bones and such are packed tightly underneath like cordwood.

73 km southeast of Salzburg

SALT MINE
(Salzbergwerk)

The entrance to the mine is on the hill overlooking the city; follow the signs to the south side of town to the cable-car station, which will take you up to the mine. Open May and mid-September–October, daily, 9:20am–3pm; June–mid-September, daily, 9am–4:30pm. Admission: 135 AS; children 4–15, 65 AS. Phone: 06134/8251/46.

Journey back in time to the year 1000 B.C.E.—on your butt. Throw dignity to the winds as you plummet down smoothly polished wooden slides, just like real miners do, to explore one of the world's oldest salt mines. Visit a subterranean salt lake and probe evidence of prehistoric visitors before riding the mine train back out into the world.

17 km southwest of Vienna

LAKE IN A CAVE
(Seegrotte)

On the road leading to the city of Giesshübl, just east of Hinterbrühl, next to the A21. Open daily, April–October, 9am–noon and 1–5pm; November–March, 9am–noon and 1–3pm. Admission: 55 AS; children 4–14, 30 AS. Phone: 0 22 36/263 64.

Europe may have more underground lakes than you ever suspected, but this one is the biggest. Walk through a labyrinthine network of underground corridors to reach the lake, then climb into a motorboat. Measuring 56,000 square feet, the glassy waters glow greenish-blue, eerily reflecting the cave's low, rocky ceiling and narrow archways. And who would have thought that the world's first jet fighter was built at this very spot? Don't miss the candlelit underground shrine.

of human freaks and bloody accident victims; sinister mechanical toys; a painting of the real Count Dracula; little suits of armor for children; and creations so intricate their makers may have gone insane putting them together. A shell grotto sprouts sea monsters, mermaids and a coral crucified Christ. Stuffed sharks dangle on chains from the ceiling.

Innsbruck

SCHLOSS AMBRAS' CHAMBER OF WONDERS
(Schloss Ambras Kunst- und Wunderkammer)

Schlosstrasse 20, southeast of downtown: Take tram 3 from the station or bus 6 ("Tummelplatz-Schloss Ambras"); shuttle buses also run back and forth from the castle to Maria-Theresien-Strasse/Altes Landhaus in Innsbruck, once a day in winter and more frequently in summer. Open April–October, Wednesday–Monday, 10am–5pm; December–March, Wednesday–Monday, 2–5pm. Admission: 60 AS; students and children, 30 AS. Phone: 0512/341 21 54 or 348 4 46.

Popular in the 16th century, lavish "chambers of wonders" mingled artworks with natural curiosities to reflect the world's strangeness. Ranging from cookbooks to sandals to abnormal antlers, Archduke Ferdinand's collection includes poison made from goat intestines; portraits

Kaag

5 km north of Edelsbach, which is just northwest of Feldbach

FRANZ GSELLMANN'S WORLD MACHINE
(Weltmaschine)

House 14 in the village of Kaag: to reach Kaag from Graz, take the train to Feldbach, and from there a bus to Edelsbach; from Edelsbach follow the signs pointing to the Weltmaschine (about a one-hour walk). Alternatively, you can get off the train two stops before Feldbach at Rohr; head up to the main road from the train station and look for the Weltmaschine sign, then walk over the hill to Kaag (one and a half hours). Or simply take a taxi from Feldbach. Open Wednesday–Monday, 9am–6pm; the proprietors usually turn on parts of the Weltmaschine whenever visitors arrive, so stick around until you get to see it in action. Admission: voluntary donation. Phone: 0 31 15/29 83.

Without the slightest mechanical or artistic training, a humble farmer named Franz Gsellmann spent 23 years creating a mind-boggling masterpiece of eccentricity, a contraption that he dubbed the *Weltmaschine*. Filling a large room at the Gsellmann farm, this whirling, spinning, frenzied machine is unlike anything else you are likely to see in this life—or the next. Amid an overwhelming concatenation of red, blue and green gears, wheels and drive shafts, you will find a xylophone, toy gondolas, hula hoops, bells, metronomes, Christmas lights, a roulette wheel, fans, chains, electric candelabras, a plastic Mary and Jesus, tiny boats, cages, clocks, bejewelled crowns, crystal decanters, miniature windmills, an iron rooster, a spaceship, model atoms, a barometer, an oxygen tank and much more, all interconnected into one vast, incomprehensible mechanism. The crucial question has always remained unanswered: What exactly does the *Weltmaschine do*? Is it a perpetual motion machine? Does it make the world go around? Gsellmann died in 1981 without ever fully revealing its intended function, though devotees think it reveals the inner workings of the human soul. See for yourself.

Klagenfurt

Near the Slovenian border, 130 km southwest of Graz

MINIMUNDUS

Villacher Str. 241, west of the center, just across the park from the eastern shore of the Wörthersee. Open April and October, daily, 9am–5pm; May–June and September, daily, 9am–6pm; July–August, Sunday–Tuesday and Thursday–Friday, 9am–7pm, Wednesday and Saturday,

9am–9pm. Admission: 90 AS; children, 30 AS. Phone: 0463/ 21 1 94 0.

But isn't that the Sydney Opera House? *Jawohl*, and just an alpenhorn's throw away from the Eiffel Tower. While it would take a long time to walk around the *real* world, it's a snap here, where over 170 famous buildings are reproduced on a 1:25 scale. Model ships glide up and down waterways, and model railroads chug along their tracks in the shadow of miniature castles and cathedrals. The shrunken landmarks, lovingly shaped and tinted down to the last minuscule brick, make the normal-sized plants growing in flowerbeds alongside them look like grotesque triffids.

Mauthausen

25 km east of Linz

CONCENTRATION-CAMP MEMORIAL AND MUSEUM
(Öffentliches Denkmal und Museum)

Just north of Mauthausen village. Open April–September, daily, 8am–6pm (last entry, 5pm); October–December 15 and February–March, daily, 8am–4pm (last entry, 3pm). Admission: 25 AS; students and children, 10 AS; former inmates, free. Phone: 07238 / 2269.

Sculptures evoking twisted menorahs, emaciated prisoners and giant barbed wire punctuate the unearthly stillness of this former death camp. Many of the stark buildings, guard towers and crematoria stand completely intact. Prisoners' uniforms are among the museum's displays, as well as hundreds of gut-wrenching photographs taken during the war. A documentary about the camp screens in several different languages.

54 km east of Graz

WITCHCRAFT MUSEUM
(Hexen-Museum)

In the castle, on the hill overlooking the town. Open April–October, daily, 9am–5pm. Admission: 85 AS; students and children, 50 AS. Phone: 03153/ 8346.

Peggau

20 km north of Graz

LURGROTTE PEGGAU

The cave's entrance is about 1 kilometer northeast of Peggau: From Graz, take a train to the Peggau-Deutschfeistritz stop; exit the station, go left, and walk for about 10 minutes until you come to the Lurgrotte sign. Open April–October, daily, 9am–4pm. Admission: 60 AS; children 15–18, 45 AS; children under 15, 35 AS; discounts for groups of two or more. Phone: 03127/2580.

Austria's biggest stalactite cave features a stunning variety of weird dripstone formations. A comfortable pathway leads along an underground river past shimmering white stone curtains, fields of needle-sharp stalactites, misshapen blobs called "The Witch's Cleft" and "The Waterfall," spooky half-lit vistas deep into the heart of the earth and a huge phallic column hanging almost to the ground, nicknamed "Prinz." If the tour only whets your appetite for more underground adventure, head down the road to Lurgrotte Semriach, which is in fact just a different entrance to the same long cave which starts at Peggau. The Semriach end is just as spectacular as the Peggau side, but you'll have to buy a separate ticket to get in.

Built around the year 1100 atop a 1,500-foot volcanic cone, the dramatic castle-fortress housing this museum is exactly the sort of place that conjures up legends of medieval magic. The twelve-room collection in its cellar shows how hellishly hard life was for witches, both real and accused, during the castle's heyday. Devices of torture and humiliation include a shame mask and a viciously spiked iron maiden. Also here are life-size dummies demonstrating an accused witch's fateful visit to a courtroom, and artworks showing the abusive nature of exorcism. Three hundred people were executed as witches in this region, but only now, centuries after the fact, does someone tell *their* side of the story.

DWARVES' GARDEN
(Zwerglgarten)

In Mirabell Gardens, in front of Mirabell Castle, near Schwarzstrasse. Visible during daylight hours. Admission: free.

DWARVES' GARDEN — SALZBURG

Bishop Wolf Dietrich built a castle for the mother of his children right in the middle of Salzburg where everyone could see it. And he expressed himself, like so many homeowners, with outdoor sculpture. His ring of larger-than-life stone dwarves, standing under the trees, goes way beyond the concept of garden gnomes. One sculpted dwarf has a hunchback, another a goiter and another has a tumescent lump on his head. Many of them appear to be screaming.

HELLBRUNN PLEASURE CASTLE'S WATER GARDEN
(Lustschloss Hellbrunn Wasserspiele)

Four kilometers south of downtown, off Hellbrunner Allee. Open April and October, daily, 9am–4:30pm; May–June and September, daily, 9am–5:30pm; July–August, daily, 9am–10pm Admission: 70 AS; students and children, 35 AS. Phone: 0662/82 03 72-0, or 0662/82 03 72-16.

You never know when you'll get squirted as you tour the tree-lined avenues, glassy ponds and fairy-tale grottoes of a prince and archbishop whose lavish practical joke has been thrilling and drenching visitors since 1612. Amid this garden's dazzling Renaissance splendor, hidden spigots lurk everywhere. Your first clue is the prince's stone picnic table and chairs—serene enough until the whole ensemble begins to spurt. Meanwhile, stone satyrs pose in the sunshine while water-powered mechanical birds tweet, organs moan and sigh, fountains toss sparkling balls into the air and mechanical figures carouse.

HOUSE OF NATURE
(Haus der Natur)

Museumsplatz 5, on the riverfront, just northwest of the Old Town. Open daily, 9am–5pm. Admission: 55 AS; students and children, 30 AS. Phone: 0662/8426 53.

On the second floor of this comprehensive natural history museum is a helpful exhibit on animal droppings, featuring the summer and winter stools of forest creatures. On the fourth floor is a taxidermed freak collection which includes the ubiquitous two-headed calf, as well as Siamese-twin calves, a three-legged duck and a lamb born without a head. A cyclopic lamb, a volleyball-headed encephalitic giraffe and a four-legged eagle extend the moment even further. Across the room from these are taxidermed cross-breeds, including a liger (lion/tiger) and a swan/goose. Also on this floor, don't miss the models of syphilitic penises, and a framed madonna made of insect parts.

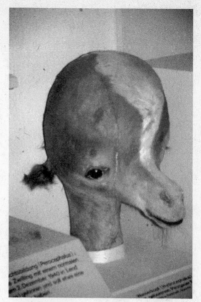

HOUSE OF NATURE—SALZBURG

Vienna

CATACOMBS IN ST. MICHAEL'S CHURCH
(Michaelergruft)

Michaelerplatz, just east of the Hofburg in the First District. Tours given May–November, Monday–Friday, at 11am and 1, 2, 3 and 4pm (tours begin inside the church in the passageway to the right of the entrance). Admission: 40 AS; students, 25 AS; children, 10 AS. Phone: 0222/533 80 00.

Dating back hundreds of years, the rows of corpses in this elegant, mostly 17th-century crypt mutely await you. Some of the dead have been naturally mummified and lie in open-lidded coffins with their hair, clothing and eyelids intact, looking as if they might get up and yawn. Many others are merely skeletons.

Vienna

CATACOMBS IN ST. STEPHEN'S CATHEDRAL
(Katakomben im Wiener Stephansdom)

1 Stephansplatz. Tours offered Monday–Saturday 10, 11 and 11:30am and 2, 2:30, 3:30, 4 and 4:30pm; Sunday at 2, 2:30, 3:30, 4 and 4:30pm. Admission: 40 AS; children, 15 AS. Phone: 0222/515 52-3526 or 3530.

This late-Baroque necropolis, first used in the 14th century and embellished through the next few hundred years, features long, cool corridors lined with the well-packaged dead. The Hapsburgs didn't seem to know that you can't take it with you; their internal organs are stored here, as are ducal corpses galore. Domed ceilings, mosaics, chiseled inscriptions and gleaming floors add to the glamour, while elaborate coffins adorned with cartouches rest neatly behind gratings and in wall niches, and lie about the rooms. Stacked bones fill other chambers.

CIRCUS AND CLOWN MUSEUM

Karmelitergasse 9, in the Second District: Take tram N or 21 to Karmeliterplatz. Open Wednesday, 5:30–7pm; Saturday, 2:30–5pm; Sunday, 10am–noon. Admission: free. Phone: 0222/369 11 11.

Some say the Viennese's abiding love of circuses springs from chronic depression. If you're like most people,

Vienna
Hundertwasser-Mania

Austria's answer to Antonio Gaudí, artist Friedensreich Hundertwasser has become an international cult phenomenon almost overnight. Little known until a short time ago, he is now a sightseeing industry unto himself. His architectural whimsies, bizarre and undulating and outrageously colorful, attract millions of devotees and awestruck gawkers every year.

It all started with the **Hundertwasserhaus**, a block-long municipal housing complex completed in 1985. Sprouting terraces, balconies and a golden onion dome, the house eschews right angles in favor of off-kilter lines and brazen fields of purple, mustard-yellow and grapefruit-pink. The roof sprouts lawns, trees, bushes and meadow flowers. Hundertwasser also designed the **façade** of a modest building nearby, with bulging columns and wild mosaics.

HUNDERTWASSERHAUS — VIENNA

The center of the Hundertwasser Universe is **KunstHausWien**, just a few blocks away. This multipurpose building houses a Hundertwasser museum, a cafe, and a gift shop selling Hundertwasser-designed souvenirs of every sort. But the main attraction is the building itself: Heaving brick floors that make you seasick, a checkerboard façade, multicolored tiles, irregular structures in glass and wood and his trademark abandonment of straight lines in favor of wavy ones.

Across town is his most striking landmark, the **Spittelau District Heating Plant**, visible for miles with its golden sphere and shimmering, colorful smokestack. Yes, it's really a functional heating plant, but it's also a hallucinatory op-art blend of medieval half-timbered farmhouse and Space Age mosque. For total Hundertwasser immersion, take a tour on the colorful Hundertwasser-designed riverboat **Vindobona**, which takes you past many of the landmarks mentioned here.

 Hundertwasserhaus: Kegelgasse 36-38, between Löwengasse and Untere Weissgerberstrasse, in the Third District. Always visible from the outside (but no entry, as it is a private residence).

Hundertwasser façade: Untere Weissgerberstrasse 27.

KunstHausWien: Untere Weissgerberstrasse 13, in the Third District. Open daily, 10am–7pm. Admission: free to wander around the building; to see the museum costs 90 AS for one exhibit or 150 AS for two (students 60 AS and 110 AS); Mondays are half price. Phone: 0222/712 04 91.

Fernwärmewerk Spittelau (heating plant): Spittelauer Lände 45, Ninth District. The best view is from the platform adjacent to the Spittelau U-Bahn station. Always visible. Admission: free.

Hundertwasser boat tours: on the *Vindobona*, leaving from Schwedenbrücke, the bridge crossing the Danube at Schwedenplatz. Tours run April–October, daily, at 11am, 1 and 3pm, and starting July also at 5pm. Tickets: 140 AS. Phone: 0222/ 727 50 222.

SPITTELAU HEATING PLANT—
VIENNA

you'll feel pure dread at the sight of so many red-nosed, baggy-suited, bewigged, funny-hatted mannequins, not to mention toy big tops and clown dolls. Homages to Buffalo Bill, P.T. Barnum and other famous figures abound, including Vienna's own Carl Godlewski, who could jump over the backs of six elephants. Props in the collection include a tiny harmonica that fits inside a matchbox, and—what could be funnier?—a trick violin that shatters at the slightest touch.

CRIMINAL MUSEUM—VIENNA

CLOCK MUSEUM
(Uhrenmuseum)

Schulhof 2 in the First District, a few blocks northwest of Stephansplatz. Open Tuesday–Sunday, 9am–4:30pm. Admission: 50 AS; students and children, 20 AS; children under 6, free. Phone: 0222/533 22 65.

Time stands still—almost—in this museum, where over 3,000 timepieces occupy three stories. Pocket watches are here in profusion, as well as miniature clocks, artistic specimens shaped like boats and animals and fruit, a cathedral clock, sundials, hourglasses, mantel clocks and an astronomical clock whose hand takes 20,904 years to go all the way around. During guided tours, many of the clocks are activated, and the place resounds.

Vienna

CRIMINAL MUSEUM
(Wiener Kriminalmuseum)

Grosse Sperlgasse 24, in the second district: take tram 21 or N to Karmeliterplatz. Open Tuesday–Sunday, 10am–5pm. Admission: 60 AS; students and children, 50 AS. Phone: 0222/214 46 78.

If you ever needed more proof that the Viennese have a fascination with death, look no further. This trip through Austrian history focuses exclusively on murder, execution and everything in between. An impressive collection of actual murder weapons and criminals' tools—hatchets, brass knuckles, scissors, revolvers—competes for space with curiously formal paintings of people being stabbed. Silently eyeing visitors is the mummified skull of a 19th-century thief who was hung on the gallows. Two centuries of bona fide horror are meticulously documented, case by case. You'll meet female serial killers from the 1860s, and one maniac who disposed of bodies in a sausage machine. In chronologically arranged cases you'll see victims' bones and other body parts shattered by anarchist bombs, as well as death masks of executed killers and assassination mementos. The 20th-century section becomes nauseatingly graphic, with large photographs showing blood-soaked victims whose heads have been smashed with hammers. The pornography and prostitution room provides some relief before the final exhibits on the death penalty which cover everything from impaling and boiling alive to execution by guillotine.

Vienna

ELECTROPATHOLOGICAL MUSEUM
(Elektropathologisches Museum)

Gomperzgasse 1–3, near the intersection of Sandleitengasse, west of the center near Kongresspark; take tram 10 or 44. S-Bahn: Hernals. Open by appointment only, for groups of at least 15 people; call ahead to make an appointment or see if you can join a group. Admission free, but each group must pay 500AS for the required tour guide. Phone 0222/489 20 80.

Ever wonder what it would feel like to have a lightning bolt flash from the sky and strike you in the head? Do you crave the sensation of grabbing a high-voltage line with your bare hands while standing in a bucket of water? The Electropathological Museum is the place for you. The hair-raising effects of electricity on the human body are explored in shocking detail. Of special interest are the turn-of-the-century wax models of body parts that have been struck by lightning—the museum was founded by a doctor interested in the medical aspects of that new-

fangled phenomenon called electricity. Elsewhere you'll find taxidermed birds that were found half-barbecued after landing on the wrong wire, clothing and other objects taken off mountaineers struck by lightning, defective electrical appliances and photos of their deadly effects, and even a section on electric chairs as a form of execution. And in case you were planning to use the microwave to make some underwater snacks while in the bathtub, the safety exhibits will explain why this may not be the best idea. We usually don't list museums that are open by appointment only, but this one is so extraordinary—unique worldwide, in fact—that we had to make an exception.

Vienna

ESPERANTO MUSEUM

Hofburg, just inside St. Michael's Gate of the Imperial Palace. Open Monday and Friday, 10am–4pm and Wednesday, 10am–6pm; closed September 1–21. Admission: free. Phone: 0222/535 51 45.

Created in 1887 by a Polish eye doctor who yearned to smash the linguistic barriers looming around him, Esperanto is an artificial language whose proponents envision world friendship through communication. As languages go, it's pretty angular and easy—no irregular verbs, no tongue twisters. The museum displays books, manuscripts, sheet music, labels, leaflets, posters, postage stamps and more, all printed in Esperanto. Over 100,000 items await the day when we can all flash the peace sign and shout in unison, *"Paco!"*

FEDERAL PATHOLOGIC-ANATOMICAL MUSEUM

In the Madhouse Tower (Narrenturm) *at the Old General Hospital* (Altes Allgemeines Krankenhaus), *Spitalgasse 2. Open Wednesday, 3–6pm; Thursday, 8–11am; the first Sunday of every month, 10am–1pm; closed in August. Admission: 20 AS. Phone: 0222/406 86 72; call before visiting.*

This historic collection comprises a picturesque horde of dead bodies, organs, limbs, bones and realistic wax models spotlighting the diseases, deformations and other bad things that befall humans and animals. Some are floating in formaldehyde, some are desiccated and mounted: 50,000 exhibits in all, dating back 200 years, are displayed in a spirit of respect, and with gratitude that future generations will be spared some of these afflictions. Don't miss the encephalitic skeleton with its huge, spherical head.

THE HOLY GRAIL, ETC.

In the Secular and Ecclesiastical Treasuries (Schatzkammer), *Schweizerhof* (Metro: Burgring). *Open Wednesday–Monday, 10am–6pm; last admission, 5:30pm. Admission: 80 AS; chil-*

dren, 50 AS; children under 10, free. Phone: 0222/533 79 31.

Quest no further: The Holy Grail is in this pompous old Viennese museum. Well, maybe. Some say the orangeish stone tureen, fifty-eight centimeters across and fitted with useful handles, has hidden amid its wavy marbling the name of Jesus, and that it is the grail. Museum sources trace it to a 4th-century Constantinople craftsman, but you never know. Gallop over to Room 8 and judge for yourself. Meanwhile, room 11 houses a lance said to be the one with which Jesus was pierced during the crucifixion. A pin lodged inside it is said to be a nail from the cross itself. Relics abound in Room IV (note that the "secular" treasures are in rooms marked with Arabic numerals, while the "ecclesiastical" ones are in rooms marked with Roman numerals). Framed in silver is a cloth with which St. Veronica is said to have wiped the dying Jesus' face. Also here is a jewel-studded crystal egg housing yet another Holy Nail, and a reliquary with splinters from the cross.

JOSEPHINUM MUSEUM OF MEDICAL HISTORY

Währinger Strasse 25/1, at the intersection of Van Swieten Gasse; museum is on the first floor; follow the signs. Open Monday–Friday, 9am–3pm. Admission: 10 AS; students free. Phone: 0222/403 21 54.

Art, science and ghoulish fascination come together in this extraordinary collection of 18th-century wax anatomical models. Crafted by Florentine artists from 1775 to 1785 at the behest of Emperor Joseph II for the purpose of training his army surgeons in the details of human anatomy (dissecting cadavers was taboo at the time), these masterworks have survived the centuries in pristine condition. The human body is laid open in all its horrifying splendor: Muscles, bones and organs, all so flawlessly rendered that they seem to be fresh from the autopsy room, await your gaze in their original rosewood cabinets. One waxen woman has dainty pink lips, a cute nose, curling hair and a chest torn open to reveal her intestines, liver and lungs; she appears to be sleeping peacefully. Another wears a lovely double strand of pearls and stares at the ceiling as her innards hang out for all to inspect. A skinless man reclines casually on his elbow, as if at a Roman banquet. Another section of the museum is devoted exclusively to tongues. One waxen man standing upright is completely intact except that his penis has been sawn off. His flayed female companion, on the other hand, gets a dainty tuft of pubic hair—we can see every muscle and organ in her body, but God forbid that we compromise her modesty.

MILITARY HISTORY MUSEUM
(Heeresgeschichtliches Museum)

 Arsenal, building 18, off Arsenalstrasse, in the Third District; take tram 18, D or O. Open Saturday–Thursday, 10am–4pm.

 Admission: 40 AS; students and children, 20 AS; admission is free on the first Sunday of every month. Phone: 0222/795 61-0.

In America we televise our assassinations; in Austria they preserve the bloody gleanings in museums. A whole room here is dedicated to what befell Archduke Ferdinand on a visit to Sarajevo in June, 1914—the event that sparked WWI, in case you didn't know. On display are the death masks of Ferdinand and his wife, as well as the fateful car in which the assassination happened. The uniform he was wearing is shown unlaundered, riddled with bullet holes and crusty with blood.

MUSEUM FOR HARNESSING, SADDLING, HORSESHOEING, AND VETERINARY ORTHOPEDICS
(Museum für Beschirrung und Besattelung, Hufbeschlag und Veterinär-Orthopädie)

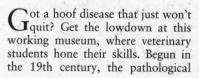 *On the campus of the University of Veterinary Medicine, Josef-Baumann-Gasse 1; museum is on the first floor of the orthopedics building on OP-Platz, across from the horse stall 200 meters to the right of the university's main entrance (take tram 26). Open Monday–Thursday, 1:30–3:30pm. Admission: free. Phone: 0222/250 77 0; call ahead to arrange a tour.*

Got a hoof disease that just won't quit? Get the lowdown at this working museum, where veterinary students hone their skills. Begun in the 19th century, the pathological hoof collection includes double hooves, claw-like hooves that grew too long and hooves with tumescent growths that look like coral. Also here are horse teeth, stirrups, feedbags, crops, a troika harness, reindeer saddles from Lapland and a WWI gas mask made especially for horses. An array of horseshoes through history includes ancient Roman leather "hipposandals." Lucky visitors will get a chance to tour the stalls and surgery area in the same building.

THIRD MAN SEWER TOURS

 Tours given several times a month, usually on Friday and Sunday late afternoons or evenings, starting at the Stadtpark U-Bahn station. Phone: 0222/774 89 01. Call ahead for exact times and admission prices, which change seasonally. A different tour guide at 0222/408 33 03 offers unofficial but similar tours of "Underground Vienna."

The sights, sounds and especially the smells of postwar Vienna come back to life during this *Third-Man*-themed walking tour. Visit many of the actual sites used as movie locations for the 1949 classic, including the notorious sewers, which Orson Welles found so repellent that he almost refused to film the legendary chase scene therein. Rumor has it that construction threatens many of the tunnels on this route, so sign up before the tour becomes part of the legend too.

TOBACCO MUSEUM
(Tabakmuseum)

 Mariahilfer Strasse 2, in the Seventh District. Open Tuesday–Friday, 10am–5pm and Saturday–Sunday, 10am–2pm. Admission: 30 AS; students and children, 20 AS. Phone: 0222/526 17 16.

Yearning for the days when no one knew that nicotine was addictive this genteel museum includes replicas of a tobacconist's shop, King William's tobacco-council chambers and a tobacco importer's countinghouse. A diverse collection of meerschaum pipes as intricately carved as church altars is the main attraction here. But Delft china pipes, African pipes, opium pipes, snuffboxes and an exhibit tracing the history of Austrian cigarettes are also nothing to sneeze at.

UNDERTAKERS' MUSEUM
(Bestattungsmuseum)

 Goldeggasse 19, in the Fourth District. Open Monday–Friday, noon–3pm by appointment, though even if you show up without calling first they'll probably let you in. Admission: free. Phone: 0222/501 95-4227.

Anyone who loves funerals will feel right at home here among caskets, cremation paraphernalia, black costumes, death masks, diagrams of hearses, drawings of cadavers, and devices to safeguard against accidental live burial. Led by an undertaker, the guided tour teaches you how funerals and attitudes toward dead bodies have changed over the years. The museum is housed in Vienna's Municipal Undertaking Institute, HQ of the city's only licensed burial firm. Music lovers won't want to miss the official death notices of Beethoven and Strauss.

SWAROVSKI CRYSTAL WORLDS— WATTENS

15 km east of Innsbruck on the A12 road

SWAROVSKI CRYSTAL WORLDS
(Kristallwelten)

Kristallweltenstrasse 1. Open daily, 9am–6pm. Admission: 75 AS; children under 13, free. Phone: (0) 5224/51080-0.

A man-made hill rises from the pristine countryside, landscaped to resemble a face staring through crystal eyes, spitting a waterfall. Commissioned by the Swarovski company—crystalmakers for Madonna and Michael Jackson—the underground "worlds" include a faceted crystal dome for that caught-in-a-kaleidoscope feeling; crystal artworks by Keith Haring and Salvador Dali; Brian Eno's moody meditation room; and a 120-foot-long crystal wall studded with twelve tons of semiprecious stones. Swarovski has given free rein to avant-garde artists who create ever more crystalline extravagances for each passing year. Outside in the sun again, wander a hand-shaped maze the size of a city park.

40 km south of Salzburg

ICE GIANTS' WORLD
(Eisriesenwelt)

On Tennengebirge, northeast of town: A 5-kilometer mountain road leads to a parking lot; then a 15-minute walk takes you to a cable railway which carries you further up the mountain; yet another 15-minute walk leads to the cave; plan on 4- or 5-hour round-trip excursion from Werfen. Open May–June and September–October, daily, 9am–3:30pm; July–August, daily, 9am–4:30pm; tours given hourly. Admission: 90 AS; children, 45 AS. Phone: 0662/84 26 90-14, or 0 64 68/52 48 or 52 91.

D on't say you're surprised to discover how very, very cold it is inside the world's largest ice-cave system, even on a hot summer day. The towering, bluish pillars, soaring slick archways and other formations that shimmer around you are all made of solid ice. Formed as water trickles down into the cave and freezes, the natural sculptures look like enormous crystal chandeliers, diaphanous clouds and wind-tossed translucent curtains. Some forty-seven kilometers of the cave have been explored so far; wooden walkways make the tour less slippery.

Zwettl

50 km northwest of Krems

MUSEUM OF MEDICAL METEOROLOGY
(Museum für Medizin-Meteorologie)

On route 36, 3 kilometers north of Zwettl, in a cloister in the adjacent village of Dürnhof. Open May–October, Tuesday–Sunday, 10am–6pm (last admission 5pm). Admission: 40 AS. Phone: 02822/531 80.

Remember how Aunt Gertie's corns would ache every time a thunderstorm loomed on the horizon? Zwettl's utterly unique Museum of Medical Meteorology takes a close look at folk medicine and its relationship to old-fashioned notions about the weather. From witchcraft to allergies, barometers to blood-letting, the exhibits embark on a remarkable multidisciplinary approach to historical analysis. One entire room is devoted to the symbolism of frogs and snakes, which supposedly have supernatural powers to ensure youthful vigor, fertility and rain for the crops (see the connection?). Elsewhere you'll learn about alchemy, divining rods, the Theory of Similarities, anti-lightning talismans and the fusing of Christian and pagan philosophies in the Central European rural psyche. The oft-pooh-poohed phenomenon of weather sensitivity is given serious consideration, as are sacred flowers, sushine recorders and magical fossils. My shoulder's acting up again—better fix that hole in the roof.

BELGIUM

here is a tiny, dungless replica of the Antwerp zoo.

Don't miss:

Antwerp

MAGIC WORLD

Hangar 15, Cockerillkaai, on the waterfront just south of St. Annatunnel. Open daily, 10am–6pm. Admission: 160 BF; disabled, 130 BF; children, 60 BF; children under 5, free. Phone: 03/237.03.29.

Life in the big city doesn't seem so intimidating after a stroll around this *little* city, a scale model of downtown Antwerp. Visitors feel eighty-seven times larger than life as tiny cars idle on the streets and model ships line the waterways. The Opera House and all the rest lie at your feet, almost as impressive and precise as the real things, while a sound-and-light show details local history. Also

Beselare

10 km east of Ieper

WITCHES' PARADE
(Heksenstoet)

Held every two years on the evening of the last Sunday in July. For more information, call 057/46 66 33.

Once dubbed "the Sorcery Parish," Beselare has a tradition of blaming old ladies for bad things that happen. The whole town participates in a parade where twenty-foot-tall witches with hook noses, buckteeth and hideous birthmarks proceed through the streets wielding giant crystal balls and baskets of writhing snakes. Amid songs and music, floats creep along and children march in pointed hats, carrying broomsticks. A mock tribunal tries and condemns a "witch" to death, and a mock burning-at-the-stake completes the jollity.

Binche

60 km southwest of Brussels

CARNIVAL OF THE GILLES

Held every year on Shrove Tuesday (Carnival), starting early in the morning and lasting all day; most of the action focuses on the Grand Place in the center of town. For more information, call (064) 33 67 27.

Early on the morning of Shrove Tuesday, thousands of locals don the traditional costumes of the *gilles*: padded full-body suits covered in red, yellow and black lion designs, crowns and stars, worn with clomping wooden shoes and thick waistbands from which dangle massive bells. After dancing around the streets all morning wearing identical masks with green wire-rim glasses, red eyebrows and handlebar mustaches, sometime around 10am each *gille* takes off his mask and puts on a billowing ostrich-plume headpiece as big as an armchair. Taking up a basket of oranges, he starts heaving fruit at spectators. In the chaos, fruit splatters everywhere. The ritual dates back to the 16th century, when local royalty staged a parade to celebrate the conquest of Peru: the *gilles* are supposed to resemble Incas, and the oranges represent Inca gold. Around 3pm everybody reassembles for a more formal parade, followed by fireworks and all-night parties.

Binche

60 km southwest of Brussels

INTERNATIONAL MUSEUM OF CARNIVALS AND MASKS
(Musée International du Carnival et du Masque)

Rue du St-Moustier 10. Open Sunday–Thursday, 9:30am–12:30pm and 1:30–6pm; Saturday, 1:30–6pm. Admission: 180 BF; children, 100 BF. Phone: 064/33 574 or 33 52 27.

The festive rites of five continents take shape here as life-size figures representing revelers, all dressed up and ready to act out their primal impulses, pose against realistic backdrops. From Binche's own fluffy-headed *gilles* to Native American kachina dancers and way beyond, the constantly changing collection gives a truly international view of partying hardy.

Bouvignes

2 km north of Dinant

MUSEUM OF LIGHTING

16 Place du Bailliage. Open May–October, Wednesday–Monday, 1–6pm. Admission: 70 BF; children, 50 BF. Phone: 082/22 49 10 or 22 45 53.

Over 500 lamps and lighting accessories show what's been happening since our ancestors learned that they had other options after the sun went down besides sitting around worrying about vampires. Ranging from prehistoric times to the present—from fire to crude lanterns to Victorian frosted glass confections and into modern times—the exhibits reveal humankind's eternal struggle against its terror of the dark.

Brugge (Bruges)

PROCESSION OF THE HOLY BLOOD
(Heilig Bloedprocessie)

Ascension Day (usually in late May); procession starts at 3pm and winds through the streets encircling the basilica until about 6pm. Grandstand tickets, 400

BF; bench tickets 150 BF. For more information, call (050) 44 86 66 or 44 86 64.

The Count of Flanders brought a souvenir home from the First Crusade in 1149: In the slender crystal vial is a substance said to be Jesus' blood. Since 1303 the relic gets an annual airing, and crowds fill the streets eager for a glimpse. Phalanxes of performers in rich costumes reenact biblical scenes—don't miss God, Moses, Roman centurions and Jesus in misery. Shields, helmets, chains and lances flash while choral voices soar and the relic in its golden portable shrine brings up the rear.

Brussels

ATOMIUM

 On the Boulevard du Centenaire in the Laken district at the northern edge of the city; from Brussels' Central Station, take the Metro line 1A to the Heysel stop. Open April–August, daily, 9am–8pm; September–March, daily, 10–6pm. Admission: 200 BF; children, 150 BF; children under 3, free. Phone: (02) 474 89 77 or 477 09 77.

Climb inside this giant metal "molecule," traipse up and down its slender tubes to probe its nine spherical "atoms" and peek out their windows. This big metallic landmark was built 165 billion times bigger than a real molecule for an expo in 1958. You can speed at fifteen feet per second to the topmost ball's observation chamber 310 feet up, for a panoramic vista of Brussels. Exhibitions in the atoms feature science and art, including 3D mockups

of the latest viruses. If all this pseudo-shrinkage makes you hungry, one of the atoms houses a restaurant.

Brussels

DAVID AND ALICE VAN BUUREN MUSEUM GARDENS

 Avenue Léo Errera 41, in the Uccle district south of the center. Open daily, 2–5:30pm. Admission: 100 BF; students, 50 BF (note that these hours and prices are for the garden only; museum admission is separate). Phone: (02)343 48 51.

Pay no mind to the pretentious art museum lodged in the former home of two wealthy collectors. The adjacent garden boasts a 1,000-square-meter maze, created in 1968 with 1,300 clipped yews to resemble King Minos' labyrinth. Yet the motif wavers. Set here and there along half a kilometer of zigzagging flagstoned alleyways are seven enclaves, each of which houses an abstract sculpture illustrating part of the *Song of Songs*. Contemplate "I am the Rose of Sharon" while hyperventilating as you strive to find your way out of the maze. Elsewhere on the grounds, a "Secret Garden of the Heart" with heart-shaped clusters of miniature pink and red roses was commissioned by Alice Van Buuren in memory of her late husband.

JEANNEKE PIS

At the end of Impasse de la Fidelité, off rue des Bouchers, near the Grand–Place. Visible at any time.

With his member in his hands, the Manneken Pis has been stealing all the attention for centuries. But this statue of a naked little girl is doing the same thing he is. And like him, this pigtailed tyke never runs dry. Nestled in an alcove, the fountain was created in 1985 by Denis Adrien Debouvrie, a sculptor convinced that female urination deserves the world's attention. All coins thrown into the fountain—a sign urges you to toss a coin and make a wish—as well as proceeds from Jeanneke Pis postcards and recordings of the *Song of Jeanneke Pis* are donated to charity.

THE LITTLE BRUSSELS MUSEUM OF THE NEST AND THE FEEDING TROUGH

(Le Petit Musée Bruxellois du Nichoir et de la Mangeoire)

Rue Louis Lumière 17, in the Forest district, southwestern section of Brussels, off Chausée de Neerstalle: From central Brussels, take the Metro to the Bourse or Horta stops, then take bus 48 southbound to the end of the line; walk south on Chausée de Neerstalle, and turn left on rue Louis Lumière (Tram 18 or 52 southbound will also get you

close). Open the first Saturday of the month, 10am–6pm, or by appointment. Admission: free. Phone: 02/376 52 97.

Even birds need a place to sleep, and this museum explains how to make nests for every different bird species. The point is, hopefully, that if you build a nice nest in your backyard, some entertaining birds will move in. There's even a display on bats. Then you move on to the feeding-trough section, which displays dozens of different techniques for distributing snacks to our wild friends. A nonprofit group of bird lovers runs this place, keeping Belgians informed on nest-construction techniques.

MANNEKEN-PIS'S COSTUME COLLECTION

In the Museum of the City of Brussels, in the Maison du Roi on the Grand'Place. Open April–September, Monday–Friday, 10am–12:30pm and 1:30–5pm; October–March, Monday–Tuesday and Thursday–Friday, 10am–12:30pm and 1:30–4pm; Wednesday, 10am–1pm. Admission: 80 BF. Phone: 23 52 55 56 81.

All day he stands on the corner of rue de l'Etuve and rue du Chene behind the Town Hall, gripping his little organ and pissing incessantly for all the world to see. Installed as a public fountain in 1619, Brussels' iconic statue has been the subject of kidnappings, maimings and assorted indignities. As this museum shows, he has also been given over 600 costumes by

well-wishers—including a gold brocade specimen from Louis XV, who
felt bad because his countrymen had
plotted a recent heist. Row upon row
of Manneken-Pis replicas model
sportswear, military garb, tribal outfits and more. He looks adorable peeing while dressed as a witch, an
African dancer, a shiek and a chef.

through France and mini-Vesuvius
erupts regularly throughout the day.
Since Brussels is the European Union's
capital, Mini-Europe has turned
increasingly political, promoting pan-
Europeanism and the brotherhood of
all nations.

MINI-EUROPE

*In Bruparck, a north Brussels
park in the shadow of the Atom-
ium: From Brussels' Central Station, take the Metro line 1A to
the Heysel stop, then follow the
signs. Open daily, April–June
and September, 9:30am–6pm;
July–August, 9:30am–8pm; October–December, 10am–6pm;
special midnight closing mid-
July–mid-August. (Last tickets
sold one hour before closing
time.) Admission: 395 BF; children under 12, 295 BF; children
under 1.2 meters tall, free.
Phone: (02) 478 05 50.*

Not just your run-of-the-mill mini-
village, this vast complex is an
entire mini-*continent*. Every single
nation in Europe—from Greece to
Sweden—has its own mini-region
bristling with astoundingly accurate
reproductions of famous landmarks.
We're not just talkin' the Eiffel Tower
and the Parthenon here: Hundreds of
obscure but striking architectural
masterpieces are faithfully re-created,
including Lübeck's Holstentor gateway, Portugal's Guimares Castle,
Austria's Melk Abbey and scores
of cute Belgian and Dutch town-
scapes. Meanwhile, mini-TGVs career

MUSEUM OF COCOA AND CHOCOLATE
(Musée du Cacao et du Chocolat)

*On the Grand'Place, in La Mai-
son des Ducs de Brabant. Open
Tuesday–Sunday, 10am–5pm.
Admission: 200 BF; students, se-
niors and children, 150 BF.
Phone: (02) 514 20 48.*

A third-generation chocolatier has
assembled this homage to chocolate, complete with free samples.
Maybe *now* you'll be grateful for all
that the Third World has done for
you. Beginning with cocoa's arrival
in Europe as a bitter taste of exotica,
the museum's collection of videos
and other exhibits reveal all the science and craft that turns beans into
the unbelievably expensive confections that rank among Belgium's
best-selling souvenirs.

MUSEUM OF SPONTANEOUS ART
(Musée d'Art Spontané)

*51 Blvd. Léopold II, in the
Koekelberg district northwest of
the Grand'Place (Metro: Ribau*

Brussels
Comic Strip Walking Tour

No other country holds cartoons and comic strips in such high esteem as Belgium does. Cartooning is considered the national art here, and most Belgians grew up reading *les bandes dessinées*—what we would call comic books. The most famous Belgian exports are Tintin and the Smurfs (*Schtroumpfs* in their native land), but dozens of other characters unknown to most Americans but beloved by Belgians include Lucky Luke the cowboy, Quick and Flupke, Spirou, and Gaston Lagaffe. To foster this obsession, civic administrators have allowed artists to paint huge murals of favorite cartoon characters all over Brussels, and you can see most of them on a convenient self-guided walking tour. The route's precise twists and turns are far too convoluted to enumerate here. Your best plan is to start at the **tourist office** on the Grand'Place and pick up a free cartoon mural walking tour brochure. Some of the sites it lists are far-flung; skip the first section of the tour and start right off the Grand'Place by heading down **rue Marché au Charbon** to the first mural near number 19. You'll pass three more murals in quick succession around rue Marché au Charbon before starting a wide loop around the city center, encountering a new mural every few blocks. Finish off your tour with three places not officially part of the route: **The Belgian Centre for Comic Strip Art**, a museum/library/art space filled with the world's largest collection of comics, and featuring statues of Tintin and Snowy and their famous moon rocket in the lobby. A few blocks away you'll come to **Hotel Arenberg**, a comic strip–themed hotel whose bar, **l'Espadon**, has cartoon murals and a free comics library for patrons. As you complete the circle coming along rue de la Colline back to the Grand'Place, stop by the elegant **Tintin Shop**, which sells an amazing if pricey array of Tintin clothing, models, figurines, watches, tea sets, books and more.

Brussels Tourist Information Office: Hotel de Ville, Grand'Place (open daily, 9am–6pm; phone: 02 / 513 89 40).
Belgian Centre for Comic Strip Art: rue des Sables 20 (open Tuesday–Sunday, 10am–6pm; admission 200 BF, students 160 BF, children 80 BF; phone: (02) 219 19 80).
Hotel Arenberg and **l'Espadon**, rue d'Assaut 15 (bar open daily, 10am–1am; phone, 02 / 501 16 16).
Tintin Shop (*La Boutique de Tintin*): rue de la Colline 13 (open Monday, 11am–6pm; Tuesday–Saturday, 10am–6pm; Sunday, 11am–5pm; phone: 02 / 514 51 52).

court). Open Tuesday–Saturday,
Phone: (02) 426 84 04.

Set in the industrial milieu of a decommissioned printshop, these 100 paintings are a far cry from the Old Masters. Treading the remote fringes of their medium, these examples of outsider art—or *art brut*—display all the disturbing imagery and obsessive stylings of more or less unhinged minds.

OMMEGANG

Held every year in the Grand'-Place during the the first week in July. Seats in the viewing stands can be reserved for 700–2,100 BF. For more information or to reserve seats, call the Tourist Information Office at 2 513 89 40.

Horses' hooves clatter, acrobats whir and horns blare as hundreds of paraders dressed in dazzling jerkins, ruffs and all the poufy splendor of Renaissance costume fill the Grand'Place for this lavish pageant honoring the fun-loving 16th-century sovereign, Charles V. Revived in 1930 to replicate Charles' glory days, the event, whose name means "to go all around" in Brussels parlance, begins with a procession and culminates in a giant chess game with horsemen acting as the pieces.

PLASTICARIUM

Rue Locquenghien 35, northwest of the city center, just off Boulevard de Nieuport (Metro: St-Catherine). Open by appointment only, and usually restricted to groups of ten or more; call to see if another group aready has a visit scheduled, and ask if you can join the tour; or hook up with nine other people. Admission: 250 BF. Phone: 02/344 98 21.

Welcome to the universe of orange plastic! This amazing collection of furniture and housewares from the heyday of plasticmania (1960-1973) makes everything that followed look positively tame in comparison. Swollen, bulbous monstrosities in yellow, red, green and orange—mostly orange—go where "retro" designers fear to tread. From armchairs, tables, couches, lamps, bookcases and garbage cans to ashtrays, TVs, briefcases, toys, ornaments and stereo speakers, absoutely everything in the museum is made entirely of vivid, shiny plastic. The exhibit is arranged as a prototypical '60s utopian house—like a full-size dollhouse for humans—where everything is artificial and the future gleams brightly in the near distance. If you currently own anything made of wood, fabric or metal, you may be well advised to avoid this neighborhood entirely.

Brussels

SEWER MUSEUM
(Musée des Égouts)

In the Pavillon de l'Octroi (Toll-house), Porte d'Anderlecht, at the western edge of the city. Tours given Wednesday at 9 and 11am and 1 and 3pm. Admission: 80 BF; children, 50 BF. Phone: (02) 513 85 87.

Human beings' various means of discarding their effluent are explored in an above-ground exhibit as your visit begins. Then, in three basement rooms, learn the technical and practical ins and outs of modern sewage treatment before descending yet further. Deep under the city, walk along a gangway to see the River Senne and Brussels' main sewer, the Chaussée de Mons. Explore over 100 feet of genuine waste disposal in action. An audiovisual montage tops off the visit, warning viewers never to forget the brave sewer workers who risk their lives every day.

Couvin

45 km south of Charleroi, near the French border

CAVES OF NEPTUNE

24 Route de l'Adugeoir in the village of Petigny, which is just northeast of Couvin on the road to Frasnes. Open April–June, daily, 10am–noon and 1:30pm–6pm; July–August, daily, 10am–6pm; October, Saturday–Sunday, 10am–6pm. Admission: 230 BF; children, 140 BF. Phone: 02/731 59 67 or 071/21 41 41.

Tour the cavern's dramatic and spookily lit natural formations, then descend to the nether regions and embark on a twenty-minute voyage down an underground river. The grand finale is a son-et-lumière presentation with frothy waterfalls rushing down rocky walls illuminated in sapphire blue, ruby red and brilliant gold, accompanied by strobe lights and New Age music.

Dinant

LA MERVEILLEUSE CAVE
(Grotte de Dinant "La Merveilleuse")

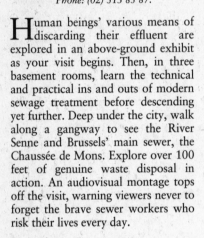

Route de Philippeville 142: From the Grand'Place in the center of town, cross the bridge over the River Meuse; turn left after one block onto Route de Philippeville and the cave will be on your left after a 5-minute walk. Open April–June and September to mid–November, daily 11am–5pm; July and August, daily, 10am–6pm; December– March, Saturday and Sunday, 1–4pm. Admission: 180 BF; students and seniors, 160 BF; children, 130 BF; children under 6, free. Phone: (082) 22 22 10.

A favorite attraction in the Victorian era, La Merveilleuse Cave is renowned for its whiter-than-white stalactites—some of which border on the translucent. The man-made infrastructure here is deliberately more "natural" than in most other caves: Meandering pathways have railings that look organic, and the lighting is straightforward (no colors or trick spotlights). Amid an overwhelming proliferation of oozing stalactites and dripstones—many of which look like frosting that's been left out in the rain—you'll find waterfalls, and (if you look closely) fossils embedded in the rock.

Durbuy

45 km south-southwest of Liège

TOPIARY PARK
(Parc des Topiares)

 Rue Haie Himbe 1, on the banks of the Ourthe River, across the bridge from the old town center. Open February–December, daily, 10am–6pm. Admission: 150 BF; small children free. Phone: 086/21 90 75.

Claiming to be the world's largest topiary garden open to the public, the *Parc des Topiares* has over 250 separate figures trimmed to green perfection. It took over twenty years to painstakingly train many of these bushes into the realistic shapes of swans (followed by a trail of privet cygnets), amphorae, crocodiles, squirrels and hundreds of other shapes. Among the most impressive bushes are the stag with a massive set of antlers, a bikini-clad woman reclining on a lawn chair, a Manneken Pis and a large elephant. You'd be hard pressed to find better topiary anywhere.

Ellezelles

6 km east of Ronse, which is northeast of Tournai

WITCHES' SABBAT

 Held every year on June 27, starting at 5pm in the place d'Ellezelles, in the center of town. For more information and to confirm the date and time, call 068/54.22.12.

This very peculiar "folkloric event" is a little like a midsummer Halloween. Locals dressed as witches with grotesque, big-nosed masks, along with others dressed as devils and a werewolf, gather in the center of town and set off on a procession through the fields to the *place à l'Aulnoit*, a secret coven meeting place reserved every year for this special purpose. Starting at 9pm, the witches and devils dance around the bonfire in a hair-raising ritual, and then give up their broomsticks to regular folks who embark on the odd "broomstick dance." Then everybody gets drunk. That much is clear. What is *not* clear, however, is what it all means: Is it an ancient ritual that somehow survived centuries of witch-burnings, or just an excuse for a rollicking good time?

Eupen

40 km east of Liège, near German border

JACQUES CHOCOLATE MUSEUM

 Industriepark, rue de l'Industrie 16. Open Monday–Friday, 9am–4:30pm; Saturday,

I11am–5pm (but usually no chocolate is produced on Saturday). Admission: free. Phone: 087/59 29 67.

Where does all that rich, creamy sweetness come from? From factory workers using big steel machines, as you can see while touring this 100-year-old chocolatier's self-described "chocolate kingdom." Watch a panoply of *superchocolat* bars being filled with hazelnuts, almonds, raisins and even banana cream, then learn about cocoa culture and history with the help of antique candy-molds, wrappers and other artifacts. A craftsperson demonstrates the old techniques.

Geel (Gheel)

45 km east of Antwerp

PSYCHIATRIC HOMECARE TOWN

 For more information, call the Tourist Information Office at (014) 57 09 55 or 57 09 92.

For centuries, the mentally ill have made a beeline for Geel, where miraculous cures are rumored to take place and where, to help matters along, local families practice a program of letting psychiatric outpatients live at home with them. It all started with Dymphna, an Irish princess who allegedly arrived here around 600 A.D., hotly pursued by her father, a king with incest on his mind. He severed her head in a fit of madness. Now Geel is one of the few places in the world where the mentally ill are fully integrated into society, and make up a substantial portion of the population. A spring festival held every five years reenacts the saint's escape attempt and martyrdom.

Geel (Gheel)

45 km east of Antwerp

ST. DYMPHNA AND HOSPITAL MUSEUM
(Sint Dimpna- en Gasthuismuseum)

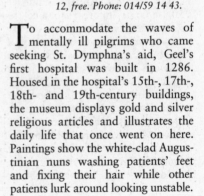 *Gasthuisstraat 1, in the town center near the church, just east of the marketplace. Open April–September, Tuesday–Friday and Sunday, 2–5:30pm; October–March, Tuesday–Friday, 2–5:30pm. Admission: 75 BF; students, 60 BF; children under 12, free. Phone: 014/59 14 43.*

To accommodate the waves of mentally ill pilgrims who came seeking St. Dymphna's aid, Geel's first hospital was built in 1286. Housed in the hospital's 15th-, 17th-, 18th- and 19th-century buildings, the museum displays gold and silver religious articles and illustrates the daily life that once went on here. Paintings show the white-clad Augustinian nuns washing patients' feet and fixing their hair while other patients lurk around looking unstable.

Genval

18 km southeast of Brussels

MUSEUM OF WATER AND FOUNTAINS
(Musée de l'Eau et de la Fontaine)

 Avenue Hoover 63, near Genval Lake. Open Saturday and Sunday, 10am–6pm; Monday–Friday, by appointment only. Admission: 80 BF; students 65 BF; children, 40 BF. Phone: 02/654 19 23.

Remembering the decorative fountains that once stood all over Europe, offering themselves to parched passersby and washerwomen, the museum offers real spurting specimens. Documented in English, German, Dutch and French, and dating back hundreds of years, the exhibits include fountains shaped like lolling marble cupids, sandstone water filters decorated with religious scenes, medieval wooden water pipes and more.

Geraardsbergen

30 km west of Brussels

MANNEKEN-PIS AND MANNEKEN-PIS MUSEUM

 At the Town Hall. Fountain visible at all times; museum is open April–September, Monday–Friday, 9am–noon and 1–5pm; Saturday–Sunday, 9am–6pm. Admission: free. For more information, call (054) 41 78 87 or 41 92 87.

Brussels' peeing fountain gets all the attention. But it's hardly the only peeing fountain in Belgium. Why, Geraardsbergen's peeing fountain, dating back to the mid-15th century, is much older than Brussels'. Mounted on the Town Hall and spurting into a wide, fluted basin, this Manneken Pis looks just like his famous cousin and is the subject of a citywide festival every spring. And like the one in Brussels, this statue has also been given fancy costumes by his fans. The museum displays this wardrobe along with displays detailing the statue's history.

Ghent (Gand)

TORTURE-INSTRUMENT COLLECTION

 In Gravensteen Castle, Sint-Veerleplein, in the northern part of the city center. Open April–September, daily, 9am–6pm; October–March, daily, 9am–5pm. Admission: 200 BF; students 100 BF; children under 12, free. Phone: 09/223 99 77 or 225 93 06.

The Middle Ages weren't a good time to thwart the law, as the implements in this disingenuously self-described "Museum of Court Paraphernalia" reveal. Built in 1150, its gray stone towers mirrored forbiddingly in the waters below, the castle—complete with dungeon—has served over the years as a fort, a mint, a cotton mill, a courthouse and a jail. A glinting guillotine is among the most imposing of the tools on display here, which are accompanied by illustrations showing how they were once used to coerce confessions out of prisoners, restrain the mentally ill and carry out death sentences.

Han-sur-Lesse

45 miles south of Liège, southeast of Dinant

GROTTOES OF HAN-SUR-LESSE
(Domaine des Grottes de Han)

On the main square of Han-sur-Lesse, off the E411 road, on the western side of the Lesse River. Daily guided visits leave from the village center to the cave: March and November at 11:30am, 1, 2:30 and 4pm; April and September–October, every hour 10am–noon and 1:30–4:30pm; May–June, every half hour, 9:30–11:30am and 1–4:30pm; July and August, every half-hour, 9:30am–11:30am and 1–6pm; Museum of the Subterranean World is open from mid-March–May and September–November, daily, 11am–5pm; July–August, 11am–7pm. Admission to cave and Speleotheme: 350 BF; students and seniors, 315 BF; children 12 and under, 220 BF; children under 3, free. Admission to museum: 120 BF; students 100 BF; children, 80 BF. Phone: (084) 37 72 13.

A mini-tram trundles you to the mouth of the cave, the Han Hole; then a guide leads you on foot into the eerily illuminated cavern with its soaring stalagmites and chambers, including the Mosque, Hall of Weapons and Nipple Gallery. A sound-and-light show punctuates the tour, with a cannon shot demonstrat-ing the echo. Then on board a barge, glide down the subterranean Lesse River. A museum displays prehistoric tools and skeletons found in the cavern, and the Speleotheme audiovisual show offers a peek at passages inaccessible to visitors.

Harelbeke

5 km northwest of Kortrijk, just southeast of Hulste

FINCH-CATCHING MUSEUM
(Nationaal Volkssportmuseum over de Vinkensport)

Hazenstraat 4. Open March–November, first and third Saturdays of the month, 2–5pm. Admission: free. Phone: 056/71.36.81, or 056/73 33 41.

It's not often that a museum can legitimately claim to be unique, but this one can. Where else could you learn so much about the sport of finch catching? Through pictures and life-size dioramas, discover how difficult it is to trick those fragile little birds into hopping inside a specially constructed finch trap. Scenes show traditional 19th-century finch-catchers' garb and explain how St. Philippus became the patron saint of *vinkeniers*, as the finch hunters are called in these parts.

Hasselt

35 km northwest of Liège

HOLLYWOOD MOVIE MUSEUM

Sint-Truidersteenweg 298. Open March–December by appointment, for groups only. Admission: 250 BF; children, 200 BF. Phone: 011/27 33 44.

Make friends fast in order to form a group and gain entrée to this remarkable ouevre. Proprietor Frans Billen isn't *exactly* a starchaser, since in an official capacity for over twenty-five years he escorted the rich and famous in his limousines during their tours through Belgium. The souvenirs they gave him are here. Original costumes from *Cleopatra*, *West Side Story* and other films pose on headless dummies everywhere, crowded in the shimmer of track lighting, countless snapshots and a Brobdignnagian replica of an Academy Award. Wax effigies of Frank Sinatra, Sammy Davis Jr. and Dean Martin lounge near a piano, wearing the stars' actual suits, while other waxworks memorialize Elvis and Madonna. Over 500 videos faithfully record Billens' meetings with celebrities ranging from Ronald Reagan to Glenn Close to the Pope.

Hotton

9 km east of Marche-en-Famenne

GROTTO OF A THOUSAND AND ONE NIGHTS
(Grotte des Mille et Une Nuits)

1 kilometer southwest of Hotton; take the road leading south toward La Roche and turn right at the sign pointing to the cave. Open April–June and September–October, daily, 10am–5pm; July and August, daily, 10am–6pm. Admission: 230 BF; students, 200 BF; children, 150 BF. Phone: 084 46 60 46.

No mere hole in the ground, this. Hidden under an isolated Belgian farmhouse, you'll find the Eccentric Gallery, the Midnight Room, the Mushrooms, the Gallery of Friendship, the Wedding Cake, the Room of Perseverance, the Pit, the Chess Game, the Drinking Trough, the Balcony and the Altar. Well, not exactly—these are the creative names applied to the varied array of weird formations and stalagmites populating this fantasy cave.

Ieper (Ypres)

CAT PARADE AND FESTIVAL
(Kattestoet)

The cat toss is held yearly on the second Sunday in May at 7pm, below the belfry in the center of town. The parade takes place every three years on the second weekend in May (after May 14, 2000, it won't be staged again until 2003); parade starts at 3pm

Sunday, while other events including carillon concerts and medieval jousts are staged throughout the weekend. For more information, call the Tourist Information Office at (057) 20 07 24.

Some say pagans used to worship a cat-goddess on the spot where Ieper's belfry stands. Another legend tells how cats, brought in to vanquish hordes of rats that threatened the local textile industry, overran the town. In either case, the streets fill with some 2,400 marchers in cat suits, led by a King and Queen of Cats as tall as telephone poles, while parade floats illustrate humankind's long love-hate relationship with cats. Even in non-parade years, the cat toss takes place: A jester on the belfry lobs velvet kitties at the crowds below. Until 1817, the ammunition was live cats. This sort of thing was once popular throughout Europe, where cats were ritually killed in hopes of banishing evil.

Izegem

12 km north of Kortrijk

NATIONAL BRUSH MUSEUM
(Nationaal Borstelmuseum)

Baron de Pélichystr 3, off Roeselaarsestraat, a few blocks south of the canal. Open March–October, Saturday, 1–5pm. Admission: 60 BF. Phone: 051 30 22 04.

Shaving brushes, lint removers and dusters are among the objects in a diverse collection that dates back hundreds of years and reflects our hatred of small flecks. Ever wondered how the brush makers pack all those bristles together so tightly and keep them in place? And how they get them all the same length? Ever wondered whether they had to slaughter the animal whose hair comprises the bristles in your brush and, if so, how many pigs or rodents had to die just so you could paint a picture? The answers are here, where homage is also paid to synthetic bristles.

Izegem

12 km north of Kortrijk

NATIONAL SHOE MUSEUM
(Nationaal Schoeiselmuseum)

Wijngaardstr. 9, off Roeselaarsestraat, a few blocks south of the canal. Open March–October, Saturday, 1–5pm. Admission: 60 BF. Phone: 051 30 22 04.

From Roman sandals to William of Orange's leather boots, from wooden clogs to orthopedic shoes to tiny, tragic, Chinese bound-foot slippers, this collection of handcrafted footwear dates back thousands of years and reveals the incessant struggle between form and function. King Leopold I's boots loom sleek and tall alongside African tribal sandals; decadent party pumps glow gold and silver; wooden Renaissance shoes perch on stilts; Mideastern slip-ons curl upward like scimitars.

North of Bruges, on the coast near the Dutch border

CASINO WITH ECCENTRIC ART

(Casino Knokke)

Zeedijk-Albertstrand 509, at Canada Square, right on the beachfront. Gambling room open 3pm–4am; other areas always open. Admission: free. Phone: 050/60 60 30, or 050 63 05 06.

Far from the over-the-top artificiality of Las Vegas and the grimy gaming dens of Winnemucca, this casino is adorned with enough original modern art to fill a major museum. The twist is that much of it is surrealistic, offbeat or downright eccentric. The showpiece is *Le Domaine Enchanté*, an immense mural painted directly on the wall by the legendary René Magritte, blending many of his trademarks into one work: Flaming tubas, sailboats made of water, tobacco leaves that transform into sinister eagles, doorways in the sky (opening onto a different sky) and a shrouded man whose headless body is a birdcage. In the lobby, beneath the world's largest crystal chandelier, is an explosively colorful Niki de Saint Phalle statue of Adam and Eve, while a large, unsettling painting by Belgian surrealist Paul Delvaux looms off to the side. The Keith Haring room is thoroughly covered in a grafitti-like mural by the American iconoclast. Changing shows focusing on the likes of Salvador Dalí and Max Ernst can be found in an adjacent exhibition room. If you get the itch, you can bet the family fortune at the baccarat table.

11 km southwest of Kortrijk

MAGIC JUKEBOX MUSEUM

Ropswalle 12; head south from the train station, turn right on Ropswalle and after 100 meters the museum will be on your right. Open September–June, Saturday–Sunday, 2–7pm; July– August, daily, 2–7pm. Admission: 100 BF, children, 80 BF; children under 6, free. Phone: 56 51 39 71.

Over sixty classic jukeboxes fill this imaginative museum, the only one in the world that sees jukeboxes for what they truly are: works of art. Luscious designs from the '40s, '50s and '60s will set off waves of nostalgia, even if you were born several decades too late to remember any of it. Especially cute are the wall-mounted mini-jukeboxes taken from diner booths, most with their original paper selection cards. And yes, almost every jukebox in the place not only works flawlessly, but also is fully loaded with oldies from both sides of the Atlantic. Many of the antique radios here work too, but their music is disappointingly modern.

BATTLE OF THE LUMEÇON

Held every year on Trinity Sunday (late May or early June); procession departs from the Collegiate Church of St. Waudru at 9:30am; battle begins in the Market Square (Grand'Place) at 12:25pm. For more information, call the Tourist Information Office at (065) 33 55 80.

After a golden coach proceeds through the packed streets bearing the skull of St. Waudru, St. George arrives on horseback to battle a green dragon whose twenty-foot pole of a tail whips around among the ecstatic spectators, who rip hairs off it for good luck. Teams of men dressed variously like dogs, in ivy leaves, and like red-horned devils waving pigs' bladders abet the fight. George always wins, not with a sword but a pistol, and the corpse is hauled through town. A children's Lumeçon is held the following Wednesday. In case you're wondering what all this has to do with Catholicism, the answer is, very little. The festival has been held continuously for at least 700 years, supposedly dating back to a time when Mons miraculously survived a plague—though its true origins probably derive from orgiastic pagan revels. The Museum of Folklore in Jean Lescarts House on rue Neuve (admission: 100 BF) has models and videos about the festival.

Morkhoven

35 km east of Antwerp

THE COURT OF SKULLS
(Schedelhof)

Bertheide 12. Open Saturday–Sunday, 10am–6pm. Admission: free. Phone: 014/26 18 13.

In the exhibition space behind his home, retired Antwerp Zoo employee Edward Geldof shows visitors the fruits of a hobby he has nur-

tured for decades: the preparing and mounting of animal skulls. Those of toothy hippopotami, horned sheep, apes, reptiles and birds are among over 700 specimens on display here, in many cases shown alongside pictures of the actual fleshed animal. Most of the exhibits aren't under glass, and visitors are welcome to stroke the bones.

Oostduinkerke

SHRIMP PAGEANT
(Garnaalfeest)

Held every year on the last weekend in June; contest is on Saturday afternoon, parade on Sunday afternoon. For more information, call (058) 51 11 89, or (058) 53 21 21.

They're too hungry to bother with shrimp boats in Oostduinkerke—fishermen on horseback charge straight into the surf, wearing slickers and wielding baskets. The annual pageant indulges a craving for crustaceans with the crowning of a (human) Shrimp Queen. She rides down the street on a float, flanked by brass bands and mounted fishermen as everyone happily scarfs Fishermen on Horseback Soup. Shrimp-fishing contests at the beach yield a twitching harvest.

Philippeville

26 km south of Charleroi

SUBTERRANEAN PASSAGES

Entrance at rue des Religieuses 2. Open July–August, daily, 2–5pm. Admission: 120 BF; children, 60 BF. Phone: 071/66 89 85.

Chiseled with surprising precision 300 years ago from the solid rock under the town, ten kilometers of tunnels connect the old fortress with other districts. After watching a multilingual film recounting the fortress's salad days and its place in local history, follow the tour guide down the ramrod-straight passages, whose arched ceilings give a subtly spiritual effect.

Saint-Hubert

45 km southeast of Dinant

HUNTERS' MASS

Held every year on Nov. 3; high mass in the basilica begins at 11am. For more information, call the Tourist Information Office at 061/61 30 10.

The town's patron saint was an 8th-century huntsman who converted after seeing an enormous stag in the Ardennes with a golden cross glowing between its ears. Now red-jacketed, black-hatted, tight-panted hunters in high boots fill the basilica for a special morning mass marking Hubert's feast day, accompanied by an international cortege of hunting-horn virtuosos. Afterward, a priest blesses local hunting dogs, priming them to go out and torment their fellow creatures.

Sint-Niklaas

20 km southwest of Antwerp

BARBER-RAMA
(Barbierama)

Regentiestraat 61-63, a few blocks northeast of the Grote Markt. Open April–September, Tuesday–Saturday, 2–5pm; Sunday, 10am–5pm. Admission: 50 BF; students and children, 30 BF. Phone: 03/777 29 42.

One look at the gas-heated curlers and monstrous 19th-century permanent-wave machines is enough to gladden the bald. This collection of clippers, combs, beard-shapers, basins, barbers' chairs, razors, ointments and other historic hairdressing equipment includes four complete replicas of vintage salons—all of which reveals fashion as the sadistic hypnotist it really is.

Sint-Niklaas

20 km southwest of Antwerp

BOOKPLATE COLLECTION
(Internationaal Exlibriscentrum)

Regentiestr. 61-63, a few blocks south of the train station. Open Tuesday–Saturday, 2–5 p.m.; Sunday, 10am–5pm. Admission: 50 BF. Phone: 03/777 29 42.

Small, fussy, personal and paranoid, the distinctive art of the ex libris emerged in order to tell the world, "This book belongs to . . ." Over 120,000 bookplates form this collection, spanning fifty different countries and many years, organized by theme and medium. Examine the intricate detail and the diverse motifs that made all those book owners confident no one would try to filch their favorite Agatha Christie mystery.

20 km southwest of Antwerp

HISTORICAL PIPE AND TOBACCO MUSEUM
(Historisch Pijp and Tabaksmuseum)

 Regentiestraat 29. Open Sunday, 10am–1pm. Admission: 60 BF. Phone: 03/766 60 60, or 03/777 32 98.

Winston Churchill smoked a big cigar, Fidel Castro smokes a bigger cigar, and Bill Clinton is a big cigar fan, but none of them ever had a cigar *this* big: over eighteen feet long, about two feet in diameter and weighing in at nearly 1,000 pounds. Sint-Niklaas's prize exhibit even has an oversize cigar band for that extra touch of authenticity. Elsewhere here you'll find exotic pipes from all over (especially European clay pipes), colorful tobacco cans, a recreated 19th-century smoker's den, antique cigarette-making apparatus and a potpourri of exotic tobacciana.

25 km southeast of Liège, just east of the town of Aywaille

REMOUCHAMPS CAVES
(Grottes de Remouchamps)

 3, Route de Louveigné, just outside town; follow the signs. Open February–November, daily, 9am–6pm; December–January, Saturday–Sunday 10am–5pm. Admission: 300 BF; children, 200 BF. Phone: 04/384 46 82.

One of the world's longest subterranean boat rides is this cave's claim to fame. The first part of your visit, however, is on foot; you'll see illuminated concretions and flowstones of every sort. Then descend to the Rubicon, which the proprietors claim is the world's longest navigable underground river. Much of the ride—in silence, mind you—is down narrow tunnels with occasionally low overhangs. Pass a waterfall and wind through the heart of darkness until you finally emerge, squinting in the sunlight.

35 km southeast of Liège

MUSEUM OF THE LAUNDRY
(Musée de la Lessive)

 Rue de la Géronstere 10, near Boulevard Chapman. Open July– August, daily, 2–5pm; September– June, Sunday, 2– 6pm. Admission: 50 BF; children, 30 BF; children under 6, free. Phone: 087/77 14 18.

Washerwomen, washing machines and detergent get their due here, where twenty different rooms reveal the unstoppable progress of laundry. Antique washing machines still in working order keep company with towering industrial laundry equipment, replicas of village water pumps and life-size tableaux about folding and ironing.

Turnhout

42 km northeast of Antwerp

NATIONAL PLAYING CARD MUSEUM
(Nationaal Museum van de Speelkaart)

 Druivenstraat 18, four blocks south of the Grote Markt. Open June–August, Tuesday–Saturday, 2–5pm, Sunday, 10am–noon and 2–5pm; September–May, Wednesday, Friday and Saturday, 2–5pm, Sunday, 10am–noon and 2–5pm. Admission: 90 BF, children, 70 BF (includes a deck of cards); or 70 BF; children 50 BF (deck of cards not included). Phone: 014/41 56 21.

As the former and present headquarters for the European playing-card industry, Turnhout is the natural place to have the continent's largest playing-card collection. Constantly rotating exhibits reveal that cards are more than something to play Go Fish with: Lush graphic designs, satirical cartoons, folk art and the social history of the last few centuries can all be found on the cards in this museum. Keep an eye out for cards made for the Asian market, including *hanafuda* decks and Chinese gambling cards. Machines used to print cards throughout the centuries are another

specialty here. The free deck you get when you enter is a reissue of a rare, beautiful 19th-century deck that is not for sale anywhere in the world.

Vielsalm

50 km southwest of Liège

WITCHES' SABBATH
(Heksensabbat)

 Held every year on July 20, beginning at 9pm. Phone: 080/21 48 03 or 21 60 80.

In local lore, *macralles* are hags with hook noses, high cheekbones, kerchiefs, long black dresses and magical powers, who roam the Salm Valley annoying their neighbors. On one night a year, townspeople dress up like *macralles* to stage a revue based on witches' rites and revels, complete with huge simmering cauldron and sound-and-light effects.

Voormezele

4 km south of Ieper

HOLY BLOOD PROCESSION

 Held every year on the first Sunday after Pentecost, usually in late May or early June; procession begins around 3pm. Phone: 057-20 13 88.

In 1152 a local abbot came into possession of a relic whose Latin inscription declared that it was a sample of Jesus' blood. Safe inside its rattle-shaped silver reliquary, topped with a silver heart, it is venerated to this day and stars in this elaborate annual procession. Flags and crosses jut every which way as over 650 townspeople act out the Passion in all its gory glory. The man portraying Jesus peers out between trickles of blood as he lugs his huge wooden cross.

Wavre

14 km southeast of Brussels

WALIBI LEISURE PARK

Open April–June, daily, 10am–6pm; July–August, daily, 10am–7pm; September–mid-October, Saturday–Sunday, 10am–6pm. Admission: 760 BF; children, 680 BF; children under 1 meter tall, free. Phone: 010/42 15 00.

Encircling its own lake, this park incorporates a man-made jungle where Belgium's own favorite cartoon character, the androgynous Tintin, faces danger again and again while visitors glide around on gondolas and watch. Also here are the OK Corral and Lucky Luke City—Wild West replicas featuring yet more Belgian cartoon stars. The park's themes blur when it comes to thrill rides, performing-seal acts, bike-riding parrots and a mock Arabian palace complete with golden domes.

Ypres (Ieper)

BELLEWAERDE PARK

Meenseweg 497, just east of town. OPen April-June, daily, 10am-6 pm; July-August, daily, 10am-7pm; September-mid-October, weekends only, 10am-6pm. Admission: 670 BF; children, 600 BF; children under 1 meter tall, free. Phone: (957) 46 86 86.

Sporting some 200,000 flowers, the park comprises "lands" lushly landscaped to replicate someone's idea of Canada, India, Mexico, the Wild West and the whimiscal "Pepinoland." Wild rides along a jungle river and down a mock Niagara Falls combine with hundreds of live wild animals, including tigers and flamingoes, to completely jar your sense of place. Watch out for those drunken Mexican pirates as archaeologist "Indiana" (sans Jones) makes off with the sacred Bengali gemstone! Ferris wheels, roller-coasters and monorails whir over native lodges, rustic forts, stone gods and off-kilter colonial splendor.

CZECH REPUBLIC

Don't miss:

Brno

CAPUCHIN MONASTERY CRYPT
(Hrobka Kapucínského Kláštera)

 Kapucínské nám. 5; entrance is to the left and below church's main door. Open Monday–Saturday, 9 am–noon and 2–4:30 pm ; Sunday, 11-11:45am and 2–4:30pm. Admission: 40 kč; seniors and children, 20 kč. Phone: 0040 6465.

The mummified bodies of numerous monks and their benefactors lie here for eternity, having been encouraged to desiccate naturally hundreds of years ago via a special air-circulation system. Some ar[e] glass-topped coffins whose detac[hed] lids adorn the wall, while the h[um]blest brothers lie on the bare e[arth] floor. The corpses' taut skin has turned the color of coffee, and their faces are in various states of disrepair. Some with their lipless jaws parted look about to say, "Y'all come back now, hear?" The corpses' feet took especially well to the mummification process, and many of these look almost bathtub-fresh. For fear of disease, burial in the crypt was discontinued by imperial edict in 1784.

Kamenický Šenov

22km east of Děčín

BASALT ORGANS
(Panská skála)

 1 kilometer south of town, off a small road leading due south toward Česká Lípa; the formations are plainly visible from a distance, next to a small lake. Visible at any time. Admission: free. For more information, call the local post office at 0424/92 309.

Perfectly sculpted hexagonal stone columns soar skyward above the mirror-like lake at their feet. The best known example of this rare natural phenomenon is Northern Ireland's Giant's Causeway (which see), but the *Panská skálá* of Kamenický Šenov is in many ways much more impressive. Formed when cooling lava fractures into crystalline geometrical forms, these thin basalt columns do indeed look a bit like the pipes of a church organ—if the organ was as tall as a six-story building. The *Panská skála* has survived the millennia almost untouched by erosion, so the flawless straight lines seem chiseled by a master mason. Even up close, you can scarcely believe the whole thing was crafted by Mother Nature.

Records, and every June holds a record-breaking festival: Czechs come from all over the country to make heroic fools of themselves performing outrageous stunts. Many of the museum's photo exhibits document past festivals.

Pelhřimov

100 km southeast of Prague

MUSEUM OF RECORDS AND CURIOSITIES
(Muzeum Rekordů a Kuriozit)

 Inside Jihlavska Gate, one of the old fortifications around the town center, east of the main square. Open April–October, daily, 9am–4pm. Phone: 0366/321 226.

A homespun, funkier version of the Guinness museums, Pelhrimov's collection documents world records being attempted or broken. Photographs depict the foolhardy and the daft testing the extremes of human endeavor, whether it be eating repellent food 'til they pop, gyrating 'til they drop or just doing things no one else would dare try. Also here are record-holding objects: the world's longest tie, a spoon big enough to bathe in, the largest picture ever made of pasta, a shaving brush worthy of Paul Bunyan, and microminiatures including pictures drawn on lentils and statues cut from toothpicks and skewers. The museum is constantly changing and growing—stop by and help knit the world's longest scarf, an ongoing interactive project (well over 200 feet at last count). Pelhrimov bills itself as the Town of

Prague

BEARDED MAIDEN ON A CROSS

 In the chapel of the Virgin of Sorrows in the Loreta Sanctuary, Loretánské nám. 7, in the castle precinct; pass through the main church to find the chapel at the corner of the corridor surrounding the courtyard, 50 feet from the exit. Open Tuesday–Sunday, 9 am–12:15pm and 1–4:30pm. Admission: 80 kč; students, 60 kč. Phone: 02/205 167 40.

Who's that hanging crucified near the mournful pietà? Realistic as a Tussaud waxwork, the sculpted figure sports a virile black beard with Cossack-style mustache to match—and a golden brocade gown, pointed satin slippers and fluffy bows. It's a girl. St. Wilgefortis was a virgin martyr who prayed for a way to ditch the marriage with a pagan fiancé her father had arranged. Her miracle came in the form of facial hair, but her father's idea of discipline didn't stop at spanking. Emerging from puffy sleeves, the saint's expressive hands are nailed firmly to a large wooden cross, while her delicate face bears the faintest trace of amusement.

DANCING FOUNTAIN
(Křižíkova Fontána)

 In the Vystaviste exhibition grounds, north of the center: Take the Metro (Line C) to the Nádraží Holešovice station; or trams 5, 12 or 17. Water-dance shows in summer, Monday–Friday, at 8, 9, 10 and 11pm; Saturday–Sunday at 3, 5, 8, 9, 10 and 11pm. Admission: 60 kč; prices vary for live shows. Phone: 2010 3224 or 2010 3280.

Monumental plumes of water leaping rhythmically toward the night sky turn psychedelic shades of orange, yellow, green and blue, to the stirring tunes of Tchaikovsky, Dvořák, Queen, Kitaro and Michael Jackson. Light and water come alive as they "dance" to melodies from *Swan Lake*, Disney's *Hunchback of Notre Dame* and whatever else is on the program. If you hear Vangelis, don't say you weren't warned.

DANCING HOUSE—PRAGUE

Somehow, slender curving columns manage to hold the whole thing up, as irregularly spaced windows stumble down one wall. Nicknamed "Ginger and Fred," The Dancing House won *Time* Magazine's "best new building" award for 1996.

THE DANCING HOUSE
(Tančící Dům)

 Jiráskovo nám. 6, on the corner of Resslova nám and Raší-novo nábřeží embankment, on the waterfront; take tram 17 to the Jiráskovo námesti stop. Always visible. Admission free.

At first sight you stop dead in your tracks: Is that building collapsing? One side seems frozen in mid-shimmy, while the other bulges as it rises, as if over-inflated and about to explode.

FOUR-LEGGED CAR STATUE

  In the rear garden of the German Embassy (Lobkovický Palace), which is at Vlašská 19 in Mala Strana; walk west on Vlasska from the embassy's entrance about 200 yards, then turn left to enter a walkway through a wall, then turn left again and follow the wooded path behind the embassy. Visible at any time. Admission: free.

Grow instantly obese as you confront your terrifying image in this labyrinth of funhouse mirrors. Housed in a historic fin-de-siecle pavilion, the mirrors will have you laughing your head off as you suddenly lose a lot of weight and grow monstrously tall.

FOUR-LEGGED CAR—PRAGUE

Incorporating an actual car, this realistic sculpture stands erect on four sturdy humanoid legs, its toes gripping the earth, poised to walk off into the current of history. Peer at it through the tall metal fence and see if it does.

 Prague

MIRROR MAZE
(Bludiště)

 In Petrin Park (Petrinske sady), west of the river, just above St. Lawrence (Sv. Vavřinec) Church; take tram 22 or bus 176 from Karlova nám. Open April–August, daily, 10am–7pm ; September–October, daily, 10am– 6pm; November–March, Saturday–Sunday, 10am–5pm. Admission: 30 kč; students and children, 20 kč.

Prague

THE MUSEUM OF THE CZECH POLICE
(Muzeum Policie ČR)

 Ke Karlovu 453/1, in the Nové Město district south of the Old Town; the nearest Metro station is I.P. Pavlova. Open Tuesday–Sunday, 10am–5pm. Admission: 10 kč. Phone: 02/298940.

A murder-scene mockup features a chalk outline of a corpse on the floor, the room in disarray from the victim's struggle. Other exhibits show the variety of weapons used by Czech criminals, including homemade guns and cannons, and actual murder weapons. The detailed recountings of famous Czech crimes from 1918 to the present would probably gross you out completely if the signs were translated into English.

Prague

ST. ADALBERT'S BONES

 In St. George's Basilica in the castle precinct, at the end of Jiřska Street where it opens onto St. George's Square; the bones are in a side chapel to the right of the main door. Open daily, 9 am–

5pm. Admission: 100 kč; students, 50 kč. For more information, call the castle visitors' center at 2437 3368 or 2437 2434.

Pray all he might, this is still where the bishop ended up. Having urged his colleagues to convert the Magyars late in the 10th century, he was justly slaughtered by heathen Prussians in Pomerania. Surrounded by paintings illustrating the saint's fate, Adalbert's skull—crowned with a dainty garland of little dried flowers—stares out through a glass pane under the altar. His other bones are neatly arranged behind the skull.

ST. JOHN NEPOMUK'S TONGUE

In St. Vitus' Cathedral, in the castle precinct; relic is behind the high altar in the back part of the church on the right side, on St. John Nepomuk's tomb. Open April–October, daily, 9am–5pm; November– March, daily, 9am–4pm. Admission: 100 kč; students, 50 kč. Phone: 2437 3368.

Today this cathedral enshrines the bones of St. Vitus himself, invisible inside an ornate box—and who can tell if they're dancing? Also here is the tongue of local hero St. John Nepomuk, a vicar who was thrown into the Vltava River for refusing to reveal certain secrets he'd heard in the confessional. Fished lifeless from the current, the martyr's body was promptly laid to rest. When by church order the remains were reexamined many years later, the tongue was reportedly fresh as a daisy. Now it

takes pride of place here, pale pink, in a glass-windowed reliquary held aloft by silver angels atop a baroque silver tomb the size of a Chevy van.

THE ST. MICHAEL MYSTERY
(Tajemství u Svateho Michala)

Michalská 27-29, in the Old Town. Open daily, 10am–8pm. Admission: 330 kč; students 270 kč; children 13–16, 250 kč; children 7–12, 200 kč. Phone: 2421 2716.

An animated multilingual bust of Franz Kafka beckons visitors to stroll through reconstructed scenes from bygone and legendary Prague. This macabre journey is housed in an 800-year-old church where elevators stall deliberately just to give you the creeps. Skulls smoke cigars, and furniture mutters forbiddingly. The crypt is stocked with genuine skeletons. Kafka keeps popping up to carp about how literature torments him. Lifelike figures posed along the route and bringing the city's history to life include Nazis, Communists and Michael Jackson.

2.5 km northeast of Kutná Hora, 65 km east of Prague

SEDLEC OSSUARY
(Kostnice)

The ticket office is at 127 Zámecka: From central Kutná Hora, take a local bus to Sedlec, or to the Kutná Hora

train station; from the station walk back 1 km toward Sedlec, past the tobacco factory, until you reach the large Church of the Assumption on Vitezna Street; turn right (north) up Zámecka Street, and go one block until you reach the ticket office at 127 Zámecka; the ossuary is half a block further up Zámecka—enter through a graveyard. Open April–September 8am–noon and 1–6pm; October, 9am–noon and 1–5pm; November, 9am–noon and 1–4pm. Admission: 30 kč; students and children 15 kč; permission to take photos (you'll want to!) an additional 30 kč. Phone: 0327/761 143.

The world's most spectacular ossuary features the bones of over 40,000 people artistically arranged into elaborate decorative motifs. Dominating the center of the room is a chandelier comprising every bone in the human body, while a series of vaulted side chapels houses vast pyramids of leg bones and skulls. The ossuary's every niche and surface is covered in bones, often fashioned into intricate designs: The jaw-dropping Schwarzenberg family coat of arms is made of pelvises, fingerbones, skulls and, of course, arm bones. From the ceiling hang long streamers and festoons of ribs, vertebrae and tibias. Your eye keeps catching whimsies such as a "fountain" of

Prague
Black Light Theater
(Černé Divadlo)

Against a black background, fluorescent props and actors alight with a strange glow appear to fly through the air, achieve impossible antigravity dance moves and float suspended. The "black cabinet" technique, created in postwar Prague, employs black-clad personnel who remain invisible against the backdrop as they scurry around manipulating everything, while music, day-glo colors and trick lighting complete the surreal effect. Several different black-light theater groups flourish in Prague today, staging productions ranging from *Faust* to classical music medleys to unnerving versions of *Yellow Submarine*.

 Most theaters have shows every night, as well as on weekend afternoons; prices vary, depending on the theater and the show
All Colours Theatre: Rytířská 31; phone, 216 10 114
The Black Theatre Animato: Národni třída 36; phone, 24 22 52 55
The Black Theatre of František Kratochvíl: Národni třída 20; phone 2491 22 46
The Black Theatre of Jiří Srnec: Stěpánská 61; phone, 232 26 36
Ta Fantastika: Karlova 8; phone, 24 23 77 63
Theatre Image: Pařížská 4; phone, 231 44 48

Caves of the Moravian Karst Region

Just north of Brno, in the heart of Moravia, the earth suddenly becomes very porous. Beneath the apparently solid ground lurks a subterranean empire of caves, tunnels, underground rivers and chasms. Called karst (after a similar geologic formation in Slovenia), the landscape is composed mostly of fissured limestone easily eroded by water. Rivers and streams seep into the ground, carve out caves and occasionally reemerge. Over 1,000 caves have been discovered here in an area no bigger than Los Angeles, and thousands more await. Though just a few are open to the public, the five listed here are a good introduction to the horrifying splendor of a cavernous world most never see. All of these can be found just east of Blansko, a mere 20 km north of downtown Brno, where the tourist office (Radnicka 8, Brno; phone, 422 110 90) can provide details on how to reach each cave.

Punkevní Caves: Tours depart from the nearby village of Skalní Mlýn. Open April–September, 8:20am–3:50pm; January–March and October–December, 8:20am–2pm. Phone: 0506/3575. The subterranean Punkna River—which you explore in boats—has created a system of caverns whose towering chambers are thick with a marshmallowy mass of stalactites, stalagmites and other gooey shapes.

Balcarka Cave:. South of the village of Ostrov. Open February–October, 10am–1pm (longer hours in summer). Phone: 0506/444 330. This modest-sized but popular cave is absolutely thick with millions of stalactites and stalagmites, like a baroque hell.

Sloupsko-Šošůvské Caves: Between the villages of Sloup and Šošůvka. Open January–March, 10am–1pm, April–September, 7:30am–3pm, October, 8am–2pm. Phone: 0506/435 335. This extensive, elaborate system of caverns has some highly unusual stalagmites formed in stops and starts when the water level in the cave heightened and dropped repeatedly long ago.

Catherine Cave: This is the cave nearest to Blansko, southeast of Skalní Mlýn. Open throughout the year with variable hours. The front part of this cave is a vast, deep cavern with such perfect acoustics that it's sometimes used for concerts; at the back you'll find what looks like an albino bamboo forest of incredibly thin stalagmites growing straight up as high as twelve feet.

Javoříčko Caves:. Several miles northeast of the other caves, west of Olomouc. Open April–October, Tuesday–Sunday, 9am–4pm (closes at 5pm May–September). Massive oozing formations call to mind hot caramel topping and heavy whipped cream.

ribs gushing from a hole in the top of a cranium, or a "bird" made of a scapula and a hand. All this started in 1511 when local monks dumped the remains from an overcrowded graveyard into this sunken chapel. In 1870, woodcarver Frantisek Rint unleashed his artistic genius on the abandoned skeletons.

Třebechovice

11 km east of Hřadec Králové

MUSEUM OF NATIVITY SCENES
(Muzeum Betlémů)

Masarykovo nám. 24. Open May–September, Tuesday–Sunday, 9am–noon and 1–5pm; October–April, Tuesday–Sunday 9am–noon and 1–4pm. Phone: 049/96053.

SEDLEC OSSUARY—SEDLEC

Hark, the herald angels are certainly numerous at this museum, which displays over fifty handcrafted creches of all types and sizes. The star of this show is the Trebechovice Bethlehem, a butterscotch-colored wooden spectacle twenty feet across, six feet high, nine feet from front to back and unbelievably detailed. Made by the devout local carver Josef Probost, its cascading flow of terraces is outfitted with over 2,000 individually chiseled trees, temples, angels, goats and all the rest—including shepherds dressed in knickers and blazers, modeled after the artist's friends. Four hundred figures move at the behest of a complex mechanism devised by their maker, who labored on the one artwork for 40 years.

SEDLEC OSSUARY—SEDLEC

Vysoké nad Jizerou

30 km southeast of Liberec, near the Polish border

KRAKONOS COLLECTION

In the Local History Museum (Vlastivědné Muzeum), Dr. K. Farského č. 130. Open Tuesday–Sunday. Phone: 0432/593118.

This small museum specializes in folk art figures of Krakonos, the local "Old Man of the Mountain." With his long blonde beard, porkpie hat, yard-long pipe, leather boots, overcoat and walking stick, the legendary giant was both worshipped and feared by the peasants of the surrounding Krkonose Mountains, which happen to be the the highest and wildest in the country. Looking and acting a little like a no-nonsense frontier Santa, Krakonos repaid good deeds with supernatural favors, and punished misdeeds with remorseless retribution. He's the champion of the peasants and the bane of the aristocrats, and all the little furry creatures love him. Hundreds of sculptured Krakonoses—from the micro to the life-size—pay tribute to this folk hero.

Zlin

80 km east of Brno, in southern Moravia

FOOTWEAR MUSEUM

Třída Tomáše Bati 1957, west of the town center, in the shoe factory. Open April–September, Monday–Friday, 8am–4pm; Saturday, 8am–2pm; October–March, Monday–Friday, 8am–3pm (hours may change; call ahead). Phone: 067/852 2203.

When Zlin's now-ubiquitous Bata shoe company was founded in 1894, its designers, buyers and salespeople traveled all over the world collecting shoes for inspiration. Their haul opened as a museum in 1931 and has been expanding ever since. Sioux moccasins and Chinese "golden lotus" slippers for bound feet are here, as well as 18th-century platform shoes, sequinned party shoes, Australian aboriginal ritual shoes made from emu feathers and human hair, and 3,000 more exotic specimens. Especially interesting are the Bata company's own experimental designs from the first half of this century.

DENMARK

Don't miss:

Aerøskøbing

On the north shore of the island of Aerø

BOTTLE-SHIP COLLECTION
(Flaskeskibssamlingen)

Smedegade 22, in the center of the Old Town, near the water. Open October–April, Tuesday–Thursday, 1–3pm, Sunday, 10am–1pm; May–September, daily, 10am–5pm. Admission: 25 DKr; children, 10 DKr. Phone: 62 52 29 51.

The 1,700 model ships trapped in bottles here comprise the lifework of Peter Jacobsen, an old seabiscuit. Before he died in 1960, "Bottle Peter" fashioned his own headstone: No less than seven bottled ships are set right into the cement. Now it's part of the collection, as Jacobsen's widow didn't want to put it in a graveyard. Other sailors' collections are here too, blending the briny and the strange.

Billund

45 km northwest of Fredericia, in central Jutland

LEGOLAND

No street address, but it's so big you can't miss it. Open April–late June and September–October, daily, 10am–8pm; late June–August, daily, 10am–9pm. Admission: April–late June and September–October (low season): 115 DKr; children, 105 DKr; late June–August (high season): 130 DKr; children, 120 DKr. Phone: 75 33 13 33.

Just about everything at this sprawling amusement complex is made of Lego bricks. Lego elephants, giraffes and crocodiles pose in the Lego jungle; Lego pirates and Lego wizards leer; Lego trains and rockets stand by for takeoff. Pan for gold with Lego cowboys at Legoldmine in Legoredo, and visit a medieval castle peopled with Lego knights and a Lego court jester. Cruise down canals past Lego versions of the Acropolis, Hamlet's castle, a Thai temple, Mount Rushmore and other works of Legoarchitecture. Wallow up to your neck in vast bins of Lego bricks—then get away from it all in the Lego-themed hotel next door.

GUINNESS WORLD OF RECORDS MUSEUM

  Østergade 16, in the pedestrian zone. Open daily, 10am–6pm. Admission: 68 DKr; students, 57 DKr; children aged 12–15, 38 DKr; aged 5–11, 25 DKr. Phone: 3332 31 31.

Waxworks, replicas, videos and hands-on simulators put you in touch with the world's largest soccer ball, the world's fastest bricklayer, the world's longest salami, the world's biggest meteor shower, the world's heaviest baby, the world's tiniest paper frog and the world's largest skirt (it's over twenty-seven feet wide). Test your skills against record-breaking boxers and racecar drivers via virtual reality, and ponder those who ate the world's largest servings of snails and prunes.

MEDICAL HISTORY MUSEUM
(Medicinsk-Historisk Museet)

 Bredgade 62 near Amalienborg Palace. Open Wednesday–Friday and Sunday; admission only with guided tours, at 11am and 1pm; in July and August guided tours are offered in English at 1pm. Admission: free. Phone: 35 32 38 00.

This museum focuses on Danish medicine, dentistry and phar-macy from 1700 to the present day. Don't roll your eyes until you've laid them on the epidemics section, especially the syphilis and bubonic plague exhibits; the pathological anatomy displays; the trepanation kit (for drilling holes in people's heads); a jar in the pharmacy section for a potion made of human fat; the Victorian-era dental drill; the "restraint chair" for violent patients, in the psychiatry exhibit; and the 19th-century barber's sign advertising his services, including enemas, bleeding with leeches and ear piercing.

MUSEUM EROTICA

 Købmagergade 24, just off the Strøget. Open May–September, daily, 10am–11pm; October–April, daily, 11am–8pm. Admission: 59 DKr; children under 10, free. Phone: 33 12 03 11.

The curator, a veteran pornographer, happily points out that groups of local schoolchildren take field trips to the museum as part of their sex-education classes. Which exhibit is more penetratingly interesting—the museum's Dildo World, its exhibit on spanking, its wall of continuous sex videos or its collection of photographs showing Great Grandma, when she was a girl, showing her muffin to the camera? Study erotica in ancient art as well as a giant carved wang and the sex lives of famous people, including Hans Christian Andersen.

POLICE HISTORY MUSEUM
(Politihistorisk Museum)

Faelledvej 20, at Skt. Hans Torv, northwest of the center. Open Tuesday and Thursday, 10am–4pm; the first Sunday of every month, 11am–3pm. Admission: 20 DKr; children under 16, free. Phone: 35 36 88 88.

Nordic crime comes alive with authentic mallets and hatchets that figured in major cases. Learn how an innocent teddy bear was roped into a crime. Drawers placed conveniently at the foot of the glass display case hold descriptions of whatever mayhem involved this necktie or that shovel. Also here—along with police motorcycles and uniforms—are relics from the day when pornography was still illegal in Denmark, including scourges, spanking paraphernalia and pictures of transvestites.

RIPLEY'S BELIEVE IT OR NOT! MUSEUM

Rådhuspladsen 57, one block from Tivoli. Open daily, 10am–10pm. Admission: 68 DKr; students, 57 DKr; children aged 12–15, 38 DKr; aged 5–11, 25 DKr. Phone: 33 91 89 91.

There's a vaguely corporate edge to the shrunken heads, costumed fleas, hand-painted potato chips, world's largest wasp nest, letter writ-ten on a grain of rice, Lord's Prayer written on a postage stamp, Siamese-twin cats, diatom art, voodoo dolls, six-legged calf, 800-foot gum-wrapper chain and other items on display at this Norse outpost of the international chain museum based on the putative findings of adventurer Robert Ripley and his minions. Then again it's so much fun.

STORM P. MUSEUM
(Storm P.-Museet)

Frederiksberg Runddel, at the intersection of Pile Allé and Frederiksberg Allé, in the suburb of Frederiksberg, west of downtown: Take bus 18 or 28. Open May–September, Tuesday–Sunday, 10am–4pm; October–April, Wednesday, Saturday and Sunday, 10am–4pm. Admission: 20 DKr; children, 1 DKr. Phone: 31 86 05 23 or 31 86 05 00.

The versatile humorist who called himself Storm P. was a Danish cross between Rube Goldberg, Bill Cosby and James Thurber. Part social critic, part comedian and part cartoonist, Storm P.'s world of philosophical bums, useless machines and acerbic witticisms is permanently branded on the Danish psyche and has earned him the status of national treasure. This one-man museum displays his cartoons, paintings and books, and has exhibits about the varied phases of his long career. Most everything is in Danish, but his vibe comes across clear as a bell. Storm P.'s impressive personal collection of pipes should assuage those who still don't get the jokes.

TOBACCO MUSEUM
(Tobaksmuseet)

 Amagertorv 9, inside the W.Ø. Larsen store. Open Monday–Thursday, 10am–6pm; Friday, 10am–7pm; Saturday, 10am–2pm. Admission: free. Phone: 33 12 20 50.

Cigar-store Indians and trick lighters shaped like guns and hand grenades are only the beginning. Antique and novelty smoking-and-sniffing paraphernalia includes engraved snuffboxes, well-preserved vintage packages, tobacco jars and cigar dispensers. Pipes from around the world include one smaller than your finger and another with three bowls. Elsewhere you'll find a box of micro-cigars smaller then the matches required to light them, a waist-high cigarette dipenser in the form of a cobra poised to strike, and a section on the black sheep of the pipe-smoking family: opium dens.

TOBACCO MUSEUM—COPENHAGEN

25 km south of Odense, on Fyn

EGESKOV CASTLE GARDENS

 Egeskovgade 18. Open May and September, 10am–5pm ; June and August, 10am–6pm ; July, 10am–8pm. Admission: 55 DKr; children, 27.50 DKr; under 4 free. Phone: 62 27 10 16.

The plump young motorcycle-riding count who owns this place wants everyone to have a fine time roaming the forty acres of immaculately manicured grounds. In the shadow of the 16th-century castle that rises from the stillness of its moat like something in a fairy tale, a baffling bamboo maze has supplanted a six-times-smaller beech maze that was used for party games in the 19th century. Also on the grounds are topiary snails and a Museum of Curiosities which explores Count Dracula's link with Egeskov.

At the western tip of Bogø island, just off the south coast of Zealand

CHOCOLATE MUSEUM
(Chokolademuseum)

 Grønsundvej 699. Open daily, 10am–6pm. Admission: 25 DKr; children, 15 DKr. Phone: 55 89 33 02.

Big burlap sacks overflowing with cocoa beans look anything but appetizing, though they're inevitable elements in the great chocolate saga. On the premises of a candy factory, this museum begins with the Mayas, then moves on to the decadence of Europe. The proprietors draw firm links between chocolate and emotions, chocolate and culture and even chocolate and human health. Free samples from the factory let you put all this to the test.

Frederikshavn

HAIR JEWELRY EXHIBIT

In the Bangsbo Museum, at Dronning Margrethesvej 1-6, off Vrangbaekvej. Open June-October, daily, 10:30am–5pm; November–May, Tuesday–Sunday, 10am–5pm. Admission: 30 DKr; children, 5 DKr. Phone: 98 42 31 11.

The jewelry on display in this local-history museum isn't made of gold and silver, but human hair. This creepy kind of macramé was a fad in the 19th century, when Swedish girls called *hårkullor* would intricately plait necklaces, bracelets, rings—even beads—and peddle their works all over Europe. Wives often wore jewelry made of their husbands' shorn tresses, while men wore watch chains made from women's hair. Families hung wreaths or plaques made from the hair of dead loved ones. You'd need a magnifying glass to properly examine the precision of these gruesome, tightly woven trinkets.

Frederikshavn

BOOKPLATE COLLECTION
(Exlibrissamling)

In the Frederikshavn Art Museum, Parallelvej 14, near the Rådhus. Open Tuesday–Friday, 10am–5pm, Saturday–Sunday, 10am-4pm. Admission: DKr 10; children, free. Phone: 98 43 16 63.

Jules Verne's bookplate, on display here, depicts a pockmarked planet and a spaceship. Others in this collection range far and wide, depending on their former owners' tastes—from ships to geishas to modern art. And Scandinavia wouldn't be the same without erotic bookplates featuring pee and nipples and the Devil honing his phallus on a whetstone. With 250,000 rare examples in the collection, you never know what'll turn up.

Hillerød

in the center of North Zealand

SKELETONS IN AEBELHOLT ABBEY
(Aebelholt Klostermuseum)

4 Aebelholt, 6 kilometers west of Hillerød toward Frederiksvaerk. Open May–August, Tuesday–Sunday, 10am–4pm; September, Tuesday–Sunday, 1–4pm; April and October, Saturday–Sunday, 1–4pm. Admission: 15 DKr; children free. Phone: 42 11 03 51.

After the abbey was founded in 1175, tales of miracles surrounding a resident French monk named Guillaume lured droves of sick pilgrims in search of cures. The large collection of skeletons on display today, excavated at the now mostly ruined abbey, shows how those who didn't find miracles ended up. Also in the museum here are the monks' surgical instruments, evoking an air of medieval illness and death. Don't miss the skeleton of a pregnant woman, forever locked in her shy, wistful pose.

Holme-Olstrup

8 km northeast of Naestved, on Zealand

BONBON-LAND

 Gartnervej 2; buses and trains to Holme-Olstrup drop passengers off near the front gates. Open May–mid-June and August–mid-September, Monday–Friday, 10am–6pm, Saturday and Sunday, 10am–8pm ; July, daily, 10am–8pm. Admission: May–mid-June and August–mid-September, 95 DKr; July, 105 DKr; children under 90 cm tall, free. Phone: 55 56 33 00.

If you've eaten a lot of Danish candy, you'll laugh your head off at this theme park whose sixty-plus attractions are based on the wacky names of popular sweets. Natives insist that no translation could properly convey the hilarity of the park's "Dog-fart Roller-coaster," where an enormous brown hound presents its butt to the riders while grimacing. Also here are a nauseous-turtle whirligig and a splash ride involving rats. An array of carousels, boats, rafts and other amusements entail such themes as skid marks, fly swat-

ters, wet diapers, ants, beavers and bird poo.

Horsens

40 km southwest of Århus, in eastern Jutland

EUROPEAN MIDDLE AGES FESTIVAL

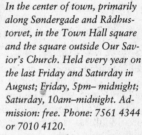 *In the center of town, primarily along Søndergade and Rådhustorvet, in the Town Hall square and the square outside Our Savior's Church. Held every year on the last Friday and Saturday in August; Friday, 5pm– midnight; Saturday, 10am–midnight. Admission: free. Phone: 7561 4344 or 7010 4120.*

The electric lights go out all over town as Europe's largest medieval festival begins at sunset. From then on, flaming torches, candlelight and open fires provide all the illumination, adding authenticity to what is already a joltingly realistic reenactment of life in the 15th and early 16th centuries. Having lavished amazing care on their costumes, over 120,000 participants become lords, ladies, beggars, witches, minstrels, lepers, pilgrims, prostitutes, bandits, brides, monks and alcoholics. Fully outfitted knights joust on horseback, while market stalls and roving troubadors pack streets whose modern aspects have been completely disguised. Medieval treats including suckling pig and gruel are served—no utensils, of course—and Gregorian chants, jousts and executions pop up throughout the affair.

Klejtrup

13 km southwest of Hobro, in north-eastern Jutland

WORLD MAP GARDEN
(Verdenskortet)

  Søren Poulsenvej 5, which runs along the shore of Klejtrup Lake (Klejtrup Sø). Open daily May and September, 9am–6pm; June–August, 9am–7pm. Admission: 20 DKr; children under 13, 10 DKr. Phone: 98 54 61 32.

It may have taken God only six days to make the world, but Søren Poulsen is running a close second: It took him only twenty-five years to make a pretty good copy. The product of his lifelong obsession, this is a series of artificially built islands in the shape of a world map. One glance at its vastness and you can see why it took him twenty-five years to finish—working alone and often ridiculed. Step off Antarctica (the mainland) onto southern Africa and you're on your way, traversing continents. Eighteen holes of transnational mini golf allow you to cross five time zones in one putt, and rowboats in the Atlantic take you over to the New World in a matter of minutes. The accuracy and detail of Poulsen's rendering greatly add to the experience: Every bump in the coastline, every island is flawlessly reproduced, from Sri Lanka to Hudson Bay. The grass is even scraped away in desert regions, and rows of rocks simulate the Himalayas. But then, as you start getting lost, crossing the Siberian tundra only to find yourself in a *different* Siberia just a short time later, you notice what gives the World Map Garden that extra tincture of individuality: Certain parts of the world crop up two or even three times, as one continent leads to another, and then another. Poulsen apparently never quite figured out how the Mercator Projection works. And that's why we love him.

Lejre

Just west of Roskilde

LEJRE RESEARCH CENTER
(Lejre Forsøgscenter)

 Slangealleen 2, west of town; from Lejre's train station take the hourly HT bus #233 direct to the research center. Open May–late June and mid-August– mid-September, Tuesday–Sunday, 10am–5pm; late June–mid-August, daily, 10am–5pm. Admission: 50 DKr; children, 30 DKr. Phone: 46 48 08 78.

The people you see wearing roughly woven garb, chopping wood with primitive axes and grinding corn at this reconstructed Iron Age village are actually Danish families who vie for a chance to spend their summer vacations living like their ancestors. Amid ongoing real-life excavations, visitors can participate in Iron Age games, crafts and even cooking as practiced circa the year 1, while exploring the labyrinth and the sacrificial bog with its suspended animal skins. Paddle around in a real dugout canoe. Make, cook and eat your own wheat patties from scratch. A reconstructed Stone Age area and a rural 19th-century area occupy farther-flung parts of the center.

On the eastern tip of Aerø island

BOTTLE-SHIP COLLECTION

In the Maritime Museum, Prinsengade 1. Open October–April, Thursday–Friday, 10am–4 pm, Saturday, 11am–3pm; May and September, daily, 10am–4pm; June and August, daily, 9am–5pm; July, daily, 9am–9pm. Admission: 25 DKr; children, 5 DKr. Phone: 45 62 53 23 31.

This museum offers a splendid collection of handicrafts that kept Danish sailors' hands off each others' dungarees. On display here is a "fleet" of over a hundred ships-in-bottles, startlingly intricate in their glassy prisons, made by old salt Mads Bøye. One of the ships is a replica of the barque *Johan*, on which Bøye himself sailed to the West Indies when he was a preteen.

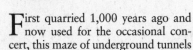

15 km southeast of Skive in Jutland

CHALK PITS
(Kalkgrube)

Kalkvaerksvej 10, just north of town. Open daily, 10am–5pm. Admission: 30 DKr; children, 10 DKr; children under 6, free. Phone: 86 64 66 66 or 97 52 32 66.

First quarried 1,000 years ago and now used for the occasional concert, this maze of underground tunnels dwarfs the visitor. Wander in the shadows cast by its curved and soaring ceilings. Contemplate the sizable colony of bats who make this their home, and study their lifestyle further in the cave's own bat museum.

On Falster Island south of Zealand in Lolland, just across the water from Germany

THE MEDIEVAL CENTER
(Middelaltercentret)

Ved Hamborgskoven 2, west of the center, across Guldborg Sound; from the train station, take Guldborg bus 2. Open May–September, daily, 10am–4pm. Admission: 60 DKr; children, 30 DKr. Phone: 54 86 19 34.

Dodge the flashing swords as chain-mail-clad knights joust at this "Center for Historical Technology." Enthusiastically reconstructed slices of late-14th-century Danish life include a huge catapult that launches real projectiles way out into the sound, and medieval ships on which you can sail into the same waters. Interactive workshops and games abound. Craftspeople, hunters, farmers, monks and other medieval types loiter around the shops, dwellings and waterfront; knights as well as ordinary folks will gladly explain to visitors what they are doing and what it means. At the banquet hall, servants in period costume deliver dishes based on 14th-century recipes.

60 km southwest of Copenhagen

FANTASY WORLD

on Eventyrvej, off Holbaekvej, across the E20 motorway, north of town. Open daily, 10am–5pm; closed January, March and late September. Admission: 60 DKr: children, 40 DKr: under 2, 20 DKr. Phone: 57 61 19 30.

Denmark's answer to "It's a Small World" features thousands of talking, singing, dancing mechanical figures arranged in fantasy scenarios. Amid the huskies in Greenland, a hip combo wails on guitar and accordion. In the Mexican Village, a fruit vendor wears a sombrero and Henry Kissinger specs. In China, the emperor wears a coolie hat. Hans Christian Andersen narrates his tales; a straw-hatted gorilla wears a grass skirt; broncos' tails drag behind them across the floor like bridal veils in Cowboyland. In Santa's Village, reportedly Europe's largest specimen of its kind, Santa's throngs of helpers are, surprisingly, not elves but little doppelgangers of Santa himself.

30 km south of Ålborg, northern Jutland

CIRCUS MUSEUM
(Cirkusmuseet)

Østerled 1. Open April–mid-October, Tuesday–Sunday, 11am–5pm. Admission: 20 DKr; children, 10 DKr. Phone: 98 51 05 55 or 98 56 26 28.

Scandinavia's sole circus museum stands next door to a wooden dodecagon which was erected in 1912 to precise Big Top specifications by Rold's noted circus clan, the Miehes. Costumes, videos, posters and other relics give insight into the lives of acrobats, barkers and trained animals in the heat of the act, as well as after the crowd goes home.

At the very northern tip of Jutland

AMBER MUSEUM
(Ravmuseum)

Bankvej 2, near the waterfront. Open January–March, daily, 10am–5pm ; March–mid-June, daily, 10am–6pm; mid-June–mid-August, daily, 10am–10pm; mid-August–December, daily, 10am–5pm. Admission: 15 DKr; children, 10 DKr. Phone: 98 44 47 33.

The petrified resin of giant pines that grew fifty million years ago has been washing up on Danish shores so long that amber was a favorite adornment as far back as the Stone Age. The Vikings wouldn't sneeze at it either, as this surprisingly interactive museum shows. Inspect over 40,000 pieces of amber containing bits of prehistoric plants and insects caught unawares. An international jewelry collection reveals that amber isn't always yellow, but comes in many colors—even blue.

Skagen

At the very northern tip of Jutland

THE BURIED CHURCH
(Den Tilsandede Kirke)

In the sand dunes between the sea and Gl. Landevej, west of downtown. Open June–September, daily, 11am–5pm. Admission: 8 DKr; children, 4 DKr. Phone: 98 44 43 71.

Hans Christian Andersen dubbed this place "the Pompeii of Skagen." All that peeks out of the wind-blown sand today is the top of a whitewashed tower, but this was once one of the region's largest churches, built in the 14th century to honor the patron saint of seafarers, and stocked with gilt figures. The sand drift started in the 16th century; 200 years later the congregation was digging its way in to attend services. By royal decree the church was closed in 1795, and soon afterward it was swallowed up almost entirely. What was once the floor is now nearly fifteen feet under the sand.

Trelleborg

8 km west of Slagelse, in West Zealand

VIKING FORTRESS AND MUSEUM
(Vikingeborgen)

Trelleborg Allé 4, north of the E66 highway; Take bus 312 from Slagelse train station.

Open April–October, daily, 10 am–5pm. Admission: 35 DKr; children 5–15, 20 DKr; children under 5, free. Phone: 53 54 95 06.

Clad in jerkins, they're practicing archery, contemplating Odin and setting out to prove that Vikings weren't merely a bunch of thugs. At this fifteen-acre, thousand-year-old, interactive ring fortress, the museum shows items found during the excavations, while the café serves mead. Ongoing workshops and demonstrations revive Viking lifestyles and include falconry, leathercraft, pony riding, wool spinning, cooking, music, ceramics and thuggish fighting.

Varde

15 km north of Esbjerg, in western Jutland

MINIATURE TOWN
(Minibyen i Varde)

Arnbjerg Park (Arnbjerg Anlaegget), just east of the center. Open May and early September, daily, 10am–4pm; June and August, daily, 10am–5pm; July, daily, 10am–6pm; late September–mid-October, Monday–Friday, 11am–3 pm. Admission: 20 DKr; children, 5 DKr. Phone 75 21 12 90.

It takes teeny-tiny bricks to make a village this small. Built on a 1:10 scale using traditional construction materials, this new replica shows exactly how Varde looked in 1860—before the town was largely destroyed, as the guide explains, by townspeople causing accidental fires. Red rooftops reach your haunches as you stride down the cobblestoned mini-streets past tiny trees and pocket-sized lawns surrounding over 250 little houses, a church and other structures.

FINLAND

Don't miss:

*free; children under 6, free.
Phone: (0)9 773 991 or (0)9 773
992 87.*

In the midst of Finland's favorite amusement park, Barbie's evolution is traced from the ultra-rare, wasp-waisted plastic gals of the late '50s to the spoiled shopaholic Barbies of today. Expect full documentation on Barbie's amazing professional careers as a doctor, rock star, horse trainer and housewife. Vote for your favorite wacky Barbie costume, many of which were made by famous Finns. Paintings by worshipful fans adorn the walls. Collections from around the world show how different cultures dress and adore the slim-thighed icon. If you dare, pose for a photograph wearing human-size Barbie fashions from the museum's collection. Then abandon all hope and enter the Barbie ice cream parlor next door.

Helsinki

BARBIE MUSEUM
(Barbie World)

In Linnanmäki Amusement Park, Tivolikuja 1: To reach the park north of downtown, take tram 3B, 3T or 8. Barbie World is in the Linnanmäki Museum, near the north gate of the park. Open May, Tuesday–Friday, 4–10pm, Saturday 1–10pm, Sunday 1–9pm; June–mid-August, daily, 1–10pm; mid-August–early September, Saturday and Sunday, 1–10pm. Admission: 15 FIM for the park and 12 FIM for the museum; students and children 6–16, 10 FIM for the park and admission to the museum is

---

Helsinki

HOTEL & RESTAURANT MUSEUM
(Hotelli- ja Ravintolamuseo)

Tallberginkatu 1 F, in the Cable Factory cultural center, west of downtown on the waterfront. Open Tuesday, Thursday and Friday, noon–6pm; Wednesday, noon–8pm; Saturday and Sunday, noon–5pm. Admission: 10 FIM if so; children free. Phone: (09) 693 1774.

What do Finnish chefs do with all those reindeer, beets and crayfish? Mouthwatering exhibits dish out all the details on Finnish food—from the forest and the lake to the table. Model cafés, kitchens, restaurants and hotel rooms welcome the invisible guest, and don't miss the collection of 40,000 menus. As for another aspect of Scandinavian hospitality, the dramatic Alko exhibit tells the story of Finnish liquor stores and the crucial role they play in this nation's culture.

MUSEUM OF MEDICAL HISTORY
(Helsingin Yliopiston Lääketieteen Historian Museo)

 Hämeentie 153 c, in the Old Town. Open August–June, Tuesday and Friday, noon–3pm; Thursday, 4–6pm. Admission: 4 FIM; students, 2 FIM. Phone: (09) 708 4822.

Relics from a medieval lepers' hospital are among the oldest items on display at this museum, which runs the medical gamut from veterinary science to dentistry to gynecology to ophthalmology to pharmacy. Don't miss the rustic tools used in days of yore to bleed patients, or the "cooling helmet" once used to subdue crybabies who thrashed around. Dr. Arvo Ylppö's historic collection of wax figures gives insight into early-20th-century childcare. Replicas of an operating theater, a hospital dining room and a patient's room are furnished with authentic accessories, many of which were donated by—you guessed it!—yet another lepers' hospital.

ROCK CHURCH
(Temppeliaukio)

 Lutherinkatu 3, at Temppelikatu. Open in summer, Monday, Tuesday, Thursday and Friday, 10am–8pm, Wednesday, 10am–7pm, Saturday, 10am–6pm; in winter, Monday, and Thursday–Friday, 10am–8pm, Tuesday, 10am–12:45pm and 2:15–8pm, Wednesday, 10am–7pm, Saturday, 10am–6pm. Admission: free. Phone: 498 804 or 494 698.

Hewn out of solid granite with only its copper cupola visible from the outside, Temppeliaukio Church is a modern spectacle consecrated in 1969. Used as an occasional concert venue as well as a Protestant house of You-Know-Who, the interior is yawning and cavernous, with its cave-like inner wall deliberately left unfinished.

SEXHIBITION EROTIC FAIR

 Tallberginkatu 1 C, in the Cable Factory cultural center, west of downtown on the waterfront. Every year, usually in late May; call for current dates. Phone: 9 694 1178, or 9 169 3757.

This is what it's like to live in a country that wasn't founded by shiploads of puritans. Every year the city sponsors a sex fair in the popular Cable Factory. The performances, exhibitors and activities change from year to year, but one theme always prevails.

On the coast of the Gulf of Bothnia, between Oulu and Rovaniemi

SNOW CASTLE

  Castle is rebuilt every year, usually from December to March; call for exact dates and location. Admission: free to the castle, but various activities and products within the castle have separate prices. Phone: (0)16 259 822, or (0)16 259 502 (Snow Castle Office).

In 1996 the people of snowbound Kemi built what they called the "World's Largest Snow Castle," replete with restaurants, hotel rooms, a concert hall and more. The project was such a success that it has now become an annual event. Since Kemi is just below the Arctic Circle in a damp seaside area, nobody need worry about whether or not there'll be enough snow: Winter here is essentially one continuous blizzard. Future snow castles promise chapels, ice art exhibitions and every amenity under the ominous dark clouds. If you've ever wanted to sleep in a hotel made of snow, this is your chance. Bring earmuffs.

Naantali

MOOMINWORLD
(Muumimaailma)

 On the island of Kailo in the harbor; a short footbridge connects the island to the northwest corner of Naantali's old town, near the Convert Church. A "Moomintrain" makes various stops near the harbor before dropping off visitors at the bridge. Open June 6–August 16, daily, 10am–6pm. Admission: 80 FIM; children 3–14, 60 FIM; under 3, free. Phone: (02) 511 1111.*

Moomins are cartoon characters that look sort of like pastel hippopotami with big, soulful eyes and no mouths. Like many of their cartoon counterparts worldwide, the Moomins and their friends learn fascinating lessons about life, friendship and the environment while living in a magical world full of surprises. Visit Moominpapa, Moominmama, the Witch, Little My, the Snorkmaiden and the rest in their five-story Moominhouse and cute little cottages. Cross the rapids on a rope bridge, roam the Whispering Woods and sweat in the turf-lined peat sauna. This children's park's unrelenting kookiness will bring a welcome dose of surrealism to your travels.

Posio

136 km southeast of Rovaniemi

INTERNATIONAL COFFEE CUP MUSEUM

 At the Pentik ceramics factory complex (Pentikmäki), just north of the center. Open mid-June–mid-August, Monday–Friday and Sunday, 9am–8pm, Saturday, 9am–6pm; mid-June–mid-August, Monday–Friday and Sunday, 10am–5pm, Saturday, 10am–4pm. Admission: 5 FIM; children, 2FIM. Phone: (0) 16-372 1819.

French coffee drinkers do it with Limoges. Italians do it with ridiculous little vessels hardly big enough to hold two mouthfuls. Gain insight into caffeine culture and customs around the world with 2,000 coffee cups from nearly 100 different countries. Along with appropriate utensils, they're on display at the headquarters of a firm that manufactures—of all things—coffee cups.

Rovaniemi

On the Arctic Circle

SANTAPARK AND SANTA CLAUS VILLAGE

5 kilometers northeast of town, 2 kilometers south of the airport on Highway 4; a free shuttle runs between Santa Claus Village and SantaPark. Open daily, late November–January, 10am–8pm; irregular hours the rest of the year, but always open on weekends and usually Friday as well. Admission for SantaPark 95 FIM; children 4–11 65 FIM, children under 4, free. Phone: (0) 16 333 0000 (SantaPark) or (0) 16 356 2096 (Santa Claus Village).

They always told you Santa lived at the North Pole, but it was a ruse. He lives here in Lapland, where they *eat* reindeer. SantaPark is a newly opened glitzy Christmas-themed underground amusement park with Disneyesque rides, real reindeer, and more elves than you can count. Can't wait til December? Here you can OD on holiday cheer any time of year. At Santa Claus Village is a workshop with fervent elves and Santa's Post Office, which stamps mail with an Arctic Circle postmark. Santa's House, the Christmas School and a reindeer park are also here. Mr. and Mrs. Claus await your whining plaints.

Savonlinna

100 km northeast of Mikkeli

RETRETTI ART CENTRE

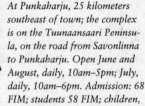

At Punkaharju, 25 kilometers southeast of town; the complex is on the Tuunaansaari Peninsula, on the road from Savonlinna to Punkaharju. Open June and August, daily, 10am–5pm; July, daily, 10am–6pm. Admission: 68 FIM; students 58 FIM; children, 28 FIM. Phone: 15 644 253.

Giving new meaning to the term "underground art," this exhibition center offers 27,000 square feet of man-made subterranean grottoes. Follow the spiral staircase down, down, down to see the artworks on display. Deep inside the earth, a 1,000-seat concert hall has been hewn out of solid stone—ceiling, proscenium arch and all, with figures carved into the wall. Performances and shows change periodically and range from Wassily Kandinsky to the art of voodoo.

Tampere

COSTUMED MEXICAN FLEAS

In the Museum of Dolls and Costumes (Nukke- ja Puku Museo), Hatanpää Mansion, Hatanpään Puistokuja 1; Take bus 21 from the city center.

Open May–August, Tuesday–Saturday, 10am–5pm, Sunday, noon–5pm; September–November and January–April, Wednesday–Sunday, noon–5pm. Admission: 30 FIM; students, 15 FIM; children, 5 FIM. Phone: (0) 3 222 6261.

The rest of the museum offers centuries' worth of rag dolls, paper dolls, china dolls, dollhouses, wedding gowns, gloves and more, but all this serves as a mere backdrop to the smallest exhibit of all. What better place than a palatial, late-19th-century neo-Renaissance mansion for a set of authentic dead Mexican fleas all dressed up in tiny, festive garments? Two are wearing frock coats, one is in an Eskimo outfit and another wears a bridal gown, though we're not sure it's a girl. As far as we know, these are the smallest costumes in the world.

Tampere

MUSEUM OF ESPIONAGE
(Vakoilumuseo)

 Tullintori Shopping Center, 2nd floor. Open daily, noon–6pm. Admission: 30 FIM; students and children, 20 FIM. Phone: (0) 3 2123 007.

Find out everything the secret agents don't want you to know. Created by serious researchers with the help of veterans from the shadowy realm of espionage, this museum spotlights famous spies as well as the world's most powerful spying organizations. Examine the kinds of devices 007 might carry on his next case, and watch demonstrations showing how to use them.

Tankavaara

230 km north of Rovaniemi

TANKAVAARA GOLDEN WORLD
(Tankavaaran Kultakylä)

  On the E75 road; look for the signs. Open June–mid-August, daily 9am–6pm; mid-August–September, daily 9am–5pm; October–May, Monday–Friday, 10am–4pm; Finnish Gold Panning Open is held the first week in August. Admission to museum: 35 FIM; children, 10 FIM. Gold panning: 20 FIM. Registration fee for Finnish Gold Panning Open: 120 FIM. Phone: (0) 16 626 158 or 626 171.

On the site of Finland's 1934 gold rush, which was launched when a Finn asleep in a haystack was guided to Tankavaara in a dream, the Gold Museum celebrates great gold rushes in Japan, Australia and twenty countries around the globe. Not only can you meet a football-sized nugget named the Welcome Stranger, but you can also wander around replicas of boomtown buildings from all over the world and try your hand at panning in Gold World's own placer. Finders keepers. If the gold bug bites hard, enter the annual Gold Panning Open.

Turku

MEDIEVAL MARKET

 Held every year over five days in late July or early August; events scheduled in the Old Market

Square, Wednesday–Friday, 4–8pm; Saturday–Sunday, noon–6pm; other events are held at Turku Castle and the Aboa Vetus Museum, in the town center. Admission: free. For more information, call the Turku Cultural Centre at (0) 2-273 8370 or 2-273 8341

Knights, minstrels, merchants, monks, jesters, archers, prisoners, princesses and priests by the thousands fill streets transformed into a bustling, late-14th century marketplace. Tents, banners and horse carts hide traces of the modern world, while dozens of booths offer medieval-style cuisine and handicrafts. For the seriously committed, a dense schedule of events includes jousting, theater, music, an outcasts' freak show, church services, mock hangings and a nostalgic procession of lepers.

An Electrochemical Iyophiligator, a Gnagg Booster and a Spacegobben are among a wacky team of Finnish artists' "defunctioned machinery and localized black holes" on display at this puzzling exhibition center. The devices are meticulously constructed, fitted with spiraling pipes and wires and polished copper tanks, and look real but are all completely useless. The Bonk company's long but fictitious history is carefully documented with grainy photographs, ersatz advertisements and official-looking but totally fake documents. Don't miss the Paranormal Cannon, or the high-density anchovy-based barbecue briquettes called "Bermuda Triangles."

Uusikaupunki

On the southwestern coast, 75 km northwest of Turku

DYNAMO CENTRE BONK

Siltakatu 2, at Sorvakon rantatie, across the bridge leading south across the harbor. Open in summer, daily, 10am–6pm. Admission: FIM 25; children, FIM 10. Phone: (02) 841 8404.

FRANCE

Don't miss:

Paris

Paris

CATACOMBS
(Catacombes)

1 place Denfert-Rochereau, 14th arrondissement; the entrance is in the center of the square, at the back of the park (Métro: Denfert-Rochereau). Open Tuesday–Friday, 2–4pm; Saturday–Sunday, 9–11am and 2–4pm. Admission: 27 F; students and children, 19 F;

children under 8, free. Phone: 01 43 22 47 63.

How many dead people does it take to fill Paris's vast network of subterranean galleries? About 6 million, most of whom were transferred here from the city's overstuffed graveyards between the 18th and 19th centuries. During World War II these cool sepulchral chambers were a favorite Resistance rendezvous. Today, some sixty feet below the street, the guided tour leads past piles and piles of neatly stacked bones and skulls and meticulously arranged skeletons. Here's yet another art form at which the French prove themselves very skilled.

Paris

CHAPEL OF OUR LADY OF THE MIRACULOUS MEDAL
(Chapelle Notre-Dame de la Médaille Miraculeuse)

140 rue du Bac (Métro: Sèvres-Babylone). Open Monday and Wednesday–Saturday, 7:45am–1pm and 2:30–7pm; Sunday, 7:20am–1pm and 2:30–7pm; Tuesday, 7:45am–7pm. Phone: 01 45 48 10 13.

The Virgin Mary is said to have visited a young nun named Catherine Labouré at this church in 1830 and given her a special message along with the design for a holy medal. Today Catherine is a saint and her touched-up corpse, removed from its tomb in 1933, lies exposed here in a glass case alongside a statue of Mary. In another glass case are the preserved remains, dressed in a habit, of St. Louise de Marillac. She cofounded the Daughters of Charity with St. Vincent de Paul, whose preserved remains lie in another church around the corner.

Paris

EDITH PIAF MUSEUM
(Musée Edith Piaf)

 5 rue Crespin du Gast, 11th arrondissement (Métro: Ménilmontant). Open Monday–Thursday, 1–6pm, by appointment only. Admission: free. Phone: 01 43 55 52 72.

The Friends of Edith Piaf operate this homage to the Little Sparrow inside a private apartment. Personal items including the singer's actual clothes, teensy little shoes, furniture, sheet music, fan letters, pictures, posters and mementoes of her concerts evoke the *chanteuse*'s life. Here's a glimpse into all the mysteries, tragedies and unanswered questions hidden behind the voice that brought you *La Vie en Rose*.

Paris

EYEGLASSES MUSEUM

(Musée des Lunettes et Lorgnettes de Jadis)

 380 rue St-Honoré, at rue Cambon, 1st arrondissement (Métro: Tuileries, Concorde); museum is upstairs from the shop. Open September–July, Tuesday–Saturday, 12:30–5pm. Admission: free. Phone: 01 40 20 06 98.

Known in the '60s as Europe's "King of Spectacles," the optician Pierre Marly created eyeglasses for stars ranging from Marlene Dietrich to Sammy Davis Jr. Today you can see the Dalai Lama's *lunettes* along with Elton John's and Jackie O's trademark specs and Maria Callas' contacts. The collection Marly spent decades assembling includes over 2,500 items, including Louis XIV-era lorgnettes. Don't miss the eyeglasses made for cats and dogs, or the fans and canes with built-in lenses. Opera telescopes, Sarah Bernhardt's monocle, and wooden Eskimo sunglasses crowd the single room along with checkered eyeglass frames, plaid frames, polka-dotted frames and frames made to resemble tennis racquets and slices of fruit and cheese.

Paris

FRAGONARD VETERINARY MUSEUM
(Musée Fragonard d'Alfort)

 In the National Veterinary School, 7 ave. du Général de Gaulle in the southeastern suburb of Maisons-Alfort (Métro: Alfort–Ecole Vétérinaire). Open during the school year, Tuesday–Wednesday, 2–5pm; Saturday–Sunday, 10am–5pm. Admission: 20 F; children, 15 F. Phone: 01 43 96 70 52.

At this no-holds-barred veterinary showplace, prepare yourself for the clitoral hypertrophy of a mare. A cyclopic veal calf's head floats in a jar, staring out of its one central eye. A pale menagerie of animal skeletons serves as a backdrop to huge tumescent bones, tubercular organs, a cow's ovarian cyst, a horse's tongue, fetal beasts twisted into improbable knots, and a skinned cat stretched out flat as a bathmat. All of this is an appetizer before you reach the huge glass case housing a horse and its human rider. Posed authentically, the man sitting erect and the horse midgallop, they're partially flayed, the skin peeled away to reveal bones and sinews. Honoré Fragonard, a relative of France's other famous Fragonards, created the spectacle in the late 18th century according to his own special secret technique, hoping to evoke a "horseman of the apocalypse." Other samples of his work are here as well, but it's the rider's enormous glass eyes that leave a lasting impression.

FRAGONARD VETERINARY
MUSEUM—PARIS

Paris

FREEMASONS' MUSEUM
(Musée du Grand Orient de France et de la Franc-Maçonnerie Européenne)

 Inside the temple complex at 16 rue Cadet, 9th arrondissement (Métro: Cadet); museum is in the Salle Saulnier at the rear of the building. Open Tuesday–Saturday, 2–6pm. Admission: 10 F. Phone: 01 45 23 20 92.

Peek into the Masons' secret world of spirituality, hierarchy and trowels. A wide assortment of dishes, cups, swords, coins, seals, documents, talismans, jewels, ceremonial leather bibs and even decorated eggs bear inscriptions revealing the fraternal organization's morass of cryptic sigils: moons, stars, suns, skulls, birds, pentagrams, ladders, crossed keys, the Tower of Babel, Hebrew letters, Stars of David, Satan, the Serpent, Father Time. . . . In one picture, knife-wielding skele-

tons threaten a terrified man. Exhibits detail Revolutionary-era Freemasons and George Washington's membership in the brotherhood. Another reveals how the Nazis persecuted French Freemasons during WWII, ransacking these premises and arresting key leaders in 1941. Thrones command attention at one end of the hall.

Paris

JIM MORRISON'S GRAVE

 In Père-Lachaise Cemetery, 20th arrondissement (Métro: Père-Lachaise); grave is in Section 6, closest to the Porte du Repos entrance off rue du Repos; maps are posted at all the entrances. Open March–October, Mon-

day–Friday, 8am–6pm, Saturday,
8:30am–6pm, Sunday,
9am–6pm; November–February,
Monday–Friday, 8am–5:30pm,
Saturday–Sunday, 9am–5:30pm.
Admission: free.

Faces come out of the rain to surround this popular pilgrimage site. In a commodious graveyard that holds the remains of Yves Montand, Edith Piaf, Chopin, Colette, Balzac, Molière and many other famous frogs, it is the Lizard King who attracts a constant stream of devoted loiterers. A cop patrols the flower-strewn grave while an international array of visitors busily snaps photos, lights cigarettes, scrawls graffiti and hums. Tomb-side rumor-mongers warn that the grave, bones and all, is to be moved sometime soon to points unknown. If Jim seems missing, ask where he's gone.

JIM MORRISON'S GRAVE—
PARIS

MEDICAL HISTORY MUSEUM
(Musée d'Histoire de la Médecine)

 René Descartes University, 12 rue de l'Ecole de Médecine, on the 2nd floor: Follow the signs once inside the building; 6th arrondissement (Métro: Odéon). Open mid-July–September, Monday–Friday, 2–5:30pm; October–mid-July, Monday–Wednesday and Friday–Saturday, 2–5:30pm. Admission: 20 F; children under 12, free. Phone: 01 40 46 16 93.

The knife with which a surgeon operated on Louis XV's fistula is here. So are the tools used to perform Napoleon's autopsy. Syringes, gastroscopes, an 18th-century combined tongue depressor and gag, an array of *les speculums* and devices for amputation, urology, skull drilling and cauterization are among this 100-year-old museum's grandly displayed exhibits dating back to the doctors of ancient Egypt. Note the carved anatomic model made of wood.

MUSEUM OF COUNTERFEITS
(Musée de la Contrefaçon)

16 rue de la Faisanderie, 16th arrondissement (Métro: Porte Dauphine). Open Monday–Thursday, 2–5pm; Friday, 9:30am– noon; Sunday, 2–6pm. Admission: 15 F. Phone: 01 45 01 51 11.

Fake brand-name products on display here, like "Chenel" perfume, prove the fearlessness of sleazy hucksters. You'll take an extra-hard look at that "Timex" watch on your wrist, that "Maidenform" bra under your shirt and the pack of "Marlboros" in your pocket after this. The museum's collection includes counterfeit liqueur, designer jeans, cigars, jewelry, toys, cash, even cookies. Most of the exhibits, displayed alongside the genuine article, have actually been the subjects of court battles. One room is devoted to bootleg videos and sound recordings, while the shoddily made counterfeit car parts and household appliances are good for a shiver.

MUSEUM OF CURIOSITY AND MAGIC
(Musée de la Curiosité et de la Magie)

11 rue Saint-Paul, 4th arrondissement (Métro: Sully Morland, St-Paul). Open Wednesday, Saturday and Sunday, 2–7pm. Admission: 45 F; children, 30 F. Phone: 01 42 72 13 26.

Taking some but not all the mystery out of sawing ladies in half, this museum is operated by experienced prestidigitators. Occupying rooms spookily made to look like caves, it traces 200 years of magic with over 3,000 artifacts, including trick cards, false-bottomed boxes, disappearing scarves, deforming mirrors, optical illusions, interactive displays and automated figures. One room is devoted to spiritualism, complete with vibrating tables and other tools used by fake mediums. You'll never feel the same about seances

again! A live magic show completes the tour.

MUSEUM OF EROTIC ART
(Musée de l'Erotisme)

72 blvd. de Clichy, 18th arrondissement (Métro: Blanche). Open daily, 10am–2am. Admission: 40 F; students, 30 F. Phone: 01 42 58 28 73.

Don't miss the elegant wooden chair fitted with its own golden dildo, or the modern Russian "icon" featuring jism-happy priests. If the Pigalle's sex clubs make you lust after fine art in a classic setting, this museum should do the trick. Artists spanning the globe and the eras put their collective spin on sensation and penetration with over 2,000 carvings, masks, toys, photographs, paintings, sculptures and implements. Nepalese temple carvings make mating seem a little scary.

MUSEUM OF PUBLIC ASSISTANCE AND PARIS HOSPITALS
(Musée de l'Assistance Publique–Hôpitaux de Paris)

47 quai de la Tournelle, on the riverfront, 5th arrondissement (Métro: Saint Michel, Maubert-Mutualité, Cité); enter through the courtyard. Open Tuesday–Saturday, 10am–5pm. Admis-

sion: 20 F; students and children,
10 F. Phone: 01 40 27 50 05.

Maybe bedpans aren't the first things that pop into your mind when you think of Paris. But the story of what the city has done with its plague victims, psychotics, invalids, military casualties, women in labor and abandoned babies gives history a whole new perspective. Paintings worthy of the Louvre, but depicting the ill, hang elegantly among enema syringes, baby bottles, rubber nipples, blood-encrusted Red Cross uniforms and vintage electroshock-therapy machines. One exhibit in the two-story complex is devoted to infanticide while others feature vaccination and skull drilling. St. Vincent de Paul, a Parisian who aided at-risk tots, is honored, and his vestments are on display.

MUSEUM OF PUBLIC ASSISTANCE—
PARIS.

ORFILA ANATOMY MUSEUM LOBBY
(Musée Orfila)

🖐 *45, rue des Saints-Pères, 8th floor, in the Université René Descartes, Faculté de Médecine building, half a block north of Blvd. Saint Germain, 6th arrondissement (Metro: Saint Germain des Prés). Lobby exhibits visible anytime the university building is open, but it has no official opening hours; usually open daily 8am (or earlier) until late in the evening. Admission: free. Phone: 01 42 86 20 47.*

No fewer than three anatomy museums hide out on the 8th floor of this nondescript university building: Musée Orfila, Musée Delmas and Musée Rouviere. To see any of them you must first take the elevator to Room 606 on the 6th floor and apply to the Secretary of the Institut d'Anatomie, who never seems to be there and who wouldn't necessarily let you in even if she were. Luckily, the exhibits in the museum's shared lobby are worth the trip all by themselves, require no permission and are visible anytime. The desiccated nude corpses of an entire family—man, woman and child, apparently all found naturally preserved—greet you as you enter, standing stiffly in a glass case. Nearby are 18th-century wax-works of male genitals, anuses and skinned faces. Another case holds rows of headless babies and Siamese twins in formaldehyde. Some jars of deformed body parts are ill-sealed, and the formaldehyde has partly evaporated. The museums, skulking behind closed doors, promise more horrors to those who charm their way in.

ORFILA MUSEUM LOBBY—
PARIS

PET CEMETERY
(Cimetière des Chiens)

4 Pont de Clichy, in the As-nières-sur-Seine suburb, north-west of the center (Métro: Pont de Clichy); cemetery is on the riverfront. Open mid-March–mid-October, Wednesday–Monday, 10am–7pm; mid-October–mid-March, Wednesday–Monday, 10am–5pm. Admission: 16 F; children, 8 F. Phone: 01 40 86 24 11.

The original Rin Tin Tin is buried here along with rows and rows of beloved cats, dogs and other pets—even a monkey. Figurines, plastic bouquets and porcelain photographs of the departed creatures adorn many of the graves, with emotional epitaphs mourning the lost Fifi, Loulou and Jules. Founded a hundred years ago, the cemetery has a run-down look today, its fountains crumbling and dozens of feral cats roaming like ghosts among the granite monuments. Useless-looking poodles comprise a majority of the dead, but a large monument remembers Barry, a life-saving but martyred St. Bernard.

ORFILA MUSEUM LOBBY—
PARIS

ASNIÉRES CIMETIÉRE DES CHIENS—
PARIS

CIMETIÉRE DES CHIENS—PARIS

PREFECTURAL POLICE MUSEUM
(Musée de la Préfecture de Police)

 In the police headquarters at 1 bis, rue des Carmes, 5th arrondissement (Métro: Mutualité);

 museum is on the second floor. Open Monday–Friday, 9am–5pm; Saturday, 10am–5pm. Admission: free. Phone: 01 44 41 52 50.

A stout wooden execution post, circa 1940-44, flanks the entrance. Note prodigious wear and tear at chest level. A Revolution-era guillotine blade, surrounded by gory paintings of crime and punishment, furthers the feeling. A model guillotine complete with a little head in a basket shows how the device works. French history buffs will want to peruse documents from the Dreyfus case, and who could resist the matchbook with which a condemned man lit his last cigarette? Nazi relics include a gun sneakily built inside a fountain pen. Criminals' death masks help illustrate sagas of 19th-century Parisian crimes. On display is a rope with which a murderer lowered his victims into a pit; a woman's skull alongside the hammer that cracked it; and the rolling pin with which a teen killed his cousin in order to steal his watch. An exhibit on explosives includes a bomb hidden in a flowerpot.

PRINCESS DIANA SHRINE

 On Place de l'Alma, at the north end of Pont de l'Alma, on the border between the 8th and 16th arrondissements; the shrine is next to the Seine on the west end of the square where it becomes Avenue de New-York (Metro: Alma-Marceau). Always visible. Admission: free.

On August 31, 1997, Princess Diana and her boyfriend Dodi Al-Fayedh died when their car crashed in the tunnel that runs beneath Place de l'Alma. When grief-stricken fans started flocking to the spot to pay tribute a few hours later, they were surprised to find that the French had already erected an elaborate memorial in her honor. Or so the fans thought. Through a strange twist of fate, a huge brass flame standing above the tunnel had been there for ten years, erected on the Place de l'Alma in 1987 to comemmorate the Statue of Liberty's centennial. But few bothered to read the plaque. Within days the monument (a replica of the flame in the Statue of Liberty's torch) was blanketed in flowers, notes and tearful tributes. Parisian city officials were not pleased, and removed all the memorials. A few days later, more appeared. The battle between Diana-worshippers and the Paris police con-

tinues to this day. It's readily apparent that Diana is ascending toward saintly status: many of the notes here are prayers to her, or votives thanking her for miraculous intercession. If you want to see the actual place where she died, cross the busy street eastward to the entrance of the tunnel on Cours Albert 1er, climb onto the lawn and peer down under the square.

Paris

ST. VINCENT DE PAUL'S BODY

In the Chapel of the Priests of the Congregation of the Mission, 95 rue de Sèvres, 6th arrondissement (Métro: Sèvres-Babylone, Vaneau). Open Monday–Saturday, 7–11:30am and 1:30–6:30pm; Sunday, 8am–noon and 1:30–3:15pm. Admission: free. Phone: 01 45 49 84 84.

Ordained in 1600, Vincent was allegedly once taken captive during a voyage and sold as a slave in Tunisia. He is said to have converted his master, who freed him, but Vincent's brush with bondage might have inspired the selfless charity for which the saint is known. It's no accident that his name crowns thrift stores far and wide to this day. His corpse, artfully coated in wax, rests in an extravagant silver-and-glass casket on a platform high above the main altar. Climb the staircase for an up-close view of the saint in his lace sleeves and trim slippers, his hands folded neatly. He looks blissfully asleep.

PRINCESS DIANA SHRINE—PARIS

STRAVINSKY FOUNTAIN—PARIS

SEWER TOURS
(Les Égouts)

 Entrance is across from 93 quai d'Orsay, next to Pont de l'Alma on the river, 7th arrondissement (Métro: Alma-Marceau). Open May–October, Saturday–Wednesday, 11am–5pm; November–December and February–April, Saturday–Wednesday, 11am–4pm. Admission: 25 F; students and children, 20 F; children under 5, free. Phone: 01 47 05 10 29.

Your journey through the mysterious world of wastewater dispersal begins with a museum and an audiovisual show. Then follow your tour guide deep into the bowels of the city to explore Paris's brightly illuminated sewage tunnels. Learn their history and function while inspecting the pipes. So *this* is where all those croissants end up. Yes, it smells. And it's mucky and slippery, so don't wear those white suede sandals.

STRAVINSKY FOUNTAIN
(Fontaine Stravinsky)

 Adjacent to the Pompidou Centre, 3rd arrondissement (Métro: Chatelet). Visible at any time. Admission free.

Shallow as a kiddie pool, this huge concrete oblong is populated with dozens of fantastic figures and mechanisms. Avant-garde artist Niki de Saint Phalle has created many of her trademark plump creatures in flashy colors that offset the gray surroundings: a revolving heart, an elephant's nodding head, a pair of red lips that spit continuously. Interspersed with these are the slightly more sinister metal sculptures of fellow artist Jean Tinguely: spinning wheels, mobile steel tubes, steel things gyrating. What draws the eye most forcefully is a giant bright blue hat that spins and spins.

STUFFED RATS

 In the window of the Arouze shop, 8 rue des Halles, 1st arrondissement (Métro: Chatelet). Visible at any time.

Specializing since 1872 in rat traps, this shop is devoted to what it calls the *destruction des animaux nuisables*—vermin. With countless deaths on their hands, its owners won't get into Buddhist heaven. Twenty huge dead rats, taxidermed and then cunningly reinserted into traps, hang suspended in the display window. Signage explains that the rats were all killed in the Les Halles district around 1925. Taxidermed mice and helpless-looking stuffed moles are on display as well, along with a roach motel that's simply full to bursting.

Just east of Pontoise, which is 25 km northwest of Paris on the N14 road

ABSINTHE MUSEUM
(Musée de l'Absinthe)

44 rue Callé. Open June–September, Wednesday–Sunday, 11am–6pm; October–May, Saturday–Sunday, 11am–6pm. Phone: 30 36 83 26.

W ho would have thought the distilled essence of anise and wormwood could ever have gotten so popular that it destroyed people's lives and then was outlawed, just like opium? Soldiers in the African army, who drank the tangy green beverage to ward off dysentery, introduced absinthe to the thirsty civilian masses early in the 19th century. Artists in particular couldn't get enough. On two floors, this museum traces the liqueur's roots to ancient times, when wormwood was recognized as an effective vermifuge. Learn how 100 years ago talented French fringe-dwellers believed absinthe aided their minds.

Paris

SUBTERRANEAN WINE MUSEUM
(Musée du Vin)

5 square Charles Dickens, off rue des Eaux, 16th arrondissement (Métro: Passy). Open Tuesday–Sunday, 10am–6pm. Admission: 35 F; seniors, 30 F; students, 29 F; includes tasting. Phone: 01 45 25 63 26.

D eep underground, in the cellars of what was once the wine-producing Passy Abbey, fifteen chambers recreate a long history. Costumed mannequins portray ancient Roman vintners as well as bar patrons, barrel makers and medieval monks hard at work over their sacramental formulae. Gray stone subterranean archways and a statue of Bacchus frame impeccably organized thematic exhibits featuring corkscrews and rare bottles. Wine samples add a welcome interactive touch.

Chartres

THE HOLY CLOTH
(La Sainte Chemise)

In Chartres Cathedral, two-thirds of the way to the rear, in the left-hand apsidal chapel behind the choir. Open daily, 7:30am–7:15pm. Admission: free. Phone: 02 37 21 56 33.

The large, whitish cloth enshrined here under the filtered light of stained glass is said to have been what the Virgin was wearing when Jesus was born. Charlemagne's grandson, France's King Charles the Bald, owned the relic in 876. When Chartres was under siege in 911, the cloth's powers were said to have protected the defenders, after which the cloth's fame grew enormously. French queens in succeeding centuries took advantage of its allegedly miraculous ability to vanquish labor pains. Having been scientifically tested, it is known to be 2,000 years old and of Middle Eastern origin.

MOSAIC HOUSE
(Maison Picassiette)

22 rue du Repos, between rue de Sours and rue St. Cheron, east of the center. Open Wednesday–Saturday and Monday, 10am–noon and 2–6pm (last admittance, 5:45pm); Sunday, 2–6pm (last admittance, 5:45pm). Admission: 10 F; children, 5 F. Phone: 02 37 34 10 78.

Raymond Isidore, an untrained artist who worked at the nearby cemetery, started decorating the outer walls of his house with bits of broken china in 1938. He kept it up for nearly thirty years until his death in 1964, mosaicking every surface outside the house and much of the inside with whimsical images of himself, his wife, the Virgin Mary, windmills, vases of flowers and the entire Chartres skyline, cathedral and all. Then he started mosaicking his furniture. Among the mosaicked pathways in his flowery garden you will also find a miniature Eiffel Tower, a chapel and other structures which Isidore built and patiently coated with bits of dishes, cup handles and shells.

30 km east of Paris, off the A4 road

LOUIS BRAILLE'S BIRTHPLACE

13 rue Louis Braille. Open October–March, Tuesday–Thursday and Saturday–Sunday, 2–5pm, Friday by appointment; April–September, Tuesday–Thursday and Saturday–Sunday, 10am–noon and 2–6pm, Friday, by appointment. Admission: 15 F; children under 12, free. Phone: 01 60 04 82 80.

If you aren't blind, then "Braille" is one of those names at once completely familiar yet totally mysterious. Who *was* the guy? Housed in Louis Braille's picturesque childhood home, this museum uses memorabilia to eagerly fill in the details on this Frenchman who, completely blinded after cutting one eye accidentally with a knife when he was three, went on to invent the raised-dot alphabet and to become a scholar in his own right, teaching algebra and music. A dramatic painting captures young Louis on the verge of seizing the fateful knife.

Elancourt

15 km west of Versailles

FRANCE MINIATURE

25 route du Mesnil (boulevard André Malraux). Open mid-March–mid-November, daily, 10am–7pm. Admission: 75 F; children 4–16, 50 F. Phone: 01 30 62 40 79.

Don't have time to rent a Citroen and tour the whole country? Here on 13 acres are miniature versions of French landmarks. Organized by region and encompassing all styles and eras, they're perfect down to the last roof tile, turret and gargoyle. Inspect no less than fifteen entire mini-villages evoking French country life from Picardy to the castle-studded Loire Valley to Corsica, not to mention a somber gray Notre-Dame and a thirty-foot Eiffel Tower. Mont Saint-Michel stands reflected grandly in its own little pool, while tiny aristocrats disembark from a tiny horse carriage in the shadow of Versailles' ruddy façade. A mini-TGV glides on its curved track past a sleek white palace and minuscule boats bob in the harbor at La Rochelle. Amphitheaters, ruins, restaurants and dozens of other buildings stand thigh-high.

Marne-la-Vallée

32 km east of Paris

DISNEYLAND PARIS

Take the RER (line A) or TGV to Marne-la-Vallée-Chessy station. Open daily, April–mid-July, 9am–8pm; mid-July–August,

9am–11pm; September–October, 10am–6pm; extended hours on weekends; reduced hours in winter. Admission: in high season, 195 F, children, 150 F; in low season, 150 F, children, 120 F. Phone: 01 60 30 60 30.

Indiana Jones and the Temple of Peril is a roller coaster. Ghosts haunt the Phantom Manor and Pinocchio looks particularly evil at this hugely expensive "cultural Chernobyl," which for a while no one thought would last. All the familiar rides and characters are here, except that Goofy talks like Gerard Depardieu. Main Street U.S.A. feels as weirdly foreign as Timbuktu. For round-the-clock disorientation, several theme-hotels here offer Americana *à la Française*. Hotel New York has skyscrapers and its own Central Park. Newport Bay Club has a New England lighthouse. Hotel Cheyenne has a chuckwagon and saloon. The Davey Crockett Ranch has log cabins, teepees and a "trading post" stocked with Disney souvenirs.

Milly-le-Foret

45 km south of Paris

THE CYCLOPS
(Le Cyclop)

In the forest just west of town, off the D837 road; follow the signs. Open May–September, Friday, 10:15am–1pm and 2–4:45pm, Saturday, 11am–1pm and 2–5:30pm, Sunday, 11am–1pm and 2–6:15pm; October, Friday, 10:15am–1pm and 2–4:15pm, Saturday, 11am–1pm and 2–4:15pm, Sunday, 11am–1pm and 2–5pm. Admission: 35 F; students, 30 F; children, 20 F;

children under 10 not admitted inside the sculpture; exterior visit, 5 F. Phone: 01 64 98 83 17 (tourist office); reservations required for Friday visits.

This gloppy, one-eyed sculpture rising more than sixty feet from the forest floor was designed by avant-garde artists Jean Tinguely and Niki de Saint Phalle. They spent three years and 300 tons of steel making it. The steel face, with its two fangs and a tongue that doubles as a slide, shines like a mirror, while complex systems of metal wheels, vertiginous ramps, girders and catwalks jut out behind. Climb a spiral staircase inside the head to view paintings, mosaics, sculptures and architectural whims on its upper levels, with structural steel a key motif. Parts of the sculpture move, enhancing the industrial ambience.

Provins

75 km southeast of Paris

SUBTERRANEAN PASSAGES
(Souterrains)

Entrance is at 16 rue St-Thibault, in the middle of the Medieval City. Open November–April, Saturday–Sunday, guided tours at 3 and 4pm; April–October, Monday–Friday, guided tours at 3 and 4pm; Saturday–Sunday, 11am–6pm. Admission: 22 F; children, 14 F. Phone: 01 64 60 26 26.

Someone named Clement chiseled his name into the wall of this underground labyrinth in 1788. Other graffitists left their marks as well, inscribing animal shapes, mysterious abstract images and other messages here and there around the vaulted tunnels under the town's old infirmary. Begun in the 12th century, the system contains as many as 150 chambers, many of which were dug out by laborers seeking loam for use in the local wool industry.

Rambouillet

18 km southwest of Paris

SHELL COTTAGE
(Chaumière aux Coquillages)

On the grounds of Rambouillet Castle, west of the center, off rue R. Poincaré. Open April–September, Wednesday–Monday, 10am–noon and 2–5:30pm; October–March, Wednesday–Monday, 10am–noon and 2–3:30pm. Admission: 40 F; students, 34 F; children under 12, free. Phone: 01 34 83 29 09.

Thousands of seashells coat the rounded walls, niches and arched windowsills of this "cottage." Created in the 18th century to augment the 14th-century castle and keep up with a current fad for shell grottoes, the chamber has complex floral designs, faux columns, hanging "ribbons" and geometric patterns all crafted in mussel shells, mother-of-pearl and marble. Another folly on the grounds is *la Laiterie de la Reine*, where Queen Marie Antoinette played at being a milkmaid.

Senlis

30 km northeast of Paris

PARC ASTÉRIX

 5 kilometers north of Charles de Gaulle Airport on the A1 road (exit at the "Parc Astérix" sign); or take the RER to Roissy Charles-de-Gaulle station, then a bus from the station. Open April–June and September–October, daily, 10am–6pm; July–August, 9:30am–7pm. Admission: 170 F; children, 120 F; children under 3, free. Phone: 33 3 44 62 34 04 or 34.

Zeus is the god of roller coasters and the Styx is a splashy raft-ride at this park that revisits history as seen by Astérix the Gaul. Just as in the popular cartoons, this little boar-hunter with the big yellow mustache pops up everywhere. The park's version of ancient Greece offers a temple and a dolphin show; ancient Rome sports a carousel and Nero's Flotilla. Lose yourself in the Druids' Forest, then telescope French history in one fell swoop with chevaliers, menhirs, musketeers, medieval castles, motorcycles and the heist of the *Mona Lisa*.

Thoiry-en-Yvelines

40 km west of Paris

WILDLIFE PARK

 At the Chateau de Thoiry. Open Easter–September, daily, 10am–6pm; October–Easter, daily, 10am–5pm. Admission: 100 F; Children under 13, 79 F. Phone: 01 34 87 52 25.

Over a thousand exotic animals live in the shadow of this Renaissance castle. Occupying a zoo and a wildlife reserve is a menagerie of hippos, bears, tigers, zebras, giraffes, elephants, dromedaries, panthers—even komodo dragons. Many species roam free in *La Reserve Africaine*, where the sight of lions lounging in the winter snow adds yet another surreal dimension. Wild beasts were housed at Thoiry as long ago as 1559. But in those days nobles hunted them for sport.

Brittany, Normandy and the North

35 km west of Caen

BALLOON MUSEUM
(Musée des Ballons)

In Balleroy Castle (Chateau de Balleroy). Open mid-March–mid-October, Thursday–Tuesday, 9am–noon and 2–6pm.

Admission: 25 F; children, 22 F.
Phone: 31 21 60 61.

After buying this Renaissance castle, millionaire Malcolm Forbes installed a museum in one of its old stables to immortalize his passion for hot-air balloons. Covering the pioneering Montgolfier brothers and modern-day balloonists, the world's first museum of its kind inspires acrophobia with historic documents, miniatures, photographs, models, vintage balloon parts and colorful dioramas. Tiny figures in three-cornered hats hail landmark launches.

Forest of Brocéliande

Everybody knows that King Arthur had a cute British accent, and that his Knights of the Round Table spent most of their time gallivanting around England in search of the Holy Grail. Everybody except the French. In truth, many of the earliest Arthurian legends took place not in England but here in Brittany's Forest of Brocéliande, nowadays also called Paimpont Forest. Despite being much smaller now than in days of yore, this ancient woodland is a virtual paradise for Grail fanatics and would-be Merlins—nowhere else in the world will you find a higher concentration of mystical sites associated with King Arthur. The forest is 40 kilometers west of Rennes, just northwest of Plélan-le-Grand and the N24 road, surrounding the town of Paimpont (which is connected to Rennes by several buses daily). Your best bet would be to first stop by the tourist offices in either Plélan-le-Grand (in the Mairie [town hall] on the central square) or Paimpont (5 Esplanade Brocéliande) and stock up on maps and brochures, without which you could quite easily get lost. Many of the sites are accessible via signposted walking trails, but getting around the forest without a car is not easy, as public transportation in the area is severely limited.

The Church of Tréhorenteuc is a logical place to start. Rebuilt in 1942 by a local priest obsessed with Arthurian legends, this small village church is bursting with mysterious symbols and images of the Holy Grail, the Knights of the Round Table and

Celtic mythology, including a remarkable stained-glass window. (Tréhorenteuc is 15 kilometers west of Plélan-le-Grand, north of the N24 on the D141 road, at the western edge of the forest; the church is in the center of the village. Open June–September, daily, 10am–6pm; October–May, daily, 10am–noon and 2–5pm.)

The Tréhorenteuc Tourist Office, nearby, will furnish you with pamphlets and maps; they also arrange guided walks (Place Abbé Gillard, Tréhorenteuc; open daily, June–September, 9am–7pm; October–May, 10am–noon and 2–6pm; phone: 02 97 93 05 12).

The Valley of No Return, which follows the course of a river just south of Tréhorenteuc, leads to a small lake called the **Fairy's Mirror**, legendary home of the magical Morgan le Fay and imprisoned spirits (follow the signs to the clearly marked walking trail leading south from the village). On hills to the south of this valley you can find ancient mystical megaliths called **The House of Viviane** (overlooking the valley next to the hamlet of la Touche-Guérin) and **The Tomb of the Giant** (a little farther south on the peak of the hill called la Butte de Tiot, 1 kilometer north of the hamlet called le Lidrio).

On the east side of the same hill is **La Chapelle St-Jean**, an old church once attended by the Knights Templar, who carry their own Grail associations (on the D312 road).

Barenton Fountain (or Merlin's Spring), farther north, is a sacred ancient ritual site. The Druids thought the water burbling from the ground here had magical properties. Many still think so: You can summon a rainstorm by sprinkling water from the fountain on the big stone nearby, or cure your insanity by taking a sip. This is also the spot where, according to a pivotal Arthurian legend, Merlin met Viviane (1 kilometer east of the hamlet of Folle Pensée, which is 5 kilometers north of Tréhorenteuc off the D141; signs indicate the walking trail).

The Chateau de Comper, a 14th-century castle perched next to a lake said to be the eternal home of the fairy Viviane, has taken advantage of its location to declare itself the **Centre de l'Imaginaire Arthurien**. Here you'll find Arthurian exhibitions, lectures, video screenings and historical re-creations throughout the summer. They also arrange guided tours to the forest (6 kilometers north of Paimpont on the D31 road; the chateau is on the east side of the village of Comper. Open April, May and September, Wednesday–Thursday and Saturday–Monday; June–August, Wednesday–Monday. Call ahead for events schedule: 02 97 22 79 96). At the northern end of the forest are two more important sites: **The Fountain of Youth** (yes, the very one—here it was under our noses all that time) and **Merlin's Tomb**. The tomb is purported to be the burial place of Merlin's body—his spirit is still alive. These stones are actually just the jumbled remains of an ancient cromlech supposedly used by ancient and modern Druids in magical rituals (1½ kilometers southwest of St-Malon-sur-Mel, which is 10 kilometers north of Plélan-la-Grand on the D59. Both sites are difficult to find without a map: head southwest from St-Malon-sur-Mel, passing through the hamlet of Tréveré until you come to the Etang de la Marette. The fountain is just beyond this lake, in a small cluster of trees; the tomb is on a hilly area nearby).

Unrepentant King Arthur addicts might consider staying the night in **Le Manoir du Tertre**, an eerie hotel that holds Celtic storytelling evenings and even sponsors ghostly nighttime walks through the forest (2½ kilometers south of Paimpont, just west of the D71; phone: 02 99 07 81 02).

Cossé-le-Vivien

55 km southeast of Rennes
ROBERT TATIN MUSEUM

In and around the farmhouse called La Frénouse; it's hard to miss. Open in summer, daily, 10am–noon and 2–7pm; winter, daily, 10am–noon and 2–5:50pm. Phone: 43 98 80 89.

Housepainter-turned-world-traveler-turned-ceramicist Robert Tatin sculpted dozens of exuberant fantasy figures all around his 6th-century stone house in the countryside. Staring with goggle eyes alongside pools and decorated walls are statues of Joan of Arc, Paul Gaugin, Vercingetorix and Tatin's other idols, created in an Olmecs-on-acid kind of style. The massive Door of the Sun pursues a yin-yang theme, while a monolithic Mary offsets the mother goddess embodied in Tatin's Door of the Moon. Gray stone images probing metaphysics and history rear up all over the property, where Tatin himself was buried after his death in 1983. Along with the artist's cryptic paintings, more sculptures fill the museum in his former house.

Granville

SHELL FAIRYLAND
(Féerie des Coquillages)

On the outcropping next to the lighthouse, west of the train station. Open March–November, daily, 9am–12:30 and 2–7pm. Admission: 40 F. Phone: 02 33 50 19 10 or 33 50 19 83.

At last, someone has come up with a use for all those millions of seashells that litter our beaches, reefs and ocean floors. Countless cowries, clam shells, scallops, sea snails and more—including over three tons of coral—have been fashioned into statuary, soaring "stained-glass" windows and miniature cityscapes displayed in this surreal museum. A rampant lion, recumbent mermaid and delicate mosque, all covered in shells, hardly prepare you for the resplendent Italian Room, complete with floor-to-ceiling columns. On one wall, each of 2,000 separate flower designs took two hours to make. Also on the premises are amazing artworks made with semi-precious stones and butterfly wings.

JULES VERNE MUSEUM
(Musée Jules Verne)

3 rue le l'Hermitage, on the waterfront. Open Wednesday–Saturday and Monday, 10am–noon and 2–5pm; Sunday, 2–5pm. Admission: 8 F; students and seniors, 4 F. Phone: 40 69 72 52.

The writer's eyeglasses and a painting of his wife add a cozy touch to Verne's reconstructed sitting-room. Other chambers in this three-story paean recall Verne's characters and futuristic creations. Captain Nemo is flanked by a diving suit, an octopus and a view of the Loire. Phileas Fogg and the rest come alive in the form of books, posters, letters, artifacts and furniture left behind by the author, a Nantes native. Note the compass and globe that Verne himself used when plotting his characters' adventures.

SCULPTED ROCKS
(Les Rochers Sculptés)

5 kilometers north of town in the suburb of Rothéneuf, on the Pointe du Christ; follow the signs from the intersection of rue Abbé Fourré and chemin des Rochers Sculptés. Open in summer, daily, 9am–9pm; winter, 10am–5pm. Phone: 02 99 56 97 64.

A local priest started chiseling these cliffs nearly 100 years ago.

LES ROCHERS SCULPTÉS—ST-MALO

The surf and sea air inspired him, and when he was done Abbé Fourré had sculpted some 300 rocks in the shapes of sea monsters and other creatures who could only have been conceived in dreams. Pathways wind in and out among the sprawling expanse of weathered sculptures, now considered a major example of *art naïf*. In the right light, the chiseled features seem to have grown naturally out of the rock.

The Loire Valley

On the Loire River

THE CHANTELOUP PAGODA
(Pagode de Chanteloup)

Just south of Amboise, off the D31 road: it's visible from afar. Open June and September, daily, 10am–7pm; July–August, daily, 9:30am–8pm; October, daily, J10am–noon and 2–5:30pm; November, Monday–Friday, 2–5pm, Saturday–Sunday, 10am–

*noon and 2–5:50pm; February,
Monday–Friday, 2–5pm, Saturday and Sunday, 10am–noon
and 2–5pm; March, daily,
10am–noon and 2–5pm; April,
daily, 10am–noon and 2–5:30pm;
May, daily, 10am–6pm. Admission: 30 F; students, 24 F; children, 20 F; children under 7, free;
half-hour boat rides on the pool,
25 F. Phone: 02 47 57 20 97.*

*C*hinoiserie—phony Chineseness—
was trendy in France when the
exiled Duke of Choiseul, former
prime minister to Louis XV, erected
this seven-story pagoda as a monument to those who had been kind to
him during his days of woe. It was
once a mere folly on the grounds of
his castle. The castle itself was later
demolished, leaving only this out-
sized garden ornament as a reminder
of past glories. Today, from the 130-
foot summit, you can see as far as the
Cathedral of Tours and across the
green Forest of Loches, while the
pagoda is reflected in a huge pool.
Visitors can play an array of 18th-
century outdoor games, including
giant dominoes and croquet.

On the Loire River

THE ENCHANTED HOUSE
(Maison Enchantée)

*7 rue du Général-Foy, between
rue Victor Hugo and rue Rabelais.
Open June–August, daily,
10am–7pm; September–October
and March–May, 10am–noon and
2–6pm; November–February,
2–5pm. Admisson: 30 F; children,
22 F. Phone: 47 23 24 50.*

*L*ittle robots dressed in the rich
velvets and brocades of yesteryear enact twenty-five different
scenes from history and literature.
Their creepy puppet faces will make
a permanent impression on your
brain. In one scene, Leonardo da
Vinci paints the *Mona Lisa* while
behatted musicians play mandolins
and flutes surrounded by faux
stained glass. In another, Doctor
Jekyll faces an identity crisis. In all,
some 250 characters jerk spasti-
cally.

On the Loire River

HOUSE OF
MICROMINIATURES
(Maison de l'Art Microminiature)

*9 rue Nationale, a few blocks
west of the castle. Open Tuesday–Sunday, 10am–7pm. Admission: 28 F; students, 25 F;
children, 18 F. Phone: 02 47 57
34 05.*

*A*ctual mosquitoes hunch over a
chessboard that's just the right
size for them, complete with chess
clock and chessmen. Not far away, an
actual dead grasshopper is posed
upright holding a finely crafted, infini-
tesimal violin. Visitors peer through
microscopes to examine such offerings
as a portrait of Rabelais carved into a
poppy seed. A four-by-five-millimeter
Mona Lisa is here, as are the micro-
miniaturist's trademark: gold sculptures mounted on a human hair. The
world's smallest book is here, measuring 0.9 mm by 0.9 mm and filled with
actual words and pictures.

Amboise

On the Loire River

LEONARDO DA VINCI'S INVENTIONS

*In the Chateau du Clos-Luce.
Open in January, daily, 10am–
5pm; February–March and mid-
November–December, daily,
9am– 6pm; April–June and
September–mid-November, daily, 9am–7pm; July–August, daily, 9am–8pm. Admission: 40 F;
students, 30 F. Phone: 02 47 57
62 88.*

Before dying here on May 2, 1519,
Leonardo spent his last four years
enjoying the Loire Valley. A modern-
day team affiliated with IBM has constructed forty of the prescient
machines he invented. Made solely of
materials available during the Renaissance, these include the world's first
airplane, the world's first car, the heli-
copter, the parachute, the tank, the
machine gun and more. Lodged in a
Renaissance manor, the structures
show how a single mind altered so
many parts of the future.

Blois

*In the Loire Valley, midway between
Orleans and Tours*

HOUSE OF MAGIC
(Maison de la Magie)

*1 place de la Chateau, across
from the castle. Open June and
September, daily, 10am–1pm
and 2–6pm; July–August, daily,
10am–6:30pm; October-Novem-
ber, Wednesday–Thursday,*

Harry Houdini borrowed his
stage name from Jean-Eugene
Robert-Houdin, a Blois-born 19th-
century master magician whose legend takes center stage here. The
house itself seems to play tricks, as a
six-headed dragon appears out of
nowhere and seemingly inanimate
objects suddenly move. Wands,
cards, dice and other magicians'
tools shed new light on stunts that
used to baffle you, and exhibits on
famous prestidigitators reveal the
public's incessant delight in not
understanding what's going on. Real
live magicians are on hand, and your
visit includes a trip to the museum's
theater. Prepare to be deceived.

Chinon

48 km southwest of Tours

ANIMATED WINE AND COOPERAGE MUSEUM

*(Musée Animé du Vin et de la Tonnel-
lerie)*

*12 rue Voltaire, 2 blocks north
of the Vienne river, just east of
the castle. Open April–September, daily, 10:30am–12:30pm
and 2–7:30pm. Admission: 24 F.
Phone: 02 47 93 25 63.*

A local man singlehandedly created all the life-size moving figures who harvest grapes, make wine
and assemble barrels in which to put
the wine amid this museum's evocative 15th-century architecture. Using
old tools, the models labor away to
the sound of a taped narration—you

can ask for the English version—in which Rabelais is merrily quoted. Naturally a free *dégustation* of Chinon wine rounds out the experience.

Dénezé-sous-Doué

15 km west of Saumur

THE SCULPTED CAVERN
(Caverne Sculptée)

Just outside the village, off the D69 road; follow the signs. Open Easter–June and September–October, daily, 2–7pm; July–August, daily, 10am–7pm. Phone: 02 41 59 15 40.

A mysterious brotherhood of 16th-century stonemasons—nobody knows quite who—carved hundreds of human figures into the subterranean stone walls of this rounded cavern. Among these carvings is what has been called the first depiction of a Native American ever made in Europe. Another clearly shows a woman nursing a child. Side by side in the yellowish stone, some hand in hand, the gowned figures seem to be doing an endless dance, their eyes staring, lips parted, fingers neatly chiseled. The anonymous artists' message remains obscure.

Doué-la-Fontaine

15 km southwest of Saumur

ZOO OF THE MINES
(Parc Zoologique "Les Minières")

At the town gates on rue de Cholet. Open in summer, daily, 9am–7pm; winter, 10am–noon

 and 2–6pm. Admission: 50 F; children, 35 F; children under 3, free. Phone: 02 41 59 18 58.

The 500 wild animals roaming in "semi-captivity" here probably appreciate the leafy, jungle-like setting. But they might be oblivious to the zoo's peculiar troglodyte charm. Lodged in an old quarry, the park occupies an extensive labyrinth of caverns and grottoes, carved out of the rock long ago by industrious miners. Today the lions, tigers, flamingoes, apes and other beasts lope from bamboo grove to waterfall, yawning and shrieking. Watch jaguars fish for their lunch; feed giraffes in a very intimate manner; and wander among carnivorous birds devouring bloody carrion in the Vultures' Quarry.

Reignac-sur-Indre

Midway between Tours and Loches, on the Indre river

LABYRINTHUS

Off the RN 143 road. Open July–August, daily, 10:30am–7:30pm; September, Friday–Sunday, 10:30am–7:30pm. Admission: 45 F; children, 30 F; children under 4, free. Phone: 02 38 98 00 80.

Every year on the same spot a group of expert mazeologists create a fantastic series of befuddling labyrinths out of growing cornstalks and flowers. No effort is spared, no detail overlooked in these ultra-sophisticated temporary mazes. Wacky sculptures, funhouse mirrors and viewing platforms are positioned at strategic locations; costumed actors prance about to entertain and confuse you. Each season the mazes are in a different theme: previous years revolved around *Alice in Wonderland*, and outer space. Future productions promise to be just as inventive.

Rochemenier

20 km southwest of Saumur

TROGLODYTE VILLAGE

Rochemenier is 1 kilometer northeast of Louresse, which is 6 kilometers northwest of Doué-la-Fontaine. Open April–October, daily, 9:30am–7pm; November and February–March, Saturday–Sunday, 2–6pm. Admission: 23 F; students, 13 F. Phone: 02 41 59 18 15.

Under the quaint little village that stands on the plain is another one twice as large. Over 200 years ago, when digging was cheaper than building, farmers in search of dry, fireproof housing dug 250 rooms out of the limy rock—forty subterranean farms in all, complete with bedrooms, barns and dining rooms. Today you can visit twenty underground rooms, a subterranean farmyard with animals, and an underground chapel. Bushes and grass sprout from the roof. An updated troglodyte house, furnished with mod cons, lends life underground an irresistible appeal.

St-Hilaire-St-Florent

4km northwest of Saumur

MASK MUSEUM
(Musée du Masque)

Rue de l'Abbaye, near the National Riding School, just west of the Thouet river. Open Easter–mid-October, daily, 10am–12:30 pm and 2:30–6:30 pm. Admission: 25 F; children, 15 F. Phone: 41 50 75 26.

This museum doesn't merely hang its prodigious mask collection on the walls. In evocative surroundings, dummies dressed in appropriate costumes model 100 years' worth of masks. An ancient Egyptian scene involves a masked mummy lying prone at the foot of a column inscribed with hieroglyphs; the nearby mural impressionistically evokes the Nile. Standing close at hand in slinky dresses are a masked Cleopatra and a servant, who smile happily, regardless of the corpse. Other dummies wear clown masks, pig masks and faces of the rich and famous.

St-Hilaire-St-Florent

4 km northwest of Saumur

MUSHROOM MUSEUM
(Musée du Champignon)

On the D751 road, just northwest of town, toward Gennes, on the south bank of the Loire. Open February 15–November 15, daily, 10am–7pm. Admission: 38 F; students and children, 20 F. Phone: 02 41 50 31 55.

Visit shiitakes, oyster mushrooms and all your favorite species on their own turf. Watch them as they thrive by the ton in the dim, fecal milieu they like best. The tour takes in a small section of the miles of subterranean galleries carved out of soft white tufa, where you can see fungi at various stages of development. Learn the differences between various species and peek at the harvesters, who wear hats fitted with lamps as miners do. Also here is an exhibition detailing over 400 wild species, and a troglodyte café for sampling a few of your own.

Savonnières

10 km west of Tours

PETRIFYING GROTTOES

(Grottes Pétrifiantes)

Off the D7 road, just south of the Cher river. Open February–March and October–December, daily, 9am–noon and 2–6pm; April–September, daily, 9am–6:30pm. Admission: 29 F; children under 15, 23 F. Phone: 02 47 50 00 09.

The mineral-rich subterranean waters in this cave have a strange power: Objects left in them get a weird, pale stony coating somewhere between ivory and barf. Objets d'art subjected to this process can be seen in an on-site Museum of Petrifaction. The cave itself, first opened in 1547, boasts concretions in all sorts of ripply shapes. Stalactites hang like chandeliers within the sound of a petrifying waterfall. Petrified animals and an ancient Gallo-Roman graveyard intensify a sense of foreboding that is softened only by wistful statues of prehistoric beasts. Rhamphorhynchus and euparkeria and their companions loiter beside the underground lake.

Tours

MUSEUM OF MASTER CRAFTSMANSHIP

(Musée du Compagnonnage)

In the Cloître St-Julien, 8 rue Nationale at Quai Anatole France, a block from the Loire. Open mid-June–mid-September, daily, 9am–12:30pm and 2–6pm, mid-September–mid-June, Wednesday–Monday, 9am–noon and 2–6pm. Admission: 25 F; students, 15 F. Phone: 02 47 61 07 93.

Consider a pagoda made of cake icing. Then consider a shiny, yard-long wooden clog. A big sugar castle and a glossy, full-size chocolate violin, complete with strings, are among the other masterworks on display here. Dozens of such items, crafted over countless hours, reveal the true skills of carpenters, joiners, roofers, bakers and members of other trade guilds. Don't miss France's most perfect wooden wheel and the miniature spiral staircase.

CHOCOLATE VIOLIN, MUSÉE DU COMPAGNONNAGE—TOURS

Southwest France

Anduze

40 km northwest of Nimes

LA BAMBOUSERAIE

 Just east of town, off the D35 road. Open March–October, daily, 10am–5pm. Admission: 32 F; children, 18 F; disabled, 15 F. Phone: 04 66 61 70 47.

Stand around watching the trees grow taller at this evocative arboretum—giant bamboos can gain three feet in height within twenty-four hours. Over 150 different types of bamboo rustle in the breeze along with a forest full of banana plants, palms and other exotic foliage. A labyrinth and a full-size replica of a tropical Asian village await curious visitors, as do waterways thick with pink hyacinths. Anyone who ever thought of bamboo as a feeble, slender waif of a plant will have a new perspective after seeing the giant species, whose thick trunks soar dozens of feet into the air.

Angoulême

100 km northeast of Bordeaux

COMIC-STRIP MUSEUM
(*Musée de la Bande Dessinée*)

 121 rue de Bordeaux, on the riverside just west of the train station. Open in summer, Tuesday–Friday, 10am–7pm, Saturday–Sunday, 2–7pm; winter,

 Tuesday–Friday, 10am–6pm, Saturday–Sunday, 2–6pm. Admission: 30 F; students and children, 20 F. Phone: 05 45 38 65 65.

The day has finally come when Charlie Brown and Snoopy number among the artifacts in a pretentious French art museum. "*Les maîtres d'Amérique*" occupy a special section of this large and distinctively designed structure, which houses over 4,000 original comic strips in all. French masters get pride of place in this exploration of techniques and themes, with due respect paid to the prolific Belgians as well as Will Eisner, Charles Schulz, Al Capp and their Yank colleagues. An on-site library holds 10,000 comic books from all over the world.

Brantôme

20 km north of Périgueux

GROTTO OF THE LAST JUDGMENT

 Behind the abbey, on boulevard de Charlemagne. Open April–June and September, Wednesday–Monday, 10am–12:30pm and 2–6pm; July–August, daily, 10am–7pm; October–December and February–March, Wednesday–Monday, 10am–noon and 2–5pm. Admission: 20 F; students and children, 15 F. Phone: 05 53 05 80 63.

Centuries ago, monks quarried away the soft stone at the base of this cliff. They gradually created a series of troglodytic chambers surrounding a spring, and during the 12th century they worshipped and

GROTTO OF THE LAST JUDGMENT—
BRANTÔME

stored their wine here in hand-hewn, cavernous chapels. Most portentous of all is the huge and acoustically intriguing Grotto of the Last Judgment, whose walls are carved with a monumental but completely cryptic bas-relief. Archaeologists have been trying for years to explain this ménage of horn-blowing angels, crowned heads, skeletons, monks, doorways and rows of faces wearing weird little hats, all surmounted by a figure on a throne. Some say it's an early medieval warning against drunkenness; others say it harks back to the region's pagan roots. On the adjoining wall is a chiseled crucifixion scene in which the grieving Mary is twice as big as Jesus.

Brantôme

20 km north of Périgueux

MEDIUMISTIC ART MUSEUM
(Musée Fernand Desmoulin)

 Boulevard Charlemagne, in the abbey complex. Open February–March and October–December, Wednesday–Monday, 10am–noon and 2–5pm; April–June, Wednesday–Monday, 10am–12:30pm and 2–6pm; July–August, daily, 10am–7pm;

 September, daily, 10am–12:30pm and 2–6pm. Admission: 15 F; students and children, 10 F; purchase tickets in the abbey gift shop, where an attendant will take you upstairs to the museum. Phone: 05 53 05 80 63.

Born in 1835, Fernand Desmoulin was a local physician. Back home after attending a friend's seance one evening, he picked up a pencil and couldn't stop drawing. The complicated portraits that resulted were, the doctor insisted, images from the "other side," drawn by departed spirits who guided his hand. Desmoulin grew famous as he devoted the next few years to conducting seances and producing dozens of pictures which now hang here. Signed not by the doctor but by his alleged spirit guides, calling themselves "Your Old Master," "Astarte" and "the Institutor," the spooky watercolors and dense pencil portraits each reportedly took only ten minutes to complete.

Brantôme

20 km north of Périgueux

ST. SICAIRE'S RELICS

 In the Church of St. Sicaire, separated by a small courtyard from the abbey on boulevard Charlemagne which dominates the western edge of town. Open daily, 10am–7pm. Phone: 05 53 05 80 52.

Remember when Herod ordered all the babies in Judea killed so that Jesus wouldn't make it to adulthood? And then his soldiers went out and massacred every male toddler in the land *except* Jesus? Well, one of those

MUSÉE FERNAND DESMOULIN—
BRANTÔME

45 km southwest of Montpellier, on the coast

MAGIC PALACE

Place Agde Marine, off quai Jean Miquel, on the waterfront. Open Easter–September, daily, 10am–noon and 3–11:30pm; magic shows daily at 5 and 11pm. Admission to museum: 25 F; children under 12, 15 F; magic shows, 10 F. Phone: 04 67 01 54 80.

This museum's Grand Illusions room unravels some of the tricks that have puzzled audiences for years. Fairground automata, trick mirrors, magicians' accessories and interactive experiments reveal yet more about how all those handkerchiefs, coins, cards and bouquets manage to appear out of nowhere, and how rabbits keep from suffocating inside hats.

babies' bodies is allegedly here, even though the massacre happened a long time ago when Jesus, still a baby himself, hadn't yet developed the following that would turn into Christianity. (Thus, you might wonder, how did anyone have the foresight to scoop up this dead baby? Ask not, friend.) A marble sculpture illustrates the killing of the infant now canonized as St. Sicaire. As the baby wails in its mother's arms, a brutish soldier in a loincloth swings a dagger. A stained-glass window depicts the same scene, only in this version the attacker wears a toga while the baby has a grown-up face and wears a long green gown. Obscured inside a cute bisque baby-doll, the relics lie in a tiny glass-and-bronze casket mounted partway up the wall. They say Charlemagne himself brought the relics here, making this church a favorite with medieval pilgrims.

45 km southwest of Montpellier, on the coast

NUDE CITY
(*Quartier Naturiste*)

Cap d'Agde is 5 km southeast of the city of Agde; the "Quartier Naturiste" (Nudist Area) of the otherwise normal city of Cap d'Agde is at the east end of town; the only access is via Avenue de la Butte, then turn right at Avenue du Bagnas. A city bus runs from both Agde and Cap d'Agde to the entrance gate. Always open. Admission to the nudist area is monitored—no oglers allowed. If you

want to visit, be prepared to take it all off. *Accommodation and meals at the various hotels and restaurants are in the same price range as in the rest of France. Phone: 04 67 26 00 26 (entry gate), or 04 67 01 04 04 (Cap d'Agde Tourist Office).*

This self-sufficient nudist resort is more than just a place to take off your clothes: it's an entire mini-city. Thousands of people live here in the summer and never get dressed for months at a time. Sure, there's a mile-long nude beach, but that's just the beginning. Here you'll find hotels, apartments, houses, campsites, shops, restaurants, cafes, supermarkets and more—all strictly nudist. Banking in the buff? You bet. About the only thing you can't find here is clothing. Cap d'Agde even boasts what are probably the world's only nudist post office and police station. Want to sail your yacht with nothing on? Go right ahead. The crowded dance floor at the resort's trendy disco has absolutely no dress code whatsoever. And you haven't truly experienced all life has to offer until you've seen a Godard film in a theater full of naked people.

CABRESPINE CAVERN
(Gouffre Géant de Cabrespine)

North of town, off the D620 road. Open March–June and September–November, daily, 10am–noon and 2–6pm; July–August, daily, 10am–7pm. Admission: 40 F; children, 20 F. Phone: 04 68 26 14 22.

The cavern's main chamber measures over 700 feet across and over 600 feet high—dwarfing the Eif-

fel Tower, as your tour guide is eager to point out. Colorful concretions in the Devil's Balcony include sturdy columnar stalagmites, but also here are striated curtains of stone and clusters of stalactites as delicate as silk strands. The Crystal Room boasts amazingly fragile twiglike formations in luminous white.

HAT MUSEUM
(Musée du Chapeau)

3 rue Cros-Mayrevieille, in the Old Town. Open daily, 10am–7pm. Admission: 20 F; students, 18 F; children, 10 F. Phone: 04 68 71 61 26.

Berets keep company with medieval hats, Renaissance hats, Napoleonic hats and many others at this museum, where mannequins model headgear with matching costumes as a bonus. Firefighters' helmets stoke that lust for men in uniform. Turbans lend symmetry to bearded heads, while military helmets make their wearers look like insects and recall the functional ugliness of war. Elaborate Louis XIV-era hats hark back to times when nobody had to run for buses.

PETRIFYING FOUNTAIN
(Fontaine Pétrifiante)

13 rue du Perou, at rue Gaultier-de-Biauzat, south of the train station. Open April–June and September, daily, 9am–noon and

2–6pm; July–August, daily, 9am–7:30pm; October–March, Tuesday–Sunday, 10am–noon and 2–6pm. Admission: 18 F; children, 12 F. Phone: 04 73 37 15 58.

Enter the magic world of "mold encrustation," where geology and art come together. Minerals in the water emerging from a natural spring here have a way of "petrifying" anything left submerged for several months. Figurines, bas-reliefs and even stuffed animals come away coated with a hard finish looking vaguely like ivory, vaguely like soap. Learn about the thermal spring, and about how over the centuries earlier generations "tamed" its transformative powers. Examine artworks in progress. Life-size, encrusted images of sheep, dogs and people occupy the on-site park.

to avoid the crowds anyway).
Phone: 05 61 65 04 11.

The real attraction here is not the multifarious stalactites, the gushing underground waterfalls or the labyrinthine passages, but rather the unforgettable sensation of taking an hour-long boat trip—entirely underground. Billed as Europe's longest navigable underground river, Labouiche is not a heart-pounding thrill ride but rather an eerie reentry into the primordial womb. The drifting, near-silent excursion, in boats propelled by subterranean sailors who pull on strategically placed rails and cables, is half dream, half nightmare, and a unique experience you won't soon forget. That is, unless you stupidly grip the edge of the boat and let your fingers get scrunched against the walls.

Foix

80 km south of Toulouse

UNDERGROUND RIVER OF LABOUICHE
(Rivière Souterraine de Labouiche)

6 kilometers northwest of Foix, on the D1 road, near the village of Vernajoul. Open April–May, Monday–Saturday 2–6pm; Sunday 10am–noon and 2–6pm; June and September, daily, 10am–noon and 2–6pm; July and August, daily, 9:30am–6pm; October–mid-November, Sunday, 10am–noon and 2–6pm (last departures 45 minutes before morning and afternoon closing times). Admission: 40 F; occasional discounts for arriving early in the morning (a good idea

Gimeaux

27 km southwest of Vichy

PETRIFYING GROTTO
(Sources Pétrifiantes)

Avenue de la Libération. Open February–December, daily, 9:30–noon and 2–6:30pm. Admission: 17 F; children, 9 F. Phone: 04 73 63 57 59.

A hundred years ago, it was discovered that hot mineral springs emerging from volcanic fissures in this picturesque cave could be coaxed to encrust whatever was submerged in them. Thus developed the popular art by which figurines, bas-reliefs and statues are gradually coated with hard whitish stuff, sort of like what dental fillings are made of. A tour through the cavern explores glistening natural formations offset with encrusted animals and artworks in progress. An audio-visual show explains the process.

La Trimouille

60 km east of Poitiers

ISLAND OF SERPENTS
(L'Île aux Serpents)

 Route de Montmorillon. Open April–September, daily, 10am–7pm; March and October–November, daily, 2–6pm. Admission: 40 F; children aged 5-16, 30 F; children under 5, free. Phone: 05 49 91 33 33.

Stroke sinuous, legless bodies and stare into beady eyes here, where over 300 snakes writhe. Boas and all their serpentine cousins do their best to dispel the story about that bit of nastiness in the Garden of Eden. Enthusiastic handlers do their best as well. An extensive collection of exotic species from all over the world is housed safely on an artificial island, à la Jurassic Park. At feeding time, watch snakes distend themselves grotesquely as they swallow whole eggs. And don't miss seeing snake babies in the "nursery." Caymans and iguanas cavort in the new legged-reptile zone.

Le Masgot

65 km northeast of Limoges

VILLAGE OF STONE SCULPTURES

 Le Masgot is a tiny village in the Creuse district, northwest of Aubusson, north of the D941 road between Ahun and St.

 Sulpice-les-Champs. Get a good map of the area before getting lost. Sculptures are visible throughout the village. A welcome center at the southwest end of town in the old bakehouse off Route du Pont de la Roche has brochures outlining self-guided walking tours, and offers guided tours at various times throughout the year. Always visible. Admission: free; guided tours start at 10 F; 15 F for two people; children under 12, free. Phone: 05 55 66 98 88.

Nineteenth-century master mason François Michaud filled his hometown to bursting with *art naif* granite sculptures. Over the course of the last century many had become lost or overgrown, but a recent village-wide beautification project has restored most of them to their former glory. Everywhere in town you'll encounter Michaud's distinctive, disarming style, reminiscent of satirical 12th-century Norman church carvings. A big-breasted mermaid is the most frequently photographed, but scores of strange and amusing sculptures are perched on walls and stuck onto houses at every turn: a rolling snake; a weird lopsided bear; allegorical busts; inscriptions in Greek, Latin, rustic French and coded symbols; a naked woman with something circular balanced on her head; Napoleon; a crusader; faces; mystery animals and cryptic decorative details galore. Most of the work seems to have had secret meanings to Michaud, but now we can only speculate. Make sure to grab a walking-tour brochure before you start—otherwise you might miss some of the more curious hidden surprises.

Limoux

12 km south of Carcassonne

CATHA-RAMA

 47 ave. Fabre d'Eglantine, in the town center. Open Easter–June and September–October, daily, 10:30am–noon and 2–6pm; July–August, daily, 10:30am–7pm. Admission: 25 F; children under 10, 21 F. Phone: 04 68 31 48 42.

Denounced as heretics and head-quartered in this part of France, the Cathars were a medieval Christian sect. They had both male and female clergy, weird ideas about sex, and a firm belief that no good existed in the material world. They also became increasingly unpopular with Church authorities, who finally launched a bloody crusade in 1209 and wiped the Cathars out. Catharama uses cutting-edge audiovisual effects to recount the Cathars' story and the massacre that ended it all. The spectacle probes legends of a rich treasure that the Cathars, sensing their impending doom, are believed to have hidden hereabouts.

Lourdes

MUSEUM OF THE RELIGIOUS STATUE
(Musée de la Statue Religieuse)

 3-13 rue des Pyrénées, southeast of the grotto and just southwest of the town center. Open Easter–October, daily, 8am–noon and 2–7pm. Admission: free. Phone: 05 62 94 27 44.

Statues of the Virgin Mary look holy but have prosaic beginnings at factories like this one, where you can watch phalanxes of freshly manufactured plaster statues standing in colorless squadrons, waiting for employees to paint their eyes in. Marys of all sizes stand with palms pressed together, awaiting their new homes, in hypnotic profusion. Statues of other saints join Mary at the accompanying museum, clearly labeled so that pathetic heathens can tell the difference between Andrew and Anthony. In vividly painted plaster, Jesus exposes his heart while the others, mounted atop pedestals, look on.

Maureillas las Illas

30 km southwest of Perpignan, east of Ceret in the Pyrenees

CORK MUSEUM
(Musée du Liège)

 Avenue Maréchal Joffre (no number). Open mid-June–mid-September, daily, 10:30am–noon and 3:30–7pm; mid-September–mid-June, Wednesday–Monday, 2–5pm. Admission: 15 F; students and children, 5 F. Phone: 68 83 48 00.

Mock-ups relating to what has long been this region's major industry reveal how cork does, in fact, grow on trees. Learn how it gets from those short, sturdy trunks into your wine bottle. Peruse many artworks and other items made from this unsung substance. Bas-reliefs depicting heroic scenes—complete with soldiers' slender arrows, muscular torsos and deftly formed faces—highlight cork's surprising sculptability.

Montpellier

AGROPOLIS MUSEUM

951 ave. Agropolis, north of the center; take bus #5 to the end of the line. Open Wednesday–Monday, 2–6pm. Admission: 25 F; students and children, 15 F; children under 10, free. Phone: 04 67 04 75 00 or 04.

At this food museum's interactive "Banquet of Humanity," you can use computers to help a group of unattractive modern sculptures representing peoples of diverse nations discuss issues of world hunger. All around a building that from the outside—if you like silver tortillas—looks somewhat edible itself, big colorful screens and CD-Roms rear up to teach how faces are fed. Hunting, fishing and *Maman*'s home cookin' are explored along with the science and spirituality of food around the globe. Farming techniques in every imaginable ecosystem are explained in detail, while a new exhibit demonstrates the importance of beverages and drinks in human history. Behind the museum is a major food research center where French scientists busily investigate the nutritional merits of quiche Lorraine and fire-roasted caterpillars.

Oradour-sur-Glane

23 km northwest of Limoges

MARTYRED VILLAGE
(Village Martyr)

Visible at any time. Admission: free. Phone: 55 03 13 73 (tourist office).

This was an ordinary town when, on June 10, 1944, an SS squadron arrived without warning. After herding everyone into the main square, the Nazis locked all the men in barns, shot them and set the barns on fire. Confined in the church, women and children were then machine-gunned, and the church was set ablaze. The massacre left 642 dead, nearly half of them children, and to this day nobody knows why. Fifteen acres of the ruined city are now a permanent memorial. In unearthly silence, shattered walls surround the old square. Tram wires hang in the air over unused tracks, and rusted cars slump into the pavement. Guided tours are given of the burned church.

Peyzac-le-Moustier

25 km southwest of Périgueux

LA ROQUE ST-CHRISTOPHE

Off the D706 road, directly overlooking the southern shore of the Vézère river. Open January–March and November–December, daily, 11am–5pm; April, daily, 10am– 6pm; May–June and September–October, daily, 10am– 6:30pm; July– August, daily, 10am–7pm. Admission: 33 F; students, 25 F; children, 17 F. Phone: 05 53 50 70 45.

With troglodyte dwellings and a fortress installed in natural shelters spanning five different levels, this cliff has housed human beings since Paleolithic times. Chiseled stairs, artwork and other touches left by 50,000 years' worth of inhabitants augment huge crevices reminiscent of Native American cliff dwellings, though these were occupied much earlier. Acrophobics won't have fun touring these lofty chambers, or what remains of the fortress once used as a refuge from Viking raiders and again during the Hundred Years War—after which the English went ahead and seized it anyway. Mannequins show the bloody fashion in which prehistoric residents dealt with their ursine neighbors.

Poitiers

FUTUROSCOPE

In Jaunay-Clan, 8 km north of Poitiers on the RN10 (Route Nationale); it is literally impossible to miss, and is probably visible from the moon: Trains and buses run to the park from Poitiers. Open daily, 9am–6pm; in summer, the park stays open until the laser show finishes, sometimes as late as 10pm. Admission: in summer, 185 F, children, 150 F; mid-season, 165 F, children, 130 F; low season, 140 F, children 110 F. Phone: 05 49 49 30 80.

No normal theater will do after a visit to this relentlessly visual theme park with its shimmering silvery silhouette. The screen in its Kinémax theater is seven stories tall. Then, in the Magic Carpet, one 2,000-square-foot screen stands before you and another lies beneath your feet for that flying-squirrel feeling. In the Omnimax, films are projected onto a huge dome. In yet other theaters on the premises, your seat moves with the action onscreen and 3D images zip out of nowhere to make you duck. Also here are a 360-degree cinema, a high-resolution cinema and holograms. Cyber Avenue lets you play with the latest technical toys. The wild, futuristic architecture is part *Flash Gordon*, part *Bladerunner*. Oh yeah, don't forget the lake with unique dancing fountains, and the nighttime laser show.

Rennes-le-Château

40 km south of Carcassonne

TOWN OF MYSTERY

Take a bus from Carcassonne south to Couiza; from there you must walk or take a taxi 4.5 kilometers on the D52 up to Rennes-le-Château (a sign on the main D118 road points the way up the hill). In the village, all the attractions are along the rue du Château; the Domaine is at one end, and the Museum and Church are at the other end, where it intersects with rue de l'Eglise. The village is so small you can't miss them. Church open for 15 minutes each hour starting at 10:45am, 11:45am, 12:45pm (summer only), 2:45pm, 3:45pm, 4:45pm, 5:45pm, 6:45pm; museum open daily, 10am–noon and 2–7pm; Domaine open daily, 10am–7pm. Admission: Church, free. Museum, 18 F; students, 12 F. Domaine, 25 F; students, 20 F. Phone: 04 68 74 14 56 (Museum); 04 68 74 31 16 (Domaine).

What secrets does this windswept hilltop village harbor? According to *The Holy Blood and the Holy Grail*, the bestselling book about the Rennes-le-Château mystery, in the late 19th century a local priest accidentally unearthed the greatest treasure in history while remodeling the town's church. Ancient coded documents he discovered hidden in a hollow pillar implied that Jesus and Mary Magdalene had children together, that these children were brought to Gaul and became the ancestors of the Merovingian Dynasty, the first kings of France. Deposed in the 7th century, the royal line has ever since been struggling to reaffirm its divine right to rule over Christendom, a struggle that has changed the course of world history. This secret about Jesus' "*sang/raal*" (royal blood) might very well be the "*san/graal*" (holy grail) everybody's been searching for all these years. In any case, the priest, Bérenger Saunière, suddenly became fabulously wealthy. His building projects around the village can still be seen

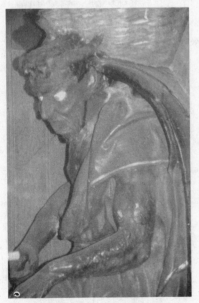

DEVIL STATUE IN CHURCH—
RENNES-LE-CHÂTEAU

today. A nascent tourist industry caters to the starry-eyed spiritual fortune-hunters that flock here seeking answers. The remodeled church features a grotesque statue of the devil at the entrance, with many images of Mary Magdalene and her boyfriend throughout. Visitors are closely monitored and kicked out after 15 minutes to keep them from tearing the place apart looking for clues. Adjacent to the church is the town museum, which explores many aspects of the convoluted story—mysterious tombs, Visigothic treasures, detritus from Saunière's digs and more—with many of the actual objects on display. The museum gift shop and a bookstore down the block called Atelier Empreinte sell every imaginable volume on the mystery. Up the street is the Domaine de l'Abbé Saunière, the estate Saunière built with his riches. Around overgrown gardens you can explore the Tour Magdala (named after Mary Magdalene's hometown), a crenellated tower with a remarkable view, built to house his library; an exhibit of his personal effects, including the page from his diary on which he records finding something in an old tomb; as well as modern speculations on what the treasure really was. Yet another mini-museum is hidden under the belvedere, with a section on the secret codes in the documents. After poking around Villa Bethania, Saunière's unremarkable house, you can wrap up your visit with his tombstone, at the very top of the cemetery behind the church. You'll find no answers here: the Abbé took his secrets with him to the grave.

Rocamadour

FOREST OF THE MONKEYS
(Forêt des Singes)

 Just outside of town in l'Hospitalet. Open April–June and September, daily, 10am–noon and 1–6pm; July–August, daily, 10am–7pm; October, daily, 1–5pm. Phone: 05 65 33 62 72.

The popcorn you acquire at the entrance isn't to eat while enjoying your stroll around these wooded grounds. It's to satisfy the greedy apes who dash right up and beg to be fed. Over 100 furry Barbary macaques, an endangered species native to Morocco's Atlas Mountains, live and breed here. Watch them swinging from trees, clambering on rocks and basking beside ponds. Watch the big-eared young cling to their mothers. Feel the scrape of their humanoid paws as they reach into your hands in search of food.

Rochechouart

30 km west of Limoges

METEORITE EXHIBITION
(Espace Météorite Paul Pellas)

 16 rue Jean Parvy, 4 kilometers west of the center. Open in summer, Monday–Friday, 9:30am–12:30pm and 2–6pm, Saturday–Sunday, 2–6pm; spring and fall, daily, 2–6pm. Admission: 17 F; children, 15 F. Phone: 05 55 03 02 70.

During that busy Jurassic period 200 million years ago, a meteorite hurtled earthward here. Good thing nobody was sitting around trying to thread a needle. Releasing energy said to be 14 million times that of the atomic bomb that destroyed Hiroshima, the meteorite left a huge crater which has eroded and can't be seen anymore. But hey, it altered the local geology forever. In the heart of a region that proudly calls itself "Meteorite Country," this exhibition uses artworks, interactive experiments, videos and actual meteorites to tell the whole percussive saga.

Romagne

40 km south of Poitiers

MONKEY VALLEY
(La Vallée des Singes)

 At Le Gureau, near Romagne; follow the signs. Open March–November, Saturday–Sunday, 1–5pm. Admission: 50 F; children, 35 F. Phone: 05 49 87 20 20.

Rediscover your ancestors among the 200 primates that wander free here on a series of forested islets, against the muted music of a waterfall. Direct contact is encouraged with the apes, some of which are endangered species. Macaques, gorillas, lemurs, gibbons and other primates peer up at visitors while romping playfully, displaying their buttocks and flashing lipless grins. If the sight of all those opposable thumbs hasn't taken away your appetite, a vast onsite picnic area awaits.

On the western end of île de Ré, an island just offshore from La Rochelle

NOAH'S ARK
(L'Arche de Noé)

Near the lighthouse at the very tip of the island. Open June–August, daily, 10:30am–7pm; April– May and September, 2–6:30pm. Phone: 05 46 29 23 23.

Agrab bag of diverse attractions are combined here in a large, flowery park, so you don't have to choose just a single one. Live birds flaunt their colorful selves in the park's Parrot Jungle, while dead birds and other unfortunate animals occupy dioramas in the Naturama. Cheer up—yet more live animals frolic in the on-site zoo, where monkeys and lemurs enjoy the sea breeze. Yet more death awaits in the shellcraft museum, where some eight million seashells from all over the world have been used to create glittering artworks. Five thousand bug comprise the butterfly-and-insect museum, but wait! In the Musicarium, a musician makes outrageous sounds with space-age synthesizers in a planetarium atmosphere. Historical tableaux and models revisit the islanders' ancestors and several millennia of sea sagas. Don't miss the little *Titanic* on its way to the ocean floor.

50 km southeast of Périgueux

GORODKA-MAGIKA

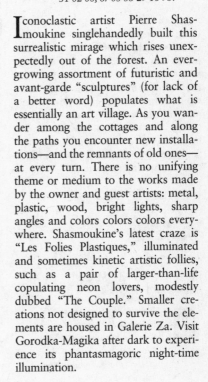

5 km south of Sarlat on the road leading toward the village of La Canéda (follow the signs pointing to "Gorodka-Galerie Za"). Open April–May, daily, 2–7pm and 9–10pm; June–September, 10am–9pm and 10pm–midnight; October, Sunday, 10am– 6:30pm; November–March, by appointment (call ahead). Admission: 25F; children, free. Phone: 05 53 31 02 00, or 05 53 29 18 93.

Iconoclastic artist Pierre Shasmoukine singlehandedly built this surrealistic mirage which rises unexpectedly out of the forest. An evergrowing assortment of futuristic and avant-garde "sculptures" (for lack of a better word) populates what is essentially an art village. As you wander among the cottages and along the paths you encounter new installations—and the remnants of old ones—at every turn. There is no unifying theme or medium to the works made by the owner and guest artists: metal, plastic, wood, bright lights, sharp angles and colors colors colors everywhere. Shasmoukine's latest craze is "Les Folies Plastiques," illuminated and sometimes kinetic artistic follies, such as a pair of larger-than-life copulating neon lovers, modestly dubbed "The Couple." Smaller creations not designed to survive the elements are housed in Galerie Za. Visit Gorodka-Magika after dark to experience its phantasmagoric night-time illumination.

Souillac

65 km north of Cahors

MUSEUM OF THE AUTOMATON
(Musée de l'Automate)

Place de l'Abbaye, on the north side of the abbey. Open April–May and October, Tuesday–Sunday, 10am–noon and 3–6pm; June and September, daily, 10am–noon and 3–6pm; July–August, daily, 10am–7pm; January–March and November–December, Wednesday–Sunday, 2–5pm. Admission: 30 F; students, 20 F; children, 15 F. Phone: 05 65 37 07 07.

Snake charmers and acrobats are among the 3,000 vintage automated figures jostling and clenching and spasming at this museum. And they're all controlled by a single electronic brain! The collection spans over a hundred years, with an automated New Orleans jazz band just bristling with racial stereotypes. Also here are automated tableaux, industrial robots and androids.

Thiviers

37 km north of Périgueux

FOIE GRAS MUSEUM
(Musée du Foie Gras)

Place Foch, across from the church in the center of town. Open July–August, Monday–Saturday, 9am–6pm, Sunday, 10am–1pm; September–June, Tuesday–Saturday, 10am–noon and 3–6pm. Phone: 05 53 55 12 50.

Pâté de foie gras isn't pretty. And it isn't pretty the way they fatten the geese and ducks whose distended livers get mushed into the final product. Spread it on baguettes, will you? This museum shows the whole process, with taxidermed birds trapped inside wooden cages too small to even move around in—a fate familiar to veal calves. Taxidermed geese, goslings, ducks and ducklings stand against rustic stone walls looking oblivious. A mannequin in regional costume force-feeds a stuffed goose by ramming a funnel down its throat and pouring grain in. Free samples await.

Toulouse

MEDICAL HISTORY MUSEUM
(Musée d'Histoire de la Médicine)

2 rue Viguerie, in the Hotel-Dieu Saint-Jacques complex, next to the Pont-Neuf, across the river from the city center. Open Wednesday–Monday, 9am–5pm. Admission: free. Phone: 05 61 77 84 25.

A wall-size cabinet for storing medicinal herbs flanks the entrance to rooms stocked with medical artworks and artifacts. One exhibit details the 18th-century enema craze. A 19th-century canvas depicts a man suffering from elephantiasis of the scrotum. Insane-asylum relics make life look pretty bad for the mentally ill, while photographs of early-20th-century autopsies don't make death look very good either. Yet another painting reveals a colorful vivisection lab where a proud scientist is in the midst of cutting apart a live dog.

THE "HOLY BODIES" CIRCUIT
(Le Tour des Corps Saints)

In the crypt of Saint-Sernin Basilica, place Saint-Sernin, midway between the train station and the river. Open July–September, Monday–Saturday, 10am–6pm, Sunday, 12:30–6pm; October–May, Monday–Saturday, 10am–noon and 2–5pm, Sunday, 2–5pm. Admission: 10 F; children under 15, free.

Consecrated in the 11th century, this is the oldest Romanesque church in the Western world. It was a popular stop on the medieval pilgrimage route to Spain, housing a veritable banquet of saints' relics. The crypt occupies two levels, more or less circular, and you can make the circuit like so many pious visitors before you, eyeing the boxed remains of St. Honoré, St. Louis, St. Simon, St. Jude and many more. The treasured relics of this church's 3rd-century namesake, St. Saturnin, are stored in what looks like a clutch purse. A glass case holds St. Exupery's 13th-century mitre and St. Remy's 13th-century gloves, their tightly woven fabric withstanding the test of time.

6 km north of Les Eyzies

PREHISTOPARC

On the D706 road just north of town. Open March–June, daily, 10am–6:30pm; July–September,

daily, 9:30am–7pm; October, daily, 10am–6pm. Phone: 05 53 50 73 19.

Lifelike models of humans and animals evoke scenes from the brutish panorama of prehistoric life, all arranged in woodsy surroundings. Based on skeletal remains excavated in the region and armed with clubs, rocks and rustic stakes, the models of shaggy-haired men hunt and fish. They paint sensitively on cave walls. They tear carcasses limb from limb, and with models of shaggy-haired women and children they enjoy family life. Models of wooly rhinoceros, mammoths and other beasts complete the picture.

Provence, the Rhône and the Alps

SEA-OF-ICE CAVE
(Grotte de la Mer de Glace)

35 place de la Mer de Glace: Take the Montenvers railway from Chamonix. Open July–August, daily, 8am–6pm (trains depart every 20 minutes); May–June and September, daily, 8:30am–5:30pm (trains depart every 30 minutes); October–April, daily, 10am–6pm (make reservations at the train station). Round-trip railway fare (includes admission to cave): 73 F; children, 39 F. Phone: 04 50 53 12 54.

Manmade tunnels jutting far into the ice of the mountainside open onto solid-ice rooms whose "furnishings" are cut carefully out of you-know-what. Armchairs carved out of solid ice are clustered cozily around an all-ice coffee table in the chilly "living room." An all-ice bathroom sports a tub and sink; an all-ice kitchen has an oven and table; an all-ice bedroom has a pillow-topped bed, a piano and more. Frequent remodeling is necessary to keep the structures intact under the pressure of a constantly shifting glacier and the vicissitudes of a medium that melts.

Chateauneuf-les-Martigues

25 km west of Marseille

EL DORADO CITY

Off the A55 road; exit at Carry le Rouet. Open July–August, daily, 10am–7pm; June, Monday–Friday, 10am–5pm, Saturday, 11am–6pm, Sunday, 10am–7pm; variable hours October–November and March–May. Admission: 60 F; children, 50 F (includes live show); to visit without attending a show, 40 F. Phone: 04 42 79 86 90.

What are these broncos doing in the south of France? Bucking, *naturellement*. This Wild West park boasts a Boot Hill, a "Dakota" waterfall, a rodeo, a gold mine, mariachis, teepees, stunt shows, a totem pole and a choo-choo train that flies French flags and gets attacked regularly by dynamite-wielding banditeaux. Mosey around the Mexican Village with its persuasive adobes, or the full-size Main Street with its dentist's office, sheriff's office, barbershop and gallows.

Costumed characters play the washboard and dance the can-can.

Cuges-les-Pins

Midway between Marseille and Toulon

OK CORRAL

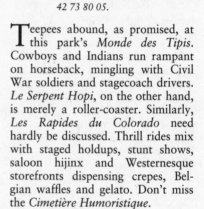

Just east of town, off the RN 8 road. Open mid-March–October, daily, 10:30am–6:30pm; November–mid-March, Wednesday and Saturday–Sunday, 10:30am–6pm. Admission: 80 F; children between 1 meter and 1.4 meters tall, 65 F; children under 1 meter tall, free (different rates for renting a teepee-campsite). Phone: 04 42 73 80 05.

Teepees abound, as promised, at this park's *Monde des Tipis*. Cowboys and Indians run rampant on horseback, mingling with Civil War soldiers and stagecoach drivers. *Le Serpent Hopi*, on the other hand, is merely a roller-coaster. Similarly, *Les Rapides du Colorado* need hardly be discussed. Thrill rides mix with staged holdups, stunt shows, saloon hijinx and Westernesque storefronts dispensing crepes, Belgian waffles and gelato. Don't miss the *Cimetière Humoristique*.

Echirolles

Just south of Grenoble

MUSEUM OF RAYON

(Musée de la Viscose)

27 rue du Tremblay in the southern suburbs of Grenoble, two blocks west of cours Jeon Jaures, near the freeway interchange.

Open September–June, Monday and Wednesday, 2:20–4:30pm, Saturday, 9–11am; July–August, by appointment only. Admission: 10 F. Phone: 76 33 08 28.

Hailed as "artificial silk" when Frenchmen invented it in 1884, rayon promptly marched on to enjoy a proud career in pocket linings, slinky dresses and countless other necessities. Founded to mark rayon's centennial, this museum shows how the slippery stuff is manufactured and then worn by men and women around the world. Discover how rayon came forward to meet the 20th century's voracious hunger for synthetic fabrics.

Hauterives

28 km north of Romans-sur-Isère

THE IDEAL PALACE OF CHEVAL THE MAILMAN
(Le Palais Idéal du Facteur Cheval)

In the middle of the village; you can't miss it. Open mid-April–mid-September, daily, 9am–7pm; mid-September–mid-November and February–mid-April, daily, 9:30am–5:30pm; December–January, daily, 10am–4:30pm. Admission: 26 F; children, 17 F. Phone: 04 75 68 81 19.

Ferdinand Cheval was a country postman and certainly not a trained architect when he started building his fantasy palace in 1879. Naturally, all his neighbors called him insane, but Cheval kept at it for nearly thirty years. Using stones and other bits and pieces he found while making his rounds, he erected a complicated castle now hailed as a national monument. Its stippled walls undulate, rising in arches, curving stairways and minarets. Like an exotic temple in a monochrome dream, it sports row upon row of columns, stupas and statuary. These and the turreted tower that surmounts it give the place a toothy look from afar. Artificial palm trees pose atop terraces. Cement vines, animals and sculpted human figures soar this way and that. Chiseled inscriptions give clues to Cheval's cosmic bent.

Jassans-Riottier

25 km north of Lyon

LIVING MUSEUM OF ADVENTURE NOVELS
(Musée Vivant du Roman d'Adventures)

410 rue Edouard Herriot. Open mid-May–September, Tuesday–Sunday, 2–6pm; guided visits at 1, 3:30 and 5pm. Admission: 35 F; children, 30 F; children under 7, free. Phone: 04 74 09 50 12.

The tour guides act out scenes and launch into dramatic readings from the imaginative works of Jules Verne, Edgar Rice Burroughs, Arthur Conan Doyle and others. Enthusiastically arranged artworks, books, posters and artifacts spotlight outer space, lost worlds, new worlds, crime and other aspects of the genre. Changing exhibitions show how, ever since Homer wrote the *Odyssey*, adventure novels have been literature's way of filling hapless readers' heads with lessons in history, mythology, geology, astronomy and paleontology.

Lans-en-Vercors

9 km southwest of Grenoble

THE MAGIC OF AUTOMATA AND SANTA CLAUS HAMLET
(Magie des Automates et Hameau du Père Noël)

West of the center, on the road to the neighboring village, Villard-de-Lans. Open daily, 10am–6pm. Admission: 39 F; children, 28 F. Phone: 04 76 95 40 14.

They've decked the halls with over 1,500 figurines embodying Santa and his elves. See Santas made of plastic, plush, velvet and paper. See Santa flying a hot-air balloon. See Santa lounging exhausted on a couch. See Santa with a pinecone for a body. See Santa wearing a white suit. See the stuffed reindeer nuzzling Santa. See Santa's bedroom. See Mickey Mouse masquerading as Santa. Elsewhere on the premises, hundreds of automated dolls gyrate and bob with the terrifying, wide-eyed stare so typical of their genre. An automated sultan rides an elephant while automated fakirs charm snakes. An automated violinist glowers. Baggy-trousered automated clowns perform tricks. For those who still can't get enough, elsewhere on the premises teddy bears wear clothes and demonstrate regional crafts.

Lyon

TONY GARNIER URBAN MUSEUM
(Musée Urbain Tony Garnier)

4 rue des Serpollières, 8th arrondissement, south of the center. Murals visible at any time;

guided tours given February–October, Saturday, 2 and 4pm. Admission: 25 F (for tour). Phone: 04 78 75 16 75.

This open-air museum celebrates early-20th-century architect Tony Garnier with 24 huge murals covering the sides of high-rises. Some 5,000 square meters of murals evoke the Lyon-born architect's dream of an "ideal city" with trompe-l'oeil majesty. Depicting a stadium, a clock tower and complicated streetscapes, the murals make you squint, their painted skies blending into the real sky. Garnier designed the nearby buildings, and the tour takes you into an apartment furnished 1930s-style to complete the picture.

Romans

67 km south of Lyon

SHOE MUSEUM
(Musée de la Chaussure)

2 rue Sainte-Marie, just east of City Hall. Open September–June, Tuesday–Saturday, 9–11:45am and 2–5:45pm, Sunday, 2:30–6pm; July–August, Tuesday–Saturday, 10am–6:30pm, Sunday, 2:30–6pm. Admission: 25 F; students, 12.50 F; children under 7, free. Phone: 04 75 05 81 30.

The Phoenicians made pointed shoes popular. Byzantium was rife with gold-encrusted leather slippers. And Louis XIV's reign saw the advent of the buckle. Thousands of sandals, shoes and boots offer a tour of the world since ancient times, showing how history shaped footwear and footwear shaped history. Learn how 19th-century missionaries in China horrified their would-be flocks with statues of a barefoot Mary. Learn how mosque protocol mandated the slip-on. Ponder the Greek fondness for pompons. Exhibits trace footwear fashions all the way from the Hittites to Diana Ross and Bernadette Peters.

Saint-Cannat

16 km northwest of Aix-en-Provence

THE VILLAGE OF AUTOMATONS
(Le Village des Automatons)

 Just southeast of town, on the N7 road heading toward Aix-en-Provence. Open April–September, daily, 10am–6pm; October–March, Wednesday, Saturday–Sunday, 10am–6pm. Admission: 45 F; children, 25 F. Phone: 04 42 57 30 30.

Over 500 automated figures of people and animals occupy fanciful structures in an outdoor setting, enacting favorite tales and bound to disturb your dreams for years to come. Sleeping Beauty is here, and an enormous Gulliver beset by Lilliputians who look like little lumberjacks. Also here are Pinocchio, Aladdin, Merlin and Tyrannosaurus Rex. Quake nervously in the shadow of artificial flowers that soar way over your head. Here, too, is your opportunity to ponder whether or not you would enjoy living in a shoe.

Salon-de-Provence

30 km northwest of Marseille

GREVIN MUSEUM OF PROVENCE
(Musée Grevin de la Provence)

 Place des Centuries, in the Old Town. Open daily, except Saturday and Sunday mornings. Admission: 20 F; students, 15 F. Phone: 04 90 56 36 30.

Augmented with appropriate sound effects and fragrances and arranged against softly painted backdrops, dozens of dreamy-eyed waxworks revive scenes from Provence's 2,600-year history. The designers' objective was to celebrate "Women and Water," and sure enough we watch Mary Magdalen disembarking from a boat on a Provençal beach, wrapped in the biblical equivalent of a towel. St. Martha tames a French dragon, and gorgeously coiffed queens sit around looking pretty and occasionally dangerous. Famous males on display include Paul Cezanne and characters from Marcel Pagnol's movies.

Salon-de-Provence

30 km northwest of Marseille

NOSTRADAMUS' HOUSE
(Maison de Nostradamus)

 11 rue Nostradamus, in the Old Town. Open Monday–Friday, 9:30am–noon and 2–6:30pm; Saturday–Sunday, 2–6:30pm. Admission: 20 F; students and children, 15 F. Phone: 04 90 56 64 31.

Nostradamus is one of those individuals whom you don't think of as having a first name, yet he did. It was Michel. That and other surprises abound in the house where he lived after arriving in Salon as a young man, and where he recorded his famous prophecies. Complete with sound effects, life-size reconstructions revive ten scenes from the strange career of a man whom bigwigs like Catherine de Medici eagerly consulted for astrological advice. See Nostradamus loitering amid glamorous and spiritual settings, contemplating the black plague and the distant future. Changing exhibitions on 16th-century themes illuminate the era that spawned the prophet.

Tarascon

TARASQUE PARADE
(Fêtes de la Tarasque)

Held every year on the last Sunday in June, beginning at 3pm; parade's route includes boulevard du Chateau, avenue de la République, cours Aristide Briand, boulevard Victor Hugo, boulevard Gambetta and boulevard Itam. For more information, call the tourist office at 04 90 91 03 52.

They say a huge green spiky monster called the Tarasque terrorized this town in the first century C.E. They say Mary Magdalene's servile sister St. Martha came along and tamed it. For at least 500 years, as mandated by Roi René, the town has celebrated its deliverance with a wacky historical parade featuring this allegorical monster. Today's model of the Tarasque measures fifteen feet from its flat face to its curly tail and looks like a hideous turtle with human features and sea-urchin spines. Concerts, fireworks and historical reenactments go on all weekend.

Burgundy and the East

Bar-le-Duc

75 km west of Nancy
SKELETAL STATUE

In the Church of Saint-Etienne, off place Saint-Pierre, southwest of the train station. Open daily. Admission: free. Phone: 87 06 16 16.

René de Chalon, Prince of Orange, died at war in 1545. He left instructions asking that his memorial statue represent him not in his prime but instead as he might appear after he had been dead for three years. A sculptor followed these directions, and today his extremely realistic marble statue commands attention in the Gothic church. Flesh tattered and clinging in shreds to half-exposed bones, the tall statue stands startlingly erect in a heroic pose. One long and wizened arm upraised, the figure gazes off heavenward through empty eye sockets, its neck a mass of cords.

Bèze

30 km northeast of Dijon
UNDERGROUND BOAT TRIPS

At the source of the Bèze river. Open April and October, Saturday–Sunday, 10am–7pm; May–September, daily, 10am–7pm. Admission: 27 F; children, 14 F. Phone: 03 80 75 31 33.

Enter the cave and glide along crystal-clear subterranean waters in a clunky boat that belies the beauty of its surroundings. Electric lights the colors of Lifesaver candies cast a cherry-red, butterscotch-yellow and lime-green glow in one huge chamber. Stalactites and stalagmites rear up and hang down, their decidedly phallic shapes reflected in the limpid shallows. Don't miss the cluster of stalagmites, just as phallic as the rest but creatively dubbed the "Mexican Hats."

Champagney

15 km west of Belfort

THE HOUSE OF *NÉGRITUDE* AND HUMAN RIGHTS

(La Maison de la Négritude et des Droits de l'Homme)

1 rue L.S. Senghor, on the town square. Open June–September, Wednesday–Monday, 10am–noon and 2–6pm. Phone: 03 84 23 13 98.

The citizens of this tiny town spoke out against slavery 200 years ago. They filed an official abolitionist grievance in 1789 while the rest of France was merely attempting to save its own *derrière*. Recounting centuries of civil-rights struggles and worldwide human-rights abuses, this museum displays heavy chains and fetters. Other slave-ship relics are displayed along with African artworks, weapons and ceremonial tools. Still more exhibits detail Martin Luther King, Jr., Toussaint Louverture and slavery's 20th-century implications, with a look at Nazism as a major human-rights abuse.

Dicy

Midway between Joigny and Montargis, off the D943 road.

LA FABULOSERIE

On rue Basse. Open Easter–October, Saturday–Sunday, 2–6pm; July–August, daily, 2–6pm. Admission: 30 F; students, 25 F; teens, 20 F; children, 18 F. Phone: 03 86 63 64 21.

Giant wooden human figures pose nude, wear suits and walk their dogs. Apes play guitars. Towers rear up and dozens of grotesque dolls lurk everywhere in this indoor-and-outdoor jungle of works by nonprofessional artists. Over thirty years ago, a local couple started collecting works created from found objects and junk by miners, farmers, masons and the like. Now it sprawls all over their house and gardens. Raw fantasy and impulse run rampant here, as in the huge "Little Pierre's Merry-go-round," made by a deaf-mute cowherd and sporting airplanes, tractors and military tanks.

Mulhouse

MUSEUM OF TEXTILE PRINTING

(Musée de l'Impression sur Étoffes)

14 rue Jean-Jacques Henner, across the canal from the train station. Open May–September, daily, 9am–6pm; October–April, daily, 10am–6pm. Admission: 36 F; students, 18 F, children under 18 and art students, free. Phone: 03 89 46 83 00.

Over 3 million samples reveal our ancestors' deep-seated dissatisfaction with solid navy blue. First displayed in 1833 as a way to show off Mulhouse's key industry, this collection has expanded to encompass increasingly modern techniques and designs. Examine the whole "*tissutheque*," starting with the flowery 18th-century fabrics from India which have influenced European design to this day. Scarves, bedspreads, shawls, gowns and even T-shirts tell the rest of the story. Ongoing demonstrations show how polka dots, for example, are born.

landscapes complete with distant temples, mountains, palm groves, elephants and big skies. Discover what homeowners around the world have chosen to surround themselves with through the ages, including tapestry-like scenarios and trompe-l'oeil images replicating baroque statues. Note the wallpapers that imitate—if you squint—marble, tile, wood and mosaics.

Nevers

ST. BERNADETTE'S BODY

At the Convent of St-Gildard, 34 rue Gildard, off rue de Charleville, north of the center.
Open April–October, daily, 7am–7:30pm; November–March, daily, 7:30am–noon and 2–7pm. Admission: free. Phone: 03 86 71 99 50.

Bernadette Soubirous was the unpopular village maiden who claimed to have had eighteen visions of the Virgin Mary at Lourdes in 1858. Mocked and lionized, she retreated to this convent and became a nun eight years later. After her death and burial, Bernadette's body was disinterred and—it is said—turned up completely intact. Retouched with wax, the remains have been dressed in a nun's habit and displayed here in a glass casket since 1925. Bernadette was canonized in 1933, and to this day her shrine attracts half a million pilgrims every year.

Mulhouse

WALLPAPER MUSEUM
(Musée du Papier Peint)

28 rue Zuber, in the Rixheim suburb, east of the center. Open June–September, Monday–Friday, 9am–noon and 2–6pm, Saturday–Sunday, 10am–noon and 2–6pm; October–May, Wednesday–Monday, 10am–noon and 2–6pm. Admission: 30 F; students, seniors and children, 20 F; children under 12, free. Phone: 03 89 64 24 56.

Wall-size panoramas depicting foreign wars, tropical beasts, myths and complicated fantasies are among the most impressive offerings in this, the world's largest wallpaper collection. Tasteful furnishings provide context for wallpaper masterworks rich in color and detail. Examine printed vistas of exotic

GERMANY

Don't miss:

Aachen

INTERNATIONAL PRESS MUSEUM

(Internationales Zeitungsmuseum)

Pontstrasse 13, northwest of the cathedral. Open Tuesday–Friday, 9:30am–1pm and 2:30–5pm; Saturday, 9:30am–1pm. Admission: free. Phone: 0241/4 32 45 08.

In the very street where Julius Reuter launched his news agency with forty carrier pigeons, this 100-year-old museum houses some 160,000 first editions, special editions and final editions of newspapers from around the world. These include the world's smallest and largest papers (cigarette-packet sized and four feet high, respectively), papers printed in the Kaffir, Telugu and Maori languages, a handwritten "jungle newspaper" and 1989-90 editions tracing Communism's last days.

Augsburg

FRED RAI WESTERN-CITY

On Bundesstrasse, north of the E14, at the Dasing exit, east of Augsburg. Open Easter–October, Friday–Sunday, 10am–6pm and on holidays. Phone: 082 05/2 25.

Will the Germans never tire of the American West? What is it about rampant gunslinging and the persecution of resident minorities that intrigues them so? The romance continues at this replica of a Western town, complete with cavalrymen, can-can dancers, trappers and ponchoed "Mexicans." The whole wild and woolly phenomenon has been configured by German showman Fred Rai, who shows up here on Sundays astride his horse, Spitzbub. Visitors can ride ponies, dine in a saloon, buy big hats in a general store and watch Indian dance performances, knife-throwing shows and shooting exhibitions. Blonde squaws and young braves lurk alongside teepees.

MEDIEVAL BANQUETS
(Mittelalterliches Schlemmermahl)

 At Welser Kuche, in the "Stiermann haus," Maximilianstr. 83, just south of the center. Served Monday–Saturday, at 8pm. Price depends on size of meal ordered. Phone: 08231 96110.

Candles drip wax picturesquely, and diners drink mead out of horns as big roasted things are brought to the table. Drawn from the recipe files of a bygone Augsburg patrician, meals ranging from four to ten courses are served on wooden planks and hand-thrown pottery, and are eaten with stilettoes. A set of mock medieval rules is imposed; disobedient diners will be clamped into wrist-irons, as everyone laughs.

40 km south of Braunschweig

WITCHES' FESTIVAL
(Walpurgisfeier)

 Held every year on the night of April 30, in some cases lasting several days. For more information, call the regional Tourist Information Office at (5321) 3 40 40; the St. Andreasberg Tourist Information Office at (5582) 8 03 36; or the Bad Sachsa Tourist Information Office at (5523) 3 00 90.

Don't it always seem to go that you don't know what you've got till it's gone? Though they tortured and killed all their actual witches centuries ago, many villages in this region now ring in the month of May with nostalgic revels. In Bad Harzburg, townspeople don witch costumes with giant heads and long spiky fingers. St. Andreasberg holds a witches' procession, a witches' play and a dance. In Bad Sachsa they dress not only as witches but also as devils, joined by a May queen. Other towns launch fireworks, while the most vicious hold rollicking mock witch-burnings.

60 km north of Nuremberg/Nürnberg

COLLECTION OF HOLY RELICS

 In the Diocesan Museum (Diözesanmuseum), Domplatz 5, adjacent to the cathedral. Open Tuesday–Sunday, 10am–5pm. Admission: DM 4; students, DM 2; children under 15, DM 1. Phone: 09 51/502-325.

Most visitors to this collection of rare religious artifacts come to see the regal medieval clothing on display. But who knows how many unnamed saints and martyrs had to die to provide raw material for the bone-relic pyramids here? St. Dionysius' head leers from behind glass, as do the brocaded skulls of two of St. Ursula's 11,000 virgins. Nearby is a skull labeled as the head of St. Luke, though we can scarcely believe it's *the* St. Luke from 2,000 years ago. A reliquary called the *"Dom Kreuz"* holds one of the biggest pieces of the True Cross left anywhere in the world: About 11 inches long and 1 inch wide, it looks like it would make a handy back-scratcher.

Berchtesgaden

*140 km southeast of Munich, in the far
southeastern corner of the country*

HITLER'S TEAHOUSE
("EAGLE'S NEST")
(Kehlsteinhaus)

*From the Berchtesgaden train
station (easily accessible from
Salzburg, Austria or Rosenheim,
Germany: Change at Freilass-
ing), take a bus to Obersalzburg-
Hintereck, and then change to a
special shuttle bus that goes
straight up the mountain to the
Kehlstein elevator, which will
then take you up to the teahouse.
Open daily, mid-May–mid-October, depending on weather and
snow conditions. Admission: bus
from Berchtesgaden to Ober-
salzburg-Hintereck, DM 6.80
round-trip (children, DM 3.40);
bus and elevator ride from Ober-
salzburg-Hintereck to Kehlstein,
DM 20 round-trip (children, DM
12); once you're there, the view
is free, but the restaurant's a bit
pricey. Phone: (0)8652/2969
(restaurant) or (0)8652/2029
(bus company).*

Even dictators need birthday presents, and this is what Hitler got
for his fiftieth. Ride one of the largest
and definitely the gaudiest elevators in
the world—elaborate gilt- and brass-
work, wide mirrors all around—
straight up through the heart of a
mountain to the Kehlsteinhaus.
Dubbed the "Eagle's Nest" (which is
why you'll sometimes see it referred
to as *Adlerhorst*) by occupying American soldiers in 1945, this mountain-
top retreat is now an elegant teahouse
and restaurant, literally perched on an
Alpine peak. All the Nazi decorations and any paraphenalia associated with *Der Führer* have been carefully removed; the whole building
was his holiday retreat, though he
rarely used it.

Berchtesgaden

*140 km southeast of Munich, in the far
southeastern corner of the country*

SALT MINES
(Salzbergwerk)

*Bergwerkstr. 83. Open May–mid-
October, daily, 9am–5pm; mid-
October–April, Monday–Saturday,
12:30–3:30pm. Admission: DM
20; children, DM 9.50. Phone:
(0 86 52) 6 00 20.*

Hitler had his mountain retreat at
Berchtesgaden, but the salt
mines both predated and outlived
him. Worked for over 480 years and
comprising five different levels, the
mines are still in use. Decked out in a
traditional miner's uniform, complete with jaunty cap, ride a tiny
train half a mile inside the mountain
into the first pit, with its nearly acre-
wide ceiling. Slide 100 feet down a
wooden ramp to the lower level,
where a salt museum and film await.
After rafting across a subterranean
lake, whooshing down another slide
and traveling on a funicular, board
yet another train for the fast plunge
back out of the mountain.

Berlin

"CHECKPOINT CHARLIE" MUSEUM
(Museumhaus am "Checkpoint Charlie")

Friedrichstr. 43-44, between Kochstrasse and Zimmerstrasse (U-bahn: Kochstrasse). Open daily, 9am–10pm. Admission: DM 8; students, DM 5. Phone: 030/253 72 50, or 251 10 31.

The real Checkpoint Charlie—a prefab wooden hut from which the Americans monitored transit between the two Berlins—was uprooted by a crane in 1990. This museum near the site dedicates itself to anguished memories of the absent Wall. Objects used in daring escapes and attempted escapes include a mini-submarine, motorized hang gliders, getaway cars and hot-air balloons. A vast array of other relics includes photos and paintings along with fire-bombs and those ubiquitous spray-paint-spattered hunks of broken concrete.

Berlin

CREEPY CABINET AND NAZI BUNKERS
(Gruselkabinett)

Schöneberger Strasse 23a, near Stresemann Strasse; entrance is set back from the street, through a gate and across a cement platform (S-Bahn: Anhalter Bahnhof; U-Bahn: Potsdamer Platz). Open Sunday–Tuesday and Thursday, 10am–7pm; Friday,

10am–9pm; Saturday, noon–8pm. Admission: DM 12; students and children, DM 9. Phone: 26 55 55 46.

"Welcome to Berlin Creepy Show!" announces the animatronic doorman, his neck a bloody stump, his grinning head balanced on his hand. A stone's throw from the notorious Führer Bunker where Adolf took his own life (not open to the public as yet), this long-abandoned air-raid shelter has been converted into a horror show/haunted house/Nazi-era historical showcase. Start on the lowest level, which has exhibits about the shelter's WWII days, with personal effects left here by Berliners during Allied air raids. In a glass case all by itself is a calling card imprinted with the name "Heinrich Himmler": apparently the SS chief dropped it during an inspection tour. The next floor features life-size scenes from medieval times: amputations with rusty saws, animal-to-human blood transfusions, impalings, torture, an alchemist's laboratory, witch burnings and the real axe of Berlin's last executioner. On the third level, vampires, zombies, rats and tacky fake skeletons lurk in a warren of dimly lit chambers. Real live "monsters" leap out of the gloom here and there, resulting in much incontinence and hilarity. Restore yourself at the Blood Bar, a ghoulish saloon serving red cocktails.

Berlin

DOG MUSEUM
(Hundemuseum)

Alt-Blankenberg 33, in the Alt-Blankenberg neighborhood (S-bahn: Blankenberg). Open

Tuesday, Thursday and Saturday, 3–6pm. Phone: (030) 481 3931.

A 1945 German draft order for dogs is one of 20,000 exhibits in this private museum, whose proprietors just can't get enough of man's best *freund.* Stuffed dogs, ceramic dogs, wooden dogs and effigies in other media show how artists through the years have responded to the irritating sound of yelping and the touch of a cold wet nose. Also here are postage stamps, cups, clocks and other domestic objects depicting or shaped like dachshunds, spaniels, terriers, retrievers, bulldogs—even poodles—proving that German shepherds are hardly the only species beloved in this canine-crazed country. Seven exhibition rooms will make you slaver and pant. The proprietors gladly dispense advice on animal rights.

Berlin

EROTIC MUSEUM
(Erotik-Museum)

Kantstrasse at Joachimstaler Strasse, one block south of Zoo Station (U-Bahn: Zoologischer Garten). Open daily, 9am–midnight. Admission: DM 10; students and seniors, DM 8; no one under 18 admitted. Phone: 030/886 06 66.

In a city famous for its erotic antics, this museum displays centuries' worth of artwork. Indian miniatures and Japanese scrolls show athletic feats. Fertility figures from around the world keep few secrets. Artifacts crafted through the ages give new meaning to the word "rigid." Learn about gay pre-war sex researcher Dr. Bernard Hirschfeld and other German pioneers, or simply study new positions. Changing exhibits focus on everything from sodomy to erotic works by famous painters.

Berlin

GAY MEN'S HISTORY MUSEUM
(Schwules Museum)

Mehringdamm 61, third floor, in the Kreuzberg district (U-bahn: Mehringdamm). Wednesday–Sunday, 2–6pm; guided tours given Saturday at 5pm. Admission: DM 7, DM 4. Phone: 6 93 11 72.

Exhibitions and film screenings—not always the kind you'd show your mother—augment this museum's library and its permanent poster and magazine archive. This bills itself as the only museum in the world devoted exclusively to homosexuality; it features an ever-changing selection of graphic arts and historical exhibits about gay men and their role in society. The archives and library are practically a museum unto themselves, with a comprehensive collection of publications going back decades.

Berlin

HEMP MUSEUM
(Hanfmuseum)

Mühlendamm 5, between Spandauer Strasse and Breite Strasse (U-bahn: Klosterstrasse). Open

Tuesday–Friday, 10am–8 pm;
Saturday–Sunday, noon–8pm.
Admission: DM 5; children un-
der 10, free. Phone: 030/242 48
27.

Is hemp the world's most delightfully versatile plant? Along with big, juicy specimens flourishing in pots, the museum displays hemp lampshades, hemp stationery, hemp jackets, hemp hats, fuzzy hemp socks, hemp pretzels, hemp cat litter, hemp soap, hemp moisturizing cream, hemp lamp wicks, hemp pet food, hemp candy, hemp beer—even sturdy hemp jeans and sensible hemp sneakers. Supporting exhibits cover medical marijuana, hemp-farming history, and pot laws and lore in cultures around the world, from Jamaica to Jordan. A café and gift shop on the premises offer opportunities to think deeply over what you've learned and sample some of what you've seen.

MEDICAL HISTORY MUSEUM
(Medizinhistorisches Museum)

In Charité Hospital, Schu-
mannstr. 20/21, in the Mitte dis-
trict; use the Spreekanal entrance
(U-bahn: Zinnowitzer Strasse; S-
bahn: Lehrter Stadtbahnhof).
Open Monday, Tuesday, Thurs-
day and Friday, 1–4pm; Wednes-
day, 1–7pm. Admission:
voluntary donation. Phone: 28
02 31 47.

Lose your appetite for schnitzel and bratwurst after perusing this venerable collection of over 1,000 body parts. Diseases and other

routes to abnormality and deformation are the big subject here, evinced by unforgettable organs, bones and bits of flesh. Visiting exhibits offer medical tidbits from around the world, while vintage microscopes and surgical instruments are also on display.

MUSEUM OF FORBIDDEN ART
(Museum der Verboten Kunst)

In the watchtower in Mauer-
park, Schlesischer Busch, Pusch-
kinallee at Schlesisherstrasse, in
the Treptower district (U-bahn:
Schlesischer Tor; S-bahn: Trep-
tower Park). Open Saturday–
Sunday, noon–6pm. Admission:
free. Phone: 204 20 49.

The old east-west dividing line used to slice right through what is now this serene park. In the former East German guard tower, steep metal stairs lead up through a trapdoor to an array, on the top floor, of relics from a vanished age. Clunky radio equipment, a dummy dressed as a guard, a field telephone, signs reading HALT! and many pictures evoke this place as it was when barbed wire surrounded it. On the second floor are changing exhibits of what would once have been "forbidden" art, depicting life in Berlin as it used to be.

PEACOCK ISLAND
(Pfaueninsel)

From central Berlin, take the S-bahn to Wannsee, then bus 316 to the Pfaueninsel stop; from there a ferry shuttles you to the island. Open May–August, daily, 8am–8pm; April and September, daily, 8am–6pm; March and October, daily, 9am–5pm; November–February, Tuesday–Sunday, 10am–4pm. Ferry to island: DM 2; students and children, DM 1. Phone: 805 30 42.

Full of faux landmarks that rear up cunningly in the distance, this island playground was the brainchild of Friedrich Wilhelm II, successor to Friedrich the Great. He commissioned it so that he and his mistress could flit from fake Roman temple to fake Swiss cottage, chasing live peacocks on the way. The structures and monuments dotting the island are meant to look best at a distance, so they look like cartoons close up. Tame peacocks still strut on the paths, lawns and flower gardens, shrieking their heads off, while golden pheasants and other exotic birds mutter in an aviary. The most prominent folly, a tiny castle near the ferry dock, has a charming but comically useless bridge connecting its two towers.

PEACOCK ISLAND—BERLIN

STASI MUSEUM

(ASTAK Forschungs- und Gedenkstätte Normannenstrasse)

Ruschestrasse 103, Haus 1, near Frankfurter Allee (U-bahn: Magdalenenstrasse). Open Tuesday–Friday, 11am–6pm; Saturday–Sunday, 2–6pm. Admission: DM 5; students and children, DM 3. Phone: (030) 5 53 68 54.

Shiver as you learn how the East German secret police—Stasi for short—kept tabs on would-be dissidents and everyone else in their jurisdiction. Marvel at surveillance equipment such as tape recorders and spy cameras hidden inside briefcases, purses and even cans. Other displays include documents, victims' reports and clunky Communist relics. Explore part of the organization's former offices and just be glad they can't interrogate anybody anymore.

SUGAR MUSEUM
(Zucker-Museum)

Amrumer Strasse 32 (U-Bahn: Amrumer Strasse). Open Monday–Wednesday, 9am–5pm; Sunday, 11am–6pm. Admission: DM 4.50; students and children, DM 2. Phone: 31 42 75 74.

TOPOGRAPHY OF TERRORS—BERLIN

Get the culinary, social, historical and scientific lowdown on humankind's most popular addictive drug. Elegant antique silver sugar bowls and serving spoons compete for space with politically correct exhibits about sugar's connection to slavery, sugar's essential role in alcoholic drinks and the technological wizardry that converts raw cane juice into glazed donuts and a thousand other more prosaic products.

black-and-white photos show the gestation and birth of the Nazi phenomenon, from Kristallnacht to the war trials. In between are images and stories of men and women held, tortured and executed here. (All the captions are in German, but a book is on sale with the English translation.) This neighborhood once housed the office for the Inspectorate of Concentration Camps, as well as Gestapo headquarters and the administrative offices of the SS. An overwhelming sense of oppression hangs in the air, and the photos will send shivers down your spine.

Berlin

TOPOGRAPHY OF TERRORS
(Topographie des Terrors)

Stresemannstrasse 110; enter on Wilhelmstrasse at Niederkirchnerstrasse (S-bahn: Anhalter Bahnhof or Potsdamer Platz); exhibit is temporarily housed in a sheltered trench while a new exhibition center is being built, set to open in the year 2000. Open spring–fall, daily, 10am–6pm; winter, daylight hours. Admission: free. Phone: 030/254 86 703.

The terrors in question are Gestapo interrogations, which were conducted for years on this site. Stark

Bonn

MUSEUM OF WOMEN
(Frauen-Museum)

Im Krausfeld 10. Open Tuesday–Saturday, 2–7pm; Sunday, 11am–5pm. Admission: DM 5; students, DM 3. Phone: (0228) 69 13 44 or 69 61 64.

Art, history—uh, make that *her*-story—and feminism are the essential ingredients for this museum, which has a decidedly female take on society. The Museum of Women has continually changing exhibits, but the underlying theme remains consistent: How women view the world through their own eyes. Changing shows celebrate women's life, work and politics; paintings, sculptures and multimedia exhibits by world-famous female artists are given equal exposure with works by lesser-known craftswomen.

BEATLES MUSEUM

Heinsbergstrasse 13, at Zülpicher Strasse, in the center (U-bahn: Barbarossaplatz). Open Wednesday–Friday, 10am–2pm and 3–7pm; Saturday, 10am–3pm. Admission: DM 5. Phone: 0221 923 13 13.

Cologne and Liverpool are sister cities, which is why you'll find this shrine to the four boys here. Relics from their hard days' nights at the Star Club in faraway Hamburg are on display, along with childhood photos, autographs, clippings, rare records and fan memorabilia. Early pop-culture artifacts—Beatles underwear, plastic Yellow Submarines, Paul puppets—open a window onto mass-media exploitation. Free beverages await all visitors, but trying on the Beatle wigs is *verboten*.

CHOCOLATE MUSEUM
(Museum für Geschichte und Gegenwart der Schokolade)

On a strip projecting into the Rhine known as Rheinauhafen, between Severinsbrücke and Deutzer Brücke. Open Tuesday–Friday, 10am–6pm (last admittance, 5pm); Saturday–Sunday, 11am–7pm (last admittance, 6pm). Admission: DM 10; students and children, DM 5. Phone: 0221/93 18 88 0.

A ceramic Mayan god sits cross-legged atop a glassed-in pyramid of cocoa beans to show who really deserves homage at this glamorous museum, operated by the Imhoff-Stollwerck candy company. Pictures and fine china tell the story of chocolate's emergence as a popular beverage—after a clever Spaniard first thought of adding sugar. All the little-known details of chocolate production, from growing and harvesting the pods straight through to the creation of chocolate bunnies, are revealed in photo exhibits, and manufacturing machines fitted with windows take the mystery out of how creamy fillings wind up inside candy eggs. In the Chocolate Cinema, vintage ads are juxtaposed with modern commercials. Meanwhile a bottomless chocolate fountain offers free samples to everyone.

GOLDEN CHAMBER
(Goldene Kammer)

In the Basilica of St. Ursula, Ursulaplatz; chamber is on the right as you enter the church; an attendant will let you in. Open Monday and Wednesday–Friday, 9:30am–noon and 12:30–5pm; Saturday, 9am–noon and 1–5pm. Admission: DM 2. Phone: 0221/13 34 00.

The walls' upper reaches are textured thickly with human bones. A veritable tsunami of ribs, shoulder blades and femurs is arranged in zigzags and swirls and even in the shapes of Latin words. Lower down, shelves support some 700 skulls. Legend tells how St. Ursula took 11,000 virgins on a voyage and they all ended up getting brutally martyred. Many of the skulls on display in this 17th-century chamber allegedly belonged to the virgins, though recent retranslations dispute the legend and claim there were actually only eleven girls, if any. Head-shaped reliquary after head-shaped reliquary stares out blankly, alternating with skulls resting in gilded encasements and wearing headgear that strongly resembles yarmulkes.

started printing their own money, and desperate Germans began trading margarine and bricks instead of paper currency. Glass cases flanking the bank's entrance and featuring knapsacks stuffed with pre-war German inflation cash are a sad testimonial to inflation around the world. Inside the bank, exhibits revealing the history of money include gold ducats, counterfeits, Manchurian vulcanized-rubber coins and the world's largest and smallest coins (two-and-a-half feet across and one-eighth-inch across, respectively). An added bonus is an international piggy-bank collection.

Cologne (Köln)

INFLATION MUSEUM
(Geldgeschichtliches Museum)

 In the Kreissparkasse bank, Neumarkt 18-24, southwest of the Dom. Open Monday–Friday, 9am–7pm; Saturday, 9am–2pm. Admission: free. Phone: 0221/227 2370 or 227 2279.

During the 1920s, inflation swung so out of control in Germany that one of several banknotes in circulation was worth 100,000,000,-000 marks. Towns and businesses

INFLATION MUSEUM—COLOGNE

Cuxhaven

100 km north of Bremen, on the North Sea coast

SHIPWRECK MUSEUM
(Wrackmuseum)

 Dorfstrasse 80, at Windeichenweg, just inland in Stickenbüttel. Open April–October, Tuesday–Friday, 9am–1pm and 3–6pm; Saturday–Sunday, 10am–1pm and 3–6pm. Admission: DM 4.50; children, DM 1.50. Phone: 04721/23341.

A lonely little two-man U-boat welcomes you into this museum, whose 1,500 artifacts were salvaged from sunken ships. An estimated 3,000 vessels went down in the rivers and sea hereabouts over the last two centuries, and the wrack on display includes propellers, portholes, rudders, figureheads, torpedo casings, cutlery and cargo from warships, liners, freighters, submarines and tugs. Many exhibits, such as a pathetic stash of gooseberries found among the provisions on a downed WWI sub, evoke a true sense of drowning and destruction. If any place is going to leave you with that sinking feeling, it's this one.

15 km north of Munich

CONCENTRATION-CAMP MEMORIAL
(Kz-Gedenkstätte Dachau mit Museum)

 Alte Römerstr. 75, on the northeastern edge of town. Open Tuesday–Sunday, 9am–5pm. Admission: free. Phone: 081 31/17 41.

Many perished in this camp from 1933 until April 1945, when American troops arrived. In 1965 the site was opened as a memorial not just to its own dead, but to all of the Nazis' victims. Sinister barbed wire spans the walls from guard tower to guard tower, and the concentration-camp buildings still stand, though they are now adorned with predictable sculptures evoking torture and pain. A documentary film (the English version screens at 11:30am and 3:30pm) provides an introduction to the on-site museum's 500-plus artifacts detailing this and other camps.

Ettal

10 km north of Garmisch-Partenkirchen, south of Munich

LINDERHOF CASTLE
(Schloss Linderhof)

 12 kilometers west of Ettal, on the road heading toward Austria; buses run regularly to the castle from Oberammergau. Open April–September, daily, 9am–12:15pm and 12:45–5:30pm; October–March, daily, 10am–12:15pm and 12:45–4pm. Admission: in summer, DM 9; in winter, DM 7. Phone: 0 88 22 / 35 12.

Bavaria's Ludwig II created an unbelievably rococo castle and the world's largest artificial cavern, an underground lake and vast artworks inspired by Wagner's operas, all of which earned him the sobriquet "mad king." He used to glide around the underground lake in a golden boat, but the exorbitant expense and excess of his beloved "dream castles" ended up getting Ludwig deposed. Tour the landscape of the mad king's visions, where the Blue Grottoes of Capri meet *Tannhauser.*

Frankfurt

STRUWWELPETER MUSEUM

 In the Schirn Kunsthalle art museum building, in the Römerberg, in the center of town. Open Tuesday and Thursday–Sunday, 11am–5pm; Wednesday, 11am–8pm. Admission: free. Phone: 069 / 28 13 33.

Struwwelpeter—"Peter the Slob"—is Bart Simpson's slightly sinister 19th-century German ancestor. A stubborn rebel who refuses to cut his hair or nails, and who sports a huge natural and curling talons, the sailor-suited preteen was created by Frankfurt writer Heinrich Hoffmann. Struwwelpeter's strong and pathological will has earned him countless fans worldwide, as evinced by books of his adventures translated into diverse languages, including Yiddish and Japanese. Don't miss the parodies, including *Struwwel-Hitler*.

Furth im Wald

70 km northeast of Regensburg, on the Czech border

SLAYING-THE-DRAGON FOLK PLAY
(Drachenstich Festspiele)

 Held every year in mid-August. Phone: (99 73) 80 10 14 (festival committee) or (99 73) 80 10 80 (tourist office).

Fake blood spews forth from the dragon's mouth, rising in a red mist over the soil—or *is* it fake? Dating back to 1431, Germany's oldest traditional folk play retells the story of a knight who rides up in chain mail and a leather jerkin to slay a pock-marked green dragon much bigger than himself. When he drives the mortal blow home at last, smoke pours from the beast's nostrils while a crimson wave gushes out between its fangs.

Füssen

100 km southwest of Munich

NEUSCHWANSTEIN CASTLE
(Schloss Neuschwanstein)

 6 kilometers southeast of Füssen; buses leave regularly from the Füssen train station and drop you off a short walk away—it's hard to miss. Open April–September, daily, 8:30am–5:30pm; October–March, daily, 10am–4pm. Admission: DM 9; children under 14, free. Phone: 08362/81035.

Lofty and white, this 19th-century castle—said to be the model for Disneyland's—was commissioned by Bavaria's Ludwig II, an idealist and patron of the hard-up Richard Wagner, who wrote operas for him. Perhaps the most extreme manifestation of eccentricity in architecture, this fantasy structure was planned by a set designer, who purposely made it look as dramatic as possible. The castle, of course, has no real function other than to look stupendous—the mark of a true folly.

Gersthofen

5 km north of Augsburg

BALLOON MUSEUM
(Ballon Museum)

Bahnhofstr. 10, in the center of town. Open Saturday–Sunday, 10am–6pm; Wednesday, 2–6pm. Phone: 08 21 / 2491-135.

More hot-air balloons take off from Gersthofen every year than from all other departure points in the world, put together. In a town where ballooning dates back to 1786, this museum occupies five stories, each with a different balloony theme. Over 1,300 artifacts include original balloon gondolas (those basket things that hang underneath), as well as the world's first attempt at 3D photography (the subject was balloons). The top floor features modern art with balloon motifs.

Hamburg

EROTIC ART MUSEUM

Nobistor 10, between Holstenstrasse and Grosse Freiheit (S-bahn: Reeperbahn); entrance is at the top of the stairs. Open Sunday–Thursday, 10am–midnight; Friday and Saturday, 10am–1am. Admission: DM 15; students, DM 10. Phone: 317 47 57.

Goya painted erections. The proof is here, in this tastefully arranged collection of original works ranging from the 15th to the late 20th centuries and all having something in common. David Hockney, Pablo Picasso, Jean Cocteau, Keith Haring and dozens of others are among an almost exclusively male coterie of artists whose impressions of orgies, enemas, mating animals, Priapus and lesbians you can admire here. Learn how some of the works by German artists were vilified and their makers victimized during Hitler's notorious campaign against "degenerate art." It's like any art museum, only less boring.

Hamburg

HOT SPICE MUSEUM
(Gewurzmuseum)

At Sandtorkai 32, second floor. On the waterfront, south of the center, just east of Niederbaumbrucke (U-bahn: Messberg or Baumwall). Open Tuesday–Sunday, 10am–5pm. Admission: DM 4; children under 12, DM 2. Phone: (040) 36 79 89.

This old spice warehouse gives off inviting aromas as you wander around dipping fingers into crates, sacks, barrels and bowls to sample bits of dried cinnamon, cassia, jalapeño and mace. Evoking realms as far away as Sarawak and Sichuan, dozens of different spices are arranged according to a rather puzzling set of themes, from cuisine to ritual, packaging, import, herbal cigarettes, teas and even art. Don't miss the model ship made entirely of cloves. Saffron, curry and mustard get their due, while a handless, grinning mannequin portrays a spice dealer.

Hamelin (Hameln)

PIED PIPER PLAY
(Rattenfänger Spiele)

Performed every Sunday at noon, mid-May–mid-September, on the Hochzeitshaus Terrace on the market square in the center of town. Admission: free. For more information, call the tourist information office at 5151/202-617 or 202-618.

The piper in his patched clothes came to town and lured its rats away, but when he wasn't recompensed he sneaked back in disguise and led 130 Hamelin children into oblivion. Today the piper wears vivid tights and a feathered hat as dozens of amateur actors portraying rats, town councillors, parents and hapless tots reenact the fateful events of June 26, 1284. Some say the story is a metaphor for the medieval recruitment of Hamelin's citizens to colonize the distant outposts of Silesia, Moravia, Pommern and Prussia.

Ingolstadt

70 km north of Munich

MEDICAL HISTORY MUSEUM
(Medizinhistorisches Museum)

In the "Alte Anatomie" building, Anatomiestrasse 18-20, near Jahnstrasse on the western edge of the center. Open Tuesday–Sunday, 10am–noon and 2–5pm. Admission: DM 3; students, seniors and children, DM 1.50; admission free on Sunday. Phone: (08 41) 30 54 93 or 30 5 1860.

What patient could stand for an ordinary sterile scalpel after viewing these vintage handcrafted rectal speculi, amputation saws, cauterizing irons, cranial chain saws, blood-letting bowls, ear funnels, hernia cutters and other implements in coral, silver and semiprecious stone? Housed in a historic building as thick with frescoes as a church, the collection occupies many rooms and includes preserved body parts and half-skinned skeletons who clench their teeth and flaunt bright veins. Don't miss the do-it-yourself enema chair.

PIED PIPER PLAY—HAMELIN

Kassel

BROTHERS GRIMM MUSEUM
(Brüder Grimm-Museum)

Bruder Grimm-Platz 4A. Open daily, 10am–5pm. Admission: DM 3; students, DM 2. Phone: 0561/103 235.

Jacob and Wilhelm Grimm, the pair who brought you Little Red Riding Hood, lived in Kassel once upon a time, before taking professorships up the road in Gottingen and then losing their nice jobs after a misunderstanding with the king. The Grimms' dishes, furniture and other personal items are here, along with illustrated fairytale books from all over the world. Versions of *Puss in Boots*, *Snow White* and all your favorite stories of betrayal and murder are here in an amusing array of obscure languages, including Basque, Breton and Sardinian.

`Kassel`

MUSEUM FOR SEPULCHRAL CULTURE
(Museum für Sepulkralkultur)

Weinbergstrasse 25-27, south of the train station. Open Tuesday–Sunday, 10am–5pm. Admission: DM 5; students, DM 3; children under 6, free. Phone: (0562) 91 89 30.

In Germany, death isn't merely a fact of life; it's a frame of mind. This brooding obsession is exposed to the light of day in this trendy museum, which mixes pretentious death-themed modern art with ancient coffins and actual tombstones to explore every facet of "sepulchral culture." Framed death notices, photographs of children on their deathbeds, painted skulls from the Hallstatt Bonehouse (which see), embalming equipment, crematoria, mourning costumes and caskets for stillborn babies compete with stark and occasionally ugly art about decaying heads and feeling miserable. Note the hair jewelry, made from tresses of the newly deceased and worn by mourners. If you wear a lot of eyeliner, mascara and black clothing and spend all day reading about vampires, you'll feel like you're in heaven.

`Kassel`

PARK OF FOLLIES
(Schlosspark Wilhelmshöhe)

Main entrance to the park is at the end of Wilhelmshöher Allee, in the Wilhelmshöhe District, at the western edge of town; there are other entrances along Mulangstrasse. Open daily during daylight hours; the platform in the Hercules statue is open mid-March–mid-November, daily, 10am–5pm. Admission: free. Phone: 0561/3 22 80.

Behind Wilhelmshöhe Castle sprawls a magnificent landscape garden liberally sprinkled with baroque follies and faux ruins, built at the end of the 18th century by Elector Wilhelm, a wannabe medieval knight trapped in the wrong century. Follow the winding trails past cascading pools and gliding swans; a fake Roman aqueduct constructed to look like an ancient ruin; the Devil's Bridge (*Teufelsbrücke*), a quaint, vaguely oriental span that connects nothing to nothing; and the park's masterpiece, Löwenburg Castle, a "medieval" structure purposely built of crumbling stone to appear in a half-ruined state, complete with a nonexistent chapel (note the stained glass) and teetering tower. Looming above it all is a massive statue of Hercules, perched on the tip of a pyramid at the top of a steep hill. If your legs are up to it, climb up along the endless waterfalls to the viewing platform at the top and look down upon your phony, crumbling empire.

Kassel

WALLPAPER MUSEUM
(Tapetenmuseum)

 Within the Hessisches Landesmuseum, Brüder-Grimm-Platz 5. Open Tuesday–Sunday, 10am–5pm. Admission: DM 5, but free on Fridays. Phone: (05 61) 78 46-222.

Hilarious, '70s floral designs lurk among dozens of wallpapers displayed—cleverly—against wallpaper. Wall-size panels dating back to the 18th century serve as a gateway to this collection, which will leave you with more interior-decorating schemes than you can afford. Hundreds of years' worth of wall coverings range from the embossed to the metallic to the 3D, from the neoclassical to Chinoiserie. Room-size wallpaper panoramas depict ancient myths, pastoral scenes, waterscapes and the Battle of Austerlitz. Don't miss the trompe l'oeil door and curtained windows, printed on wallpaper to make a large room look enormous.

Leipzig

STASI MUSEUM

 Dittrichring 24, main entrance (Haupteingang), at the western edge of the city center, southwest of the train station. Open Wednes-

 day–Sunday, 2–6pm. Admission: free. Phone: 341 961 24 43.

East Germany's secret police—the Stasi—had its headquarters and interrogation center in the building nicknamed "Round Corner" (*Runden Ecke*), which now houses this museum. Founded by members of the citizens' committee that seized the place in 1989, the chilling collection includes phone-tapping devices and other secret microphones; guns, bludgeons, and propaganda posters; as well as piles of intercepted letters and shredded documents. A row of glass jars contains fabric swatches that Stasi officers rubbed against dissident pamphlets in hope of later identifying the distributors by their scent. A woman's purse and a strap-on false stomach contain hidden cameras with which to photograph demonstrations; also here are wigs and other disguises. It might leave you with the sense of having walked into the middle of a propaganda movie, but it's real.

STASI MUSEUM—LEIPZIG

BAVARIA FILMTOUR

Bavariafilmplatz, just south of the city in Geiselgasteig (U-bahn: Silberhornstrasse, then tram 25 to Bavariafilmplatz). Open March–October, daily, 9am–4pm. Admission: DM 15; children, DM 10. Phone: 64 99 23 04.

You won't see the *Psycho* house or Gilligan's Island on this studio tour, but as a diminutive Teutonic answer to Hollywood, it offers its own stars, stunts and sets. Walk through those ever-popular sets from *Das Boot* and lots of German movies you have probably never seen, and watch a soap opera being filmed. Stuntmen survive explosions, gunshots and hair-raising falls, solely for your entertainment.

CENTER FOR UNUSUAL MUSEUMS

Zentrum für Aussergewohnliche Museen (Z.A.M.)

Westenriederstr. 41, near Thomas-Wimmer-Ring (U-bahn: Marienplatz; S-bahn: Isartorplatz). Open daily, 10am– 6pm. Admission: DM 8; students and children, DM 5. Phone: 089/ 290 4121.

The last word in chamber pots, padlocks, pedal-cars, perfume, the Easter Bunny and Austria's Empress Elizabeth comprise permanent collections, while one rotating exhibition yields continually changing surprises. A spiked Iron Maiden welcomes visitors at the door. The world's only Easter Bunny collection has over 1,000 effigies of the egg-producing rodent in porcelain and plush, not to mention cutely dressed taxidermed rabbits. A Roman urine flask and a British bowl with Hitler's face printed inside it are among the chamber pots. Five thousand perfume bottles help tell the story of scent, and the lionization of Empress Elizabeth may baffle you completely.

FAIRGROUND, PUPPET-THEATER AND MUSICAL INSTRUMENT COLLECTIONS

In the Munich City Museum (Münchner Stadtmuseum), St.-Jakobs-Platz 1, in the southern part of the city center (U-bahn and S-bahn: Marienplatz); puppetry and fairground collections are on the third floor, music collection on the fourth floor. Open Tuesday and Thursday–Sunday, 10am–5pm; Wednesday, 10am–8:30pm. Admission: DM 5; students, and children, DM 2.50. Phone: 089/233-22370.

A puppet Paul Klee made for his son in 1916, and surrealistic puppets from the '30s, are among devil puppets, shadow puppets, life-size puppets and 25,000 others in an exhibition space that includes its own theater. Nearby, the fairground collection includes an eight-foot automatronic King Kong (it bites!) and sideshow waxworks including a lifelike horned woman. Tibetan human-skull drums and flutes made of leg bones punctuate the musical-instrument collection, along with an elephant-tusk trumpet, an automated brass band and more tubas than you're likely to see in any single location anytime soon.

KARL VALENTIN MUSEUM
(Valentin-Musäum)

In the Isartor, a tower at the intersection of Thomas-Wimmer-Ring and Im Tal (S-bahn: Isartor). Open Monday, Thursday, Friday and Saturday, 11:01am–5:29pm; Sunday, 10:01am–5:29pm. Admission: DM 2.99; students and children, DM 1.99; 99 years old or older, free. Phone: 22 32 66.

This museum's hours and admission prices—which are hilarious to the German public, so accustomed to neat, round numbers—give a taste of the hoots that lurk up the spiral staircase. Munich-born Karl Valentin, who died in 1948, was an absurdist folk-hero comedian, kind of a cross between Harpo Marx and Red Skelton. Valentin earned legions of fans, including Hermann Hesse and Bertolt Brecht, who would probably laugh their heads off at this museum's barrage of visual jokes and the decor that clutters the tower. It's all documented in a Bavarian dialect that native German speakers can hardly understand, and they think that's hilarious too.

MEDIEVAL BANQUETS
(Mittelalterliches Shlemmermahl)

At Welser Kuche, in the "Feldherrnkeller," Residenzstr. 27. Served nightly at 8pm. Admission: DM 58; children under 10, free. Phone: 089/29 65 65.

Stab large carcasses with the dagger that is your only implement at an eight-to-ten-course, three-hour banquet. The hearty, heavy dishes are based on recipes prepared in local kitchens 450 years ago. At vast tables, break bread with strangers, swig local brew and get punished if you break any of the restaurant's whimsical rules.

55 km northeast of Augsburg

SHELL GROTTO

In the garden of the castle (Schloss Neuberg an der Donau), Residenzstr A2. Open Tuesday–Sunday, 10am–5pm. Admission: DM 4; children, DM 3. Phone: 0 84 31/88 97.

Against walls painted smooth azure, thousands of mussel shells taken from the Danube have been shaped into pictures and designs—the brainchild of Renaissance dandies with too much time and too much nacre on their hands. All around the Blue Grotto, tracing its arched doorways and filling its shrine-like niches, shells ingeniously form floral motifs and flowing ribbons, vases and spirals, bands and whorls. On the ceiling, a complex pattern comprising concentric circles, curlicues and letters marking the four directions is centered around whimsical renderings of zodiac symbols, all fashioned from shells.

DUNGEONS WITH TORTURE CHAMBERS
(Lochgefangnisse)

Under the Town Hall. Open Tuesday–Sunday, 10am–4:30pm, with guided tour only. Admission: DM 4; students and children, DM 2; children under 6, free. Phone: 233 61 32 (tourist office).

Here in the "Prison of the Holy Roman Empire," medieval inmates had no chance of either escaping or whiling away their confinement with a friendly chat. Ironclad doors separated the cells from one another. Peek in and see their short plank beds still sporting wooden-board pillows. Follow the guide along a claustrophobic warren of low tunnels to the torture chamber, stocked with original instruments and replicas including stocks, tongs, crushers, pliers and spiked wrist clamps. (The English translation of the narrative insists that torture was alien to the Germanic people until the Catholic Church forced it on them in the 14th century, ha ha.) Medieval prisoners—arsonists, slanderers and such—lived in total darkness here. The only room with a shaft of natural light is the hangman's.

UNDERGROUND ART TUNNELS
(Kunstbunker Felsengange)

Entrance is behind the Albrecht Durer statue in Albrecht-Durer-Platz, a few blocks north of St. Sebald's Church in the Old Town. Visits with guided tour only; tours depart daily at 11am and 1, 3 and 5pm. Admission: DM 7; students, DM 5; children under 10, free. Phone: 0911/22 70 66.

Deep under the streets of the Old Town, roam this cool, 900-meter warren of smoothly hewn tunnels, first known to have been used as early as 1380. Because the conditions here were found to conserve art perfectly, the city's most highly prized works—including many by Durer—were stored in these tunnels for safekeeping during the first world war and again during the second, when bombs reduced Nuremberg to rubble.

Plech

35 km northeast of Nuremberg

FRANCONIA'S WONDERLAND
(Fränkisches Wunderland)

Zum Herrlesgrund 13, on the A9 Nürnberg-Berlin road; follow the signs. Open April–mid-October, daily, 9am–6pm (last admission, 5pm). Admission: DM 19; children, DM 16; children under 3 feet tall, free. Phone: 09244/9890.

Plump Teutons in cowboy costumes loiter around an ersatz Wild West habitat which includes a saloon, ranch, sheriff's office, gold mine, gallows, blacksmith's shop and Mexican café. The Indian village has tribal dancers and gargantuan teepees. These share the park with huge model dinosaurs, figures from Grimms' fairy tales and piano-playing skeletons who occupy a ghost town and dutifully perform in a Ghost Show.

Potsdam

Just southwest of Berlin

FILMPARK BABELSBERG STUDIO TOURS

Off Grossbeerenstrasse near August Babel-Strasse, east of the town center: From Berlin, take the S-bahn to Babelsberg station, then bus 690 or 692 to the Ahornstrasse stop. Open March–October, daily, 10am–6pm. Admission: DM 28; children under 12, DM 21. Phone: 0331/721 27 50.

Relive your favorite moments from *Das Boot, Metropolis, The Neverending Story* and other German classics at the studio where they were created. The tour includes sets from various sci-fi, fantasy and horror films as well as a nauseous simulated dive on the *Das Boot* set. Leap at an opportunity to watch a talk show being filmed and stunt actors diving through flames. A Wild West section demonstrates this country's endless love affair with cowboys. Spacemen, wizards, fancy ladies and acrobats strut about the wacky backlot sets.

Potsdam

Just southwest of Berlin

SANSSOUCI PARK FOLLIES

West of the city center: There are dozens of entry points, and it's so big you can't miss it (S-Bahn: Potsdam Stadt). Open Tuesday–Sunday, 9am–dusk. Admission to the park is free; if you want to go inside the buildings, each has its own admission price and hours. Phone: 3 31/969 4200 or 4202.

The eccentric 18th- and 19th-century buildings scattered throughout immense Sanssouci Park are hard to categorize: part folly, part baroque extravagance, part architectural sculpture. As you stroll around, keep an eye out for these: **The Chinese House:** It doesn't look Chinese at all, but features much over-the-top Chinoiserie, including an umbrella-toting Mandarin on the roof. **The Dragon House:** The architects did their homework on this phony pagoda, which actually resembles the real thing. **The Hill of Ruins:** At the park's far northern end are custom-made "ancient ruins." **The Roman Baths:** a simulated Roman Villa, which *wasn't* made as purpose-built ruins and looks perfectly brand new. **The Historic Windmill:** For some reason, in the 18th century, windmills were considered exotic and bizarre, so every good folly park had to have one. **The Church of Peace:** a fake medieval Italian church. **The "Mosque" Steam Engine Building:** This pumping station for Sanssouci's fountains (actually outside the park on Breite Strasse) is masterfully and convincingly disguised as a Near

Eastern mosque, complete with minaret. **The New Palace:** One of this huge complex's features is a top-notch shell grotto, with mosaics of dragons and cherubs made not only with shells but also with fossils, minerals, petrified wood, colored stones and quartz crystals. The gardens are among the biggest in Europe, so it's a good idea to grab a free map of the grounds (from the tourist office or the castle) before you set out, or at least follow the signboards placed throughout the park.

HOTEL BÄREN

Hofbronnengasse 4-9, near the Market Square in the Old Town. Accommodations start at DM 150. Phone: (09861) 944-10.

Dating back to the 11th century and staffed by workers in period costume, the Bear Hotel is one of Germany's oldest inns. At medieval banquets served in its restaurant, diners eat and drink from earthenware vessels, using daggers and their bare hands. They say the ghost of Count Rugger III haunts the place; after every banquet, guests are given a peek at Rugger's skeleton. It's the real thing, and it lies moldering in a wooden coffin, clutching a sword.

MEDIEVAL CRIMINAL MUSEUM
(Mittelalterliches Kriminalmuseum)

Burggasse 3-5, just south of the town hall in the Old Town. Open April–October, daily, 9:30am–6pm; November and January–February, daily, 2–5pm; December and March, daily, 10am–4pm. Admission: DM 5; children, DM 3. Phone: 0 98 61/53 59.

Spiked chairs, chastity belts and goofy metal pig-masks are among the devices in this expansive collection. Four floors are stocked with well over 100 exhibits revisiting the days when public shame was the sentence for such crimes as drinking too much, violating dress codes or baking overly small loaves of bread. Among the "shame masks," made to be worn outdoors, are a long-tongued one for gossips. Lazy students were made to ride the wooden "shame donkey," while incompetent musicians were forced to wear the huge "shame flute." Stocks, a gibbet, torture instruments and all the rest are conveniently illustrated and explained in multilingual text.

70 km south of Hamburg

HEIDE-PARK

On the A7 road between Hamburg and Hannover. Open March–November, daily, 9am–6pm (last admittance, 4pm). Admission: DM 34; chil-

HEIDE-PARK—SOLTAU

 dren under 4, free. Phone: 51
91/91 91.

This park's trained alligators strive
to give their species a good
name. And its Electronic Bird Theatre might remind you of Disneyland's Tiki Room. But where else this
side of Japan could you find a large,
lifelike replica of a Dutch town complete with windmill, drawbridge,
canal and thirty-two authentic
houses? Homesick Yanks will yell
"Ahoy" and climb aboard a paddle-
wheel steamboat for a voyage down
the "Mississippi River." *This* river
sports a Statue of Liberty, reconstructed on a 1:2 scale. She lifts her
lamp to salute a sparkly white U.S.
Capitol, complete with fluttering
American flags and café tables.

PLAYING-CARD MUSEUM
(Spielkarten-Museum)

 Schönbuchstrasse 32, at Lengen-
feldstrasse, in the Leinfelden-
Echterdingen district south of the
center. Open Tuesday–Saturday,
2–5pm; Sunday, 11am–5pm. Ad-
mission: free. Phone: (0711) 7 56
01 20.

A great deal of decks comprise
Europe's largest open-to-the-
public card collection. Over 400,000
cards span 600 years and five continents, adorned with images and in-
jokes reflecting the obsessions of their
times. Playing cards, fortune-telling
cards and trick cards range from the
primitive to the postmodern, many of
them too profound for pinochle. A
futuristic tarot deck's version of the
Wheel of Fortune depicts Satan and a
soccer ball. Myriad kings, queens,
jokers and jacks are here, but so are
round cards, sexagonal cards and
cards no wider than your finger.

90 km northeast of Göttingen, in the
Harz Mountains

WITCH TOWN

  The Witches' Dance Floor is in
the hills south of town: Follow
the signs down Walpurgisstrasse,
left on Friedrichsbrunner Strasse,
and along the hiking trail up the
hill (40 minute walk); or you can
take the gondolas (Kabineten-
bahn) which leave from
Goetheweg a few blocks south-

*west of the train station.
(May–September, 9:30am–6pm,
October–April, 10am–4:30pm;
Admission: DM 8, children, DM
5). The Walpurgishalle is also on
the hill, a few hundred meters
from the Hexentanzplatz, down
a clearly marked trail (open daily, May–October, 9am–5pm);
Walpurgisnacht celebrations
happen on the hill (and throughout the town) on the night of
April 30–May 1. Phone: (03947)
2597 or 2277 (tourist office).*

Get a glimpse of what the world would have been like if Europe had never been Christianized. The Witches' Dance Floor *(Hexentanz-platz)* above Thale is an ancient pagan ritual site, now converted into a tourist attraction. Grotesque bronze statues of witches, demons, monsters and familiars adorn the boulders in a forest clearing where a legendary witch met her fate and where actual Teutonic goddess-worship rituals were held long ago. Down the trail you'll find the Walpurgishalle, a museum about the witchy history of the Harz Mountains, with many a dubious exhibit about devil worship and magic. Witch-themed businesses are everywhere: Witch snack booths, witch hotels, witch souvenir shops and witch restaurants, and the town's witch logo is stamped on everything else. Real-life witches, pagans and drunken revelers descend on the *Hex-entanzplatz* every April 30 for a Walpurgisnacht celebration that can be authentic, tacky, hilarious, orgias-tic or spooky, depending on where you go, whom you meet and which rituals you attend.

 Ulm

GERMAN BREAD MUSEUM
(Deutsches Brotmuseum)

 *Salzstadelgasse 10, a few blocks
northwest of the cathedral. Open
Tuesday and Thursday–Sunday,
10am–5pm; Wednesday,
10am–8:30pm. Admission: DM
5; students, seniors and children,
DM 3.50. Phone: 0731/69955.*

Even at the Last Supper, they were wolfing it. Over 10,000 artworks and artifacts celebrate bread's 8,000-year history. Works by Picasso and Chagall containing images of bread mingle with ancient Egyptian tomb sculptures, ovens, baking utensils, grindstones, ration cards and the replica of a 19th-century German bakery amid three floors of elegantly mounted displays. Entire exhibits are devoted to bread's role in world religions and the fight against world hunger. Others are devoted to cake ("the housewife's pride") and the history and culture of pretzels.

 Weitnau

85 km south of Ulm

MINIATURPARK ALLGÄU

 *Between the towns of Isny and
Kempten, off the B12 road.
Open mid-March–mid-Novem-
ber, daily, 10am–6pm. Phone: 0
83 75/16 07.*

Little synthetic pedestrians pose under awnings along a Parisian cityscape—complete with lampposts and café umbrellas—which doesn't even come up to your knees. Curving waterways reflect pee-wee versions of the Leaning Tower, Bavarian castles and exotic milieux, including a jungle, China and Texas. Tower over the minarets of a miniature mosque which basks atop a rock in the spiky shade of palm trees. Don't miss your chance to loom over the Great Wall.

GREAT BRITAIN

Don't miss:

London

London

BRAMAH TEA & COFFEE MUSEUM

The Clove Building, Maguire Street on the south bank of the Thames at Butler's Wharf, just east of Tower Bridge (Tube: London Bridge or Tower Hill). Open daily, 10am–6pm. Admission: £3.50; students and children, £2. Phone: (0171) 378 0222.

Learn the fateful link between opium and tea. At this wharf 300 years ago, 6,000 tea-chests were unloaded every day from clipper ships sailing up the Thames. Now, at this museum operated by a former tea planter, 1,000 tea- and coffeepots augment colorful displays. Learn the differences between Chinese, Japanese and Indian teas and inspect numerous tea cosies. Meditate on the march of time while perusing exhibits on percolators, coffee roasters, chemistry, espresso, instant coffee and the relentless ascendancy of the teabag.

London

THE CLINK

1 Clink St., SE1, between London Bridge and Southwark Bridge (Tube: London Bridge). Open May–September, daily, 10am–10pm; October–April, 10am–6pm. Admission: £4; students and children, £3. Phone: (0171) 403 6515.

Skeletons wrapped in rags and locked in gibbets welcome you beside the stone portals of a medieval prison whose name is now slang for "jail." Between the 14th and 17th centuries, debtors and prostitutes were among the prisoners who faced an unhappy future within these halls, where visitors now peruse instruments of restraint, punishment and execution. Gregorian chants wheeze through speakers, and torches flicker on the walls to illuminate blades, chains and merciless spikes. For an additional £1, a guided tour provides further insight into the torture devices' fine points.

CUMING MUSEUM

In the Newington Library Building at 155-7 Walworth Road, SE17, in the Southwark borough (Tube: Elephant & Castle). Open Tuesday–Saturday, 10am–5pm. Admission: free. Phone: (0171) 701 1342.

Fascinated with wart cures, curses, lucky bones and the like, Edward Lovett hung around in junk shops after the turn of the century collecting so many items relating to London superstitions that his wife left him. In 1916 he gave his superstition collection to this museum. These thousands of artifacts include a cow's heart jammed with pins; a mandrake; "lucky" boots; a crystal ball; a child's caul in a bag; and dozens of other things said to safeguard against drowning, lightning, diarrhea, nightmares, poverty and the evil eye.

EMBASSY OF TEXAS

Pickering Place, off St. James' Street, between King Street and Pall Mall, SW1 (Tube: Green Park). Always visible. Free admission.

From 1842 to 1845, Texas was an independent nation. Its embassy in London was located along this narrow passageway, hardly wide enough to walk through with your arms outstretched. How ironic for a state that prides itself on bigness! Pickering Place may very well be the smallest street in London. A plaque in the passageway marks the spot.

THE FAN MUSEUM

12 Crooms Hill, off Greenwich High Road in Greenwich, just southeast of London (Docklands Light Railway Station: Island Gardens). Open Tuesday–Saturday, 11am–4:30pm; Sunday, noon–4:30pm. Admission: £3.50; students and children, £2.50. Phone: (0181) 858 7879 or 305 1441.

Adorning two Georgian townhouses are over 3,000 fans made of silk, paper, wood, lace, ivory and more—enough to cool a genteel army. At this museum, the world's first of its kind, rotating exhibitions explore various themes depicted on fans, while a workshop offers demonstrations on the crepuscular art of fan making.

GOLDERS GREEN CREMATORIUM

 On Hoop Lane, just east of Finchley Road, in Golders Green, northwest of the center (Tube: Golders Green). Open Monday–Friday, 9am–5pm; to visit the mausoleum containing the ashes of Sigmund Freud and Anna Pavlova you must first ask permission in the office. Phone: (0181) 455 2374.

The ashes of T. Rex's Marc Bolan, mounted high in a brick wall here, lure pilgrims from far and wide. Many other beloved figures also chose cremation and wound up here in distinguished company. Make your way around the chapels and grassy grounds, paying visits to Keith Moon, Rudyard Kipling, T.S. Eliot, Dorothy Sayers, H.G. Wells, Vivien Leigh, Peter Cook, Neville Chamberlain and, among thousands of others, the Maharajah of Cooch-Behar. Analyze the sleek, decidedly vertical and arguably phallic tomb of Sigmund Freud. Nearby is Anna Pavlova's final resting place. Peter Sellers is memorialized with a humble rosebush.

SIGMUND FREUD'S URN—GOLDERS GREEN CREMATORIUM, LONDON

GRAND LODGE MUSEUM

 Great Queen Street at Wild Street, WC2 (Tube: Holborn); in two parts at either end of a second-floor corridor. Open Monday–Friday, 10am–5pm; Saturday, 10am–3pm. Admission: free. Phone: (0171) 831 9811.

What secrets lurk in the Grand Hall of the Masons? This fraternal society, hundreds of years old, has had illustrious members ranging from kings to Peter Sellers. Framed by nougaty marble and vaulted ceilings, the museum displays items inscribed with the Masons' seemingly contradictory symbols. Ponder pentagrams and Stars of David, daggers, ladders, smiling suns and staring eyes. "The world in pain our secrets to gain," reads one dish. Guided tours lead deeper into the sanctum sanctorum. Note the items handcrafted by Masonic POWs.

HISTORY HOUSE

18 Folgate St., at Liverpool St., Bishopsgate (Tube: Liverpool St.). Open the first Sunday of every month, 2–5pm; reservations required. Admission: £7; children under 14 not admitted. Phone: (0171) 247 4013.

HOUSE OF DETENTION—LONDON

A Londoner has painstakingly turned his own home into that of the fictional 18th-century "Jervis" family. As you walk through the rooms, every detail has been arranged to imply that the Jervises have just stepped out. Smells waft through the air, furniture and accessories are positioned just so, and countless nuances trick your senses into believing you have just intruded on a busy household in the midst of its life. Visitors under fourteen are banned because the proprietor believes adolescents' powers of perception aren't strong enough to grok the experience.

HOUSE OF DETENTION

Clerkenwell Close, off Sans Walk, in the Clerkenwell district, E1 (Tube: Farringdon). Open daily, 10am–6pm (last admission 5:15pm). Admission: £4.50; students £3.50; children, £2.50; children under 5, free. Phone: (0171) 253 9494.

Make way for mannequins portraying what the taped narration calls "base wretches, improvidents, hulking unwashed men and drunken people." They occupy 20,000 square feet of subterranean passages comprising what was Victorian London's busiest prison. In its heyday this dank institution admitted 10,000 prisoners a year. The site was used as a prison as early as 1616, but the ambience here today is decidedly Dickensian. Waistcoated pickpockets await their gloomy fate and dummies dressed as inmates prepare gruel.

HUNTERIAN MUSEUM

At the Royal College of Surgeons of England, 35-43 Lincoln's Inn Fields, just northeast of Covent Garden (Tube: Holborn). Open Monday–Friday, 10am–5pm. Admission: free, but technically the museum is open only to doctors, scholars and artists (we like to think that all our readers are scholars, or arty, or perhaps both). Phone: (0171) 405 3474 ext. 3011.

This is the mother of all anatomy museums. Case after case brims with ovaries in jars, aborted quadruplets, fetal animals and much, much more, all displayed in a claustrophobic Victorian style. Human penises and an elephant's vagina are among the attractions here, with explanations in helpful binders attached to each case. Don't miss a placenta from the birth of octuplets, a sample of gum scurvy, the skeletons of dwarfs and giants, and a skull with an overgrown tooth emerging out of its nose. The museum's namesake, anatomist John Hunter, performed experiments including the transplantation of a spur from a rooster's leg to its head. The results are on display here. Syphilitic skulls, an unborn manatee—just imagine what *else* this collection contained before German bombs damaged it during WWII.

London

JEREMY BENTHAM'S BODY

In the main building of University College, entrance at 210 Gower St., one block south of Euston Road (Tube: Euston Square); enter building through the far right door. Open Monday–Friday, 8am–5pm. Admission: free.

University College founder Jeremy Bentham died in 1832. He asked in his will that his skeleton be clad in his Sunday clothes and displayed prominently on campus. This was his sarcastic attempt to demonstrate fleshly transience and thus encourage people to donate their corpses to medicine—at that time, students only had access to the cadavers of executed criminals. Today Bentham sits upright in a glass-fronted cabinet, his waxen face beaming mildly. A photo exhibit nearby shows the old lawyer's bones being inserted into the stuffing under his clothes. Bentham's actual head used to rest between the seated fig-ure's legs, but now it languishes in a safe.

London

LAWN TENNIS MUSEUM

At the All England Lawn Tennis Club on Church Road, just north of St. Mary's Road, Wimbledon (Tube: Southfields or Wimbledon). Open Tuesday–Saturday, 10am–5pm; Sunday, 2pm–5pm. Admission: £3; students and children, £2. Phone: (0181) 946 6131.

Tennis grew from a gentle Victorian amusement with medieval roots to a multimillion-dollar international sport. This museum shows how, while offering views of Wimbledon's famous Centre Court. Lifesize tableaux recreate a racquetmaker's workshop, a players' dressing room and a garden party. Videos let you relive the agony and ecstasy of last year's championships, and interactive quizzes let you pick the winners.

London

THE LONDON DUNGEON

28-34 Tooley Street, between Stainer Street and Joiner Street, SE1, a few blocks from London Bridge (Tube: London Bridge). Open April–September, daily, 10am–6:30pm (last admission 5:30pm); October–March, daily, 10 am–5:30pm (last admission 4:30pm). Admission: £8.95, children, £6.50, children under 15

must be accompanied by an adult. Phone (0171) 403 0606.

The Grim Reaper beckons as you glide in a boat along misty waterways, past re-creations of bygone horrors. Guillotines, blood, Jack the Ripper, vampires, battering rams and the like are all very well and good. But after you've waited hours to get in and paid a terrifying admission price, you might expect something a bit less insultingly cheesy. Even the automated figures smeared with artificial gore look sheepish.

MOCK-MEDIEVAL HOUSES–LONDON

London

MEDIEVAL BANQUETS

At the Beefeater Restaurant, in Ivory House, St. Katherine's Dock, E1 (Tube: Tower Hill). Doors open nightly at 7:45pm; dinner is served at 8pm and show begins at 8:15pm. Admission: £37.50; children under 14, £20. Phone: (0171) 480 5353.

As diners eat a four-course meal, knights joust and nobles loiter, and a putative Henry VIII presides. Dancing girls, magicians, minstrels and a parade of other characters dish out merrie olde Englande by the tankardful. After two hours of this, the Middle Ages ebb away and they clear the floor for an hour of reassuring disco.

London

MENTAL PATIENTS' ARTWORKS

At Bethlem Royal Hospital, Monks Orchard Road in Beckenham, a southern suburb of London, in Kent. Open Monday–Friday, 9:30am–5pm; call first to make an appointment. Admission: free, but donations welcomed. Phone: (0181) 776 4307.

If the location of the museum rings a bell, that's because the name of this mental hospital, founded in 1247, is the root of our familiar word "bedlam." On display here are artworks expressing the ids and inner contortions of mental patients. See how Richard Dadd, Vaslav Nijinsky and other "outsider artists" found solace in ink, paper and paint. Also here are chilling exhibits on the hospital's history.

MOCK-MEDIEVAL HOUSES

Surrounding the intersection of Buck Lane and Highfield Avenue, in the northwestern suburb of Kingsbury.

As if England didn't already have enough castles and bona fide cottages, architect Ernest Trobridge designed these diminutive fakes with nostalgic flair. Scattered around the intersection are several evocative apartment houses and single-family dwellings that give you a fairytale feeling right in the middle of suburbia. Some of these creations sport turrets and balconies befitting Rapunzel, others have showy thatched roofs. Some have that hardy, half-timbered effect.

MUSEUM OF GARDEN HISTORY

In the former parish church of St.-Mary-at-Lambeth, Lambeth Palace Road at Lambeth Road (Tube: Waterloo or Victoria). Open Monday–Friday, 10:30am–4pm; Sunday, 10:30am–5pm. Admission: free, but donations accepted. Phone: (0171) 261 1891.

Britain's insatiable royal gardeners roved worldwide 300 years ago collecting fruits and flowers for the king. The world's first museum dedicated to gardening history is housed in a 900-year-old church, long derelict, that was narrowly saved from the wrecker's ball. The churchyard has been turned into a garden based on a 17th-century design, blooming with plants found in England at that time. In the garden, you may be startled to find the tomb of Admiral William Bligh, of *Bounty* fame. But there it is.

MUSEUM OF THE MOVING IMAGE

South Bank, beneath Waterloo Bridge, near Belvedere Road, between the Royal Festival Hall and the Royal National Theatre, SE1 (Tube: Waterloo). Open daily, 10am–6pm. Admission: £6.25; students, £5.25; children, £4.50. Phone: (0171) 401 2636 or (0171) 928 3535.

Real live actors quip and mug as they guide visitors around this vast museum celebrating movies, TV and video. Nearly fifty exhibition areas and interactive displays explore actors, auteurs, animators and the technology that lurks behind it all. Over 1,000 video sequences run continuously, while film clips race past at breakneck speed on other screens. Learn about the media from their earliest and most embarrassing days to the high-tech present, as costumes, props and other relics pay homage to the stars.

ODONTOLOGICAL MUSEUM

At the Royal College of Surgeons of England, 35-43 Lincolns Inn Fields; enter through the Hunterian Museum (which see for special admission requirements) (Tube: Holborn). Open Monday–Friday, 10am–5pm. Admission: free. Phone: (0171) 973 2190.

Teeth retrieved from the battlefield at Waterloo are part of this dental collection. Only 10 percent of the museum's 3,500 specimens are on display at any one time, but that's enough to keep anyone flossing forever. Malformed jaws, 18th-century dentures and the sad results of periodontal disease share shelf space with Anglo-Saxon skulls and simian skulls associated with England's Piltdown Man hoax. Don't miss the human cyclopean skulls, each with a single huge gaping eye socket and no incisors.

OLD OPERATING THEATER & HERB GARRET

9a St. Thomas' Street, Southwark (Tube: London Bridge). Open Tuesday–Sunday, 10am–4pm. Admission: £2.90; students, £2; children, £1.50. Phone: (0171) 955 4791.

Hundreds of years ago London's wealthy women had surgery while lying on their kitchen tables. Poor women had surgery here. With-

out anesthetics or antiseptics, the city's best doctors could amputate a limb in under a minute. Its rudimentary pallet surrounded with bleachers for eager medical students, this restored 1822 operating theater lacks only the pus of yesteryear. The adjoining museum displays tools used for amputation, bloodletting, skull cutting and childbirth. Also here are the hospital's old apothecary and materials on medieval healthcare.

RAINFOREST CAFE

Shaftesbury Avenue at Rupert Street, in Piccadilly Circus, W1 (Tube: Piccadilly Circus). Open Sunday–Thursday, noon–11pm; Friday–Saturday, noon–midnight. Phone: (0171) 437 1799.

Twitching animatronic gorillas and towering elephants peer through rising mists and thick tangled vines. Diners sit in a synthetic jungle-basement listening to the taped shrieks of tropical birds while munching Rasta Pasta and Jurassic Chicken. Waterfalls and fake rain patter in the periphery, thunder rumbles and lightning flashes. The restaurant employs an animal curator and the waitstaff wears safari

RAINFOREST CAFE—LONDON

London
Unusual Walking Tours

London hides more macabre secrets than perhaps any other city in the world. As you wander aimlessly and ignorantly through the streets, with every step you pass crime scenes, haunted mansions, curiosities and weird cultural landmarks without even knowing it. The solution to unenlightened strolling? Take a guided walking tour put on by one of several companies that specialize in pointing out the ghastly and humorous side of The City. No need to make a reservation—just show up at the appointed time and place. All walks listed here cost £4.50 per person.

The Original London Walks [(0171) 624 3978] is by far the largest organization, with dozens of different tours on a variety of deliciously horrible topics. Their famous "Jack the Ripper Haunts" tour focuses obsessively on history's most famous serial murderer, reborn as a cult anti-hero (every night, 7:30pm, Tower Hill tube station). "The Ghosts of the West End" is one of their many spine-chilling ghostly tours (Mondays and Thursdays, 7:30pm, Embankment tube station). "The Beatles 'In My Life' Walk" explores film locations from *A Hard Day's Night* and *Help*, Paul's and Ringo's former homes, the Abbey Road studios and more (Tuesdays and Saturdays, 11am, Baker St. tube station Baker St. exit). Our favorite is "Spies' and Spycatchers' London," revealing the actual sites of Cold War espionage deceptions and fiascoes (Saturdays, 2:30pm, Piccadilly Circus tube station, exit 3). Call for details of other tours, with themes ranging from "Sherlock Holmes" to "Eccentric London."

Stepping Out [(0181) 881 2933] has several unique tours ranging from the macabre to the mod, including "Rebels, Radicals and Rough Justice" focusing on martyrs and revolutionaries (Thursdays, 11am, Farringdon tube station); "Apparitions, Graveyards and Alleyways," as chilling as it sounds (Sundays, 7:30pm, Blackfriars tube station ticket hall); and "Fire, Fish and Foul Murder" (Mondays, 2:30pm, Monument tube station, Fish St. Hill exit).

Historical Walks of London [(0181) 668 4019] features "Graveyards, Ghouls and Ghosts of the Old City" (Mondays, 7:30pm, Farringdon tube station); "London's Historic Curiosities—The Buried City" looks above and below ground for offbeat sites (Saturdays, 11am, Blackfriars tube station, exit 1); and, of course, their own take on "Jack the Ripper—The Whitechapel Murderer" (Tuesdays, 7:30pm, and Saturdays, 7pm, Whitechapel tube station).

Cityguide Walks [(01895) 675389] offers "Crime and Punishment in the City," a look at the blood-soaked history of inner London, on occasional Saturdays at 2pm at the Monument tube station (£4; call for dates).

Other companies running Jack the Ripper tours (Whitechapel sidewalks are literally jammed with Ripper aficionados bumping into each other at all hours) include **Ripping Yarns** [(0171) 702 9987], **Original Guided Walks** [(0181) 530 8443], and **Historical Tours** [(0181) 668 4019].

gear. Live parrots occupy the gift shop upstairs which sells rubber snakes and endangered species souvenirs.

SHERLOCK HOLMES MUSEUM

221b Baker St., NW1 (for some reason, although it bears the number 221b, the museum is actually located between 237 and 241 Baker Street) (Tube: Baker St.). Admission: £5; students, seniors and children, £3; children under 8, free. Open daily, 10am–6pm. Phone: (0171) 935 8866.

Misguided fans have actually been writing to Holmes and Doctor Watson at this address for over 100 years, asking them to help find missing persons. Well, they aren't here. Several rooms have been painstakingly furnished as Sir Arthur Conan Doyle described them in his stories, complete with pipe, deerstalker hat, violin and a clutter of Victoriana. In the room made up like that of Holmes' landlady, Mrs. Hudson, you can read some of those pitiful letters. The restaurant's waitstaff wears period costume. On the menu are Holmes-and-Watson favorites like toad-in-the-hole and Dover sole.

SIR JOHN SOANE'S MUSEUM

13 Lincoln's Inn Fields, WC2 (Tube: Holborn). Open Tuesday–Saturday, 10am–5pm. Admission: free, but donations are welcomed. Phone: (0171) 405 2107 or 430 0175.

The home of a famous architect is jammed with trivia and booty from all over the world. Bits of ancient marble snatched from Rome; Hogarth's portraits of prisons and Whigs; an Egyptian sarcophagus. Soane established his home as a museum shortly before his death in 1837 with the stipulation that everything stay where he left it. Marvel at how a British gentleman was able to blithely fill dozens of rooms, floor to ceiling, with archaeological loot. Note Soane's fantasyscapes, such as a crypt, catacombs, colonnade, *duomo* and the "Monk's Parlour."

WELLCOME MUSEUM OF ANATOMY

At the Royal College of Surgeons of England, 35–43 Lincolns Inn Fields, fourth floor, just northeast of Covent Garden (Tube: Holborn). Open Monday–Friday, 10am–5pm. Admission: free, but entrance is theoretically restricted to those "in medicine or the arts"; request a visitor's pass at the desk in the Hunterian Museum, which is also in this building. Phone: (0171) 973 2190.

Eyes stare moodily from human heads in various stages of dissection. Partially flayed limbs, organs, torsos and pelvises, encased in clear plastic, reveal more about the iridescence of membrane and the curve of bones and blood vessels than you probably want to know before lunch. Babies' disembodied arterial systems look like colorful fountains, and helpless severed hands and sphincters float in formaldehyde while faces are sliced neatly into thin pieces. Those staring eyes are fringed with lashes.

WELLCOME MUSEUM OF PATHOLOGY

At the Royal College of Surgeons of England, 35-43 Lincolns Inn Fields, second floor, just northeast of Covent Garden (Tube: Holborn). Open Monday–Friday, 10am–5pm. Admission: free, but entrance is theoretically restricted

WELLCOME MUSEUM OF PATHOLOGY — LONDON

to those "in medicine or the arts"; request a visitor's pass from the desk in the Hunterian Museum, which is also in this building. Phone: (0171) 973 2190.

Goiters, gangrenous feet and diseased body parts aplenty are housed in clear plastic boxes. Pick them up and examine them from all sides. Note the leg so big with elephantiasis that the foot is scarcely visible. Note the garnet-like malignant melanoma. Note the cross section of a baby's head complete with flowing auburn hair, and the collection of anuses. Chilling displays chart the progress of hideous afflictions that make skulls grow as big as volleyballs and bones become as brittle as Cheez-its. Tongues, bowels, skin and twisted skeletons show what can go wrong.

Southeast England

Brighton

THE ROYAL PAVILION

 Between North Street and Church Street at Old Steine, a few blocks from the waterfront. Open June–September, daily, 10am–6pm; October–May, daily, 10am–5pm. Admission: £4.50; children under 16, £2.75; students, £3.25. Phone: (01273) 290 900.

For an English palace, this sure looks a lot like the Taj Mahal. It's hard to imagine Queen Victoria kicking back in this white wonderland of turban-shaped domes, arched entryways, minarets and Moorish openwork. Amid the faux-Asian finery inside, gold and silver dragons slither up walls and clasp chandeliers while cast-iron palms and thickets of gilt bamboo rise ceilingward.

Eastbourne

MEDIEVAL FESTIVAL

  At Herstmonceux Castle, 4 miles northeast of town, off the A271 road. Every year on the last weekend in August; sieges held Saturday–Monday at 11am and 3pm; throughout the festival weekend, shuttle buses run between British Rail's Polegate station and the castle. Admission: £9; children, £4. For more information, call (01273) 723 249.

Listen to the clank of chain-mail, the swish of broadswords and the blasting of cannons as hundreds of costumed fighters storm the castle walls twice each day. They're members of Britain's Medieval Siege Society, and this is Britain's largest three-day medieval fête. Knights joust, minstrels stroll, archers test their skill and banners flap. Craftspeople hawk their wares as witches and soothsayers court the cosmos. Fire-eaters and falconers amuse the crowds by risking their lives, 15th-century style. Some 20,000 tankard-waving wannabes gather here every summer, and revel among hogs roasting on open fires.

Groombridge

4 miles southwest of Royal Tunbridge Wells

THE ENCHANTED FOREST

 At Groombridge Place, on the B2110 road near the Spa Valley Railway's Groombridge station. Open April–October, daily, 9am–6pm (or dusk, if that comes earlier). Admission: £5.50; students, £4.50; children, £3.50. Phone: (01892) 863 999.

Who could choose between a jousting-field, a mock Gypsy camp complete with caravans, a trout-feeding pond, a Sherlock Holmes museum (Arthur Conan Doyle lived nearby), a vast U-pick field of giant sunflowers, a falconry center, a garden with disturbingly huge vegetables, a maze and mysterious pools and grottoes said to be the homes of strange beings? Flanking gardens of insurmountable beauty, this "forest" isn't sure what it wants to be, but gives you an absorbing grab bag.

SHIPWRECK HERITAGE CENTRE

Rock-a-Nore Road, on the waterfront in Old Town. Open April–October, daily, 10:30am–5pm. Admission: £2.20; children, £1.25. Phone: (01424) 437 452.

What is it about Hastings that lures ships to their splintery deaths? At low tide the coastline here has one of Europe's largest permanent displays of wrecked vessels. The museum offers exhibits and lore detailing centuries' worth of nautical disasters. Potter about with live radar. Monitor shipping in the Channel and, at the push of a button, inspect underwater riches. The accompanying audiovisual program is narrated by Christopher Lee, who once portrayed a pirate.

SMUGGLERS ADVENTURE

St. Clements Caves, West Hill, just west of the High Street, in the Old Town. Open Easter–September, daily, 10am–5:30pm; October–Easter, 11am–4:30pm. Admission: £4.50; students, £3.75; children, £2.95. Phone: (01424) 422 964.

Hewn by hand centuries ago, this underground labyrinth comes complete with a domed ballroom, a statue of Napoleon, a chapel and fake caveman art. For years it was a 19th-century tourist attraction. Now it is peopled with mannequins portraying the smugglers who hid here and outwitted local tax collectors in centuries past. Actually they look like burned-out rock 'n' rollers. Lively tableaux include a jail, a gibbet, a hanging and drunken hilarity. Skeletons and weapon-wielding figures pop up right and left. An interactive exhibit lets you chase smugglers and hit them.

65 miles southeast of London, on the coast

BONE CRYPT

In St. Leonard's Church, on Church Road at the northern edge of the center. Open May–September, Monday–Saturday, 10:30–noon and 2:30–4pm; Sunday, 2:30–4pm. Admission: 50p; children, 10p. Phone: (01303) 263 739.

Located under a church built in 1080, this is said to be England's last surviving medieval charnel house—a place where unearthed bones go when graveyards get too full. Some 8,000 thighbones dating back to before the Norman Conquest are stacked like canned goods on the shelves in the crypt. They're accompanied by 2,000 skulls. Do the math. That leaves another 2,000 people's heads and sundry body parts unaccounted for.

9 miles east of Brighton

GUY FAWKES NIGHT (BONFIRE NIGHT)

Held every year on November 5; processions begin at 5:30pm with the most spectacular ones beginning around 7:30pm at St. Anne's Crescent, on the western edge of the center; the last processions start around 9pm and lead to bonfire sites encircling the town. Phone: (01273) 483 448 (tourist office).

Seventeen Protestants were burned at the stake during the reign of the Catholic Queen Mary I, aka "Bloody Mary." With this in mind, Bonfire Night also recalls the arrest of Guy Fawkes, a Catholic terrorist who in 1605 planned to blow up the Protestant King James I and his parliament with thirty-six barrels of gunpowder. It's a nationwide holiday celebrating religious intolerance, but Lewes' celebrations are Britain's hottest and brightest. The town fills with torchlight processions, glittering fireworks and leaping bonfires into which effigy after effigy of the pontiff is hurled while crowds chant. Mock archbishops deliver pretend death sentences.

Southeast of London

DOG-COLLAR MUSEUM AND MAZE

4 miles east of Maidstone, at Leeds Castle. Open March–October, daily, 10am–5:30pm; November–February, daily, 10am–3:30pm. Admission: £8.80; students, £6.80; children, £5.80. Phone: (01622) 765 400.

Home to six medieval queens and Henry VIII, this archetypal, 900-year-old castle stands surrounded by a moat and extensive parklands. Its aviary houses psychedelically vivid tropical birds. The 2,400 yew trees forming its huge maze are arranged to resemble a castle, complete with towers and bastions. Follow the maze to a mound, inside which is a grotto covered in seashells and bones, with sculptures of mythical creatures jutting from the walls. The castle's dog-collar museum spans 400 years and comprises the world's largest collection of its kind. Don't miss the medieval spiked collars for dogs who went bear hunting.

16 miles northeast of Canterbury

SHELL GROTTO

On Grotto Hill (a street), between Dane Road and Northdown Road, a few blocks from the Lido in the area of town called Cliftonville. Open Easter–October, Monday–Friday,

10am–5pm; Saturday–Sunday, 10am–4pm. Admission: £1; children, 50p. Phone: (01843) 220 008.

Discovered by accident in 1835, this underground labyrinth probably has its origins in the shell-grotto craze of the 18th century, although the proprietors will try to tell you the place is a "temple" and that it is 2,000 years old. Millions of seashells in swirls, stripes, circles and other patterns cover the passageways' walls, ceilings and gothic archways, creating that "whoops-I'm-a-mermaid" effect. Needless to say, nobody knows who made the place.

Portsmouth

OVERLORD EMBROIDERY

In the D-Day Museum, Clarence Esplanade, on the waterfront in Southsea, south of the center. Open April–October, daily, 10am–5pm; November–March, Tuesday–Sunday, 10am–5pm, Monday, 1–5pm. Admission: £4; students and children, £2.40. Phone: (01705) 296 905.

Winston Churchill smokes a cigar as jeeps roll by in this 272-foot-long artwork created over five years by twenty women from the Royal School of Needlework. Learn the story of D-Day as only thread can tell it. Inspired by France's Bayeux Tapestry, the world's largest embroidery uses thirty-four panels to illustrate history's largest seaborne invasion—from preparation to landing to victory on the beaches of Normandy.

Ventnor

On the southern coast of the Isle of Wight

MUSEUM OF SMUGGLING

1 mile west of town, in the Botanic Garden. Open April–September, daily, 10am–5:30pm. Admission: £2.20; students and children, £1; children under 7, free. Phone: (01983) 853 677.

Life-size dummies in this big basement extravaganza recall famous smugglers who fought the law, and sometimes won, along this coast. Over 300 exhibits focus on weapons, examples of contraband and the vessels in which clever smugglers hid their goods. It wasn't always barrels.

The West Country

Bolventor

10 miles northeast of Bodmin

POTTER'S MUSEUM OF CURIOSITY

On the A30 road, in the courtyard of the Jamaica Inn. Open in summer, daily, 10am–8pm; winter, daily, 11am–4pm. Admission: £1.95; children, £1.50. Phone: (01566) 86 838 or 86 250.

Victorian taxidermist Walter Potter stuffed thousands of cute fuzzy animals and arranged their dressed-up corpses in all kinds of human-like environments. Row upon row of dead rabbits in various colors line up side by side at desks, studying from little books, in Potter's Rabbit School. Dead kittens in gowns and suits stage a lavish wedding while still more dead kittens schmooze at a tea party. The necropolis of a museum has been around for over 100 years, and it also includes freaks and assorted novelties. A taxidermist is on staff to keep the corpses shipshape.

Boscastle

5 miles north of Camelford, Cornwall

THE MUSEUM OF WITCHCRAFT

 In "The Witches' House," on the north side of the harbor. Open Monday–Saturday, 10:30am–5:30pm; Sunday, 11am–5:30pm. Admission: £1.50; children, 75p; naughty children, £10. Phone: (01840) 250 111.

Spell casting, shape shifting, cursing and divining come alive through this collection of ritual objects and other artifacts. Many were donated by practicing witches. In the face of occasional criticisms from local Christians, the museum details English witchcraft past and present, emphasizing witches' healing powers and their commitment to a Horned God who is not—repeat, is not—Satan. Crystal balls are here, and a severed hand. Don't miss the little doll, created to effect a curse, with human pubic hair sewn onto it.

Cerne Abbas

8 miles north of Dorchester

THE CERNE ABBAS GIANT

 Carved into Giant Hill half a mile northeast of the village; the giant itself is fenced off and not accessible to the public, but it is clearly visible from a distance.

He's holding a huge notched club and he's got big staring eyes. Those aren't the only big things he's got. This 180-foot-tall figure was carved into the grassy, chalk hillside by pagan artists long ago. Resplendently white against the green, he has an erection as big as his head. They say he's an ancient fertility figure. Duh.

Cheddar

20 miles southwest of Bristol

CHEDDAR SHOWCAVES AND GORGE

 Just northeast of the village on the B3135 road. Open Easter–September, daily, 10am–5 p.m; October–Easter, daily, 10:30am–4:30pm. Admission: £6.90; children, £4. Phone: (01934) 742 343.

Made of sturdy limestone and not cheese as its name might indicate, Britain's largest gorge comprises several attractions in one. Chiseled by a subterranean river, the roomy and subtly colored Gough's Cave evokes a quiet cathedral. Narrower Cox's Cave is gaudily lit. The Heritage Centre puts you among scantily clad and shaggy-haired mannequins representing paleolithic cavedwellers whose ancient remains, like that of 9,000-year-old Cheddar Man, have been found here. And the Crystal Quest is an underground fantasy scenario unsurprisingly peopled with model dwarves and wizards and flashing lights.

Culbone

8 miles west of Minehead

ENGLAND'S SMALLEST CHURCH AND LAST ISOLATED VILLAGE

In a remote glen on the Devon North Coast Path. From Minehead, go west through Porlock to Porlock Weir, from which a walking trail leads westward 1.5 miles to Culbone. A longer trail runs from the A39 coast road. Open daily during daylight hours. Phone: (01643) 702 624 (Minehead tourist office).

This tiny house of You-know-who is the smallest church in England to still offer regular worship services. At twelve by thirty-five feet it's no bigger than a suburban garage and seats no more than thirty parishioners at one time. A tidbit of medieval perfection, all thick walls and cool interiors, it's plenty roomy when you're all alone here. The presence of a church elevates the hamlet of Culbone to the status of village: What sets this village apart from all others is that it is the last one in the entire country that is not connected to the rest of England by road. The only way to get here is on foot along a trail from Porlock Weir or the coast road. Residents with cars drive overland through cow pastures.

Exmouth

11 miles south of Exeter, on the Cornwall coast

A LA RONDE

Summer Lane, 2 miles north of the center of Exmouth off the A376 road. Open April–October, Sunday–Thursday, 11am–5:30pm. Admission: £3.20; children, £1.60. Phone: (01395) 265 514.

This legendary 16-sided cottage is the reigning queen of 18th-century English eccentric architecture. Two whimsical, nonconformist cousins, the Misses Jane and Mary Parminter, returned home in 1795 after a ten-year-long vacation in Europe and immediately proceeded to build their wild new home, as if possessed. Inside on the main floor, sixteen rooms surround the central hall perfectly symmetrically: eight are pentagonal, eight are triangular, and most have diamond-shaped windows. The drawing room is decorated with a frieze made of feathers, and quaint murals, decorations and 18th-century exotica are scattered about. A La Ronde's crowning glory is its stunning Shell Gallery, normally reached by a shell-encrusted secret staircase, but now only visible on closed-circuit television. Here in one of the strangest rooms in England every square inch is covered in fossils, broken plates, animal bones, rare minerals and every imaginable variety of seashell, all arranged into luscious geometric patterns, while occasional wall "paintings" are made of feathers and seaweed.

Merton

7 miles south of Great Torrington, in Devon

BAROMETER WORLD & MUSEUM

 In the Quicksilver Barn, on the A386 road, opposite the village garage. Open February–December, Monday–Saturday, 9am–5pm. Admission: £2; children, 25p. Phone: (01805) 603 443.

Weather means a lot to Britons, islanders that they are. Devon alone once boasted no fewer than thirty barometer makers. Charting the 300-year development of these indispensible mercury-based pressure gauges, this museum houses ship barometers, traveling barometers, desk barometers, artistic barometers and more. One novelty is a mahogany specimen formerly owned by the poet William Wordsworth. Don't miss the smallest known version, no bigger than a ten-pence coin.

Minehead

HOBBY HORSE

 Held every year on May 1 and the days immediately surrounding it. For more information, call (01643) 821 040.

Six feet tall, constructed of canvas and balanced on a man's shoulders, the beribboned Hobby Horse careens through the crowded streets of Minehead and neighboring Dunster to ring in the May. Some say he's an ancient pagan fertility figure, but others link his origins to a strange story about a cow that washed ashore here after an 18th-century shipwreck. Another theory posits the ritual was meant to scare away ancient Danes marauding along the coast.

Padstow

THE 'OBBY 'OSS PROCESSION AND PADSTOW MUSEUM

 Procession occurs every May 1, beginning around 10am (if May 1 falls on a Sunday, the procession is held the day before or after). Museum is located at the Institute, in the Market Place, Broad Street at Duke Street. Open Monday–Friday, 10:30am–6pm; Saturday, 10:30am–1pm. Admission: 50p, children 30p. Phone: (01841) 532 470 or 532 574.

Six feet across, black and circular, with a pointed head and a man inside bobbing and weaving down the streets of town, this 'oss doesn't look like a horse at all. A white-clad "Teazer" with a padded prod goads the 'oss, which lies down and pretends to die, then comes back to life while drums pound. Crowds sing, heralding the first day of May as viewers all over England watch the procession on TV. No one can agree on what lusty pagan rites spawned the 'oss, though the museum has it on display year round, along with drums and other accessories.

WOOKEY HOLE CAVES

2 miles northwest of Wells

Open in summer, daily, 10am–5pm; winter, daily 10:30am–4:30pm. Admission: £6.70; children, £3.60. Phone: (01749) 672 243.

Carved out of the Mendip Hills by the subterranean River Axe, these caves were inhabited as many as 70,000 years ago. They were famous in Roman times and have been a tourist attraction since the 18th century. Now they're heavy with myth and schlock and billed as the lair of a medieval witch whom a monk turned to stone. Guided tours wind through half a mile of illuminated chambers, past the waters of the Axe and the "petrified witch." A light-and-music show forms a finale. You will be hard pressed to flee the complex's Edwardian penny arcade, a "fairground by night" display, a paper mill, a mirror-maze and more.

Central England

20 miles southeast of Stoke-on-Trent

ABBOTS BROMLEY HORN DANCE

Held every year on the first Monday after the first Sunday after September 4—but never on September 5. Festivities begin at 7:45am and last until 8pm. Phone: (01283) 840 157.

Twelve men, at least one of them dressed as a woman, dance all around the parish throughout the day—carrying not horns but reindeer antlers. It's one of Britain's oldest and most mysterious festivals, beginning early in the morning when the antlers are collected from the village church, where all year they are kept under the vicar's care. One dancer is dressed as a fool, another as a hobby horse, one as an archer and one as a husky Maid Marian. Methodically, grasping the towering antlers, they make their way from farm to farm, pub to pub and finally back to the church to have the antlers blessed and put away till next year. Though the dance is said to have inspired a scene from *As You Like It*, and carbon-dating has shown one antler to be over 1,000 years old, many suspect these "horns" arrived on Viking ships.

Alton

12 miles east of Stoke-on-Trent

ALTON TOWERS

On the B5032 road; it's impossible to miss, as signs point to the park from all directions. Open mid-March–mid-November daily 9:30am–mid-evening; opening times vary from day to day. Admission: £19.50; children 4–13, £15.50; children under 4, free; half price after 2pm. Phone: (01538) 703 344, (01538) 702 200, or (0990) 20 40 60.

England's most extravagant amusement park started as an eccentric country garden filled with 19th-century follies. Now surrounded by thrill rides, the quaint garden still serves as the spiritual heart of Alton Towers. The architecturally accurate pagoda fountain shoots plumes skyward; the faux Greek "Choragic Monument" holds a bust of the Earl of Shrewsbury, the oddball aristocrat responsible for founding the gardens; and amidst exotic plants and statuary you'll encounter canals, rockeries, topiary and architectural bagatelles galore. The modern amusement park is a worthy successor, with an overwhelming profusion of incomprehensible theme areas—such as Forbidden Valley, Cred Street and X-Sector—and goofy entertainments like The Doodle Doo Derby and The Black Hole. At night, crash at the Alton Towers Hotel: request the Cadbury's Chocolate Room for sickly sweet dreams.

Ashton

27 miles southeast of Leicester

NATIONAL DRAGONFLY MUSEUM

At Ashton Mill, half a mile south of the Oundle roundabout on the A605 road. Open mid-June–September, Saturday–Sunday, 10:30am–5pm. Admission: £2.80; children, 80p. Phone: (01832) 272 427.

Dragonflies can reach speeds up to 40 mph. But can they escape extinction as the world's wetlands diminish? This museum sings the plight of the dragonfly and its delicate cousin, the damselfly. Learn all about these elongated creatures with the help of videos, live larvae, images of dragonflies in art and a terrifying TV-microscope displaying magnified insect heads. Learn how these speedy predators mate and eat and can live up to seven years. The grounds outside offer dragonfly trails, watery habitats and observation platforms from which on sunny days you can watch nature's divebombers in action.

Beaconsfield

6 miles east of High Wycombe, west of London

BEKONSCOT MODEL VILLAGE

Warwick Road, one block south of Ledborough Lane, just north of the Beaconsfield train station. Open mid-February–October, daily, 10am–5pm. Admission: £3.60; children, £1.80. Phone: (01494) 672 919.

This legendary miniature city is the granddaddy of them all: First built in 1929, Bekonscot was the world's first model village, and inspired an entirely new genre of weird tourist attractions. Decidedly more modest than some of its flamboyant successors, Bekonscot Model Village nevertheless exudes a homespun quaintness you just can't find elsewhere. The theme is purely rural England: one and a half acres of castles and cottages, churches and gardens, moving models and miniature trains that traverse the countryside. The clusters of 4-year-olds that flock to this place as if it was some kind of sacred shrine totter about among the tiny houses like infantile Gullivers.

Berkeley

13 miles southwest of Gloucester

JENNER MUSEUM

The Chantry, Church Lane, off High Street next to the castle. Open April–September, Tuesday–Saturday, 12:30–5:30pm and Sunday, 1–5:30pm; October, Sunday, 1–5:30pm. Admission: £2; children, 75p. Phone: (01453) 810 631.

For centuries, smallpox wrought havoc. Even when it didn't kill its victims, the disease often left them blind, brain-damaged and grotesquely disfigured. Then in 1796, banking on popular folk wisdom that had been around for some time, Berkeley's Dr. Edward Jenner used cowpox to successfully vaccinate a child against smallpox, and thus changed history. The museum offers disgusting photographs of smallpox sufferers as well as other illustrations and lore. Out back is the "Temple of Vaccinia" (no, there wasn't really a Roman goddess of vaccinations—Jenner just made it up), actually just a hut where the local peasants would line up for the miracle cure.

Bournville

4 miles southwest of Birmingham

CADBURY WORLD

Off Linden Road, north of the train station. Hours vary widely; call to check. Admission: £6.25; students £5.25; children, £4.50; children under 4, free. Phone: (0121) 451 4159 or 451 4180.

Ride a "beanmobile" through a storybook chocolateland at this interactive sweetfest which may leave you craving brown rice and tofu. A mannequin dressed as Montezuma flaunts impressive pecs and bare thighs while lording it over the conquistadors. Free samples and glimpses of candymaking in action augment exhibits on the cocoa bean. Follow its journey from America to England, where no doubt it contributes to this country's dental crisis. View the replica of a set from

CADBURY WORLD—BOURNVILLE

Britain's beloved soap opera *Coronation Street*—storefronts, pavement and all are made out of chocolate by the team that brought you Wallace and Gromit.

Bourton-on-the-Water

23 miles east of Cheltenham

MINIATURE WORLD

High Street, just north of Station Road. Open Easter–October, daily, 10am–5:30pm; November–Easter, Saturday–Sunday, 10am–5:30pm. Admission: £2; children, £1.50. Phone: (01451) 810 121.

Squint at pinhead-size dice and delicate Wedgwood pitchers that could easily fit up your nose. They furnish tiny handcrafted scenarios that range from delicatessens to bomb scenes. A well-appointed kitchen is complete with tiny hams and sleeping cats the size of bees. A miniature husband arrives home to his miniature bedroom and discovers his miniature wife in flagrante delicto with her miniature lover. In tiny palatial surroundings, Henry VIII and Anne Boleyn sup on tiny potatoes alongside a tapestry containing over 2,000 stitches to the square inch.

Bourton-on-the-Water

22 miles south of Stratford-upon-Avon

MODEL VILLAGE

In the Old New Inn, on High Street. Open in summer, daily, 9am–6pm; winter, daily, 10am–4pm. Admission: £2; children, £1.50. Phone: (01451) 820 467.

The relentlessly charming village of Bourton-on-the-Water is replicated one-ninth its actual size, with houses made of pale Cotswold stone. Miniature flowerbeds bloom lavender, yellow and white in miniature typical English backyard gardens. A tiny river runs under tiny bridges. Miniature cherry trees, chestnuts and beeches faithfully duplicate the real town's normal-sized ones. Issuing from a tiny model church is the sweet recorded music of the town's actual choir. Naturally, the model village contains a model of the model village.

Bury St. Edmunds

82 miles northeast of London

BOOK MADE OF HUMAN SKIN

In Moyse's Hall Museum, Cornhill, west of the abbey. Open Monday–Saturday, 10am–5pm; Sunday, 2–5pm. Admission: £1.50; students and children, 95p. Phone: (01284) 757 488.

In a nearby barn, local farmer William Corder is said to have murdered his lover, Maria Marten, in 1827. Her body wasn't found for nearly a year, by which time Corder was a newlywed, having advertised for a wife and gotten one. He was tried and executed, pleading innocent until he mounted the scaffold and confessed. More people came to see the pig-nosed Corder's execution than comprised the town's entire population. Now the museum displays relics of the "Red Barn Murder," including Corder's toothy death mask, pistols and the record of his trial, bound in Corder's own tanned hide.

Chipping Campden

11 miles south of Stratford-upon-Avon

COTSWOLD OLIMPICK GAMES

Held every year on the first Friday evening after the English spring bank holiday (usually late May or early June); games take place at Dover's Hill, about a mile northeast of town. Admission: £2.50; children, £1. Phone: (01386) 841 206 (tourist office).

B egun early in the 17th century, this completely English competition doesn't include Swedish bobsledders or spoiled little girls in leotards doing handsprings. The rough-and-tumble sports you'll see here during a whole weekend of partying include sack races, swordfighting, sledgehammer tossing and shin kicking. The festival traditionally marks the beginning of summer in these parts. In olden times the shin-kickers wore metal-tipped boots, but today they wear sneakers and stuff their pant legs for extra protection.

Downham Market

11 miles south of King's Lynn

THE COLLECTORS WORLD OF ERIC ST. JOHN-FOTI

Off the A1122 road, just north of the center. Admission: £4; children, £2; children under 5, free. Phone: (01366) 383 185.

T he owner's policy is to never throw anything away. It's convenient that he lives on a 250-acre estate. Various buildings are packed with a numbing jumble of ships' instruments, religious artifacts, Dutch clogs, coats of armor, Celtic crosses, busts, military items and more. A whole room is devoted to the achievements of romance novelist Barbara Cartland. Another pays homage to Horatio Nelson. On the guided tour you can visit the bell tower, refectory and chapel as well as a horse-drawn carriage museum, a car museum, a replica boot shop, an apothecary, a cracker shop, a jail and dummies posing in Dickensian garb.

Gloucester

THE ROBERT OPIE COLLECTION AT THE MUSEUM OF ADVERTISING & PACKAGING

The Albert Warehouse, Gloucester Docks. Open April–September, daily, 10am–6pm; October–March, Tuesday–Sunday, 10am–5pm. Admission: £3.50; students £2.30; children, £1.25. Phone: (01452) 302 309.

T his collection of cans, packets, bottles, advertisements and boxes began when Opie bought a snack from a machine as a teen in 1963. He suddenly realized that mass-produced wrappers, made to be thrown away, can teach us a lot about ourselves. In the museum, vintage TV commercials screen constantly as you peruse containers of Vim, Zog, Oxydol and other British products dating back to the dawn of packaging some 120 years ago. Over 200,000 artifacts celebrate favorite brands as well as those that long since went the way of Pop Rocks. You'll be glad you were born too late for Bile Beans and Liver Salt.

19 miles north of London

ELIZABETHAN BANQUETS

At Hatfield House, the Old Palace, in Hatfield Park, just east of Hatfield train station. Banquets served January–March, Tuesday, Friday and Saturday; April–December, Tuesday, Thursday, Friday and Saturday; reception begins at 7:45pm; dinner is served at 8:30pm. Admission: Tuesday: £29.50; Friday: £31; Saturday, £33. Phone: (01707) 262 055 or 272 738.

In the Virgin Queen's actual childhood home, a five-course, two-hour meal is accompanied by minstrels, jesters, jugglers and lots of mead. As befits the era, the night is rife with suggestive lyrics and arcane customs. A woman impersonating Elizabeth herself presides, though the dishes and flatware look suspiciously like the ones used today on airplanes. On Tuesdays and Fridays, the festivities delve deeper into the past to evoke the era of Elizabeth's father, Henry VIII.

58 miles north of Cardiff

THE "TOWN OF BOOKS"

Bookstores are scattered throughout the town. Opening hours vary. Admission: free. For more information, call the tourist office at (01497) 820 144.

At last count, well over a million books were for sale in Hay-on-Wye. With only some 1,500 residents but over a dozen booksellers, the town is said to have the world's highest concentration of secondhand titles. That's more tattered, tea-and-mutton-spattered volumes of *Beowulf* and *The Satanic Verses* on the shelves at any one time than you can shake a spear at. Spend a rainy day combing shop after shop, tracking down that definitive version of *The Happy Hooker*.

8 miles west of Nottingham

AMERICAN ADVENTURE WORLD

Off the M1 road; follow the signs. Open April–November, daily, 10am–5pm (sometimes later in summer). Admission: £12.99; children, £9.99; children under 0.9 meters tall, free. Phone: (01773) 531 521.

Of all the themes they could have chosen for this theme park, they chose America. What nerve! Roller coasters called "Nightmare Niagara" and the "Missile" pretty much sum up our entire culture. Also here are a mock gold-rush town, an Aztec ride, a runaway-train ride, a fort, a buffalo-stampede ride, a log ride, a paddle-wheel-boat ride and that true Yank institution, go-karts. Little covered wagons circle skyward on the ferris wheel. Costumed cowboys and jazzmen twirl lassos and blow horns. Stagecoaches and phony cacti stand around. And you don't want to know what culinary indignities are lurking at the Frisco Wharf restaurant.

Kelvedon Hatch

28 miles northeast of London

KELVEDON HATCH SECRET BUNKER

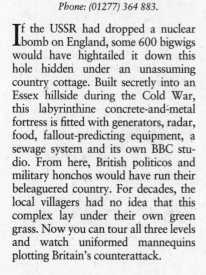

On the A128 road between Brentwood and Chipping Ongar. Open March–October, Monday–Friday, 10am–4pm, Saturday–Sunday, 10am–5pm; November–February, Thursday–Sunday, 10am–4pm. Admission: £5; children, £3. Phone: (01277) 364 883.

If the USSR had dropped a nuclear bomb on England, some 600 bigwigs would have hightailed it down this hole hidden under an unassuming country cottage. Built secretly into an Essex hillside during the Cold War, this labyrinthine concrete-and-metal fortress is fitted with generators, radar, food, fallout-predicting equipment, a sewage system and its own BBC studio. From here, British politicos and military honchos would have run their beleaguered country. For decades, the local villagers had no idea that this complex lay under their own green grass. Now you can tour all three levels and watch uniformed mannequins plotting Britain's counterattack.

Kilpeck

9 miles southwest of Hereford

SHEELA-NA-GIG

On the Church of St. Mary and St. David, near the entrance to the village. Visible at any time.

Among the appealingly grotesque stone carvings that ring this church, one stands out especially. It's the figure of a woman displaying her genitals. Called a "sheela-na-gig," this image was once common on churches all over the British Isles and beyond. Some say it harks back to goddess worship; some say it banishes evil. This early-12-century church, like many others, fell victim to rampaging Victorians. Yet an impressive array of its carvings, including dragons, birds, cryptic beasts and the sheela, managed to survive. Thus the saints, or *someone* up there, must have a soft spot for art—or women's genitals.

Lichfield

20 miles north of Birmingham

PANCAKE RACE

Held every year on Shrove Tuesday (Mardi Gras); race begins at 12:15pm in front of the Guildhall and continues down Bore Street, in the town center. Phone: (01543) 252 109 (tourist office) or (01543) 250 011 (city council).

Over 300 years ago—long before Aunt Jemima and Mrs. Butterworth were born—this town held its annual fair. The pancake race, a 20th-century addition, is now the fair's main event (pancakes are a Shrovetide tradition throughout England). In the Market Square at noon, an actual town crier opens the festivities. Then the revelers gather at the Guildhall to watch the race begin. Each competitor grips a frying pan with a pancake inside. The runners must keep flipping their pancakes as they charge through the center of town. It's said that a thick and heavy pancake works better than a light and fluffy one.

Maldon

42 miles northeast of London

MALDON MILLENNIUM EMBROIDERY

In the Maeldune Centre, High Street at Market Hill. Open daily, 10:30am–4:30pm. Admission: £1.50; students and children, 75p. Phone: (01621) 851 628.

More than eighty-five women stitched for three years to complete six panels comprising forty-two feet of embroidery. Recounting 1,000 years of history, the huge stitchery begins with the Vikings' arrival in Maldon, fresh from the sacking of Ipswich. They march on futureward, celebrating local salt production, seashells, sheep, swans, ships, a giant mace, railroads, the poorhouse, windsurfing and the local football club.

Mistley

12 miles southeast of Ipswich

ESSEX SECRET BUNKER

Crown Building, Shrublands Road, in the center of town: follow the signs. Open Good Friday–September, daily, 10:30am–4:30pm; October–November and February–Good Friday, Saturday–Sunday, 10:30am–4pm. Admission: £4.75; children, £2.75. Phone: (01206) 392 271.

Top secret for nearly fifty years, this vast, sunken bunker would have served as the underground Essex government headquarters had nuclear war erupted. Now sound effects enhance the creepiness of this sprawling maze. Tour concrete corridors, radio and map rooms, dormitories and more—including the canteen where slavering survivors would have squabbled over emergency rations. Shiny red "war telephones" are among many artifacts that make an attack feel imminent. Watch an audiovisual show that vividly evokes a nuclear assault, including tapes of actual vintage emergency television warnings announcing the end of the world. Then calmly peruse Cold War souvenirs in the gift shop.

Mow Cop

9 miles north of Stoke-on-Trent

MOW COP FOLLY

Between Castle Lane and the High Street, east of the village center. Visible at any time. Admission free.

One preposterous story goes that a gentleman built a castle as a summer home here on the border between Staffordshire and Cheshire. But—the story goes—boundary disputes kept him from ever moving in, so it fell into sad disrepair. But the dominant theory is that this imposing structure with its lonesome stone tower, broken walls and empty Gothic arch was erected exactly this way, as an ornamental ruin, in 1754. You can't deny that it improves the view.

THE CAVES OF NOTTINGHAM

Drury Walk, in Broad Marsh Shopping Centre. Open Monday–Saturday, 10am–5pm (last admittance, 4:15); Sunday, 11am–5pm (last admittance, 4pm). Admission: £2.95; students and children, £1.95. Phone: (0115) 924 1424.

The citizens of Nottingham have resorted to their manmade underground realm time and time again over the last 700 years. It served as a subterranean tannery during the leather-happy Middle Ages. Then publicans took advantage of its cool, constant temperature and stored barrels of beer here. A hundred years ago, the poor actually lived underground. On the audio-tour, clad in a colorful helmet, you can examine cooking facilities and the remnants of a subterranean slum. During World War II, when Nottingham was pelted with hundreds of German bombs, the caves served as an air-raid shelter.

THE TALES OF ROBIN HOOD

30-38 Maid Marian Way, near Friar Lane, southwest of the Old Market Square. Open in summer, daily, 10am–4:30pm; winter, daily, 10am–4pm; medieval banquets are served at 7pm (call for current schedule). Admission: £4.50; students, £4; children, £3.50; medieval banquets, £28.50. Phone: (0115) 948 3284.

Robin would flex his muscles and smirk at the "adventure cars" in which you lazily ride around revisiting wild and invigorating scenes from his legend. Sound and smell effects and live actors in medieval garb augment tableaux that inspire insurrection. Games, film screenings, storytelling sessions and exhibits featuring Robin, the Merry Men, the Sheriff and Maid Marian give sneaky messages about crusaders and the monarchy. Medieval banquets, served by "wenches," come with free lager and end with a historically accurate round of disco.

COSTUMED FLIES

In the Pitt Rivers Museum: Enter through the Oxford University Museum of Natural History, on South Parks Road, off Parks Road, opposite Keble College; flies are on the ground floor. Open Monday–Saturday, 1pm–4:30pm. Admission: free. Phone: (01865) 270 949 or 270 927.

A pair of Brazilian flies meticulously dressed in ballerina costumes is displayed among the museum's ethnological and anthropological fare. Also here are mummies, blowpipes, magical charms, knuckledusters, native clubs, shrunken heads, firearms and narcotics (imprisoned safely behind glass). The flies are small, but a staffer will gladly point them out.

THE OXFORD STORY

 6 Broad St., east of the train station. Open July–August, daily, 9am–6:30pm; April–June and September–October, daily, 9:30am–5pm; November–March, daily, 10am–4pm. Admission: £4.75; students £4.15; children, £3.75. Phone: (01865) 790 055.

A s you glide along this three-level ride, your vehicle is an automated wooden desk. Lifelike (and thus unattractive) dummies occupy well-appointed scenarios evoking the long history of Oxford University—an institution that Queen Elizabeth I, among other luminaries, held close to her heart. See scientists and other geniuses of bygone centuries pondering the secrets of the universe. See Oxford don Lewis Carroll conjuring up his masterpiece *Alice's Adventures in Wonderland*. See students burning the midnight oil, armed with cups of tea.

SHARK HOUSE

 4 New High Street, in the suburb of Headington, 2 miles east of the center. Visible at any time. Admission free.

A prodigious fiberglass shark, nearly as long as the house is tall, appears to have dived headlong into a suburban roof. The house's then-owner had this twenty-four-foot fish installed in the mid-'80s, with broken roof-tiles scattered around its flanks for that sudden-impact effect. He meant it as a bold statement on the helplessness of ordinary citizens in the hands of "man-eating" public officials. Neighbors complained. Public officials did, too. Court battles flared, but in 1992 Britain's department of the environment ruled that the shark could stay put. Today its proud silhouette, from pectoral fins to pointed tail, looks impressive against the gray sky.

ROYSTON CAVE

  Melbourn Street, near Kneesworth Street. Open Easter–September, Saturday–Sunday, 2:30–5pm Admission: £1; unaccompanied children, 20p; children free when accompanied by an adult. Phone: (0176) 324 2587.

H ewn out of the chalk by persecuted Knights Templar nearly 700 years ago, this subterranean domed chamber measures seventeen feet across. It lay abandoned and

ROYSTON CAVE—ROYSTON

15 miles northeast of Northampton

RUSHTON TRIANGULAR LODGE

4 miles northwest of Kettering, 1 mile northeast of Rothwell, just west of Rushton and Rushton Hall on an unnamed road leading to Desborough. Open April–September, daily, 10am–6pm. Admission: £1.10. Phone: (01536) 710 761.

hidden under the town's butter market for four centuries until its air vent was discovered by accident in 1746. Immensely rich and powerful before falling into royal disfavor and being accused of heresy, the "warrior monks" held mysterious lamplit rites down here. They covered the chamber's walls in chiseled images: a profusion of crucifixes, hearts, martyrs, angels, swords, concentric circles, hands, a flaming cross and other cryptic figures. Among these is an anatomically accurate female displaying her you-know-what. A human skull found here is said to have been a ritual object.

In 1593 (which is 3 x 3 x 3 x 59), Sir Thomas Tresham (the root "Tres-" in his name means three) finished building his three-themed masterpiece, the Triangular Lodge. Tresham was obsessed with the number three, partly because of his name but mostly because, as a Catholic, for him the Holy Trinity was the foundation of religious thought. Every imaginable aspect of the structure revolves around the number three. It has three sides, three floors, three triangular peaks on each side, three windows (many with triangular windowpanes) on each of the three sides of its three floors. Each side is 33⅓ feet long; across the top are three quotes from the Bible, each 33 letters long, while elsewhere are other quotes, always in multiples of three. Inside, all the rooms are triangular or hexagonal. Nowhere else in the world has Catholic numerology ever been taken to such extremes.

Ruyton-XI-Towns

10 miles southeast of Oswestry, on the River Perry

TOWN WITH A REMARKABLE NAME

 For more information, call (01939) 260 626 or 261 121.

The world's only city incorporating Roman numerals in its name, Ruyton-XI-Towns is actually pronounced "Ruyton-of-the-Eleven-Towns." In 1308 the presiding earl decided to create a brand-new borough within a manor—English geography is so comprehensible, isn't it? This process entailed lumping together the eleven towns of Old Ruyton, Wikey, Felton, Coton, Shelvock, Shotatton, Tedsmore, Haughton, Sutton, Rednal and Eardiston. The resultant community has survived through the centuries, only to be saddled with its extensive name—one of the strangest in a country that brought you towns called Ugley, Great Snoring, Westward Ho! and Buttock's Booth.

Thorpeness

28 miles northeast of Ipswich

HOUSE IN THE CLOUDS

  Off the B1353 road, opposite the windmill and facing the lake. Visible at any time; accommodations start at £220 per night. Phone: (0171) 252 0743 or (0850) 851 203.

Soon after this seaside resort was erected in 1910, someone decided a water tower was too prosaic a structure to leave standing around undisguised. So they made it look like a big red house with a charmingly peaked roof and tall white chimney—perched high atop a slender five-story tower. Today it's outfitted as a self-catering hotel and you can rent the whole thing, which sleeps twelve and comes with a dishwasher, microwave, snooker facilities and more.

Ware

2 miles northeast of Hertford

SCOTT'S GROTTO

 On Scott's Road, near Ware College, one third of a mile south of the Ware train station. Open April–September, Saturdays, 2–4:30pm. Admission: £1. Phone: (01920) 464 131.

Samuel Johnson arrived in 1773 to tour this folly, which had been dug sixty-seven feet into a hillside by his poet friend, John Scott, who in turn had been inspired by an ornamental grotto built by Alexander Pope. Today it helps to carry a flashlight while roaming the underground chambers, niches, archways and passages, all coated in seashells and pretty stones. It's frightful to realize that the place was slated for bulldozing in the 1960s and just managed to escape its fate. Toyko's Mikimoto pearl company contributed a lot of the oyster shells used in the restoration, but you will also see large scallops and other species.

Warwick

10 miles south of Coventry

WARWICK CASTLE

Castle Lane at Castle Hill, a few blocks south of the train station. Open April–October, daily, 10am–6pm; November–March, daily, 10am–5pm. Admission: £9.25; children, £5.60. Phone: (01926) 406 600.

Explore the dark dungeon and instruments of torture, displayed with helpful illustrations showing how to use them. This turreted and allegedly haunted medieval castle is outfitted by its operators, the Tussauds waxwork people, with impeccably realistic figures evoking 600 years of aristocratic pain and passion. The astounding exhibition A Royal Weekend Party 1898 recreates a big fête once hosted here. Waxwork guests—you can see their very veins—enact intrigues amid gilt furniture. You can actually smell a lavender scent rising from the bathwater. Annual events at the castle include jousting tournaments and medieval games.

West Wycombe

32 miles west of central London

HELL-FIRE CAVES (WEST WYCOMBE CAVES)

2 miles west of High Wycombe, a few hundred yards north of the village of West Wycombe; a path leading up to the church on the top of the hill goes past the signposted entrance, which has an

imposing brick façade you can't miss. The caves are not on the grounds of Dashwood's West Wycombe House, which is south of the village. Open March–October, daily, 11am–5:30pm; November–February, Saturday and Sunday, 11am–5:30pm. Admission: £3; students and children, £1.50. Phone: (01494) 533 739 or (01494) 524 411.

Sir Francis Dashwood was the archetypal smart-aleck 18th-century aristocrat, traipsing the globe and inflicting cruel practical jokes on the locals wherever he went. At home he was up to nonstop shenanigans, the most notorious of which was his so-called Hell-Fire Club, a secret society of wealthy dandies and intellectuals who met in these caves to get drunk, hold mock rituals and in general turn society on its ear. Legends are rife—all-night orgies, Satanic masses, unspeakable blasphemies—but the truth of what went on here will never really be known. All we have now are the caves themselves, populated by hilarious waxworks depicting Dashwood and his cohorts. The caves are actually a disused chalk mine that was enlarged into a series of mysterious and symbolic passageways. The waxen Lord Sandwich and his rascally baboon can be found in The Circle. Further along you'll find Dashwood and Benjamin Franklin—who was a frequent visitor—and then The Triangle, said to be symbolic of "a certain part of the female anatomy." At the end, past several more spooky spots, you'll come to the Inner Temple, where a rather tame waxwork party is under way.

Weston-under-Redcastle

10 miles north of Shrewsbury

HAWKSTONE PARK AND FOLLIES

¹/₂ mile east of Weston-under-Redcastle, on the road leading to Hodnet; signs point the way; Weston-under-Redcastle is just east of the A49, which runs from Shrewsbury to Whitchurch. Open April–November, daily, 10am–dusk; December–February, Saturday and Sunday, 10am–dusk. Admission: £4.50; students, £3.50; children, £2.50; prices slightly higher on holidays, slightly lower in winter. Phone: (01939) 200 611 or 200 300.

This grandiose and bizarre 18th-century fantasy park only recently reopened after lying abandoned and forgotten for nearly 100 years. Around 1750, Sir Rowland Hill transformed 100 acres of dramatic Shropshire countryside into a fairyland of secret passageways, hidden tunnels, clifftop pathways, incongruous follies and mysterious grottoes. As you follow the trails that twist and turn through the secluded valleys and rocky outcroppings, with every step you come across some new, unexpected extravagance. The Swiss Bridge is a rickety, handmade picturesque wooden walkway that connects bulbous stone pinnacles over a deep cleft. The Gingerbread Hall is a rustic thatched folly hut hidden in the woods. The Grotto is a creepy underground hall of columns cut into the rocky hillside. The only landmarks to keep you from getting lost are abundant folly buildings, built for the sole purpose of looking quaint. The park supposedly has Arthurian connections, so naturally you'll find waxworks of King Arthur and his followers hiding out in one of the caves.

Windsor

23 miles west of London

LEGOLAND WINDSOR

On Winkfield road, 2 miles southwest of the center. Open mid-March–mid-July and September–October, daily, 10am–6pm (or dusk, if that comes earlier); mid-July–August, daily, 10am–8pm. Admission: £16; children, £13. Phone: (0990) 040 404, or (01753) 626 111.

Made entirely of plastic Lego bricks, a tarantula as big as a house hangs over one of twenty-one rides at this British outpost of the Danish theme park. A shrunken version of St. Paul's Cathedral, built entirely of Lego and flanked with little double-decker buses, is one of several historic buildings reproduced in the park's 20,000-brick Miniland. Meanwhile, Lego knights and jesters populate a castle that doubles as a roller coaster.

Woburn

45 miles north of London

WOBURN ABBEY GROTTO

7 miles southeast of Milton Keynes, 2 miles southeast of the town of Woburn, off the B518 road, just west of the M1; signs point the way. Open January–mid-March and October, Saturday and Sunday, 11am–4pm; mid-March–September, Monday–Saturday, 11am–4pm, Sunday, 11am–5pm. Admission: £7.50; children £3. Phone: (01525) 290 666.

Forget about this stately home's world-class collection of classical paintings, its amazing antiques and its acres of elegant interior design, and head down to the Grotto. Here at ground level lurks one of England's classiest and largest shell grottoes. Lush, detailed mosaics made of shells have converted this open-sided room into an aquatic fantasyland. The stonework has been carved to resemble seaweed and stalactites; angels, tritons, and nereids float about on heaving shell waves, while the ceiling is a mesmerizing swirl of mother-of-pearl patterns. The chairs themselves are in the shapes of shells, and look as if they come from Neptune's parlor. Even the pretty "flower" bouquet is made of coral and large tropical seashells. Other follies to look for on the abbey's grounds include the "oriental" Chinese Dairy and, in the private gardens, a maze.

Northern England

Bamburgh

58 miles north of Newcastle-upon-Tyne

GRACE DARLING MUSEUM

Radcliffe Road, in the village center, opposite the castle. Open Easter–September, Monday–Saturday, 10am–5pm; Sunday, noon–5pm. Admission: free. Phone: (01668) 214 465.

Grace Darling was a lighthouse-keeper's daughter. One morning in 1838, at the age of twenty-three, she rowed with her father into a howling storm to save nine people from a shipwreck. Named a national heroine for her bravery, and thoroughly lionized, she lived only another five years. Established on the shipwreck's centennial, the museum displays relics of the rescue, including the fateful lifeboat as well as poems about the event by the likes of Wordsworth and Swinburne, and songs and books retelling the story. Also here is Grace's christening robe—as if that was relevant.

Bradford

THE COLOUR MUSEUM

Perkin House, 1 Providence Street, off Grattan Road. Open Tuesday–Friday, 2–5pm; Saturday, 10am–4pm. Admission:

£1.50; students and children, £1.
Phone: (01274) 390 955.

Can dogs see red? Why bother wearing eye shadow? Find the answers while wandering among slickly designed displays and hands-on experiments probing color perception, color in daily life, color-blindness and the use of color in fabric. Make rainbows, see like a bee, play with colored lights, freak out over wrongly hued road signs and food. In the Colour & Textiles Gallery, take on the troubles of a dye-factory boss and discover how, out of the blue, fashion-industry whims can give even the worst shades of yellow their fifteen minutes of fame.

Chester

COBWEB MADONNA

In Chester Cathedral, on Werburgh Street; the picture is in a niche in the north transept. Open daily, 7:30am–6:30pm. Admission: technically free, but a "voluntary" £2 donation is welcomed. Phone: (01244) 324 756.

If this painting of a wistful, pale madonna cradling her fat child has an ethereal and misty quality, that's either because you're experiencing an epiphany or because this "canvas" is made entirely of cobwebs. The webs were layered inside a wooden frame, then dipped in milk of all things, and allowed to set until the surface was flat enough to paint. Made in the Austrian Tyrol some 200 years ago, it is one of only two such works known to exist in the world.

Egremont

3 miles west of Whitehaven, in the Lake District

CRAB FAIR

Held every year on the third Saturday in September. Phone: (01946) 820 693.

It's not a beauty contest. For the fair's main event, which is called "gurning through a braffin," contestants put horse harnesses around their heads and see who can make the ugliest face. Who needs a Halloween mask when you can make faces like these folks do, swallowing their noses and dissolving their chins. Foreigners have competed, but for some reason it is always the British who run away with the championship. This grand tradition is said to have begun centuries ago with locals mocking a village idiot.

Kendal

TOPIARY AT LEVENS HALL

5 miles south of town on the A6 road. Open April–mid-October, Sunday–Thursday, 10am–5pm. Phone: (015395) 60 321.

For over 300 years, the yews flanking this Elizabethan house have been clipped to look like huge birds, corkscrews, cones, a coach and horses, doughnuts, domes and more. Designed in 1692 by Guillaume Beaumont, the famous topiaries are meticulously maintained in their original shapes.

CUMBERLAND PENCIL MUSEUM

At Southey Works, Greta Bridge, off Main Street, just northwest of the center. Open daily, 9:30am–4pm. Admission: £2. Phone: (07687) 73 626.

Where would English litera-ture—not to mention English mathematics—be without pencils? Enter the museum through a replica of the nearby graphite mine that spawned the world's pencil industry 350 years ago. Then explore pencils in all their sharpness, versatility and power. Trace the history of their manufacture—an interesting exhibit explores hollow wartime pencils made to carry secret maps. Get a few tips on proper pencil care and use. Don't miss the seven-foot "longest pencil in the world." A video reveals clever techniques for getting the most out of your writing implements.

THACKRAY MEDICAL MUSEUM

Beckett Street near Bayswater Road, northwest of Leeds City Station and the River Aire. Open Tuesday–Sunday, 10am–5:30pm. Admission: £3.95; students, £3; children, £2.75; children under 4, free. Phone: 245 7084 or 244 4343.

Rampant gross-outs including a Pain, Pus and Blood exhibit and a giant walk-through bowel await, cloaked in a thin yet respectable veneer of science. Roam a recon-structed Victorian slum complete with festering health hazards. Learn which diseases afflict the characters within, and follow their miserable fates to the end. Listen to a huge fake stomach rumbling, experience imminent motherhood in a preg-nancy simulator and watch a horri-bly mangled mannequin undergo surgery. Cutting-edge interactive displays make polio, leeches and prosthetic limbs that much more meaningful.

ANYTHING TO DECLARE? HM CUSTOMS & EXCISE NATIONAL MUSEUM

Incorporated within the Mersey-side Maritime Museum, at Albert Dock, off Strand Street. Open daily, 10am–5pm. Admission is by the National Museums & Galleries of Merseyside "8-pass," which allows one year's unlimited entry to all eight NMGM venues and costs £3; children and students, £1.50. Phone: (0151) 478 4499.

Instructive displays here show you how to smuggle drugs in your shoe, sneak fake designer brands past the customs agents, and avoid paying all those nasty import taxes. Learn about contraband through hands-on dis-plays that help you chase and "catch" wily smugglers. One exhibit features items confiscated by customs, includ-ing ten Beatles gold records seized thirty years ago. Another examines the Channel Tunnel as a prime smuggling route. The accompanying maritime museum is one of Europe's largest, comprising seven acres. In the section on transatlantic slavery, you can step into a life-size plantation scene and a slave's hut.

Liverpool

THE BEATLES SHOP

31 Mathew Street, in the Cavern Quarter. Open daily, 9:30am–5:30pm. Phone: (0151) 236 8066.

Money can't buy you love, it's true, but it goes a long way toward acquiring Sergeant Pepper keychains and Paul puppets. Fab gear fills the shelves in the world's largest repository of Beatles-themed merchandise.

Liverpool

THE BEATLES STORY

Britannia Vaults at Albert Dock, off Riverside Walk. Open April–October, daily, 10am–6pm; November–March, Monday–Friday, 10am–5pm, Saturday–Sunday, 10am–6pm. Admission: £6.45; students, and children, £4.75. Phone: (0151) 709 1963.

Twist and shout your way past eighteen life-size replicas of Beatles milestones. Revisit Liverpool's Cavern Club, Hamburg's Star Club (complete with a loitering dummy dressed as a prostitute), Abbey Road Studios, a yellow submarine and more. The boys' authentic collarless coats, instruments and other artifacts are on display, while videos and music do their best to resurrect John.

Liverpool

BEATLE WEEK (INTERNATIONAL BEATLES FESTIVAL)

Held every year at various venues, throughout the week surrounding the last weekend in August. Phone: (0151) 236 9091 (Cavern City Tours).

"Help!" shout thousands of fans. They converge on the city every year for concerts, tours, late-night parties, artifact viewings and enough retro rampaging to please, please them. Cover bands and lookalikes from as far away as Japan and Brazil (an acknowledged hotbed of Beatle doppelgangers) pay nonstop homage to the Fab Four and even, loyally, to their solo careers. Monday's convention features a huge flea market, guest speakers, videos, a music marathon and more impersonators than would fit in a yellow submarine.

Liverpool

MAGICAL MYSTERY TOUR

Departs daily at 2:20pm from the Albert Dock Bus Stop (opposite the Pump House Pub) and at 2:30pm from the Merseyside Welcome Centre in Clayton Square; additional tours depart at 11:50am on Saturdays year-round as well as daily in July and August. Admission: £8.95; reser-

vations recommended. For more information and to reserve seats, call (0151) 236 9091 (Cavern City Tours) or (0151) 709 3285 (Merseyside Tourism).

Your ticket to ride buys two hours in a brightly painted replica of the wonderful bus from the Beatles' psychedelic 1967 TV special *Magical Mystery Tour,* which was later released as a film. Cruise up and down Liverpool's long and winding roads gawking at the Beatles' birthplaces, childhood homes, schools, concert venues and more. Keep your eyes peeled for looking-glass people eating marshmallow pies. Discover that Penny Lane and Strawberry Field are real places after all. The famous Cavern Club awaits at tour's end.

Malton

18 miles east of York

EDEN CAMP

On the Malton bypass, off the A64 road. Open January–mid-February, Monday–Friday, 10am–5pm; mid-February–December, daily, 10am–5pm. Admission: £3.50; children, £2.50. Phone: (01653) 697 777.

During WWII, POWs were confined here. Now it's a theme park where guard towers overlook grim huts in which Italian captives once lolled, pining for espresso. Each hut is now furnished with sets, sound effects and hilarious automated mannequins evoking wartime scenarios. You'll meet Hitler, U-boats, the blackout, rationing, munitions plants, the Red Cross, air-raid precautions, fashions of the '40s, POWs and the horror of the Blitz. The huts even re-create weird wartime smells. Be sure to sample the canteen's Soup of D-Day.

Manchester

GRANADA STUDIOS

Water Street near Irwell Street and the River Irwell, a few blocks west of the town hall. Open in summer, daily, 9:45am–4pm; winter, Wednesday–Sunday, 9:45am–3pm (exact off-season dates vary slightly year to year). Admission: in summer, £6.99; in winter, £5.99. Phone: (0161) 833 0880 or 832 4999.

Britain's version of Universal Studios brings to life popular TV programs of which you may never have heard. The original set from *Coronation Street* is here, as is a replica of Sherlock Holmes' Baker Street and more. In the mock House of Commons you can try your hand at an ongoing debate. Hedging its bets, the studio also inexplicably offers thrill rides in which you whiz around upside down. In one ride, you must endure motion-simulators while staring helplessly at high-speed action on a screen. Most gruesomely instructive is the "Deadly FX" show that explains the deception behind violent cinematic special effects.

Northwich

SALT MUSEUM

162 London Road, half a mile south of the center. Open Tuesday–Friday, 10am–5pm; Saturday and Sunday, 2pm–5pm. Admission: £3; children, £1. Phone: (01606) 41 331.

Before it wound up encrusting your fish and chips, where did salt come from? Even the Romans ate salt from here in Cheshire, where for 2,000 years the rock-salt beds have done their bit to bolster British cuisine. Salt and brine, millions of gallons of which are pumped here yearly, form a far-reaching local industry which this museum explores with the help of mannequins dressed as salt miners. Look at sparkling salt crystals and consult a wheelbarrow-sized salt-detecting tongue while you learn where salt comes from, how we get it, who gets rich off it and how it keeps you alive.

Sedgefield

10 miles southeast of Durham

FREE-FOR-ALL FOOTBALL

Held every year on Shrove Tuesday (Mardi Gras); game begins at 1pm on the village green. Phone: (0191) 384 3720 (Durham Tourist Office).

The players wear shin-guards. It's not only okay to viciously kick your fellow players during this once-a-year rugby-like match, it's pretty much mandatory. After the ball is thrown into the air over the village green and strikes earth, the men of Sedgefield chase it all over town in a no-holds-barred free-for-all. Nobody's a gentleman for the duration, and neighbors work out a whole year's worth of repressed spite as they career all over the streets, the ball and each other. The first goal wins the match—but no matter what, the game must end by 6pm.

Southport

Between Blackpool and Liverpool on the coast

THE BRITISH LAWNMOWER MUSEUM

106-114 Shakespeare St., just south of the center. Open Monday–Saturday, 9am–5:30pm. Admission: £1; children, 50p. Phone: (01704) 501 336.

Oh no, they're not just for cutting grass. This museum's curator is a lawnmower-racing champion who built some of the world's fastest lawnmowers. They're on display here along with more pragmatic members of the species. Restored to pristine condition, over 200 specimens span 170 years. These include lawnmowers once owned by Prince Charles and Princess Diana, a Rolls-Royce lawnmower and a half-ton monster of a lawnmower. Don't miss the two-inch lawnmower—it works. Learn how lawnmowers were invented in Gloucester in 1837 by a man whose neighbors thought he was nuts.

15 miles southwest of Windermere

LAUREL AND HARDY MUSEUM

4c Upper Brook St., near the Marketplace, a few blocks north of the train station. Open February–December, daily, 10am– 4:30pm. Admission: £2; children, £1. Phone: (01229) 582 292.

But Ollie, I don't *like* museums. Nonetheless, this one pays homage to Ulverston-born Stan Laurel who along with his equally unattractive partner starred in over 100 films. Unaccountably hailed as humorous, the pair's oeuvre is remembered here with the world's largest collection of Laurel-and-Hardy memorabilia: posters, waxworks, dolls, props, photographs— the works. Visitors can puzzle over vintage films and inspect Laurel's own personal toilet seat.

Whitby

WHITBY MUSEUM

In Pannett Park, off St. Hilda's Terrace at Stakesby Road. Open May–September, Monday–Saturday, 9:30am–5:30 pm, Sunday, 2pm–5pm; October–April, Tuesday, 10am–1pm; Wednesday– Saturday, 10am–4pm, Sunday, 2pm–4pm. Admission: £1.50; children, £1. Phone: (01947) 602 908.

"Hands of glory" were long considered powerful amulets. Supposedly cut from a freshly executed criminal, then bled dry, embalmed and sun-dried, the hand was fitted with a candle made of hanged-man's fat and Lapland sesame. Burglars carried these into houses, where the hands' magical powers were said to keep the sleeping occupants from waking up. The Whitby Museum has the only Hand of Glory on exhibit anywhere in the world. Also in the museum is a 19th-century "tempest prognosticator" made of glass tubes, hammers, whalebone and wire, and designed to hold multitudes of leeches. And don't miss the huge collection of ships, scenes and figures encapsulated inside light bulbs.

York

JORVIK VIKING CENTRE

In the Coppergate shopping district near the town center, between Piccadilly and Castlegate. Open April–October, daily, 9am–5:30pm; November–March, daily, 9am–3:30pm. Admission: £4.95; students, £4.60; children, £3.50; children under 5, free. Phone: (01904) 643 211.

Blend Disneyland with history class on this adventure-ride as you glide past toothy dummies portraying the Vikings who once called York home. Created with the help of skulls that were found nearby and scanned with lasers, these figures reveal how wild-eyed and horsey the Norsemen and Norsewomen really were. Watch them tend farm beasts, bake bread and spin wool in a series of scenes running the gamut from ship to market to fireside. Actual Viking archaeological finds are exhibited alongside their recreated former owners. A yearly Viking festival in mid-February brings the Viking-mania up to a fever pitch.

Scotland and Northern Ireland

Armagh

40 miles southwest of Belfast, Northern Ireland

SAINT PATRICK'S TRIAN

40 English St. Open September–June, Monday–Saturday, 10am–5pm, Sunday, 2pm–5pm; July–August, Monday–Saturday, 10am–5:30pm, Sunday, 1–6pm. Admission: £3.30; children, £1.75. Phone: (01861) 521 801.

So many different things have happened in Armagh that they had to combine several eras inside this single attraction and call it a *trian*, meaning a monastic settlement. In Armagh Story, life-size figures enact the city's history since its pagan days. Celts roar, monks clutch scriptures dourly and a mannequin impersonating an architect gives a lesson on Georgian buildings. Then St. Patrick, Least of All the Faithful reenacts the life and work of the Irish favorite. In The Land of Lilliput, a nod to Swift's stint in Armagh, a twenty-foot giant gives the last word on Gulliver.

Ayr

30 miles southwest of Glasgow

ELECTRIC BRAE

9 miles south of town on the A719 road; signposted. Visible at any time.

It's not electric, but a famous optical illusion on this hillside gives the definite impression that you're driving down the slope when in fact you are climbing. A driver who lifts a foot off the gas to "coast" downhill head-first will be startled to find the vehicle slowing down and actually drifting *backward*. A driver who stops at the "crest" will find the vehicle seeming to roll uphill. Pragmatists have explained the conundrum of Croy Brae—its real name—as an effect of converging horizons along the road and nearby woods. Others hail the phenomenon as supernatural. It's a good thing this isn't a major freeway.

Bushmills

6 miles east of Portrush, Northern Ireland

GIANT'S CAUSEWAY

The causeway is a stretch of coast just north of Bushmills (signs clearly point the way); the Giant's Causeway Centre is at 44 Causeway Road, on Causeway Head, 2 miles north of Bushmills on the B146 road; minibuses circulate between the causeway and the centre daily from April–September; a National Trust coastal footpath extends the length of the causeway. Centre is open July–August, daily, 10am–7pm; shorter hours rest of year. Admission to causeway is free; admission to center is £1; children, 60p. For more information, call (01265) 731 855 or 731 159.

They say these 40,000 angular, basalt columns rearing up like fangs out of the foaming sea got here when legendary Ulster giant Finn MacCool got the hots for an extremely large woman living in Scotland. They say he erected a set of stepping-stones for her. A duller story suggests that the four-, five-, six-, seven- and eight-sided columns appeared after a volcanic eruption 60 million years ago. Various jutting formations include the Grand Causeway, the Giant's Organ, the Honeycomb, the Wishing Chair and Lord Antrim's Parlour; a large sea cavern is open to explorers.

*7:30pm. Admission: £4.50, students, £3.50, children, £2.50, children under 7, free; phone: (0156) 450 218. **The Original Loch Ness Monster Exhibition** is open in winter, daily, 9am–5pm; summer, daily, 9:30am–9:30pm. Admission: £3.50, students, £2.75, children, £2.50. Phone: (01456) 450 342.*

The real mystery here is why two extremely similar enterprises with confoundingly similar names battle it out practically next door to each other. Each strives to lure its share of curious visitors who can't bring themselves to leave the Highlands without brooding over this murky lake and the large suggestive pieces of driftwood that float around in it. Each center offers, as their names promise, exhibitions showing how tales of local lake monsters date back to medieval times. Learn about attempts at underwater observation (oops, the water's just too darn murky!) and the use of sonar in tracking the putative Nessie. Peruse grainy photographs galore.

15 miles southwest of Inverness, on the western shore of Loch Ness

THE OFFICIAL LOCH NESS MONSTER EXHIBITION CENTRE AND THE ORIGINAL LOCH NESS MONSTER EXHIBITION

*Both are on the lakefront and impossible to miss. **The Official Loch Ness Monster Exhibition Centre** is open September–February, daily, 10am–3pm; March–June, daily, 9:30am–4:30pm; July–August, daily, 9am–*

2 miles north of Airth

THE DUNMORE PINEAPPLE

1 mile south of Dunmore on the B9124 road. For more information, such as on how to rent the pineapple, call the tourist office at (01786) 445 222.

The Fourth Earl of Dunmore, governor of New York, Virginia and the Bahamas, had this place built for himself as a summerhouse in 1761. And what evokes summer better than a giant fruit? Forty feet tall, expertly crafted in stone and designed by an unknown architect, the realistic-looking pineapple crowns a broad stone structure where visitors can spend the night. Like many pineapples, this one overlooks a large garden. Steps lead up into an elegant room hidden inside the fruit itself.

Edinburgh

WITCHERY TOURS

 Office is at 352 Castlehill on the Royal Mile near Edinburgh Castle; tours depart from the Witchery Restaurant in the same location. Tours start in the evening (call for current time); Murder & Mystery Tour is held year-round, Ghosts & Gore Tour in summer only; reservations required for all tours. Admission: Murder & Mystery Tour, £7; Ghosts & Gore Tour, £7, children £4; ticket price includes a Witchery Tales book. Phone: (0131) 225 6745.

Taking on the persona of an executed highwayman, the pallid tour guide makes spectral jokes while tracing a route through the Old Town. Hear true and legendary tales of the plague and other forms of death as you walk along, investigating the dark side of the city. Here and there throughout the tour, walkers are startled by the sudden appearance of costumed figures who jump out from behind corners and doorways. These include a werewolf, a prisoner, a human-size flea, a nun with traces of facial hair, a ghostly girl wearing plaid, a ferocious Highlander and

Mary, Queen of Scots. Oops, now you know.

Florencecourt

12 miles southwest of Enniskillen, Northern Ireland

MARBLE ARCH CAVES

 On the road called Marlbank Scenic Loop just west of Florencecourt, near the Irish border. Open late March–May and September, daily, 10am–4:30pm; July–late August, daily, 10am–5pm. Admission: £5; students, £3; children, £2. Phone: (01365) 348 855.

Electrically powered boats cruise down underground waterways past waterfalls, terraces and circuitous, mysterious passages. Coated in milky calcite, the cave's brightly lit chambers are fanged with stalactites and delicate mineral formations. Part of the tour goes on foot along strategically positioned walkways.

Glasgow

ST. MUNGO MUSEUM OF RELIGIOUS LIFE AND ART

 2 Castle Street, in the Cathedral Precinct, near Cathedral Street. Open Wednesday–Saturday and Monday, 10am–5pm; Sunday, 11am–5pm. Admission: free. Phone: (0141) 553 2557.

Probing our attempts at finding meaning in a more or less senseless universe, this museum doesn't

dis anybody's gods. Three galleries are stylishly decked out with a comprehensive global array of ritual items, artworks and scripture—not to mention effigies of enough pagan deities to make John Knox wilt (he's here, too, offering a cheerless creed in the Scottish Gallery). A Zen garden is out back; the café is strictly vegetarian, and labels on the museum's displays are printed in English, Urdu, Punjabi, Chinese and Gaelic. Don't be surprised if you walk out of here chanting sutras and yearning to be circumcised.

Inveraray

INVERARAY JAIL

On Church Square, on the waterfront. Open April–October, daily, 9:30am–6pm (last admission 5pm); November–March, daily, 10am–5pm (last admission 4pm). Admission: £4.30; children, £2.10. Phone: (01499) 302 381.

What looks at first like a forbidding waterfront castle is a huge 19th-century jail. Inside, morose mannequins and real live costumed guides pose in the cells, bathtub, restraint jacket and airing yards to illustrate the fate of law-breaking Scots. Watch and listen as dummies hold a "trial" in the courtroom, and don't miss the Torture, Death and Damnation exhibition, with a kilt-wearing nogoodnik hanging from a noose, as well as a sober examination of facial branding.

Lamb Holm Island

1½ miles south of St. Mary's on the main Orkney island, connected to the main island by a causeway

ITALIAN NISSEN HUT CHAPEL

Just east of the main road leading from St. Margaret's Hope to Kirkwall. Open April–September, daily, 9am–10pm; October–March, daily, 9am–4:30pm. Admission: free. Phone: (1856) 872 856.

During WWII, several hundred Italian POWs were sent north to build concrete causeways in the chilly Scottish seas. It was a true punishment. Homesick prisoners with time on their hands turned two adjacent Nissen huts into a makeshift yet charming replica of an Italian chapel. The ceilings and windows are lushly painted with saints and angels. The altar is molded concrete. The tabernacle is driftwood. The chapel sports a candelabra, a dainty wrought-iron rood screen and plasterboard painted to look like bricks. An elaborate façade out front is complete with cement columns and a bell. The Italians went home in 1945, but the chapel remains as good as new.

Oban

McCAIG'S TOWER

On Battery Hill at the junction of Ardconnel Road and Laurel Road, a few blocks inland from the North Pier. Visible at any time.

Poised above a quaint Scottish harbor, this huge stone monument resembling a sort of Gothic Colosseum is also known as "Skyline Folly." Perforated with empty windows, it definitely dominates the skyline. Art critic and philosopher John Stuart McCaig, who was born on Lismore island, which is visible from the folly, commissioned the structure in 1895 in order to give unemployed masons something to do. He wanted the gray granite circle, 190 feet across, to eventually house an art gallery and chapel, but he died before that came to pass. The vast fake ruin remained empty. Today it encloses gardens and offers views of the sea.

Oyne

25 miles northeast of Aberdeen

ARCHAEOLINK

1 mile off the A96 road. Open daily, 10am–5pm. Admission: £3.90; students and children, £2.35. Phone: (01464) 851 500.

Millennia ago, the locals painted themselves blue and dragged megaliths around. Learn all about it from your comfortable seat in the Archaeodome. Myths and legends, Celts and stones—this park brings them closer to you. The truly fearless can don costumes and attempt ancient crafts. Scattered around forty acres are the remains of an Iron Age fort, a reconstructed Iron Age farm, a Roman camp and hands-on activities that let visitors pretend to be either archaeologists

or ancients. Don't miss the Pict Fresh Café.

St. Andrews

East coast of Scotland

SCOTLAND'S SECRET BUNKER

5 miles south of St. Andrews at the Underground Nuclear Command Centre, Crown Buildings, Troywood, on the B9131 road near where it intersects the B940, north of Anstruther. Open April–October, daily, 10am–5pm. Admission: £5.95; children, £3.25. Phone: (01333) 310 301.

If Soviet Intercontinental Ballistic Missiles had ever rained down on Scotland, turning the countryside into a radioactive wasteland, this is where the government would have hidden out, planning the counterattack and coordinating the relief effort for the millions of casualties. Declassified only in 1993, this amazing subterranean maze of high-tech military equipment and survival gear has been preserved exactly as it was left. Protected by umpty-ump million tons of concrete, tungsten rods, 10-foot-thick walls and blast doors, the secret bunker was a veritable underground city, with sleeping areas, movie theater, TV stations, chapel, power plant, police station, restaurant and more. But the most fascinating rooms are those for coordinating the military operations, which give a chilling look into Cold War "mutual assured destruction" mentality. Be careful where you wander: parts of the bunker are still classified and off-limits to visitors. Spooky.

Wales

20 *miles north of Swansea, on the A4067 road*

DAN-YR-OGOF SHOWCAVES

 Just north of the village, on the western side of the Haffes river. Open Easter–October, daily, 10am–shortly before dusk. Admission: £6.50; children, £4. Phone: (01639) 730 284 or 730 800.

A dinosaur park and replicas of Iron Age and 19th-century farms flank the entrances to a trio of 300-year-old caves, forcing visitors to careen from era to era. As if the illuminated caves' underground waterfalls were not enough, the operators also throw in a snowless "dry" ski slope, a museum, a theater and a riding school. A brontosaurus glowers over the Iron Age huts, while another dinosaur menaces the ski lodge.

South Queensferry

8 miles west of Edinburgh

THE BURRY MAN

 Held every year on a Friday in early August. The museum is at 53 High Street, on the waterfront; open Monday and Thursday–Saturday, 10am–1pm and 2:15–5pm; Sunday, noon–5pm. Admission: free. Phone: (0131) 331 5545.

For nine hours every year, a man parades mutely through the hot streets clad scalp-to-ankles in a flannel suit completely covered with prickly burdock burrs. Clutching flower-trimmed walking sticks and burdened by his heavy costume, he traces the town's boundaries. Only his eyes and mouth are visible as, accompanied by two helpers, he silently begs for money door-to-door. The 250-year-old tradition may have started as a harvest festival, or a way to scare demons. No one is sure. Meet a full-size Burry Man model in the town museum.

Colwyn Bay

Just southeast of Llandudno, Wales

DINOSAUR WORLD

 In Eirias Park, off the A55 expressway, west of the center. Open Easter–September, daily, 10am–6pm, weather permitting. Admission: £2.50; children, £1.50; children under 3, free. Phone: (01492) 518 111.

Grazing in the grass, wallowing in mud, arching their long, fiberglass necks—dozens of huge model dinosaurs pose amid the green Welsh countryside. Staring stupidly, they lash out at one another with bared glistening fangs. You won't find this many dinosaurs hanging out together anywhere else in Britain. Enjoy screenings in the Dinosaur Video Room, and create dinosaur-themed brass rubbings. And like all members of victorious species, you can feast on sandwiches in the picnic area while listening to the dinosaurs' pathetic growls.

Corris

5 miles north of Machynlleth, Wales

KING ARTHUR'S LABYRINTH

At the Corris Craft Centre, on the A487 road between Dolgellau and Machynlleth. Open April–October, daily, 10am–5pm. Admission: £4.10; children, £2.95. Phone: (01654) 761 584.

Saunter into a dank Welsh cave, climb aboard a cute little electric boat, cruise down an underground river and disembark deep in the bowels of the earth. Here in the dark, moist and chilly depths, a series of carefully constructed waxwork scenarios recounts the legend of King Arthur: dragons, climactic battles and more. You'll also be regaled with rather more obscure Welsh myths, such as the story of the Head of Bendigeidfran, which perches malevolently on a rock. A cluster of pseudo-medieval Welsh craftsmen await as you return to the light of day.

Fishguard

13 miles southwest of Cardigan, in southwestern Wales

THE LAST INVASION TAPESTRY

(Tapestri Brodwaith y Goresgyniad Olaf)

In St. Mary's Church Hall. Open March–October, Tuesday–Saturday, 10am–5pm, Sunday, 2–5pm; November–April, hours vary. Admission: £ 1; children 8–16, 50p; children under 8, free. Phone: (01348) 874 997.

Seven hundred years after the Norman Invasion was recorded on the Bayeux Tapestry, the French were up to their old tricks once again. They invaded Fishguard in 1797, when Britain was still licking its wounds after the American Revolution. This French incursion is remembered as the last time England was ever invaded by a foreign power. Embroidered by seventy local women, the 100-foot tapestry depicts the whole debacle. High-masted ships arrive flying the French flag. French soldiers in their red-white-and-blue trousers skulk around looking impotent while the brave Welsh hold their own. Even the local farm animals get into the act.

Llandudno

THE ALICE IN WONDERLAND CENTRE

At the Rabbit Hole, 3-4 Trinity Square. Open Easter–October, daily, 10am–5pm; November–

*Easter, Monday–Saturday,
10am–5pm. Admission: £2.75;
children, £2.25. Phone: (01492)
876 413 or 860 082.*

The real-life little girl named Alice for whom Lewis Carroll wrote his books spent her summers in this Victorian resort town. Today, automated versions of the March Hare, the White Rabbit, the Mad Hatter and a huge-handed, stupefied Alice sip tea and consult pocketwatches amid faux foliage in this "warren" of life-size mobile tableaux based on Alice's adventures.

Llanfairpwllgwynwyll-gogerychwyrndrobwlllan-tysiliogogogoch

5 miles west of Bangor

TOWN WITH THE LONGEST NAME IN EUROPE

Called "Llanfair P.G." for short, this Welsh village's name has fifty-eight letters. In Welsh, it means "The church of St. Mary in a hollow of the white hazel near to the rapid whirlpool and to St. Tysilio's church near to a red cave." The town used to have a normal-sized name; it was actually extended to its present length as a 19th-century tourist lure. Travelers have snapshots taken of themselves in front of the train-station sign. You can also buy souvenir train tickets, suitable for framing.

Machynlleth

CELTICA

Just south of the center, in the Y Plas mansion, on Aberystwith road. Open daily, 10am–6pm. Admission: £4.65; students and children, £3.50; children under 5, free. Phone: (01654) 702 702.

Special effects throughout this walk-through exhibition immerse you in the deliciously pagan world of the Celts. Scenarios outfitted with model animals and shaggy-haired humans daubed in blue face-paint help you learn about this culture's poetic prowess, martial heroics and clever handicrafts. Sounds and strange visuals abound, but not a single written word interrupts the drama as you roam through the Corridor of Time wearing a headset. After inspecting a replica of an ancient foundry, move on to the Celtic village, circa the year 50 C.E. Use high technology to "meet" village residents such as a bard, a slave, a blacksmith, a warrior, a Druid and even a female chieftain.

Portmeirion

2 miles southeast of Porthmadog, in northern Wales

THE PRISONER VILLAGE

*Open year-round, daily,
9:30am–5:30pm. Admission:
£3.70; children, £1.90; children
under 4, free. Phone: (01766)
770 000.*

"I am not a number. I am a free man!" shouted the intelligence agent dubbed "Number 6" in TV's *The Prisoner*. At the time, he was lodged in a beautiful Italianate village from which it seemed he could never escape. The village where the show was filmed was real, yet it wasn't. Architect Clough Williams-Ellis, striving to counteract all the destruction he saw in WWI, spent forty-seven years building his fantasy village. Colonnades, promenades, a dome, gardens, turrets, statuary, semitropical foliage, tile-roofed houses, a hotel, cottages and towers the colors of after-dinner mints evoke the sunny Mediterranean.

GREECE

Don't miss:

Kalambaka

In central Thessaly, 80 km west of Larissa

METEORA MONASTERIES

The monasteries are grouped about 4 kilometers north and east of Kalambaka, near the village of Kastraki. There are various roads and trails winding among the rocks; depending on which route you follow and how many monasteries you see, your visit could take all day. Public buses run very infrequently in the area; if you're not up to walking fifteen to twenty kilometers, you may want to join one of the guided tours arranged by the many travel agencies in Kalambaka. Open daily, 9am–1pm and 3:30–5pm (appproximately), though each monastery sets its own hours and some occasionally close one day a week.

Admission to each monastery:

400 dr; students: 200 dr. Note that there is a strict dress code. Basically, don't dress like a hippie or a dorky tourist: Keep arms and legs covered, no long hair for men and no pants for women. Phone: (0432) 222 77 (Varlaam), or 78 (Great Meteoron) or 79 (Agios Stefanos).

Perched precariously on soaring pinnacles of stone, the monasteries of Meteora almost make reclusive asceticism seem fun. Familiar to Westerners as the dramatic location for the climax of the 1981 James Bond thriller, *For Your Eyes Only*, Meteora in fact has a history that goes back 1,200 years, when hermits first settled here. The construction boom, however, happened between the 14th and 16th centuries, when monks fleeing the worldly life scaled impossibly sheer cliffs to build monasteries in the clouds. Of the twenty-four original monasteries, only five are still occupied today. The biggest and highest, Great Meteoron, houses wonderful Orthodox frescoes and an impressive church. Nearby Varlaam can only be reached by climbing 195 acrophobic steps, but be thankful: Until this century the only way up was by clambering into a net which was then drawn up via hand-cranked winch, as you dangled hundreds of feet in the air. If your hair needs straightening, creep carefully across the terrifying bridges to Roussanou convent, perched precipitously on the very edge of a sheer cliff. You're lucky that you can't visit the picturesque ruins of Agia Moni, since you'd probably die of fear just tying to ascend its absolutely vertical shaft. Agias Triadas and Agios Stefanos are a short distance away, and offer ever more vertiginous religiosity.

Firewalking Rituals of Northern Greece
(Anastenaria)

Clasping icons of St. Constantine and St. Helen, ordinary Greek villagers put themselves into a trance and literally dance on hot coals. They feel no pain, and afterward their feet appear completely unharmed. This annual ritual is supposed to commemorate a medieval miracle in which icons of the region's mother-and-son team of patron saints cried out to be rescued from a church fire. When the villagers dashed in to save the images, they emerged from the flames unscathed. Ever since, on the saints' feast day—May 21—the rescue is reenacted just after dusk in a smattering of northern Greek villages in Macedonia and Thrace. The dancers, called *anastenarides* ("moaners") because of the cries they make as they work themselves into a frenzied trance, step rhythmically through the flames and across the coals, over and over, to the sounds of music and encouragement from the crowd. This strange custom, say the historians, is stranger than you think: It has nothing to do with Greek Orthodox Christianity at all, but is actually a remnant of prehistoric Dionysus worship that survived almost unchanged for 3,000 years. Impossible? This just happens to be the exact area where the Dionysiac religion originated, and the actions of the *anastenarides* closely mirror those of Dionysus' ancient followers. The Orthodox church, aware of the festival's pagan roots, has tried to put the kibosh on it, so there's no guarantee that it will take place in all three of the towns listed below every year. But the ritual's popularity with the general public and the media has kept it alive at least for now. Call the information offices in Serres ([0321] 67.613) or Thessaloniki ([0394] 22318) a few days ahead of time to confirm this year's locations. The three villages to look for are:

 Agia Eleni (10 km south of Serres); **Langadas** (19 km northeast of Thessaloniki); **Meliki** (50 km west of Thessaloniki).

Klima

On the Cycladean island of Milos

CATACOMBS

 2 kilometers south of the capital city of Plaka; signs on the road leading to Klima point the way to the catacombs. Open Monday–Tuesday and Thursday–Saturday, 8:30 am–2 pm. Admission: free. Phone: (0287) 21 620 or 625.

Early Christians dug out these underground avenues. Now electrically lit and fitted with wooden walkways, they serve as a silent testament to the roots of a dominant religion that today feels no need to hide. Wide, arched niches make a dark scalloped pattern against solid rock tinted reddish in the lamplight.

On the Ionian island of Kefalonia

SNAKE-HANDLING FESTIVAL

Held every year on August 15 at the Church of Our Lady. Markopoulo is at the southern end of Kefalonia, just inland from Cape Katelios. For more information, call the Tourist Information Office at 0671/24466.

Little snakes crawl out of the wilds and stream all over the village church every year on Assumption Day, the holiday marking Mary's departure for heaven. Townspeople gather to touch and embrace the serpents, which stream enthusiastically all over the courtyard, bell tower and icon of the Virgin. Is it mere coincidence that snakes were considered sacred among the ancient Greeks? Nobody knows why the animals come, or why they depart just as abruptly at day's end. But the faithful are quick to point out tiny black markings on the snakes' heads, which they say is the sign of the cross.

Mount Athos

The easternmost prong of the Halkidiki peninsula, in Macedonia

NATION OF MONASTERIES

To visit Mount Athos, you must be male, at least 18 years old, state that you have a religious or scholarly reason to visit, and obtain a special visa. Here's how to get one: First contact your local

consular authority, or the State Department, and request a letter of recommendation. Then call or write to either the Ministry of Foreign Affairs, Directorate of Churches, Academias 3, Athens (phone: 362 6894), or the Ministry of Northern Greece, Directorate of Civil Affairs, Platia Diikitiriou, Thessaloniki (phone: 031 270 092), and request an application. Once you get it, complete it satisfactorily and send it along with the letter to either address above. Hopefully, you'll be granted a visa within a few weeks. Once you have your visa, make your way by bus from Thessaloniki to Ouranoupolis or Tripiti at the northern end of the peninsula, and take a hired boat down the coast to the only legal entry point on Mt. Athos, the port of Dafni. From there you will be taken to the only village on the peninsula, Karies, where you will be admitted to the community. There are no roads or land access to Mt. Athos.

The most exclusive all-male club anywhere on earth, Mt. Athos is an independent religious state, even though a treaty signed in 1926 essentially makes it a protectorate of Greece. The 1,700 or so monks who live here take their religion *seriously* and follow a lifestyle that hasn't changed in a thousand years. According to a chrysobull (edict) issued in 1060 by Byzantine Emperor Constantine Monomahos, women and young boys are absolutely forbidden to set foot on Mt. Athos. Incredibly, the edict remains in effect, as well as other laws and rules from the Middle Ages. Mt. Athos, or "Holy Mountain" as the Greeks call it, is actually a peninsula, though it has no roads connecting it to the mainland. The twenty monasteries dotting the landscape—each independent of the other—are repositories for an uncountably huge number of icons, artworks, antique artifacts and relics, including the hand of John the Baptist at Grigoriou monastery. Visitors are allowed to stay four nights, each in a different monastery of their choosing. The lifestyle is severe, the carless roads between monasteries are long and unpaved, but it's an experience you will not soon forget.

Nemea

40 km west of Corinth

NEMEAN GAMES

In the excavated ancient stadium. Held every four years, one to three months before the summer Olympics (2000, 2004, etc.). Admission: Free to watch, and anyone over 12 may enter after registering at no charge in advance. Phone: (510) 642-5924 (in the U.S.) or 30-746-24. 125 (in Nemea).

An American archaeologist has revived these games, now staged in the same ancient stadium where they were held 2,300 years ago. At that time they were just as famous as the ones held at Olympia. Barefoot and clad in scanty Greek-style chitons, dozens of athletes from many different countries turn out for the competition. Runners draw lots from a helmet to get their lane assignments, then race 100 and 200 meters in the ancient stone grooves. With obeisance solemnly given to Greek gods, the winners receive simple palm branches while their families watch from the sidelines. This is the way the Olympics *ought* to be, with truly amateur athletes, pagan rituals and low-tech authenticity. The emphasis is on international peace and understanding. Music—played on ancient Greek instruments—and other festivities put the revelers in a Hellenistic mood.

Perama

4 km north of Ioannina, in Epirus

PERAMA CAVE

On Goritsa hill, on an unnamed road just outside the village; a sign points the way. Open daily, 8am–5pm. Admission: 1,000 dr; children, 500 dr. Phone: (0651) 81521.

This cave's claim to fame is the world's only cross-shaped stalagmite, proof that even Pluto, god of the underworld, must be a churchgoing Christian. Elsewhere on the guided tour you pass several very picturesque pools—rather optimistically described as "lakes"—and stalactites in every shape *except* a cross. The cavern—also referred to as Goritsa Cave—is perfectly horizontal; none of your underground acrophobia here.

Petralona

40 km south of Thessaloniki, on Halkidiki

PETRALONA CAVE

800 meters from the center of Petralona, on Mt. Katsika; follow the signs. Open daily,

Not only does this cave have innumerable knitting-needle stalactites, stone curtains, accretion disks and misshapen columns, all tinted a distinctive shade of red, but it also happens to be the site where Europe's oldest human remains were found. Yes—the original cavemen, over 700,000 years old. Even back then we had good taste in interior decoration: One never imagines prehistoric man's cave dwellings as being so picturesque. A museum shows what life must have been like for our grunting forefathers.

Pirgos Dirou

80 km south of Kalamata

GLIFADA CAVE

12 kilometers south of Areopolis, 4 kilometers from Pirgos Dirou, on the Mani peninsula; buses run from Aeropolis directly to the caves. On foot from Pirgos Dirou, follow the signs on the cave's special access road. Open daily in summer, 8am–4pm; in winter, 8am–2:30pm. Admission: 2,800 dr; students and children, 1,400 dr. Phone: (0733) 52222.

Women's Domination Days
(Gynaecocratia)

On January 8 every year, scattered villages around Thrace and Macedonia still celebrate the ancient custom of *gynaecocratia*, or women's rule. For this one day, men and women voluntarily reverse roles. In Greece this means that the women get to lounge around in tavernas playing cards and backgammon while the men sit at home and take care of the kids. Theoretically, the women take over the village's political structure as well, but since not much ever happens politically in a Greek village, there's not much for them to do. Should the men venture outside, they risk getting doused with buckets of water, so in practice they usually just stay at home and watch a lot of TV. Around 5pm both sexes gather in the tavernas, where the men prepare and serve a lavish meal for the women, and everyone gets drunk and parties all night. The origins and significance of *gynaecocratia* are lost in the mists of time; most scholars agree it is an extremely antique Thracian practice that predates the arrival of Christianity in the area by hundreds or even thousands of years. The most famous celebrations are in **Monoklissia** (20 kilometers southwest of Serres) and **Nea Petra** (25 km southeast of Serres), though from all accounts many untouristed villages around **Kilkis** (45 km north of Thessaloniki), **Xanthi** (58 km east of Kavala, in Thrace), and **Komotini** (40 km east of Xanthi, in Thrace) still celebrate too. Call the Serres Prefecture office at (0321) 67. 613 or 63. 960 for current locations.

If you've ever wanted to take a cruise ship to hell, here's your chance. At this staggering complex of caves isolated in the Greek countryside, interconnected subterranean lakes extend deep into the earth. Climb aboard one of the sturdy wooden ships and cruise past multicolored stalactites in thick clusters, then disembark halfway to Hades and wander around relatively unmonitored—a rarity for cave visits in Europe. Trick lighting heightens the effect of the stygian formations. Peer into the waters and try to catch sight of the legendary cave eels said to live here. Note that the cave system goes by many names, including Diros Caves, Pirgos Dirou Cave, Alepotrypa Cave, and Glifada Cave, but they all refer to the same attraction.

On the east coast of Kefalonia island

MELISSANI CAVE LAKE AND DROGARATI CAVE

 Melissani is 3.5 kilometers north of Sami, just outside the village of Karavomilos. Open April–

 October, daily, 8am–8pm. Admission: 900 dr; children, 450 dr. Phone: (0647) 22215.

When the roof of this amazing underground lake partially collapsed long ago, it turned out to be a blessing in disguise. Now as you drift about on the crystalline water in rowboats, the sun's rays pierce the darkness, strike the water and unleash a kaleidoscope of blues and aquamarines. The colors slowly shift as the minutes pass, and you enter a dreamy state of altered consciousness. Think of it as color therapy. Recently, scientists discovered that the water in the cave is actually seawater that originates from the *other* side of the island; after being sucked into sinkholes, it somehow takes two weeks to travel uphill seventeen kilometers under the ground, to emerge here and reenter the sea. Geologists are still trying to figure it out, but we think they just like drifting about on those boats. As a side trip, take in nearby Drogarati Cave (4 kilometers south of Sami, off the road to Argostoli, near the village of Haliotata; open April–October, daily, 8am–8pm; Admission: 800 dr), a modest-size, spooky cavern with freaky stalactites and perfect acoustics.

HUNGARY

Don't miss:

Aggtelek

50 km northwest of Miskolc, on the Slovakian border

BARADLA CAVE
(Baradla-barlang)

The cave system has three entrances: one just northwest of the town of Aggtelek (the entrance is clearly signposted); and another 5 km northeast of Aggtelek near the village of Jósvafö (entrance is 1 kilometer west of the village; again, follow the signs); and another at Vörös-tó, a spot on the road between the two villages. Buses run from both Eger and Miskolc to Aggtelek in the morning, and return in the afternoon.

Buses also run infrequently between Aggtelek and Jósvafö, or you can hike between the two in an hour. Open mid-April–mid-October, daily, 8am–6pm (last admission, 5pm); mid-October–mid-April, daily, 8am–4pm (last admission, 3pm). Admission: 500 Ft; students and children, 300 Ft. Phone: 48/343-073 or 48/350 006.

The puny term "cave" hardly describes this 25-kilometer-long marvel that is also—and more accurately—called "The Aggtelek Cave World." The system is so long, actually extending far into Slovakia, that three different tours are given at three different entrances. The most popular tour leaves from Aggtelek, leading past flowstones, draperies, stalactites, helictites, coralloids, stalactites and rimstone dams with nicknames like Minerva's Helmet, the Xylophone, Santa Claus, the Diamond Castle, the Turtle and the Pagoda. Musical shows are staged in the Concert Hall, and the Mirror Hall has a perfectly flat small lake that reflects the ceiling spectacularly. The Vörös-tó tour leads past brightly colored formations like the Yawning Crocodile, the Weeping Willow, the Igloo, the Octopus, Noah's Ark, the Zeppelin and the Observatory, which at fifty feet is Hungary's tallest stalagmite. The highlight is the Hall of Giants, an expansive cavern resplendent with wild shapes and colors. The third tour, from Jósvafö, takes you straight to the Hall of Giants and back. Total caveaholics can arrange a special seven-kilometer tour to seldom-seen areas.

CHILDREN'S RAILWAY
(Gyermekvasút)

Travels back and forth between Hüvösvölgy and Széchenyi-hegy, in the Buda Hills; to reach the terminal, take tram 56. Operates mid-March–October, Monday–Friday, hourly, 9:05am–5pm; Saturday–Sunday, every 45 minutes, 8:45am–5:30pm; November–mid-March, Monday–Friday, every two hours, 9:05am–4pm; Saturday–Sunday, every 45 minutes, 9:05am–5pm. Admission: 180 Ft (for a round-trip ticket); children, 90 Ft. Phone: 397-5394.

What's so bad about child labor, anyway? Almost all by themselves, clad in snug blue uniforms topped off with jaunty caps, kids aged ten to fourteen operate this big red-and-white train on its lofty 12-kilometer route. Conductors, switchmen—sure enough they're all rugrats. This is the world's only full-fledged railway run entirely by children.

GEZA KRESZ MUSEUM OF THE AMBULANCE SERVICE
(Mentömúzeum)

Markó u. 22, in the Fifth District, on the second (which Europeans call the first) floor; enter the building through the right side of the ambulance driveway (Metro: Nyugati pu.). Open daily, 9am–1pm. Admission: 60 Ft; children, 20 Ft. Phone: 344-3737 or 344-4188.

Stretchers, oxygen tents and emergency-rescue dummy heads evoke a sense of crisis in this series of dusty rooms along a silent hallway. Syringes, neck braces, photographs and relics of the *Titanic* trace the history of accidents and rescues from ancient times to the present. (Don't miss the Roman illustration of a man with a crotch injury.) Exhibits focus on hypothermia, head injuries and people thought dead and accidentally buried alive, only to be rescued at their own funerals.

GOLDEN EAGLE PHARMACY MUSEUM
(Arany Sas Patikamúzeum)

Tárnok u. 18, in the First District on Castle Hill. Open Tuesday–Sunday, 10:30am–5:30pm. Admission: 60 Ft; children, 20 Ft. Phone: 175-9772.

In a reconstructed alchemy lab, a bat and stuffed cayman dangle from the ceiling and an octopus lies coiled in a jar, while gold stars glitter on deep blue walls and a human skull, swordfish sword and other ingredients wait on the alchemist's table. Instructional alchemy books dating back hundreds of years provide clues in many languages, while artworks on the walls memorialize alchemists at work. Pharmacists' supplies include a mummified head (mummy powder was long considered a cure-all) and an 18th-century microscope made entirely of wood.

The guide won't let you miss a single thing.

HUNGARIAN MUSEUM OF COMMERCE AND CATERING
(Magyar Kereskedelmi és Vendéglátóipari Múzeum)

 Fortuna ut. 4, in the First District, on Castle Hill; the two halves of the museum are across the hall from each other. Open Wednesday–Friday, 10am–5pm; Saturday–Sunday, 10am–6pm. Admission: 100 Ft; students, 50 Ft. Phone: 175 62 49.

Puzzlement over why these two topics have been lumped together fades away as you roam this proud and wistful memorial to Budapest's bygone glory as a hospitable capitalist hotbed of café culture and fancy silk underwear. The catering section includes a reconstructed rococo hotel room and sine-qua-non eating utensils salvaged from bygone Budapest restaurants, including a crab fork, a beer warmer, an asparagus clipper and a dainty plate for spat-out bones. Stocked with Hungarian packages and products that vanished at the onset of war, the commerce section celebrates a century of brilliant advertising gimmicks.

HUNGARIAN MUSEUM OF COMMERCE AND CATERING—BUDAPEST

LABYRINTH OF THE BUDA CASTLE
(Budavári Labirintus)

 Úri utca 9, on Castle Hill in Buda. Open daily, 9:30am–7:30pm (later summer closing times are planned). Admission: 750 Ft; students, 600 Ft. Phone: (36 1) 212 0207.

Natural caverns once inhabited by prehistoric humans were expanded during the Middle Ages into storage rooms, and then into a series of interconnected cellars running underneath Buda's Castle Hill. Later they were put to military use and extended further, and became a tourist attraction in the Communist era as a down-at-the-heels historical monument. But now the seemingly endless maze has been converted into a cutting-edge subterranean theme park centered around the notion of the labyrinth as a personal and spiritual journey. Various "zones" include the Prehistoric Labyrinth, which has reproductions of paleolithic cave paintings with an emphasis on the shamanistic. The Historical Labyrinth traces Hungarian history from the distant past to the Renaissance, including waxworks and a section on the Huns, the early Magyars and the "Tartar Corridor." Deep in the tunnels, the Ivy Grotto is a confusing rhythmic pagan shrine meant to inspire deep reflection on the meaning of life. By prior arrangement, you can tour the Personal Labyrinth, a special area that in theory leads to a personal reawakening—if that's your idea of a good time. Also here are an underground café and a gallery showing temporary exhibits of labyrinth-themed art.

MARXIM RESTAURANT

Kisrókus u. 23, in the Second Disrict in Pest. Open Monday–Friday, noon–1am; Saturday, noon–2am; Sunday, 6pm–1am. Phone: 06-1/31-602-31.

"Censored" symbols and images of nude construction workers with huge hard-ons are stenciled all over the walls of this bar/pizzeria dedicated to the death of Communism. Barbed wire and tattered hammer-and-sickle flags surround cell-like booths where from a menu loaded with in-jokes, you can order Pasta Marxissimo (with three different kinds of meat), a Marxicana salad, or pizzas named after Lenin, Stalin and other monolithic figures. The "Gulag" pizza features pineapple.

PÁLVÖLGY CAVE
(Pálvölgyi Barlang)

Szépvölgyi ut. 162, in the Buda Hills, west of downtown: Take bus 6 from central Budapest (Nyugati tér) to Kolosy tér, and then bus 65 up the hill. Open Wednesday–Sunday, 10am–4pm; tours depart every hour. Admission: 200 Ft; students and children, 100 Ft. Phone: 325-9505.

Formed by thermal springs and tectonic fissures, the longest of several caves in the Buda Hils extends for thirteen kilometers, though the tour only takes you along 500 sparkly meters. Crystals, stalactites and stalagmites along with concretions in intriguing shapes offset the mildly strenuous up-and-down workout comprising the tour. The Stone Bat is not a stalactite, but a startling light-and-shadow illusion in the ceiling that looks like a gargantuan winged creature flying right at you. Inside these cool passageways with their walls like melting ice cream, it's easy to forget how close you are to the big bustling city. The nearby cave called Szemlö-Hegyi Barlang at Pusztaszeri ut. 35 is less spectacular but has rare "popcorn" and "coral" formations, left by long-gone hot springs, encrusting the walls.

ST. STEPHEN'S HAND
(Szentjobb)

> *In the Sacred Right Hand
> Chapel, at the rear of St.
> Stephen's Basilica, on Szent
> István tér, off Bajcsy-Zsilinszky
> út, in Pest. Open daily,
> April–September, 9am–5pm; Oc-
> tober–March, 10am–4pm. Ad-
> mission: free.*

The severed, mummified fist of Hungary's beloved first Christian king rests behind glass for all to admire in a gold-encrusted, church-shaped reliquary. Credited with brutally converting this land, "Good King Stephen" is said to have dismembered his cousin in a battle over the throne. Crusty and brown like a piece of fried chicken, the clenched fist still exudes an aura of power and authority. Every year on August 20, this most dearly treasured relic—hailed as the Holy Right Hand—is brought out of the basilica and carried around the neighborhood in a grand procession, as crowds applaud and weep.

SEMMELWEIS MUSEUM OF MEDICAL HISTORY
(Semmelweis Orvostörténeti Múzeum)

> *I., Aprod u. 1-3 at the foot of
> Castle Hill: Take tram 18 or 19.
> Open Tuesday–Sunday,
> 10:30am–5:30pm. Admission:
> 120 Ft; reserving a tour with an
> English-speaking guide, which is
> possible but not necessary, costs
> 500 Ft extra. Phone: 175-3533.*

A shrunken head and Neolithic fetishes flank the entrance to one of several rooms packed with medical souvenirs. You are required to don embarrassing felt slippers over your shoes (the slippers come in two sizes) as you inspect the antique surgical implements, chastity belt, ancient Egyptian mummified head, mummified foot and what looks like a mummified pigeon, as well as a bellows for reanimating apparent corpses—central Europeans have a phobia about being buried alive. Artworks depict angels assisting at a medieval amputation. A virtuosic Florentine 18th-century beeswax cadaver has flowing blonde hair and a dreamy face. Its severed breasts are thrown apart like Dutch doors to reveal intricate guts. Other beeswax models include heads, brains and bowels.

STATUE PARK
(Szoborpark)

> *At the corner of Balatoni út and
> Szabadkai út in South Buda's
> 22nd district (XXII.ker): From
> central Budapest, take bus 7 to
> the terminal at Kosztolányi Dez-
> so tér, and then the yellow Volán
> Bus leaving from stall 6; alterna-
> tively, take bus 3 and transfer at
> Jókai utca to bus 50. Open mid-
> March–mid-November, daily,
> 10am–dusk; mid-November–
> mid-March, Saturday–Sunday,
> 10am–dusk. Admission: 200 Ft;
> children and students, 100 Ft.
> Phone: 227-7446.*

Socialist statues once loomed portentously in public places throughout the country. But now many of them have been put out to pasture here. A "cemetery for the recent past," this suburban park comprises a parade of monumental Lenin statues and memorials to worker-heroes and movements, now rendered pitiful. The Hungarian Communist Party Printing House Memorial is typical of what arguably makes this park Europe's most revealing memorial to the Communist era. In the capitalist spirit, the souvenir shop sells CDs full of revolutionary hits like *The Happy Pioneer* and *We Thank You, Comrade Rákosi.*

Hortobagy ∘

35 km west of Debrecen

PUSZTA MIRAGES
(Délibáb)

Visible on sunny days in the countryside around Hortobagy and the plains further south. Admission: free. Phone: 52 369 119 (Hortobagy tourist information).

The best time to spot a mirage in the sky above the hot, flat plain known as the *puszta* is on blazing summer afternoons, in an area where the plain extends clear to the horizon. Many sightings have been reported in the national park around Hortobagy, but you have a good chance anywhere in the flat region bounded roughly by Debrecen, Szeged and Kecskemét. Mirages are caused by light rays reflecting off layered atmospheric distortions, so each is unique and usually fleeting. Farms, trees or whole villages seem to float in the sky, often (but not always) upside down. Sometimes only the upper parts of the

town are visible, which is why disembodied church spires are frequently reported. The best mirages involve multiple reflections of the same image, inverted and then reinverted repeatedly, so that a small cluster of dilapidated farm buildings looks like a Shangri-La in the clouds.

Kecskemét

80 km southeast of Budapest

NAIVE ART MUSEUM
(Naív Müvészek Múzeuma)

Gáspár András u. 11, near Hoffmann J. u., on the western edge of the center. Open mid-March–November, Tuesday–Sunday, 10am–5pm. Admission: 100 Ft. Phone: 76/324-767.

Paintings and statues by Hungarian "outsider" artists—untrained amateurs and those living on the fringe—give a refreshing glimpse into what would happen if every art school in the world were burned to the ground and their students set free. Several rooms show a rotating selection of the museum's large collection, so you never know which surprising, primitive, wild and eccentric visions you might encounter.

In the far south, on the Danube

BUSÓJÁRÁS PROCESSION

Held every year beginning on the Sunday seven weeks before Easter and lasting till Shrove Tuesday; parade begins at Koló Square and proceeds to the main square; celebrations continue on the riverbank. For more information, call 69 322 330 or 69 311 828.

The Turks invaded in 1526, and 20,000 Hungarian soldiers, including the king, died in what is still known as the "Mohács disaster." Some say this annual festival, where townspeople wear toothy, horned *busó* masks made of carved willow and wool while carousing through town shaking chains and ringing cowbells, recalls the disaster and repels any lingering Turks. Yet the loud and popular parade is also an age-old Carnival rite heralding spring and banishing winter. As a grand finale, revelers—whose masks are traditionally painted with animal blood and whose underwear is stuffed with straw—burn a coffin.

TARODI CASTLE
(Taródi Vár)

Csalogány köz 28, west of town in the hills above the Lövér baths. Bus #1 from the center of town will take you to within a few blocks of the castle. Visible from the outside at any time. There are no set hours for inside visits; if one of the family members is at home when you show up, they'll show you around. Admission: no set charge; but the owners usually ask for a donation.

Hungary has its share of medieval castles, but this one's a big fake. A local guy named István Taródi became fascinated with the grand old architecture hereabouts and decided to give it a try himself. In 1951 he began with a wooden castle, then later he refashioned it in stone. He and his family kept on building and building, while filling the tortuous passageways inside with an ever-increasing collection of antique miscellania. Today their oeuvre is a lofty confection, worthy of a fairytale but totally counterfeit, complete with towers, terraces, bastions and turrets. For total Taródi immersion, consider staying the night: the family often accepts paying guests.

BUSÓJÁRÁS PROCESSION—MOHÁCS

BORY CASTLE
(Bory Vár)

Máriavölgy ut. 54, at the north-east edge of town: From the train station take bus 31 or 32, or from the center of town take bus 26 or 26A; ask the driver where to get off. Open March–November, daily, 9am–5pm. Admission: 100 Ft; students and children, 50 Ft. Phone: 22/305-570.

Jenö Bory spent forty years single-handedly building his dream castle on the outskirts of his hometown. Not only is it the world's only castle ever built solely by one person, but it's also a monument to Bory's love for his wife and his romantic notion of how castles ought to look. Towers, balconies, archways, spiral staircases, statues and architectural flights of fancy all mesh into a medieval fairytale wonderland—which was completed in 1959. Inside is a thicket of Bory's sculptures and artwork, and a special chapel dedicated to his wife, whose portrait crops up everywhere. Because Bory was a trained artist and a genius with concrete and brick, his castle is not an unstable, crumbling pile of masonry, but rather a sturdy fortress that looks as if it could stand for a thousand years.

30 km north of Budapest, on the east side of the Danube

MEMENTO MORI

Marcius 15. tér 19 (i.e. March 15th Square, #19), on the west side of the plaza in the center of town. Open Tuesday–Sunday, 10am–6pm. Admission: 250 Ft; students and children, 125 Ft. Phone: 06-27 316-160 (Vacs Tourinform).

In 1994, workmen renovating a church stumbled upon an 18th-century burial crypt containing over 160 bodies, all naturally mummified in their pretty coffins. Many were transferred here across the square to a formerly dank basement, now rebuilt as an elegant exhibit space. Many of the most beautiful coffins line the walls and stand in neat stacks: Painted in rich blue, yellow or pink, most bear delicate images of angels, flowers, hourglasses, swirling floral motifs or rustic versions of the crucifixion. The mummies are here as well, dressed as they were at their funerals 200 years ago in woolen socks, bonnets and ruffled white gowns with flowing ribbons. Their eyes are sunken but otherwise they appear peaceful and newly dead, like a more relaxed version of Pompeii. Personal effects are in display cases: jewelry, rosaries, last wills and a small silver ring inscribed "Babette."

IRELAND

Don't miss:

Ballyvaughan

On the north coast of County Clare

AILLWEE CAVE

Just south of town, off the N67 road. Open March–October, daily, 10am–5:30pm, tours depart continuously; November–February, three tours daily depart at 11:30am, 1:30 and 3pm. Admission: £4.50; children, £2.50. Phone: (065) 77036.

Millions of years ago, streams drifting underground on Aillwee Mountain started carving passages into the limestone. Today the formations left behind include stalactites, stalagmites, rippling buttery sheets and other shapes which—ever since a local farmer discovered the cave in 1944—have been given fanciful nicknames belying their age and majesty. After inspecting the remains of a long-extinct bear, follow your tour guide past the Praying Hands and the Bunch of Carrots and along raised walkways through huge rocky caverns, one of which reverberates with the sound of an underground waterfall.

Bunratty

7 miles northwest of Limerick

MEDIEVAL BANQUETS

At Bunratty Castle, on the Limerick-Ennis Road. Held twice nightly at 5:30 and 8:45pm. Admission: £32; children 10–12, £24.25; children 6–9, £16.50; children under 6, free. Phone: (061) 360788 or 361511.

Sip honeyed mead and toast the Earl of Thomond as the singing starts in the stony depths of this impressive castle, built in 1425 by the McNamara Clan and abandoned for years, but now stocked with Ireland's most extensive collection of medieval furnishings. Women in low-cut dresses dole out four earthy courses with wine as other women in low-cut dresses offer songs and music. The tastiness of the food is a terrible historical inaccuracy that really ought to be rectified. Note also the sheela-na-gig, an ancient exhibitionist carving, in the window of the hall of the castle's great keep.

Burncourt

9 miles southwest of Cahir

MITCHELSTOWN CAVE

Just west of Burncourt off the N8 road between Cahir and Mitchelstown in County Tipperary. Open daily, 10am–6pm. Admission: £3; students, £2.50; children, £1. Phone: (052) 67246.

Discovered in 1833 when a local man accidentally dropped his crowbar into a crack while quarrying limestone, the caves are lush with stalactites, stalagmites and calcite formations, including a thirty-foot column dubbed the "Tower of Babel." Nearly half a mile of electrically lit walkways lead through three separate caverns, one of which is stunningly large, measuring some 200 feet across.

Castleisland

15 miles northeast of Killarney
CRAG CAVE

1 mile north of town, off the N21 road in County Kerry. Open March–May and September–November, daily, 10am–6pm; June–August, daily, 10am–7pm. Admission: £3; children, £1.75; under 6 free. Phone: (066) 41244.

For a long time, the locals knew that something big was lurking under here. Yet this cave was only discovered in the early '80s. Today visitors can tour 350 yards of its four kilometers, winding this way and that through colorfully illuminated chambers festooned with stalactites. Along the path, the sound of underground water and many dark entrances leading to mysterious passageways hint at the cave's hidden depths.

Clonakilty

30 miles southwest of Cork City
MODEL RAILWAY VILLAGE

On Inchydoney Road (no number), on the beach just south of town; follow the signs. Open February–June and September–October, Monday–Friday, 11am–5pm, Saturday–Sunday, 1–5pm; July–August, daily, 10am–6pm. Admission: £3; students, £2; children, £1.25. Phone: (023) 33224.

Begun as a project to boost sagging employment in the region, the miniature town shows West Cork as it was in the 1940s. Stroke the dark rooftop of a knee-high factory and wonder whether a miniature God occupies the little cathedral, complete with stained-glass rose window, from which a pair of minuscule newlyweds are emerging. Pastel houses stand surrounded by green lawns, flowerbeds and a working model train, which replicates in miniature the now-extinct West Cork Railway.

Cork

CORK CITY GAOL

On Convent Avenue (no number) off Sunday's Well Road in the Sunday's Well district, north of the River Lee, a half mile west of the city center. Open March–October, daily, 9:30am–6pm (last admission 5pm); November–February, daily, 10am–5pm (last admission 4pm). Admission: £3.50; stu-

dents, £2.50; children, £2.
Phone: (021) 305022.

Slip on a set of headphones to hear prisoners and wardens recounting their stories on tape as you stroll through the corridors. This monumental jail operated between 1824 and 1924; the tour gives insight into social conditions that sparked many a life of crime. In furnished cells, mannequins languish, dawdle, argue, regret the past and even nurse babies against peeling walls while sound effects evoke the listless shuffling of feet and other claustrophobic noises. A film introduces locally famous inmates, putting them in a courtroom scene and letting them tell a judge how they got here.

BLOOMSDAY

Held every year on June 16; celebrations are focused around the James Joyce Museum, located in the Joyce Tower on the beach at Sandycove, just south of Dublin's Dun Loaghaire suburb. For more information, call the James Joyce Cultural Centre at (01) 878 8547 or the museum at (01) 280 9265.

Dedicated readers from all over the world gather each year to celebrate Leopold Bloom's sojourn in this Martello tower where Joyce's Parisian publisher, Sylvia Beach, created a museum in the author's honor. Joyce himself stayed for a while in the tower, and it is from here that the author gives readers a glimpse of the "snotgreen" sea as *Ulysses* opens. Food and drink and yes yes yes yes yes yes yes yes yes yes yes yes yes readings from the daunting but celebrated novel mark the anniversary of Bloom's epiphany.

KILMAINHAM GAOL

Inchicore Road (no number) at South Circular Road, just southwest of Heuston Station, in the Kilmainham district. Open April–September, daily, 9:30am–6pm (last admission 4:45pm); October–March, Monday–Friday, 9:30am–5pm (last admission 4pm), Sunday, 10am–6pm (last admission 4:45pm). Admission: £3; students and children, £1.25. Phone: (01) 453 5984.

First opened for "guests" in 1792, this cavernous and multitiered expanse of bars and guardrails is now one of Europe's largest unoccupied prisons. Before it ceased operation in 1924, many famous Irish rebels were held and even executed here, some of them now hailed as heroes and martyrs. A tour of the jail includes chilling exhibits and an audiovisual presentation that helps put in perspective the country's complex history and the inevitable links between Irish political struggle and prisons.

Kilkenny

DUNMORE CAVE

In Ballyfoyle, 7 miles north of Kilkenny, off the N78 (Castlecomer) road. Open mid-March–mid-June and mid-September–October, daily, 10am–5pm; mid-June–mid-September, daily, 10am–7pm; November–February, Saturday–Sunday, 10am–5pm. Admission: £2; students and children, £1. Phone: (056) 67726 or (056) 51500 or (01) 661 31111, ex. 2386.

Known to travelers as early as the 9th century, these caverns were reportedly the scene of a terrible Viking massacre in the year 928. Today not a Viking is in sight as you follow the tour guide along catwalks to explore a series of million-year-old chambers, their gloppy calcite formations illuminated to effect deep shadows and moody hues. An adjacent visitors' center has exhibits on the hole's history.

Kilkenny

THE SMALL WORLD EXHIBITION

In the Shee Alms House, Rose Inn Street (no number), just west of the River Nore in the town center. Open May–August, daily, 9am–4:30pm; September–April, Monday–Friday, 9am–4:30pm. Admission: free. Phone: (056) 51500.

Squint at the miniaturist as he fashions tiny houses and paints tiny paintings whose rich reds and browns evoke the Old Masters. Changing exhibitions feature postage-stamp still lifes, as well as historic buildings ranging from an ancient Roman merchant's house to an 18th-century manor to a medieval castle.

Killinaboy

35 miles northwest of Limerick

SHEELA-NA-GIG

Over the south door of the ruined church. Visible at all times. Admission: free. For more information, call the Ennis Tourist Information Office at (065) 28366.

The naked female figure carved out of stone and holding her labia open atop a door in this 12th-century monastery is one of many such marvels that once adorned churches and other buildings all over the British Isles. Nobody knows how the tradition began, or what these figures really mean, for their staring eyes and often acrobatically grotesque postures bespeak something other than mere decoration. Some say the sheela-na-gigs are vestiges of goddess worship, or that they depict vanity and lust, or that their fierce attitude is intended to scare away evil forces.

Killorglin

11 miles northwest of Killarney

PUCK FAIR

Held every year on August 10, 11 and 12. The goat platform is in the center of town on The

Square, where Upper Bridge Street meets Langford Street. Admission: free. For more information, call (066) 62366.

A billygoat is crowned, draped in regal purple robes and led to a raised platform, where he is dubbed King Puck for the remainder of the festival and stands chewing calmly while thousands roister in the streets below. Ireland's oldest traditional fair fills the town with music and hilarity as revelers come from near and far to pay mock homage to the goat. Does this hark back to a time when the pagan Irish worshipped a horned god? Many think so, and regard this as one of the most overt pagan holdovers into the Christian era. After three days of busking competitions, bartender races, face-painting, horse-trading and nonstop musical entertainment, the goat is defrocked and sent back out to graze when the festival ends.

Kinvara

15 miles south of Galway

MEDIEVAL BANQUETS

At Dunguaire Castle, on the Clare–Galway Road. Held twice nightly, May–October, 5:45pm and 8:45pm. Admission: £30; children 10–12, £22.75; children 6–9, £15.50; children under 6, free. Phone: (061) 360788.

The plaints of thespians accompany an ersatz medieval repast in a strikingly stark castle perched beside Galway Bay. Drawing on the bardic tradition of nonmedieval Irish literary lights William Butler Yeats, George Bernard Shaw and Oliver St.

John Gogarty (who actually owned the place in the last century and appears as a character in Joyce's *Ulysses*), the actors perform scenes that reveal slices of Celtic life while making you marvel at the number of writers this rainy island has produced. Aside from the setting not much is medieval, but then again, you probably wouldn't want to come within bone-chucking distance of a *real* medieval banquet.

Murrisk

6 miles southwest of Westport

CROAGH PATRICK MOUNTAIN-CLIMBING PILGRIMAGE

Held every year on the last Sunday in July: Murrisk is on the road to Louisburgh in County Mayo; follow the signs from there to Croagh Patrick. For more information, call the Westport Tourist Information Office at (098) 25711.

Croagh Patrick is a softly symmetrical, 2,510-foot peak on whose slopes St. Patrick is said to have spent forty days fasting and praying. From here, he is said to have banished Ireland's snakes. More than 1,500 years later, devotees show their faith throughout the seasons by climbing the peak. The major pilgrimage, held every year on Reek Sunday, draws over 60,000 climbers from far and wide who gather at Murrisk Abbey before dawn carrying flashlights. Many pilgrims raise the stakes by making this one-to-two-hour climb up the rocky trail in their bare feet. Masses are held in the church perched on the windy summit.

12 miles west of Waterford City

SHELL GROTTO

On the grounds of Curraghmore House, off the R680 road between Waterford and Carrick-on-Suir. Open Monday–Friday, by appointment. Admission: £2. Phone: (051) 387102.

Catherine Poer, who was Countess of Tyrone and Waterford County's first countess, collected thousands of shells from all over the world to decorate this grotto on the grounds of her imposing house in 1754. Unlike many of her fellow 18th-century aristocrats who embraced the shell-grotto craze, Catherine designed, built and adorned the grotto herself. Today the walls of the circular chamber are still resplendent, floor to ceiling, with the patterns she envisioned and pressed into place.

6 miles southeast of Ennis

CRAGGAUNOWEN, THE LIVING PAST

6 miles east of Quin, off the Sixmilebridge-Quin road. Open April–October, daily, 9:30am–6pm (last admission, 5pm). Admission: £4.20; students, £3.30; children, £2.60. Phone: (061) 367146 or 367178.

Actors in homespun garb haul wood, tend pots and stoke fires while portraying Bronze Agers who lived here long ago. Reconstructions

on the site include a ring fort, a 4th-century farmhouse and the *crannóg*, a reed-and-wattle dwelling built on a lake to protect it from marauding warriors. Era-appropriate animals such as wild boar snuffle around the grounds. Also here is *Brendan*, the hide-hulled boat in which Irishman Tim Severin replicated the voyage on which St. Brendan may have discovered the New World 1,000 years before Columbus.

6 miles southeast of Ennis

MEDIEVAL BANQUETS

At Knappogue Castle. Held twice nightly, April–October, at 5:30 and 8:45pm. Admission: £32; children 10–12, £24.25; children 6–9, £16.50; children under 6, free. Phone: (061) 360788 or (091) 61788.

Belly up to long wooden tables in a massive 15th-century dining hall as banners flap above and a rather practiced pageantry unfurls. Singers, musicians and storytellers clad in Technicolor gowns punctuate the lengthy meal with elaborate tales of Celtic women both mythical and real. Learn about beloved saints and haughty sovereigns, a female pirate and various strong-willed "sinners" who have made their names among the not-totally-patriarchal Irish.

25 miles east of Cork City

SHELL GROTTO AND MAZE

In the Ballymaloe Cookery School garden; turn off the N25 road at Castlemartyr and follow the signs to Shanagarry. Open April–October, daily, 9:30am–6pm. Admission: £3. Phone: (021) 646785.

Wondering what to do with all the mussel and clam shells her students discarded, this cooking school's proprietor found inspiration in romantic gardens created 200 years ago. In 1995 she commissioned an artist to create a shell grotto and this is the result, though it required even more shells than the cooking school had on hand. Octagonal, with graceful gothic windows, the chamber has walls, ceiling and even window sills completely covered in shells of all types and colors, forming floral designs, bands, checkers and meandering curves. Also in the garden and evoking the past is a yew maze, designed to get lost in.

Strokestown

12 miles west of Longford

FAMINE MUSEUM

In Strokestown Park House off the N5 Dublin-Ballina road, in County Roscommon; museum is housed in buildings in the stable yards. Open April–October, daily, 11am–5:30pm. Admission: £3; children, £1.25. Phone: (078) 33013.

Hunger prevails in this museum where letters, documents and artifacts chart the Great Irish Famine of the 1840s. Exhibits show how the famine affected the wealthy family who once lived in this vast house and how it affected their poorer compatriots across the whole island. Strokestown's landlord at the time attempted to evict his starving tenants; in desperation, they killed him. Parallels are drawn with other famines happening around the world today. Your country might be next.

Tralee

15 miles north of Killarney, on the west coast

KERRY THE KINGDOM

In Ashe Memorial Hall, Denny Street (no number). Open mid-March–July and September–December, daily, 10am–6pm; August, daily, 10am–7pm. Admission: £5.50; students, £4.75; children, £3. Phone: (066) 27777.

Several different attractions on separate floors include Geraldine Tralee, named for the Fitzgerald family which controlled Kerry, Cork and Limerick during the Middle Ages. Visitors ride around in little cars viewing life-size tableaux showing the town as it was in medieval times. Toothy knights in chain-mail wield swords while amputees hobble around on peglegs past merchants and taxidermed chickens. Others bury their faces in their hands, look preoccupied and hurl household waste out of second-story windows. Sound effects and pumped-in odors add to the ambience.

ITALY

Don't miss:

Rome

Rome

BROKEN-POTTERY MOUNTAIN
(Monte Testaccio)

Between the Tiber and the Aventine Hill, just east of Piazza Giustiniani; via de Monte Testaccio circles the mountain (Metro: Pyramide). Visible at any time.

The ancient Romans had their junk heaps, just like anyone. They used massive quantities of amphorae and other clay vessels to transport food on voyages, and when cargoes were unloaded at the nearest port, the emptied vessels were thrown here. Each layer of shattered pots was coated in quicklime to keep down the vermin as the mountain grew higher and higher. They say Monte Testaccio took 600 years to develop, and that it was even higher before the locals started using it as a quarry. Today the peak is a protected archaeological site, but from certain vantage points at street level you can clearly see that the entire mountain is composed of nothing but millions of broken pots. Masses of orange and yellow shards still peek through silt and weeds; modern restaurants, bars and garages around the hill's base are literally tunneled out of history.

Rome

COLUMN OF FLAGELLATION

In the church of Santa Prassede, via Santa Prassede 9/a, off via Merulana near Largo San Alfonso, a few blocks south of Termini station; column is to the left as you enter, off the Chapel of St. Zeno. Open daily, 7am–noon and 4–6:30pm. Phone: 488 2456.

A two-and-a-half-foot column of smooth black-and-white marble is said to be part of the post to which Jesus was tied when his tormentors whipped him. A big mural showing the episode is on the wall of the church's gift shop, with the column prominently featured and instantly recognizable.

GROTESQUE FRESCOES

In the church of Santo Stefano Rotondo, via de S. Stefano 7, on the Caelian Hill just southeast of the Colosseum. Open Tuesday–Saturday, 9am–1pm and 3:30–6pm; Monday, 3:30–6pm.

This unusual church—circular, as its name suggests—dates back to the 4th century. But what made an impression on Charles Dickens when he visited were the dozens of Counter-Reformation frescoes ringing Santo Stefano's sleepily serene interior. Each painting depicts the martyrdom of a different saint. In soft pastel hues, we see one saint being torn apart by wild beasts, another being stoned to death, another strung up and speared. One saint hangs crucified, while various others are being prepared for dismemberment or burning. Tied to a post, one is being whipped to death. And yet another takes one last look at the world before being buried alive.

HOLY MANGER
(Santo Presepio)

In the church of Santa Maria Maggiore, Piazza Santa Maria Maggiore, a few blocks south of Termini Station. Open daily, 7am–7pm.

How many times have you sung "Away in a Manger" and wondered exactly where that manger is today? Uprooted from its original setting amid humble sheep and asses, the bed where Jesus was born is now in Rome, if you believe the faithful. They gather here to venerate the stout wooden planks, enshrined in a sunken niche with a cranky-looking bronze baby Jesus on top.

HOLY STAIRS
(Scala Santa)

Piazza di Porta San Giovanni, diagonally across from the Basilica of San Giovanni Laterano. Open April–September, daily, 6:15am–noon and 3:30–6:45pm; October–March, daily, 6:15–noon and 3–6:15pm. Free, but donations are suggested.

Said to be the original staircase from Pontius Pilate's house and

HOLY STAIRS—ROME

said to be stained with Jesus' actual blood, this steep marble staircase was lugged here in the year 326 from the Holy Land, like so many relics, by Rome's acquisitive St. Helen. Now sheathed in dark wood, with windows cut into it here and there to show the alleged bloodstains, the stairs lure busloads of pilgrims from around the world. A plenary indulgence is granted to those who climb all the way up on their knees on Fridays during Lent. A partial indulgence is granted on all other days if the climber truly repents. Having your photograph taken with one knee on the bottom step and then standing up and walking away does not count.

HOUSE OF THE MONSTERS—ROME

Rome

HOUSE OF THE MONSTERS
(Casa dei Mostri)

 Via Gregoriana 30, just downhill from the top of the Spanish Steps.

Who needs a welcome mat when the door of your home is actually the gaping mouth of a huge stone monster? As if that didn't get the message across, the faces of two more snarling monsters frame a pair of windows, which are of course barred. Standing on a sleepy street flanked by ordinary buildings, the beige house's baroque chiseled façade belies its actual history. As a wealthy artistic family's home for many years, it is known to have been a hub for visiting intellectuals throughout the 17th and 18th centuries.

Rome

JESUS IN A LOINCLOTH

 In the church of Santa Maria Sopra Minerva, via Beato Angelico 35, in the Centro Storico just east of the Pantheon. Open daily, 7am–noon and 4–7pm. Phone: 679 3926.

Michelangelo sculpted a naked and anatomically correct marble Jesus. But even the master himself couldn't get away with it, and church officials ordered that Christ be clothed. A bronze loincloth was mounted over the holy family jewels, where it remains to this day, its shiny folds and stiff metal fringe only serving to spotlight the savior's rather sumptuous thighs. Gripping a tall

JESUS IN A LOINCLOTH, SANTA
MARIA SOPRA MINERVA—ROME

cross, the statue also wears a single
bronze shoe—added because the
kisses of countless pilgrims' pious
lips were eroding Jesus' toes.

MUMMIFIED MONK, CHIESA
IMMACOLATA CONCEZIONE—ROME

Rome

MUMMIFIED MONKS

*In the crypt of the Chiesa Imma-
colata Concezione (aka Santa
Maria della Concezione), via
Veneto 27, at via Cappuccini
(Metro: Barberini); crypt is to
the right of the church's main en-
trance. Open Friday–Wednes-
day, 9am–noon and 3–6pm.
Admission: voluntary donation.
Phone: 48 71 185.*

The scrambled remains of several
thousand Capuchin monks adorn
this complex, with one room dedicated to skulls, another thoroughly
done in pelvises. Covering walls
and ceilings, the bones are arranged
in floral patterns and other shapes,
including an ominous hourglass
and a mock angel made of a skull
with scapulae for wings. Dressed in
the trademark brown Capuchin
habit that gave cappuccino its
name, several mummified monks
recline leisurely amid their brothers' bones, while others stand
around. Assembled between the late
18th and mid-19th centuries, the
crypt's collection also features the
little skeleton of a Barberini
princess, which dangles from the
ceiling clutching a sickle.

MUSEUM OF THE SOULS OF THE DEAD
(Museo delle Anime dei Defunti)

In the Church of Santa Cuore in Suffragio, Lungotevere Prati 12, in a room to the right of the worship area. Open Monday–Friday, 7–10am and 5:30–7:30pm; Saturday–Sunday, 7:30am–noon and 5:30–7:30pm. Admission: free, but donations accepted. Phone: 688 065 17.

Sometimes the dead will do anything just to get attention—even grab their surviving relatives with burning hands. At this tiny museum, a long glass case displays nightgowns, hats, Bibles and other articles bearing charred fingerprints and other markings said to have been made by souls in Purgatory begging the living to pray for them. Collected from all around Europe over hundreds of years, the array includes a man's shirt allegedly singed by his deceased mother. Also here is cash that a dead priest allegedly gave to his surviors in exchange for their conscientious prayers.

MUSEUM OF THE SOULS OF THE DEAD—ROME

NATIONAL PASTA MUSEUM
(Museo Nazionale delle Paste Alimentari)

Piazza Scanderberg 117, a few blocks south of the the Trevi Fountain; enter through vicolo Scanderberg off via della Dataria. Open daily, 9am–8pm. Admission: L 12,000; children, L 8,000. Phone: 699 1109.

Learn more about spaghetti, fettucine, macaroni, rigatoni, canneloni, ravioli, manicotti, lasagna and wagon wheels than you ever could by merely eating them. A curiously pretentious approach to noodles features artworks, utensils, diverse pasta specimens, pasta-making machinery and documents dating back to the 12th century. Photographs of Ingrid Bergman and other notables eating noodles are here, along with details on human digestion. It's all a valiant attempt to persuade you that the Italians invented noodles and didn't merely steal the idea from the Chinese.

PANORAMA THROUGH A KEYHOLE

Piazza dei Cavalieri di Malta 3, at the intersection of via di S. Sabina and via di Porta Lavernale, on the Aventine Hill. Visible at any time.

This parking lot belongs to the Knights of Malta, and is adorned with the brotherhood's cryptic symbols. But who can explain why, when you peek through the keyhole in the huge green door set into a forbidding stone wall, a perfect view of the city crowned by St. Peter's dome unfolds before you? Framed by an avenue of neat greenery in the foreground, the panorama expands, shimmering in the sunlight like an unnerving painting. It looks just too symmetrical and too precise to be an accident. Be prepared to wait your turn at the keyhole, as it's a favorite with Romans and their out-of-town guests.

ST. FRANCIS XAVIER'S ARM

In the Church of the Gesù, Piazza del Gesù, off Corso Vittorio Emanuele II in the Centro Storico east of Piazza Navona. Open daily, 6:30am–12:30pm and 4–7:30pm. Phone: 678 6341.

The church's more famous occupant is St. Ignatius Loyola, founding father of the Jesuits, whose

Rome
Catacombs

Around the outskirts of Rome, hundreds of kilometers of underground passageways crammed with dead bodies line the major imperial roads that lead away from the city. These **catacombs**, as they have come to be known, were the burial places of the earliest Christians, who—like everyone else in ancient Rome—were not allowed to bury their dead inside the city limits. Instead, they started carving tombs out of the soft tufa outside the town walls; as the centuries passed and the number of faithful swelled, the underground cemeteries grew and grew until they became a subterranean metropolis practically as big as Rome itself. Only five separate sections of the many catacombs are open to the public, and the guided tours at each site only take in a tiny fraction of the seemingly endless maze of tunnels and passageways. The catacombs of **San Callisto** contain the burial places of sixteen early popes, and 3rd-century Christian frescoes. The burial places under the church of **San Sebastian** were the first in the world to be called *catacombs*, from the Greek *kata kymbas* ("near the caves"), referring to nearby quarries. The name spread to the other burial complexes, and then to any maze of tunnels. Here you will find frescoes and paintings of peacocks, sheep, fish (an early Christian symbol) and of course bits and pieces of ancient corpses. **Domitilla** has some pagan tombs and frescoes whose iconography was later adopted by the Christians who moved in—there goes the neighborhood. Way across town, the catacombs of **Priscilla** are managed by a group of no-nonsense nuns who lead you past oodles of desiccated bodies and some very early Christian paintings, including what some argue is the world's first depiction of the Virgin Mary. **Sant'Agnese** is the least famous of the catacombs, and consequently the best preserved and least crowded, with more skeletons and bones than you care to count and a general air of hushed mortality.

San Callisto: via Appia Antica 110. Open April–September, Thursday-Tuesday, 8:30am–noon and 2:30–5:30pm; October–January and March, Thursday–Tuesday, 8:30am–noon and 2:30–5pm. Admission: L8,000. Phone: 513 01580, or 51 36 725. Take Metro line A to Colli Albani, then bus 660 to the catacombs.

San Sebastiano: via Appia Antica 136. Open April–September, Monday–Saturday, 8:30am–noon and 2:30–5:30pm; October and December–March, Monday–Saturday, 8:30am–noon and 2:30–5pm. Admission: L8000. Phone: 785 0350, or 788 70 35. Take Metro line A to Colli Albani, then bus 660 to the catacombs.

Domitilla: via delle Sette Chiese 282. Open April–September, Wednesday–Monday, 8:30am–noon and 2:30–5:30pm; October–December and February–March, Wednesday–Monday, 8:30am–noon and 2:30–5pm. Admission: L8000. Phone: 511 0342.

 Priscilla: via Salaria 430. Open April–September, Tuesday–Sunday, 8:30am–noon and 2:30–5:30pm; October–December and February–March, Tuesday–Sunday, 8:30am–noon and 2:30–5pm. Admission: L8000. Phone: 862 06272.

 Sant'Agnese fuori le Mura: via Nomentana 349; enter through the church, on the left nave. Open Tuesday–Sunday 9am–noon and 4–6pm; Monday, 9am–noon. Admission: L8000. Phone: 861 0840.

gold-encrusted house of worship this is. The Basque soldier's remains lie under a shrine whose fixtures could finance a small African nation. But on the right side of the nave, flanked by silver foliage and mounted in a glass reliquary atop a gleaming altar, St. Francis' right arm juts ceilingward. The saint became famous for sailing away and converting more Asians than he had a right to. The lion's share of his body lies far across the sea, but Rome has his wizened arm, which lures its share of pilgrims.

Rome

ST. PHILIP NERI'S MUMMY

 In La Chiesa Nuova (aka Chiesa Santa Maria in Vallicella), on Piazza Chiesa Nuova, a few blocks west of Piazza Navona; the mummy is in a chapel on the left side of the nave, toward the back. Open daily, 8am–noon and 4:30–7pm. Phone: 68 75 289.

Mother-of-pearl disks and coral are inlaid into the dark marble surrounding St. Philip's see-through casket. This gives his chapel an almost Hawaiian feel, which contradicts the Rubens paintings that adorn the church's main altar. Known for aiding the poor and for founding the order headquartered in this church, he lies today behind a glass pane and golden latticework. His face has been covered in silver and surmounted by a metal ring denoting a halo, but his hands remain au naturel. The corpse is over 300 years old, and the hands—note their prominent knuckles—show their age.

ST. THOMAS' FINGER AND OTHER RELICS

 In the church of Santa Croce in Gerusalemme, Piazza di Santa Croce in Gerusalemme, on the Esquiline Hill; entrance to the relics chapel is at the rear and on the left side of the church. Open daily, 8:30am–noon and 3:30–6:30pm. Phone: 70 14 769.

The corridor leading to what is hailed as one of Catholicism's most precious collections of relics sports a big hunk, some five feet long, of what is said to be the cross of the "good thief" who was crucified a stone's throw away from Jesus. The angular chapel houses three chips said to be the largest extant remnants of the True Cross itself. A piece of plank enshrined here is the alleged remains of the original sign reading INRI—a Latin acronym for "Jesus of Nazareth, King of the Jews"—ubiquitously replicated on crucifixes worldwide. Two spikes said to be from the Crown of Thorns are also here, along with an imposing nail whose alleged role in the crucifixion you can easily imagine. Part of the alleged Pillar of Scourging and a rock said to be from the manger in Bethlehem join the other relics in

St. Thomas' finger, Santa Croce in Gerusalemme—Rome

their big glass case amid gold and silver trimmings. The disembodied finger on display is said to be the one with which the dubious St. Thomas prodded Jesus' wounds.

TORRE ARGENTINA CAT SANCTUARY

 Via de Torre Argentina at via Florida; sanctuary is downstairs, at the edge of the ruin. Open daily, 11am–11pm. Admission: free, but donations accepted. Phone: 0348-384 5853.

Hundreds of thousands of abandoned feral cats live among Rome's ancient ruins. They bask atop broken columns all over the city while the occasional kindhearted Roman brings food and water, without which the felines would starve. Founded on an archaeological site in the early '90s, the volunteer-operated sanctuary at Torre Argentina is Rome's only organized cat shelter. Visitors can pet as many kitties as they like; over 300 cats including some really sick ones are housed, fed, nurtured, medicated and sterilized here. City officials frown on the place, whose feline population is continually bolstered by Romans who dump their unwanted pets on its doorstep, sometimes in plastic bags.

TRAFFIC BLESSING
(Benedizione delle Automobili)

Held every year on the morning of March 9, on the traffic circle around the Colosseum. For more information, call the Tourist Information Office at 06/488 991.

Italy has Europe's highest road-accident death rate, and after a few minutes in Rome it's easy to see why. With this in mind, a priest stands in a safe place one morning a year and blesses all the passing vehicles. Nominally, the rite is held in honor of Santa Francesca Romana—a pious medieval aristocrat whose feast day this is—although she never saw a car and, given her penchant for asceticism, would probably rather walk if she had a choice.

WAX MUSEUM
(Museo delle Cere)

Piazza Venezia 67, at Piazza Santi Apostoli. Open daily, 9am–8pm. Admission: L 7,000. Phone: 679 6482.

Inspired by a 1953 visit to Madame Tussaud's, this wax museum filled with chunkily crafted figures lavishes attention on earth-shaking Italians. Enrico Fermi is here, and Dante Alighieri, Guglielmo Marconi, Verdi, Puccini, Garibaldi, Paganini, da Vinci, the Medicis, Nero, a gaggle of cardinals and a room full of friendly Fascists. They take their places alongside Adolf Hitler, Heinrich Himmler, Richard Wagner and "Giuseppe Stalin." Most of the waxworks' heads are tilted to one side, giving these historical figures an air of innocent wonderment.

Near Rome

55 miles north of Rome

THE MYSTERIES OF ST. CRISTINA
(I Misteri di Santa Cristina)

Held every year on July 23–24, on streets running through the center of town. For more information, call the Church of Santa Cristina at 0761/799067.

Cristina was a pious Christian maiden of Bolsena who defied her father. The irate old pagan responded with a series of harsh punishments, but the resilient girl took a long time to die. She was boiled in oil, bitten by venomous snakes, stretched on a Catherine wheel and shot full of arrows, among other things—all of which the town reenacts every year at this festival with costumes, choreography and stage design befitting an opera. A series of elaborate tableaux vivants revisits Cristina's tortures. Not a drop of fake blood is spared as half the punishments are reenacted the first day, the rest on the second.

Bomarzo

20 km northeast of Viterbo

MONSTER PARK
(Parco dei Mostri)

Just northwest of town. Open daily, 8:30am–dusk. Admission: L12,000; students, L8,000. Phone: (0761) 924 029.

Say you're a 16th-century nobleman with a nice piece of property in the lovely Italian countryside. Why not fill the place with monumental stone carvings of hideous monsters, cruel gods and voracious beasts? That's what the brooding Signore Orsini did. At this park, droll Latin sayings are chiseled into the mossy gray stone offsetting dozens of sculptures: freaked-out sculpted elephants; slavering canines; a giant tearing a woman apart. A sculpted leaning house tweaks your equilibrium; and a big bearded staring head nicknamed *l'Orco* (the Ogre) waits with flared nostrils for you to walk right into its gaping jaws.

Nettuno

60 km south of Rome, on the coast

ST. MARIA GORETTI'S MUMMY

In Sanctuario-Basilica Madonna delle Grazie e Santa Maria, at the end of via Amerigo Vespucci, on the waterfront. Open daily, 7am–12:30pm and 3–6:30pm.

Downstairs in the church's stark cement crypt, wearing a frothy dress and clutching what looks like a dime-store rosary, lies the body of a local girl who died in 1902 while guarding her virginity against the knife-wielding boy next door. Popular with pilgrims and prettified with a wax coating, the corpse looks curiously petite— partly because Maria's arm and ribs were removed and given to her mother. Flanking the gift shop upstairs, glass cases contain pictures, personal effects and documents concerning the saint, whose legend is illustrated in lurid cartoon form across one wall.

Tivoli

31 km east of Rome

VILLA D'ESTE

On the southern edge of town; entrance is on Piazza Trento. Open in summer, Tuesday–Sunday, 9am–6:30pm with occasional nighttime illuminated fountain shows; winter, Tuesday–Sunday,

9am–4pm, though officially the park closes one hour before dusk. Admission: L 8,000. Phone: (0774) 312 070.

Hundreds of spigots spurt playful jets in this sprawling garden commissioned in the mid-16th century by Cardinal Ippolito d'Este, Lucrezia Borgia's son. Diverted underground, river water feeds the Passage of 100 Fountains (*Viale delle Cento Fontane*) and the Organ Fountain, where hydraulic power activates actual music. With true Renaissance elegance, other fountains fashioned after birds, dragons and other fanciful figures make sundry noises while leaping and cascading in every direction.

Italian Ghost Towns

The American Wild West does not have exclusive rights to the romantic notion of the ghost town. You can even find ghost towns in the densely populated, urbanized Europe of the 21st century. Of course, one must make a distinction between a ghost town and an archaeological site, especially in Italy. Envision a ghost town as an ancient ruin in the making—a city that has been left derelict, but has not yet totally disintegrated or been swallowed up by the earth. There are no fewer than three ghost towns in the immediate vicinity of Rome, all abandoned about two or three centuries ago because of endemic malaria (don't worry—it's been eradicated in the interim). **Ninfa**, the best-kept of the three, is actually on the grounds of a large country garden, so all the 17th-century buildings, including an impressive square tower, dozens of houses and desolate streets are holding up pretty well. The adjacent stagnant lake—source of the malarial mosquitoes, no doubt—adds the perfect melancholy touch. The garden setting makes Ninfa seem like a folly—but it's *real*. (Ninfa is 55 kilometers southwest of Rome, 15 kilometers northeast of Latina, near the towns of Norma and Sermoneta.) **Galeria** is amazingly close to Rome—the contrast between urban frenzy and the completely desolate alleys of Galeria is striking. Unlike their wooden American counterparts, Italian ghost towns like this one are constructed mostly of stone, so they tend to hold up against the elements and encroaching vegetation much better. (Galeria is 20 kilometers northwest of Rome, just south of road 493, about 1 kilometer west of Santa Maria di Galeria, the town that replaced it. A small road runs out to the ruins from the modern town.) **Monterano** has had a miserable history, beset by mosquitoes and rampaging soldiers until its residents threw in the towel and abandoned the city 200 years ago. Its location in a nature reserve has helped it survive the 20th century. Trees and plants are slowly reclaiming the town—making it all the more picturesque. (Monterano is 50 kilometers northwest of Rome, west of Lago di Bracciano, about 4 kilometers west of the new city of Canale Monterano, which is accessible by train. The walk from the train station to the ghost town, on the north side of the road leading to Tolfa, takes about an hour.)

Viterbo

70 km north of Rome

ST. ROSA'S TOWER PROCESSION
(Macchina di Santa Rosa)

Held every year on September 3, starting at 9pm; the procession route winds for a kilometer

through the town, passing through Piazza Fontana Grande, Piazza del Plebiscito, Corso Italia and Piazza Verdi. For more information, call the tourist office at 30 47 95.

It takes 100 men to lift the 100-foot structure shaped like a graceful church tower and illuminated against the night sky. Dressed in white with crimson cummerbunds and kerchiefs, upholding a centuries-old spiritual

Infioratas in Lazio

The Lazio region around Rome plays host to the world's highest concentration of **infioratas**, religious "flower festivals" that are also celebrated in other parts of Italy and a few other countries. Most *infioratas* are held on the Catholic holiday called Corpus Christi, a Sunday in June that just happens to fall right in the middle of wildflower season (purely coincidental, mind you). Locals fan out into the countryside weeks ahead of time and gather as many flowers as they can. These are brought back and stored in cool cellars, where the petals are plucked off and sorted according to color day and night by dozens of busy hands. Meanwhile, the streets of town are prepared with artistic sketches, often in chalk, surrounded by wooden frames. The night before the Sunday of Corpus Christi, each *infiorata* team—which can add up to half the population of the town—"paints" the pavement with millions of petals. Come morning, the boulevards are alive with vividly colored pictures made entirely of flowers; the floral art show can be as much as thirty feet wide and hundreds of yards long. The designs range from bold and geometric to solemn and religious; some look as if they were taken from a Sunday-school coloring book, while others are subtle and impressionistic. They all meet the same fate: After a suitable pause for civic admiration, beautiful pictures that took weeks to create are obliterated by tromping feet as religious processions grind the petals to a paste.

No one knows when this unusual custom began, but many a scholar sees its origin in pre-Christian seasonal rituals. If you're visiting Italy in June, keep an eye out for these towns, or ask around if any villages nearby are having their own *infioratas*, as there are many more than can be listed here:

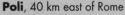

Genzano, 30 km southeast of Rome (the largest and most famous)
Poli, 40 km east of Rome
Montelanico, 70 km southeast of Rome
Genazzano, 48 km east of Rome
Spello, 10 km south of Assisi (not in Lazio, but a good one)

tradition so dangerous that the Church disavows it, the bearers balance the enormous five-ton *macchina* partly on their heads as they carry the tower through the streets of town to honor a saint whose body lies exposed for all to see, anytime of year, in the Santuario di Santa Rosa, just east of Plaza Verdi. Their faith helps them keep the unbelievably heavy tower aloft, they claim. But occasionally gravity wins. If you arrive on any day *but* September 3, you can check out the museum devoted to the festival (*Museo della Macchina di S. Rosa*) at via S. Pellegrino 60 (open Wednesday–Sunday, 10am–1pm and 4–7pm; free), which has plenty of photos of the procession.

with Alba's annual truffle fair, celebrating this region's fungal jewel.

Bologna

C. TARUFFI MUSEUM OF PATHOLOGICAL ANATOMY AND HISTOLOGY
(Museo di Anatomia e Istologia Patologica <<C. Taruffi>>)

 9 via Massarenti, east of the center at the intersection of Viale G. Ercolani, on the campus of Ospedale Sant'Orsola, on the first floor of Building 18, called the Instituto Anatomia Patologica. If you enter the campus from via Massarenti, go straight until you pass the snack

The North

Alba

60 km southeast of Turin

DONKEY PALIO
(Palio degli Asini)

 Held every year on the first Sunday in October. Phone: 535 181 or 535 901 (tourist office).

Parodying the pomp and circumstance of Siena's famous palio and all its pretentious imitators, this race pits not horse against horse but donkey against donkey. Looming grotesquely large atop their mounts, the riders wear colorful retro costumes with muttonchop sleeves and Renaissance-specific tights. They wield the reins with skill amid a cheering carnival crowd. The race coincides

C. TARUFFI MUSEUM OF PATHOLOGICAL ANATOMY AND HISTOLOGY—BOLOGNA

bar, then turn left and look for
Building 18; if you get lost on
the campus, ask for directions
to the Museo Taruffi. Open
Monday–Friday, 9am–4pm; Saturday, 9am–1pm. Admission:
free. Phone: 391 540.

This is definitely *not* for children.
An astounding collection of
anatomical freaks, assembled by 19th-
century professor Cesare Taruffi, lines
the walls of a room inside a medical
research center. Bodies and organs
preserved in formaldehyde share the
shelves with skeletons and wax models of human deformities beyond your
worst nightmares. Twins with two
heads and one body; two bodies and
one head; two heads, two arms, and
three legs; and the preserved, dried
flesh and skeleton of a baby born
with two half-bodies and *no head*.
Brace yourself for models of
supernumerary breasts and syphilitic
lesions. Others depict cyclopic
babies with one central eye, and a
baby apparently born without bones
that looks like a puddle of pancake
batter. Still others replicate babies
born without brains, and an open-
chested man whose organs were all
backwards. Real body parts include
six-fingered hands and six-toed feet,
spinal columns twisted into impossible shapes, gangrenous extremities

C. TARUFFI MUSEUM OF
PATHOLOGICAL ANATOMY AND
HISTOLOGY—BOLOGNA

and an ovarian cyst two feet across.
The "babies in formaldehyde" section features malformed corpses
sliced in half vertically to reveal their
misshapen organs, as well as more
Siamese twins, cyclopeans and
acephalic fetuses. It's horrifying,
dumbfounding, mesmerizing.

Bologna

MUSEUM OF COMPARATIVE ANATOMY

*Via Selmi 3 on the university
campus; second floor; follow the
signs. Open Monday–Friday,
9am–1pm. Admission: free.
Phone: 35 42 43.*

The intestines of a dromedary are
much larger than you want to
imagine, and the intestines of a
rhino are even larger. Various
anuses and colons, hippopotamus
skeletons and monkeys' heads are
among hundreds of inflated organs
and other body parts in a collection
begun during the early 19th century
and meant to record the marvels
of diversity. A platypus skeleton
looks like a junior high school art
project. A narwhal skeleton looks
like the work of the same artist several years later. Human fetuses are
hardly exempt, their fragile skulls
wide-eyed behind glass.

RELICS OF ST. DOMINIC AND OTHERS

 In the Basilica of San Domenico, Piazza San Domenico 13, via Garibaldi, in the southern part of the town center. Open Tuesday–Saturday, 7am–1pm and 2–7pm; Sunday–Monday, 2–7pm. Phone: 051 640 04 11.

A big X-ray showing the comfortable jumble of St. Dominic's bones hangs on the wall beside his tomb—a vast white affair sculpted by famous men. The saint's skull stares out of a golden reliquary visible through a window in the tomb. Another lure here is a waxwork replicating the mercenary-turned-monk, Blessed James of Ulm. Lying in a glass casket at the rear of the church, not far from the urn holding James' actual relics, the waxwork sports dark eyebrows and resembles someone's favorite uncle who has, unfortunately, just died. Meanwhile, in a wall niche just to the waxwork's left, what looks like the shipshape mummified top half of a man cradles a crucifix. In fact, this figure with its head at a pensive angle is the mortal remains of a noted Dominican theologian, deftly coated in papier-mâché.

ST. CATHERINE'S MUMMY

 In Chiesa della Santa (aka Corpus Domini, aka Museo della Santa), via Tagliapietre 19, in the southern part of the historic town center. Open daily, 10am–noon and 4–6pm (these are the chapel's hours; note that the church itself has longer hours). Phone: 051 331 277.

Ring a buzzer to the left of the nave and the doors will open to a chapel where the body of Bologna's own St. Catherine sits upright in a brilliant golden chair. Surrounded by a dazzling assemblage of trompe l'oeil paintings and rococo statuary befitting an expensive hair salon, the saint (not to be confused with Italy's numerous other Catherines) holds a Bible in her lap and wears an enormous cross. The body has turned very dark, giving Catherine's face a featureless quality under the bright lights. In life a 15th-century ducal maid of honor who became a nun and then an abbess,

PAPIER-MACHE THEOLOGIAN'S BUST, ST. DOMINIC'S CATHEDRAL— BOLOGNA

colleagues over nine years to make. Real bones are embedded in wax ligaments, tendons, muscles, organs and tissues to create full-size male and female faux cadavers. They stand erect, posing with arms aloft like flayed mannequins, gazing soulfully from lolling eyeballs. One hefts a sickle, another leans sportily on a post. Also here and mounted on plaques are a waxen anus, waxen legs with dangling veins, a foot-long waxen eye, a giant brain, a waxen tongue and more. A partly dissected wax cadaver wearing pearls lies prone, its cut-open belly revealing a fetus.

WAX MUSEUM OF ANATOMY—
BOLOGNA

the saint was good at calligraphy but claimed to be tormented by visions of the devil.

Bologna

WAX MUSEUM OF ANATOMY

 Via Irnerio 48, upstairs on the "first" floor. Open Monday-Friday, 9am–1pm. Admission: free. Phone: 24 44 67.

A floor-to-ceiling avenue of skulls marks the entrance to this collection of waxworks replicating the dead with virtuosic skill. Funded by Pope Benedetto XIV to aid medical research, the waxworks took 18th-century master Ercole Lelli and his

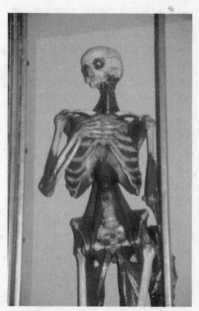

WAX MUSEUM OF ANATOMY—
BOLOGNA

Brescia

80 km east of Milan

ST. ANGELA MERICI'S MUMMY

In the Casa Sant' Angela, via Crispi 23, off via Spalto San Marco, southeast of the center. Open Tuesday–Saturday, 9am–noon and 3–6pm, but it is necessary to call the nuns first and make an appointment. Phone: 295 675.

Light brown and smooth, the mummified face of this nun, who was born right nearby and died in 1540, looks as small as a child's. Dressed in white, she lies armed with a book detailing the Ursuline order which she founded here after a pilgrimage to the Middle East and which brough Angela enduring fame as an educator of young women. Her glass casket is surmounted by trompe l'oeil art.

Capriate San Gervasio

Midway between Milan and Bergamo on the A4 motorway

FANTASY WORLD/MINITALIA

Via V. Veneto 52. Open March, daily, 9:30am–6:30pm; April–July and September–October, daily, 9:30am–7:30pm; August, daily, 9:30am–10:30pm. Admission: L 20,000; children, L 18,000. Phone: 02 90 90 169 or 02 909 13 41.

A miniature Italy—complete with Leaning Tower, a convincing Colosseum, ruined temples and other faithfully reproduced landmarks—occupies a boot-shaped artificial island in a lake in the midst of this amusement park. Ride a monorail around the lake, or for a closer view of the miniatures you can stride up and down the island's paths past waist-high basilicas and volcanoes, all immaculately detailed. Teeny toy people stand around in pee-wee piazzas, while tiny gondolas float in the lake.

Ciliverghe

10 km east of Brescia

MUSEUM OF THE WOMAN AND THE CHILD
(Museo della Donna e del Bambino)

In the Villa Mazzucchelli, via Mazzucchelli 2. Open September–July, Saturday–Sunday, 9am–noon and 3–6:30pm. Admission: L 8,000; children under 10 and seniors, L 4,000. Phone: 030/212 0975.

Those curious creatures called women, and the howling objects to which they give birth, become museum fodder here. Each of twelve rooms is dedicated to a different aspect of femalia. Purses fill one room, bridal gowns fill another. Bedsheets and other household linens fill a third. Other rooms house buttons, hats and—as if you couldn't guess—priests' vestments sewn by women. Pictures of females from around the world augment the collection, which includes enough underwear to intrigue the most closeted fetishist.

Collodi

North of Pescia, between Florence and Lucca

PINOCCHIO PARK
(Parco di Pinocchio)

 Via San Gennaro 3. Open daily, 8:30am–dusk. Admission: L 11,000; students and children, L 6,000. Phone: 0572/42 93 42.

The adventurous tale of the malcontent puppet was a book before it was a movie. Its author called himself "Carlo Collodi" after his hometown. What better place for a park filled with modernistic metal sculptures and mosaics dedicated to this saga of perfidy, backstabbing, and rigid protuberances that suddenly grow larger? The artworks revisit characters and scenes from the book: Pallbearers, pirates, snails and snakes, and a huge whale whose open mouth invites visitors to walk right inside.

Dozza

Southeast of Bologna, just west of Imola

PAINTED WALLS
(Muri Dipinti)

 For more information, call the Bologna Tourist Information Office at (051) 218 459.

Not folk art but fine art covers the walls of this fortified village. A biannual festival inspires talented residents to take up brushes and colors and paint museum-quality pictures across the outsides of their homes. Portraits, pastoral scenes, trompe l'oeil and even expressionistic pieces are designed to evoke disturbing feelings—a walk through the streets any time of year reveals a diverse array.

Florence

"LA SPECOLA" ZOOLOGICAL MUSEUM

 Via Romana 17, south of the Arno, just southwest of the Pitti Palace. Open Thursday–Tuesday, 9am–1pm (anatomy room has shorter hours; call for current schedule). Admission: L 6,000; students and children, L 3,000. Phone: (055) 228 82 51.

Opened in 1775, this is Europe's oldest science museum, lodged in the observatory (*la specola*) of a palace once owned by a grand duke. Along with thousands of animal specimens is a huge collection of realistic anatomical waxworks. Vintage waxen cadavers lie on satin pillows in elegant glass cases, while others stand erect showing off their veins. Waxen organs and other body parts are mounted artfully. But the real masterpieces are tableaux evoking the plague, syphilis and other pathways to eternity.

PRATOLINO SCULPTURE GARDEN

At Villa Demidoff, via Bolognese, just north of Florence. Open April–September, Thursday–Sunday, 10am–8pm; March, Sunday, 10am–6pm; October, Sunday, 10am–7pm. Admission: L 5,000; students and children, L 3,000; under 6 free. Phone: 055/409 427.

Acquired by Francesco de' Medici in 1568, this property was soon surrounded with artficial grottoes, amusing sculptures and trick fountains. Later abandoned, it fell to ruin but was finally restored over the last two centuries. Today visitors can once again wander its wooded pathways, contemplating the foppish fantasies that spawned a place like this. Cupid's Grotto was built in 1577, while a series of oblong shrimp ponds yielded many a meal for the aristocrats. Towering above the rest is Appenino, a colossal mountain of a man carved out of a natural rock outcropping.

18 km south of Assisi

QUINTANA TOURNAMENT
(*Giostra della Quintana*)

Main contest is held the second Sunday in September; return contest the third Sunday in September; both take place in the town stadium, three blocks from the train station, just outside the old town walls. Phone: (0742) 354 459 (Tourist Office).

Wearing tight trousers and puffy sleeves, ten knights on horseback representing the town's ten districts gallop at top speed with lances aloft, attempting to seize a set of increasingly smaller hoops. Meanwhile the crowd roars. It began with a 17th-century tournament in which knights proved allegiance to their ladies and lieges. On the eve of the contest, a procession of 600 people in Renaissance costume makes its way through the streets, and a week after, the horsemen come back for more.

27 km northeast of Brescia, on the western shore of Lake Garda

IL VITTORIALE

On the hillside overlooking the lake. Open October–March, Monday–Friday, 9am–noon and 2–5:30pm, Saturday–Sunday, 9am–noon and 2–6pm; April–September, daily, 8:30am–8pm. Admission: to the house only, L 8,000; to the house and museum, L 16,000. Phone: (0365) 20130 or 20581.

Apparently plunging down the forested slope, a big Italian warship gleams against lush foliage. Poet and WWI hero Gabriele D'Annunzio created a twenty-two-acre complex in which his home, a villa crammed claustrophobically full of exotica, stands surrounded by a Pompeii-inspired amphitheater, gardens and the huge *Puglia*. The Italian Royal Navy gave him the ship in 1925 and D'Annunzio embedded it in the hill with its prow pointing lakeward. Art deco fittings, statuary, marble columns, chinoiserie and over 3,000 books crowd the house. On the grounds are the poet's own mausoleum and the funerary urns of his luckless wartime chums. Also here is the little airplane in which he flew over Vienna in 1918, showering the city with propaganda.

Genoa

THE HOLY GRAIL
(Il Sacro Catino)

In the Treasury of the Cathedral San Lorenzo, on Piazza San Lorenzo, off via San Lorenzo, just west of Piazza G. Matteotti. Open Tuesday–Sunday, 9:30–11:45am and 3–5:45pm. Admission: L 8000; students and children, L 6000 Phone: 010/296 695.

Whoops—here it is again! That darn Holy Grail keeps popping up everywhere—even if you aren't looking for it. Never mind those competing grails in Vienna and Valencia (which see); as far as the Genovese are concerned, this one's the real deal. This *Sacro Catino* (Holy Bowl)—the sort of greenish glass goblet you might win in the dime-toss game at a carnival midway—was allegedly used by Jesus at the Last Supper. As to the other rumor that it holds the secret to mankind's salvation, we offer no guarantees.

Gignese

Between Lake Maggiore and Lake Orta

MUSEUM OF UMBRELLAS AND PARASOLS
(Museo dell' Ombrello e del Parasole)

Viale Golf Panorama 2 bis. Open April–September, Tuesday–Sunday, 10am–noon and 3–6pm. Admission: L 2,500; students and children, L 1,000. 0323/208 064.

Whether made to shield their owners from the sun or the rain, Italy's "little shadows" have done their job dutifully, as this museum attests. The only collection of its kind, it follows umbrella history and technology through the centuries, focusing on locally made varieties. These range from ladylike, fringed, silken specimens to slim black umbrellas that would make a mafia don proud.

Gubbio

35 km northeast of Perugia

"CERI" RACE
(Corsa dei Ceri)

Held every year on May 15; race begins in the Old Town, continues up Mt. Ingino and finishes at the basilica. Call the tourist office at 922 06 93 for more information.

Weighing about 800 pounds each, the *ceri* are three wooden towers topped with images of St. George, St. Anthony and the town's patron, St. Ubaldo. It's his death on May 16 that this event commemorates. Teams of youths in color-coordinated outfits shoulder the towers and dash through the town, only to face the grueling climb uphill. A cheering mob follows in hot pursuit.

Ivrea

50 km northeast of Turin

BATTLE OF THE ORANGES
(Battaglia delle Arance)

Held every year on the Thursday before Shrove Tuesday (Carnival). Phone: (012) 541 0215 (cultural affairs office).

Back in the hoary mists of time, a medieval tyrant tried to exercise his first-night rights with a local miller's daughter, who ended up dead. This event, with its feudalism-is-evil permutations, acquired a special cachet during the French Revolution and thus has been the focus of Ivrea's carnival for over 200 years. Mock power struggles mark the festivities, and a girl portraying the miller's daughter glides through town on a float. Then groups representing feudal militias and local districts fight it out using juicy oranges, pelting each other mercilessly while dressed in vivid costumes. Some wear helmets to deflect the fruit.

Lucca

ST. ZITA'S MUMMY

In the Church of San Frediano, Piazza San Frediano, off via Fillungo in the northern part of the walled city; mummy is in a chapel to the right, past the gift shop, as you enter the main door. Open Monday–Friday, 7:30am–noon and 3–6pm; Saturday–Sunday, 9am–1pm and 3–6pm.

Although it's in a rather advanced state of decay, the exposed corpse of Lucca's own St. Zita is hailed as "incorrupt." Shriveled and crumbling, yet garlanded with flowers, the 600-year-old corpse lies fully dressed in a glass case, surrounded by big paintings illustrating the humble saint's charitable activities. A pious woman who worked as a rich family's servant, Zita was—as the paintings show—always incredibly generous to the poor, even if it meant swiping food from her bosses.

Mantua (Mantova)

37 kilometers south of Verona

APARTMENT OF THE DWARVES

In the Ducal Palace (Palazzo Ducale), Piazza Sordello, at the northern end of the Old Town, next to the waterfront. Open Tuesday–Saturday, 9am–2pm and 2:30–6pm; Sunday–Monday, 9am–2pm. Admission: L 12,000. Phone: 0376-320 283.

No Renaissance court was complete without a contingent of

dwarves to amuse the lords and ladies. Usually employed as jesters and servants, these dwarves are not to be pitied too much; they often lived in splendor in the palaces of their employers. The most remarkable artifact of this social custom is Mantua's Apartment of the Dwarves in the Palazzo Ducale. The Gonzaga family built a cluster of rooms as living quarters for their beloved dwarves, taking care to make everything as comfortable as possible for them. The rooms were small with low ceilings and shrunken furniture, which is now mostly gone. But the rooms, perhaps the smallest living quarters ever built for adults, are still on display.

The game was to be played with living chessmen on a giant chessboard in front of Dad's castle. Marostica has been reenacting the contest ever since. Hundreds of performers in early Renaissance costumes cavort for three days straight, as the town fills with jugglers, soldiers, slaves, knights, clowns and the ubiquitous fire-eaters. At night everyone assembles for the game, which even has cavaliers on real horses playing the knights. There's not much tension—everyone knows who's going to win, and most of the onlookers don't even know how to play chess. But the spectacle is one of the most historically accurate anywhere.

Marostica

28 km north of Vicenza

LIVING CHESS GAME
(Partita a Scacchi a Personaggi Viventi)

On the square in front of the castle. The match takes place during even-numbered years (2000, 2002, etc.) on the second Friday, Saturday and Sunday in September; preliminary pageantry lasts all day, and the game starts around 9pm. Tickets for seats of varying quality must be reserved in advance through the tourist office; call 0424 72127, or 0424 470995.

In 1454, two knights were dueling for the hand of a lady when the lady's father stopped them, unwilling to see such virile young manhood go to waste. He proposed, instead, a game of chess, with his daughter as a prize for the winner.

Milan (Milano)

MUSEUM OF CRIMINOLOGY AND ANCIENT WEAPONS
(Museo della Criminologia e Armi Antiche)

Via Carducci 41, at Via San Vittore, west of the Duomo (Metro: S. Ambrogio). Open Monday–Friday, 10am–1pm and 3–7:30pm; Saturday, 10:30am–1pm and 3–7:30pm; Sunday, 10am–1pm and 3–7pm. Admisson: L 15,000. Phone: 02-805 35 05.

Medieval towers make a perfect setting for this collection of weapons, armor and over 100 gruesome torture implements. Explanatory text is printed in English to help you fully understand the meaning and purpose of these blades, chains, spikes and rods, dating back to the days when the term "cruel and unusual punishment" was taken literally.

Montefalco

30 km south of Assisi

ST. CHIARA'S MUMMY AND HEART

In the Chiesa Santa Chiara on via Cavour, just outside the town walls; follow the signs. Open in summer, daily, 9am–noon and 1:30–6pm; winter, 9am–noon and 1:30–5pm. Phone: 0742/379 123.

Chiara was a Montefalco-born nun who devoted herself to energetically contemplating the crucifixion. Near death in 1308, she is said to have announced to companions that Jesus' agony was "imprinted on my heart." Later extracted from her corpse, Chiara's heart attracted widespread attention as it allegedly bore the imprinted shapes of a scourge, a spear and Jesus on the cross. Today the saint's time-darkened but delicately featured body, wearing a habit, lies in an ornate glass shrine, a gold ring shining on one sinewy finger. Ring the bell and ask a nun to unlock the little hatch behind which rests the extracted heart. It looks like a bit of sponge; its famous markings have not withstood the years.

Padua (Padova)

ST. ANTHONY'S TONGUE, JAW AND VOCAL CORDS

In the Basilica di San Antonio, Piazza del Santo. Church open in summer, daily, 6:30am–7:45pm; winter, daily, 6:30am–7pm;

relics chapel open 7am–1pm and 2:30–6pm. Phone: 049/878 97 22.

Snapshots of wrecked cars and the smiling survivors of auto accidents are attached to the tomb of St. Anthony. Pilgrims line up to stroke the marble that conceals the saint's bones while his tongue, jaw and vocal cords are on display in a separate chapel. The jaw rests in a head-shaped glass contraption crowned with jewels. The vocal cords, venerated along with these other bits because of Anthony's famous eloquence, are a spongy brown mass residing in a crystal ball resting on golden flames. In another reliquary the tongue, hailed as "incorrupt," is still surprisingly pulpy for a 700-year-old muscle.

Peschiera

On the southern shore of Lake Garda, 42 km east of Brescia

GARDALAND

The park is 2 kilometers northeast of Peschiera; free shuttle buses run back and forth between Peschiera's train station and the park. Open April–June, 9:30am–6:30pm; July–mid-September, 9am–midnight. Admission: L 35,000; children under 10 but more than 1 meter tall, L 31,000; children under 1 meter tall, free. Phone: 045/644 9777.

Flee a bacteriological crisis the best way possible: by riding straight down a 120-foot vertical tower at top speed. Besides this ride with its curiously horrifying theme, other attractions at this amusement park replicate dense jungles, outer space, erupting volcanoes and the most terrifying threat of all: Colorado. Out of the sand arise impressive simulated Buddhist temples, a hieroglyphics-riddled replica of Abu Simbel, an Aladdinish souk and Elf Village. Medieval jousts and a pirate ship further juggle time and space.

BATTLE OF THE BRIDGE
(Gioco del Ponte)

Held every year on the last Sunday in June starting around 4pm, on the Ponte de Mezzo. For more information, call the Pisa tourist office at 56 04 64, or 422 91.

Fierce rivalries used to sizzle between Pisa's Mezzogiorno neighborhood south of the Arno River and the Tramontana district to its north. In 1568 an annual ritual was instituted so that citizens from both sides could act out the old hostilities. Despite many interruptions and rules changes (*Gioco*s of yore were often fatal to participants), the brutal ritual continues to this day. *Gioco* means "game," but the reverse tug-of-war staged every year on the bridge leaves team members bruised, their bright 16th-century costumes much the worse for wear. Preceding the game, which begins at dusk, townspeople parade in period costumes through the streets of town.

Prato

17 km northwest of Florence

ST. CATHERINE DE' RICCI'S MUMMY

In the Basilica of St. Vincent Ferrer and Catherine dei Ricci, off via D. Mazzamuti, at the western edge of the old city. Open variable hours. For more information and current schedule, call the Tourist Information Office at 0574-2 41 12.

Clad in a black habit and silver slippers, her face the soft black of neglected bananas, Catherine's corpse lies in a glass casket near the high altar. Centuries ago she ditched her wealthy girlhood to become a nun, at which point began a series of visions now duplicated in sculptures mounted around the church walls. In one, the saint kisses Jesus' hand as he hangs on the cross. In another, Jesus gives her a betrothal ring: The statue is underlined with the caption, "*Amore perfetto*"—"perfect love."

Siena

PALIO OF SIENA

In the Piazza del Campo, in the center of town. The races take place every year on July 2 and August 16, theoretically beginning around 7pm. Phone: 280 551 (tourist office).

Every year, ten out of Siena's seventeen neighborhoods (*contrade*) are chosen by lot to compete in a bareback horse race three times around the town's main piazza. Now Italy's most famous festival, this is in fact an ancient religious ritual rife with primitive customs and rules often described as "barbarian." The neighborhoods—each identified by a mascot such as Caterpillar, Unicorn or Porcupine—stage pre-race strategy sessions and festivities, each attempting to outwit and sabotage the others. The *palio* is not the race itself but the trophy: a banner depicting the Virgin Mary. It is drawn in a cart pulled by pure white oxen in the spectacular Renaissance procession that precedes the competition. Shortly before the race each horse is blessed in church, where it is hoped the beast will defecate. As a cannon shot signals the start, jockeys are equipped with three-foot dessicated bull penises with which they frequently whip their opponents. Cheating before and during the race is encouraged, as the jockeys pull every kind of trick to come out on top. In fact, the winning horse often crosses the finish line unencumbered by a jockey, most of whom are unseated by a sharp turn or a penis in the face. Be forewarned that Siennese hotels are booked up a year in advance for Palio days, and even standing room is scarce.

 winter, daily, 9am–7pm; 30-minute castle tours depart regularly. Admission: L 5,000; students and children, L 3,000. Phone: 011/6699372.

The recorded sounds of hoofbeats, birdsong and Gregorian chant accompany the tour guide's voice in the fortress/castle's kitchen, dungeon, courtyard, chapel and corriddors, all painted with heraldic images. The armory is stocked with swords and helmets; dead animals hang skewered in the pantry; the tiled roofs of a cobblestoned village appear through the windows, and it's all so medieval—except that it's not. It's a fake. The castle and its surrounding village were created a hundred years ago for an exhibition, when a team of Piedmontese artists and intellectuals replicated the best of 15th-century Italian architecture to create this persuasive impostor.

Turin (Torino)

MEDIEVAL VILLAGE AND FORTRESS
(Borgo e Rocca Medioevale)

In Parco del Valentino, viale Virgilio, on the waterfront. Fortress/castle open Tuesday–Sunday, 9am–7 pm; village open in summer, daily, 9am–8pm;

Turin (Torino)

MUSEUM OF PIETRO MICCA AND THE SIEGE OF 1706
(Museo Pietro Micca e dell'Assedio di Torino del 1706)

Via Guicciardini 7a, near the Porta Susa train station west of the center. Open Tuesday–Sunday, 9am–7pm. Admission: L 5,000; students and children, L 3,000. Phone: 54 63 17.

Turin has been the coveted prize in many political tugs-of-war throughout the centuries. But the suicidal ingenuity of an 18th century Piedmontese soldier thwarted Louis XIV's plans. When the king's army

Medieval Village and Fortress— Turin

besieged Turin in 1706, brave Pietro Micca ignited gunpowder to keep the marauders from invading via the city's system of underground tunnels. Micca died in the explosion, and the resigned but determined look on his mustachioed face as he swings the flaming torch is captured in the museum's paintings and sculpture. Tour the tiered underground passageways, which are still intact, and examine scale models and souvenirs recalling the siege.

Turin (Torino)

SHROUD OF TURIN REPLICA
(La Sacra Sindone)

In the Cathedral (Duomo San Giovanni) on Piazza San Giovanni, off Via XX Settembre; the

Chapel of the Holy Shroud, connected to the cathedral, is closed for repairs at the time of this writing (a replica of the Shroud is on display in the cathedral's left aisle). Opening hours to be determined after repair work is completed. Admission: free. Call the tourist office at 535 181 or 535 901 for updates on opening times.

The world's most famous relic almost became the world's most famous pile of ashes after a fire gutted its chapel in 1997. Rarely taken from its casket for public display even in the best of times, the Holy Shroud has been hidden away while restoration work is in progress. Never mind that carbon dating determined the Shroud was about 1,400 years too young to be the real burial cloth of Jesus. Its image of a bearded corpse—an ancient "photograph" on cloth that still baffles scientists—is proof enough for the faithful. A decent replica is exhibited in the church today.

Vergemoli

30 km north of Lucca, southwest of Gallicano

WIND CAVE
(Grotta del Vento)

From Lucca, head north on the SS12 and then the SS445 to Barga, then turn left and take the dead-end access road that goes through Gallicano and ends up at the entrance to the caves. Open April–September, daily, with one-, two- and three-hour tours available throughout the

day; October–March, one-hour tours only are given on weekdays with a full schedule on Sundays; call for current tour schedule. Admission: one-hour tours, L 10,000; children, L 8,000; two-hour tours, L 18,000; children, L 15,000; three-hour tours: L 25,000; children, L 20,000. Phone: 058 372 2024.

Underground rivers, waterfalls and lakes make dappled reflections in a sprawling subterranean space. The longer tours take a decidedly vertical approach on ladders up and down the walls of the abyss, past translucent formations that look like giant shower curtains. Tunnels, stalactites, pinnacles and chambers make this a very diverse cave, where the temperature is always 53 degrees and the humidity is always nearly 100 percent. Don't miss the Lake of Crystals and the Chamber of Voices.

The Pyramids of Zone easily rank as one of Europe's most bizarre geological curiosities, so seemingly impossible that you can scarcely believe they occur naturally. The needle-like towers of crumbling soil shoot straight up as high as 100 feet. When you notice that each tower has an absurdly huge boulder balanced precariously on top, you can only wonder how it got there. The scientific answer: The boulders have *always* been there. The soil around Zone is a muddy natural cement that erodes easily when directly exposed to water, yet which remains quite strong when dry. The boulders were all once at ground level, but decades of rain eroded away all the soil *except* for the thin columns directly underneath the stones, each of which kept the ground beneath it dry. The end result is a thin pillar of dirt with a massive, heavy rock at the very tip. Locals call the pyramids "Stone Witches": At dusk, in silhouette, the boulders look like heads, the columns like bodies.

Zone

40 km north of Brescia, on the eastern side of Lago d'Iseo

THE PYRAMIDS OF ZONE
(Piramidi d'Erosione)

The pyramids are in the valley below the town, along the road coming from Marone (which is 8 kilometers to the southwest on the lake): Infrequent buses run from Marone past the pyramids to Zone; be prepared to hike. Visible during daylight hours. Admission: free. Phone: 987 0913 (Natural Reserve of the Pyramids of Zone office).

The South

Messina

On the eastern tip of Sicily

FATA MORGANA MIRAGE

Visible across the strait of Messina on hot afternoons.

By definition, mirages are elusive phenomena. Yet here's a remarkably reliable one which occurs so regularly that no one need ever die without the quasi-mystical experience of having seen at least a single mirage. Look across the strait toward the mainland's Calabrian coast—it helps to stand on a promontory, or better yet in a boat off the Sicilian shore. The hotter the day, the better. Prepare yourself for the spectacle of a glittering city suspended in the sky. When the 11th-century Norman invaders saw the supernatural vision for the first time, they named it after the magical Celtic fairy Morgan-le-Fay, which explains how an Arthurian name made it to Sicily. Scientists will tell you the mirage is caused by thermal inversions and so on—but where's the romance in that?

Naples

THE LIQUEFACTION OF SAN GENNARO'S BLOOD

Every year on September 19 and the Saturday preceding the first Sunday in May; in the cathedral (Duomo), off via del Duomo in the northeastern part of the city center; crowds begin arriving around 7am. Phone: 449 097

When the city's patron saint was decapitated on September 19 in the year 305, someone had the foresight to scoop up some of his blood. Long since dried to a chunky powder and now stored in vials, the blood is said to have suddenly liquefied in 1389 on the anniversary of Gennaro's death. It is said to have happened again on the anniversary of the day his relics were brought to Naples. Now every year, the vials are brought out from their safe and held aloft while excited crowds clamor in the church awaiting a miracle. The chunks go liquid and Naples goes wild. Scientists have identified hemoglobin in the vials, but suggest that certain solids simply transmute when shaken. No one gives a hoot. On the few years when the rite has been held and the blood failed to liquefy, volcanic eruptions and epidemics befell the city.

Palermo

CAPUCHIN CATACOMBS
(*Catacombe dei Cappuccini*)

In the Convento dei Cappuccini, on via Cappuccino near Piazza Independenza, west of the center. Open daily, 9am–noon and 3–5pm. Admission: voluntary donation. Phone: 21 21 17.

Over 8,000 corpses are all dressed up with nowhere to go. For several hundred years until the late 19th century, Capuchin monks industriously preserved and stored the dead here in a huge macabre network of niches and caverns. Today the results range from sartorially splendid skeletons to mummies in various stages of decomposition. Examine their sunken eyes and contorted limbs, their trousers and hair ornaments. The Capuchins were fastidious about who was who and how to organize them: bodies are segregated by gender, age and profession. Children have their own post-mortem kindergarten, and all the lawyers stick together even in death.

LUXEM-BOURG

Don't miss:

★★★★ Echternach:
The Hopping
Procession of
St. Willibrord   232

THE HOPPING PROCESSION OF ST. WILLIBRORD

Held every year on the Tuesday following Whitsunday, in late May or early June; begins at 9am on the bridge over the River Sûre and ends at the Basilica. For more information, call 72 02 30.

To honor the Anglo-Saxon saint who died here in 739, thousands converge on this town and hop rhythmically down the weathered pavement. Holding white hankies, the dancers jump five steps forward, three steps back as marching musicians play a haunting tune over and over. The first recorded procession was in 1604; some say it has pagan roots and dates back at least to Willibrord's time if not earlier.

Grevenmacher

25 km northeast of Luxembourg City, on the Moselle River

BUTTERFLY GARDEN
(Jardin des Papillons)

On the Route du Vin, northeast of the center. Open April–mid-October, daily, 9:30am–5:30pm. Admission: 180 LF. Phone: 75 85 39/7 55 45.

Exotic species flutter around sampling tropical flowers in a hothouse that's hot and humid, just the way butterflies like it. A hatchery reveals the creatures' two-month life cycle—from egg to caterpillar to pupa and beyond.

Luxembourg City

BOCK-CASEMATE TOURS

Entrances on Place de la Constitution and Montée de Clausen. Open March–October, daily, 10am–5pm. Admission: 70 LF; children, 40 LF. Phone: 22 28 09 or 22 75 65.

Built to last atop a massively fortified rock known as the *Bock*, Luxembourg City has been ruled by many nations but takes no prisoners. Under the streets, a vast network of tunnels was rammed through solid rock during the 18th century. It once housed thousands of soldiers—not to mention their horses and cannons and their workshops, kitchens and slaughterhouses. Today visitors can tour over five miles of casemates, climbing from level to level on huge, winding stone staircases. Firing slots in the walls offer sweeping panoramas of the valley below.

Rumelange

24 km southwest of Luxembourg City, near the French border

NATIONAL MINING MUSEUM
(Musée National des Mines)

On the western edge of town; follow the signs. Open Easter–October, daily, 2–5pm. Admission: 120 LF; children, 60 LF. Phone: 56 31 21 1.

R ide a cute little train into a world where the sun never shines. Nearly 300 feet underground, a thousand yards of mineshaft are stocked with old and new mining equipment, diagrams, mannequins portraying miners and more. Rough wooden beams overhead and sallow lanternlight boost the claustrophobia quotient.

MONACO

Don't miss:

★★★★ Monte Carlo:
Exotic Garden
and Observatory
Cave   234

Monte Carlo

EXOTIC GARDEN AND OBSERVATORY CAVE

(Jardin Exotique et la Grotte de l'Observatoire)

62 *boulevard du Jardin Exotique, at the western edge of the principality, in the Moneghetti district. Open May 15–September 15, daily, 9am–7pm; September 16–May 14, daily, 9 am–dusk. Admission: 38 F; students and children, 18 F. Phone: 93 30 33 65.*

After losing your fortune in the casino, what could be more soothing than walking around on the edge of a cliff? Some of these rare cacti stand nearly fifty feet tall and many others are specially earmarked as "vegetable monstrosities." With a view extending to Italy, footbridges and paths wind past 7,000 strange specimens. Then you can descend 150 feet under the garden into illuminated caverns that sprout stalactites and stalagmites and weird limestone concretions.

Monte Carlo

THE NATIONAL MUSEUM AND COLLECTION OF DOLLS AND AUTOMATONS OF YESTERYEAR

(Automates et Poupées d'Autrefois Collection de Galéa)

17 *avenue Princesse Grace, east of the casino. Open Easter–September, daily, 10am–6:30pm; October–Easter, daily, 10am–12:15pm and 2:30– 6:30pm; automatons are set into motion daily at 11:30am and 3:30, 4:30 and 5:30pm. Admission: 26 F; students and children, 15 F. Phone: 93 30 91 26.*

Madame Galéa's retinue of 19th-century dolls pose charming and rigid amid miniature furniture, tiny dishes, wee musical instruments and other conveniences. Also here is a collection of Parisian-made automatons who are not content to share the fate of their unmechanized brethren. A cigar-smoking Buffalo Bill as well as clowns, artists and other jointed figures startlingly "come to life" several times a day.

NETHER-LANDS

Don't miss:

Alphen aan den Rijn

Just north of Gouda, off the A12 road

ARCHEON

*Archeonlaan 1. Open April–June
and September–October, Tuesday–Sunday, 10am–5pm;*

*July–August, daily, 10am–6pm
(closing days vary month to
month in the off-season). Admission: 20 Fl; children, 15 Fl; admission includes main course of
meal. Phone: (0172) 44 77 44.*

This theme park wants to show
you that Dutch history goes back
farther than Rembrandt to the times
when Roman gladiators battle women
in sandpits and monks rocked out on
accordions. In boats on the pond,
at the Roman army camp, in the cloister, the fields and all around the
wooded grounds, the park's "archeo-
interpreters" patiently explain why
they are wearing armor, leading oxen,
holding tournaments and, among
other retro activities, swallowing fire.
Various millennia are juggled here,
and then visitors are served a
medieval-style meal to eat from earthenware dishes with their fingers.

Amsterdam

CAT GALLERY
(Kattenkabinet)

*Herengracht 497. Open Sun-
day–Friday, 9am–2pm, Saturday,
9am–5pm (though the hours
change frequently). Admission:
10 Fl; children under 12, 5 Fl.
Phone: (020) 626 5378.*

This private museum has a very
clearly defined focus: priceless
original artworks from around the
world that depict cats. Tintoretto,
Rembrandt, da Vinci and Picasso are
all represented here—and that's just
clawing the surface. The elegant displays also feature Egyptian bronzes

of cat goddesses, Japanese wood-block prints and Staffordshire china cats. Photographs, posters, statues and etchings intensify that feline feeling.

EROTIC MUSEUM

Oudezijds Achterburgwal 54. Open Sunday–Thursday, 11am–1am; Friday–Saturday, 11am–2am. Admission: 5 Fl; students, 4 Fl. Phone: (020) 624 7303.

Now that other European cities are copycatting Amsterdam and opening sex museums of their own, the Dutch capital has no choice but to go further and open a second one. Not to be confused with the Sex Museum, the *Erotic* Museum is five floors of funky fun. Start with a wax model of disease-ravaged genitalia and mannequins putting bananas where they're not supposed to go. Then move on to an around-the-world tour of erotic art. Note John Lennon's original sketches of himself and Yoko having more than breakfast in bed. Spend a few minutes in the kiddie room watching a fascinating version of

EROTIC MUSEUM—AMSTERDAM

Snow White, then climb up to an exhibit on early-20th-century pornography. An entire floor re-creates Amsterdam's red-light district—hardly necessary, since the real thing is right outside. Another floor is devoted to S & M, with leather-clad mannequins whipping each other.

THE HASH MARIHUANA HEMP MUSEUM

Oudezijds Achterburgwal 148. Open daily, 11am–10pm. Admission: 8 Fl. Phone: (020) 623 59 61.

A live garden flourishes alongside displays detailing the devil weed around the world. Don't miss the exhibit exposing Louis Armstrong as a stoner. Pipes and roach-clips are here in great variety, as is an 1836 Dutch Bible made of hemp. Other products such as hemp shampoo, hemp clothing and a hemp tennis ball make it obvious that all other manufacturing materials may as well be dispensed with. A glass case stocked with items in which unfortunate persons attempted to smuggle hash across national borders is a chilling diversion: Note the hash-filled hollow dildo. California's medical marijuana initiative gets a thumbs-up, and American joints with their pure-pot fillings and uniquely tapered ends are treated as if they were from outer space. In Amsterdam, as in much of Europe, weed is mixed with tobacco and spliffs look like real cigarettes.

THE KIDS' CAFE
(Het KinderKookKafé)

*Oudezijds Achterburgwal 193.
Open for dinner on Saturday
6–8pm; for high tea on Sunday
from 5–6pm. Admission: children aged 2–4, 5 Fl; aged 5–12,
10 Fl; aged 13–99, 15 Fl; over
99, free. Phone: (020) 625 32
57.*

Young cooks between the ages of five and twelve prepare and serve all the meals at this cafe. During the week it doubles as a culinary school where the kids learn their chops (and their omelets) from grown-ups. Lamps made of sifters and whisks illuminate tables whose seats are made to resemble huge fried eggs. Throughout the café are artworks crafted from candy and pasta, with an overall licorice-allsorts motif. The kids prepare couscous, cakes, soups and other dishes from world cuisines. Adult daycare workers who initiated the program and operate the café keep the cooks from picking their noses.

MUSEUM VROLIK

*Meibergdreef 15; in the far southeastern suburbs of Amsterdam,
on the grounds of the AMC (Amsterdam Medical Center), in the
Department of Medicine (Metro:
direction Gein to the Holendrecht
stop). Open Tuesday–Wednesday,
2–5pm. Admission: free. Phone:
(020) 566-9111.*

A father-and-son team of 18th- to 19th-century anatomists, Gerardus and Willem Vrolik spent two lifetimes amassing this collection of human and animal specimens. Exhibits range from the perfectly healthy to the pathological, all the way out to the severely teratological (monstrously deformed), which is where other anatomy museums fear to tread. Just try tearing yourself away from one of the world's most extensive collections of genetically defective fetuses and newborn babies—150 of them perfectly preserved for eternity in formaldehyde. Also interesting is a display of human bones weirdly misshapen by disease, injury and bad genes.

THE NARROWEST HOUSE

*Oude Hoogstraat 22, near
Kloveniersburgwal. Visible at
any time. Admission: free.
Phone: (020) 42 72 229.*

Only 6 feet wide and 15 feet deep, the slimmest house in a city of slim houses rises three-and-one-half stories high. Despite competing claims from the owners of other narrow buildings throughout Amsterdam, this one holds city administrators' official seal of approval. Now housing a gift shop, the house was built in 1700 and expanded—upwards—in 1730. Legend says the house once served as a storage space for bodies en route to their funerals at a nearby church.

centuries-long battle between oval and round. Monocles, lorgnettes, sunglasses, spectacles, optical toys and eye-shaped ex votos all find a place here too.

SEX MUSEUM VENUSTEMPEL

 Damrak 18, between Centraal Station and Dam Square. Open daily, 10am–11:30pm. Admission: 4.50 Fl; no children under 16 admitted. Phone: (020) 622 8376.

Well-endowed with sex toys, folk art, fine art and photographs explicit enough to straighten your hair down there, this museum reveals that people had sex in ancient Rome, and they haven't stopped since. As you enter, note the continuous-loop screening of a 1920s X-rated silent film, perhaps the earliest such movie ever made. Pass masturbating mannequins and erotic artifacts from early civilizations. One room bears a sign warning away the faint-hearted: Inside are uncensored fetishist photos. Marvel at bestiality (pigs, dogs, snakes, donkeys), fecal thrills, a downright clairvoyant scene involving a cigar, snapshots of Long Dong Silver, and close-ups of stuff squirting out of holes.

THE NARROWEST HOUSE— AMSTERDAM

NATIONAL EYEGLASSES MUSEUM
(Nationaal Brilmuseum)

 Gasthuismolensteeg 7, between Singel and Herengracht. Open Wednesday–Saturday, noon–5:30pm. Admission: 10 Fl. Phone: (020) 4 212 414.

Upstairs from a high-priced optometry shop, the "National" Eyeglasses Museum (one supposedly earns such a title by being the only one in the country) traces the history of this fashion accessory/medical device from the tiny wire frames of Schubert to the glittering extravagances of Dame Edna. Marvel at glasses shaped like butterflies, chessboards, the Eiffel Tower, sharks, hearts, bats and more, and follow the

TATTOO MUSEUM AND TATTOO STUDIO

Museum: Oudezijds Achterburg-wal 130. Open Tuesday–Sunday, noon–5pm. Admission: 5 Fl; children under 8, free. Phone: (020) 625 1565. Studio: Oudezijds Voorburgwal 141. Open May–September, Monday–Saturday, 11am–9pm; October–April, Monday–Saturday, 11am–6pm. Admission: free.

Flesh preserved in formaldehyde is among the artifacts collected by tattoo artist Hank Schiffmacher, who has left his mark on the skins of Pearl Jam, the Red Hot Chili Peppers and the Ramones. Mummified arms and pictures of perforated celebrities are here, as are designs, dolls and tattooing tools from India, Laos, Japan and elsewhere. Don't miss the exhibit on Russian prisons, where inmates do the job with semen, razors and shoe polish. Photos offer glimpses of Schiffmacher in Borneo tattooing penises. Around the corner, at the artist's studio, are more tattoo-related curios as well as Siamese-twin pig fetuses and an inexplicable penis in a jar.

TORTURE MUSEUM

Damrak 20–22, between Centraal Station and Dam Square. Open daily, 10am–11pm. Admission: 7.50 Fl; students, 5.50 Fl; children, 4 Fl. Phone: (020) 639 2027.

Among the displays here is a metal armchair fitted with a spiked seat, spiked headrest, spiked backrest and spiked footrests—with spiked restraints to keep the guest in place. Inquisitors' tools are among the grisliest, making death by guillotine seem as easy as taking a bath. Explanatory artworks fill in the historical tapestry, while descriptions in a variety of languages explain how each item was used, as if it wasn't self-explanatory. Shame masks, iron maidens, pillories, stocks and nameless concussive and piercing devices round out the collection.

87 km southeast of Amsterdam

APE PARK
(Apenheul)

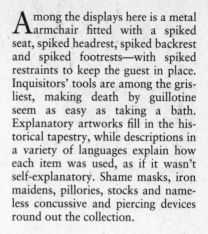

J.C. Wilslaan 31, west of town. Open April–May and September–October, daily, 9:30am–5pm; June–August, daily, 9:30am–6pm. Admission: 17.50 Fl; children, 12.50 Fl. Phone: (055) 357 5757.

Twenty-six different kinds of ape swing freely from trees, perform whimsical tricks, leap onto visitors' shoulders and rifle through pockets. Wander among hundreds of lively and inquisitive primates including no fewer than 100 squirrel monkeys. They live here along with macaws, tortoises, otters and the extremely large and hideous rodents known as capybaras. However, you cannot mingle with the twenty resident beasts that comprise the world's largest captive colony of gorillas. They live on a separate inaccessible island, as do the park's notoriously horny bonobos.

Just southeast of Nijmegen

AFRICAN MUSEUM
(Afrika Museum)

Postweg 6. Open April–October, Monday–Friday, 10am–5pm; Saturday–Sunday, 11am–5pm; November–March, Tuesday–Friday, 10am–5pm; Saturday–Sunday, 1–5pm. Admission: 10 Fl; children, 5.50 Fl. Phone: (024)-684 12 11, or (024) 684 20 44.

Forget all about windmills as you wander through a full-size reconstructed Ghanaian living compound, with stilt houses from Benin and an entire village from Mali. Erected in the wooded coutryside, these African replicas are complete with thatched roofs, ovens, scattered accessories and other details to evoke a lived-in feeling. Also on the premises is a huge collection of African masks, toothy figurines, fetishes and other religious articles, as well as a living compound from Lesotho, a pygmy camp and an Ndebele house.

Baarle-Nassau and Baarle-Hertog

17 km southwest of Tilburg, on the Belgian border

TWIN TOWNS

Visible at any time. Phone: (013) 507 99 21 (Tourist Office).

Though entirely surrounded by territory belonging to the Netherlands, the "town" of Baarle-Hertog is officially Belgian. Actually, it's inextricable from its Dutch Siamese twin, Baarle-Nassau, as the two make up a single urban agglomeration. The international border is a nightmare: Twenty-two separate Belgian enclaves all have unmarked borders that zigzag wildly across the map, so you never know from one step to the next which country you're in. The only way to keep track is to look at the address plates on the houses, which by law have color-coded markings indicating whether they are in Belgium or the Netherlands. It all started in the 12th century, when a bunch of dukes, lords and counts wrestled over the territory. A 1648 treaty only worsened the problem, so when the official international border was finally drawn in 1843 you could hear the surveyor sobbing in the background. Now the border cuts right through people's living rooms and slices a café in half. Two sets of police, post offices, banks, government offices and fire departments work side by side.

60 km southeast of Zwolle

SALT MUSEUM

(Zoutmuseum)

Langestraat 30, near the train station. Open April–October, Monday–Friday, 11am–5pm, Saturday–Sunday, 2–5pm; November–March, Tuesday–Sunday, 2–5pm. Admission: 5 Fl;

children, 2.50 Fl. Phone: (074) 376 4546.

Shaped like everything from lambs to (big duh) Dutch girls, over 2,000 salt shakers evoke Pavlovian flashbacks to plates of French fries and scrambled eggs. Situated in the heart of this country's salt basket, the museum uses cartoons, photos and a model factory to probe the versatility and value of sodium. Visitors are offered a chance to join fact-finding "treasure hunts" throughout the museum and test their salt expertise. In the video theater, films about salt screen continuously.

FROG MUSEUM
(Kikkermuseum)

Frederik Hendriklaan 38, near Johan van Oldenbarnevetlan in Scheveningen. Open the first Sunday of every month, 1–5pm. Admission: 2.50 Fl; children, 1 Fl. Phone: (070) 355 4385.

Begun nearly thirty years ago with three frog figurines and now overflowing the living room in a private home, this collection boasts over 5,100 effigies in all media and from around the world—though the proprietor admits that many of them depict toads. Made of clay, glass, wood, plaster, neon and gingham, the amphibians leap, lounge, stare, embrace, eat sandwiches, strum guitars, smoke cigars, wear clothes, sip tea and say, "I love you."

MADURODAM

George Maduroplein 1; west of the center of town; buses and trams run regularly from Den Haag's central train station. Open September– March, daily, 9am–5pm; April– June, daily, 9am–8pm; July–August, daily, 9am–10pm. Admission: 19.50 Fl; children, 14 Fl. Phone: (070) 355 3900.

Narrow houses, cathedrals, government buildings and skyscrapers, brilliantly detailed and landscaped, come up to your chest in this sprawling complex which recreates the Netherlands' best-loved sights on a 1:25 scale. Peer down at miniature versions of Dam Square, Alkmaar's cheese market, even a mini-Schiphol Airport stocked with planes the size of baguettes. Windmills whirl, canal boats glide on the waterways and trains zip around the world's largest miniature railway. At dusk, 50,000 tiny lights come on. Also on the premises is a panoramic history of the Netherlands, sculpted in sand.

The Hague ('s Gravenhage, Den Haag)

PRISON GATE MUSEUM
(Museum Gevangenpoort)

 Buitenhof 33, west of the train station. Open Tuesday–Friday, 11am–4pm; Saturday–Sunday, 1–4pm. Admission: 6 Fl; children 4 Fl. Phone: (070) 346 0861.

Used as a prison from 1420 to 1828, this gateway to a former count's castle now houses all you need to know about incarceration and torture. Branding irons, racks and other novelties are augmented by paintings and prints that helpfully illustrate the implements' optimum use. A slide show and guided tour expand the vicarious misery even further.

Heerlen

20 km east of Maastricht

DREAM CASTLE
(Droomkasteel)

 Ganzeweide 113-115, in Heerlerheide, a northwestern suburb of Heerlen; it's a 3 kilometer walk from the Heerlen train station: go north up Kloosterweg and look for Ganzeweide, which runs parallel with Terhoevenderweg. Open May–September, daily, 10am–6pm. Admission: 4 Fl; children under 15, 3 Fl. Phone: (045) 521 17 67.

This wildly off-kilter garden filled with homemade statuary comprises a dizzying profusion of large cement animals, fairytale figures, phantasmagorical monsters and ordinary people. They crowd the meandering pathways and bridges of the Droomkasteel's domain. Here and there among the hulking neckless baboons, life-size giraffes (nibbling a tree), snapping alligators and unidentifiable life forms are factory-made cupids, gnomes, puppies, Victorian gentlemen and copies of Roman busts, all of which lend a stylistic incongruity to the proceedings. A masterpiece of "outsider art," the Droomkasteel itself is a forty-five-foot high cement-and-stone pyramid thickly coated with goofy statues, pathways and dank hollows.

Kaatsheuvel

12 km north of Tilburg

EFTELING

 Europalaan 1 off the N261 highway; signs point the way. Open April–June and September–October, daily, 10am–6pm; July–August, daily, 10am–10pm. Admission: 35 Fl; children under 4, free. Phone: (0416) 273 535 or 288 1111.

First opened in 1952, predating Disneyland by many years and filled with artistry, this could well be the mother of all theme parks. At its core is the Fairytale Wood, where elaborate tableaux recall stories of princesses, kings and dwarfs—but with a truly creepy spirit. Other mind-blowing scenarios reside in a vast Arabian palace and an ornate villa where a "curse" has turned everything upside down. An Indian temple, a fakir's retreat and a haunted castle are set amid thrill rides and elaborate exotica. The park also includes an animatronic village occupied by hideous, beer-swilling babies; and over the whole proceedings a pagoda is poised high in the air like the Space Needle. Everywhere you look, there's another spectacle blending folklore and fear.

CASEMATES
(Kazematten)

Enter at the Waldeck Bastion, near Tongerseplein, part of the old defensive fortifications on the west side of town. Tours September–June, Sunday, 2pm; July–August, daily, 12:30 and 2pm. Admission: 5.50 Fl; children under 13, 3.25 Fl. Phone: (043) 325 21 21.

Ten kilometers of tunnels give new meaning to the word "claustrophobia." Ancient mines converted to military use over a period of centuries, the *Kazematten* were a secret defensive network, often used to fend off besieging armies. Dutch soldiers would gather inside and burst out behind enemy lines for surprise attacks; at other times the *Kazematten* were used to stage unexpected bombing raids or track enemy movement. The tour leads through only a limited section of the tunnels—otherwise it would take all day. But that's more than enough to evoke the gunpowder, sweat and blood that once permeated these dank subterranean passages.

THE CAVES OF MT. ST. PETER
(Grotten St. Pietersberg)

Northern System (Grotten Noord): entrance at Luikerweg 71; enter through the Chalet Bergrust, on Luikerweg, 1 kilometer south of the center of town, across the street from the entrance to Fort St. Pieter. Tours given March–June and September–October, daily, 12:30, 2 and 3:30pm; July–August, daily, 10:45am–3:45pm hourly; November–March, Wednesday and Friday, 2pm; Saturday and Sunday, 12:30 and 2pm. Dates vary from year to year.

Zonneberg Caves: Slavante 1; enter behind the Casino Slavante, on the riverfront 1.5 kilometers south of the town center, on the other side of the hill from the Northern System. Tours given April, daily, 12:45, 1:45 and 2:45pm (no 12:45pm tour on Sunday); May–September, daily, 10:45am–3:45pm hourly (tours start at 1:45pm on Sunday); October, Monday–Saturday, 1:45pm, Sunday, 2:45pm; November–December, Sunday, 2:45pm. Dates vary from year to year. Admission to either entrance: 5.50 Fl; children under 13, 3.25 Fl. Phone: (043) 321 78 78.

An apparently normal hill on the south side of town harbors a deep secret: Twisting for miles under the surface are 20,000 passages, carved out over the last two or three millennia by industrious people seeking soft marl, a versatile building material. The walls of the passageways, which branch off in a million different directions, are thickly covered with ancient graffiti, some dating back to the 1570s. Even Napoleon, on his way through town, stopped in to carve his signature. An hour-long tour leads through artistically lit tunnels past fossils, ovens and chapels (from the time when the passages were used for refuge during wars) and bas-reliefs carved into the walls. The Room of the Muses has renderings of Calliope, Clio and the gang, etched high on the wall by a talented artist. Elsewhere are scenes of prehistoric animals, a whopping crucifixion and various heavenly creatures. The guide explains the system's fascinating history, including an underground battle with the French that happened here in 1794. Each entrance covers a different section of the whole system, so if you like one, try the other.

of relics relating to the Virgin Mary. Start with a lock of her hair, a piece of her veil and a thorn from her son's party hat, all jumbled together in a single reliquary. Another reliquary holds a hunk of her belt. Nearby is her wedding ring (given by Joseph, not God), or at least an ancient copy of it. Close scrutiny also reveals the luscious locks of Mary Magdalene—the very ones with which she washed Jesus' feet. More thorns are here, along with bits of the True Cross, a splinter from Baby J's crib and a potpourri of bones, arms and other leftovers recalling fifteen centuries of martyrdom. If this doesn't satiate your appetite for relics, the treasury of the St. Servaes Basilica (*Schatkamer St. Servaasbasiliek*), a few blocks away on Keizer Karelplein, has some more body parts of saints and pieces of the cross.

Maastricht

COLLECTION OF HOLY RELICS

In the treasury (schatkamer) *of the Basilica of Our Beloved Lady (Onze Lieve Vrouwebasiliek), on O.L. Vrouweplein, in the center of town; entrance to the treasury is inside the basilica, on the left side near the back. Open Easter–October, Monday–Saturday, 11am–5pm; Sunday, 1–5pm. Admission: 3.50 Fl; children, 1 Fl; children under 6, free. Phone: (043) 325 1851.*

The treasury of this 1,000-year-old church has one of the world's most formidable collections

Middelburg

In Zeeland, in the southwestern corner of the country

MINIATURE WALCHEREN (Miniatuur Walcheren)

Koepoortlaan 1, a few blocks north of the center of town, in the area called Molenwater. Open April–June and September–October, daily, 10am–5pm; July–August, daily, 10am–6pm. Admission: 12.50 Fl, children, 9 Fl. Phone: (0118) 612 525 or 415 400.

As if Zeeland's Walcheren island wasn't cute enough in real life, now its trains, bridges, houses, farms, sheep, dikes, windmills, amusement park and all have been duplicated on a 1:20 scale. It was done in 1954 to commemorate the locals' success at rebuilding after the war. Radio-controlled boats glide calmly around the little lake.

OPEN-AIR BIBLE MUSEUM
(Bijbels Openlucht Museum)

Profetenlaan 2, at Heilig Land Stichting, just south of Nijmegen. Open late March–October, daily, 9am–5:50pm. Admission: 12.50 Fl; students, 10.50 Fl; children, 6.50 Fl. Phone: (024) 382 3110.

Thirteen acres are lined with full-size replicas of biblical-era buildings, mostly constructed between 1918 and 1940 in an effort to promote worldwide religious tolerance. Complete with a synagogue, the Middle Eastern village replicates a hamlet in what is now Jordan. A furnished Roman house is authentic right down to the deliberate reek of lentils and fish in the kitchen. Actors clad in togas and peplums lounge under columns and potter about with amphoras. Also here are a Greek house, an Egyptian house, Bedouin tents, an indoor Bible museum and a café serving dishes just like those the martyrs used to make.

Oudeschild

On Texel island, 5 km south of Den Burg

MARITIME AND BEACHCOMBERS' MUSEUM
(Maritiem en Jutters Museum)

Barentszstraat 21. Open January–June and September–December, Tuesday–Sunday, 10am–5pm; July–August, daily, 10am–5pm. Admission: 8 Fl; children, 4 Fl. Phone: (0222) 314 956.

Way up here in the North Sea, the surf has no mercy. Beachcombing—collecting flotsam and jetsam, bits of broken masts and crates of cargo from wrecked ships—has become part of the local culture, as this museum reveals. Along with items that never quite made it to Davy Jones' locker are exhibits detailing the area's lifeboat association.

Oudewater

20 km west of Utrecht

THE WITCHES' WEIGH HOUSE
(De Heksenwaag)

Leeuweringerstraat 2. Open April–October, Tuesday–Saturday, 10am–5pm; Sunday, noon–5pm Admission: 2.50 Fl; children under 12, 1.25 Fl. Phone: (0348) 56 34 00.

In the name of witch-hunt justice, 16th-century women were systematically weighed to see if they were light enough to fly on broomsticks.

Emperor Charles V, furious at corrupt village weighmasters who declared their victims nearly weightless, found that the weighmaster in Oudewater was trustworthy. Charles authorized him to issue official certificates citing the bearer's true weight, and women flocked to Oudewater. Today you can climb onto the old scales and earn a certificate of your own. A museum upstairs details the witch hunts.

Rotterdam

TAXATION AND CUSTOMS MUSEUM
(Belasting- en Douanemuseum)

Parklaan 14-16, near Veerhaven, on the waterfront south of the train station. Open Tuesday–Sunday, 11am–5pm. Admission: free. Phone: (010) 436 5629.

Smugglers who swallow cocaine stashed in knotted condoms are merely modern versions of those who hid liquor in sausage skins and opium in hollow pennies. These and other failed attempts to outwit revenue officers and border guards are illustrated here, but what about the ones that got away? Fine art and artifacts, including a 3,000-year-old Egyptian funerary statuette depicting a taxman, tell the long history of tolls and tithes; a special section is devoted to tax revolts.

Steenwijk

35 km north of Zwolle

FAIR AND CIRCUS MUSEUM
(Kermis- en Circusmuseum)

Onnastraat 3, near Gasthuisstraat. Open February–June and September–December, Tuesday–Friday, 11am–4:30pm; July–August, Monday, 1–4:30pm; Tuesday–Saturday, 11am–4:30pm. Admission: 4 Fl; children, 2 Fl. Phone: 0521-518 687.

Feel uneasy around clowns—their painted smiles, the sound of tootling horns? Then do not, repeat, do not cross this threshold, past which lie rooms stocked with model fairs and circuses, not to mention tiny dolls and towering mannequins dressed as you-know-what. Painstakingly detailed miniature merry-go-rounds and other rides are fitted with minuscule fairgoers who raise their plastic arms in joy while lights wink on and off all around them in the miniature caravans, snack-bars and fortune-telling booths. Illuminated by relentless strings of bulbs, vintage fairground figures revive old fears. A carousel ride awaits outdoors.

SCRYPTION MUSEUM OF WRITTEN COMMUNICATION
(Scryption Museum voor Schriftelajke Communicatie)

 Spoorlaan 434a, one block from the train station; turn right as you exit. Open Tuesday–Friday, 10am–5pm; Saturday–Sunday, 1–5pm. Admission: 6 Fl; students and children, 4 Fl. Phone: (013) 580 0821.

From our ancestors' chiseled hieroglyphs to word processors and beyond, this sleek museum explores the ways in which people write to one another. Ancient scripts are examined alongside collections of inkwells, pens, computers, stenciling apparatus, check-writing machines and even desk furniture. Don't miss the floor-to-ceiling wall of typewriters with its tiny antique specimens and big black hulks.

Utrecht

MOLUCCAN HISTORY MUSEUM
(Moluks Historisch Museum)

 Kruisstraat 313, near Biltstraat, east of the train station. Open Tuesday–Sunday, 1–5pm. Admission: 4.50 Fl; children, 3 Fl. Phone: (030) 236 7116.

Those industrious Dutch laid claim to the fertile Spice Islands, down New Guinea way, 300 years ago, thereupon reaping a fortune in nutmeg, mace and bird-of-paradise plumes. Japanese troops seized the islands in 1942, spelling crisis and pain for Dutch colonists and ethnic Moluccans alike. After the war, many Moluccan soldiers emigrated with their families to Holland's chill flatlands. This museum traces their torturous integration into Dutch culture, with special exhibitions on the tropical world they left behind.

Vaals

Far southeastern corner of the country, next to Aachen, Germany

THREE COUNTRIES MAZE
(Labyrint Drielandenpunt)

 Viergrenzenweg 97, south side of town, right on the border. Open: April–October, daily, 10am–6pm (last admittance 5pm). Admission: 5 Fl; children under 12, 4 Fl. Phone: (043) 306 5200.

Built, symbolically, at the point where the Netherlands, Germany and Belgium meet, this triangular labyrinth of impenetrable hedges is no stroll through the park: One wrong turn and you'll be drenched by sneaky jets of water that spurt out unexpectedly. Three strategically placed raised bridges give you a chance to survey the tangle of pathways below and chart a course to victory. Once you reach the center (*if* you reach the center), climb the observation tower and chortle over the antics of losers wandering wet and lost amid the greenery.

12 km east of Maastricht

CAVE AQUARIUM
(Grottenaquarium)

Trichtergrubbe 2, off Cauberg. Open April–October, daily, 10:30am–5pm. Admission: 10 Fl; children aged 13–16, 8 Fl; children aged 4–12, 5 Fl. Phone: (043) 601 2336 or (043) 604 2929.

If the fish in this aquarium had brains larger than lentils, they might puzzle over why they're here, lodged in tanks hewn out of cave walls. Dozens of tanks set into solid rock, deep underground, house piranhas, catfish, electric eels, seahorses, sturgeon and many non-fish species including crocodiles, iguanas and giant toads.

12 km east of Maastricht

FAIRYTALE WOODS
(Themapark Sprookjesbos)

Sibbergrubbe 2-A, on the hill on the south side of town. Open mid-April–mid-July, Monday – Saturday, 10am–5pm, Sunday 10am–6pm; mid-July –August, daily 10am– 6pm; first half of September, daily, 10am–5pm; second half of September, Saturday and Sunday, 10am–5pm. Admission: 13 Fl; children 10 Fl. (043) 601 29 85.

This all-over-the-map park has a Fantasia section with big diora-

mas evoking scenes from seventeen different fairy tales. This section also has a water-organ whose plumes of colored water "dance" to music. But the Amerika section lures visitors away with a Wild West show and a Wild West town populated with staring, costumed figures. Meanwhile, the Afrika section awaits, stocked with a menagerie of elephants and zebras.

12 km east of Maastricht

PREHISTORIC MONSTER GROTTO
(Prehistorische Monstergrot)

Plenkerstraat, just west of Wilhelminalaan and the center of town. Open in summer, daily, 10am–6pm. Phone: (043) 601 49 92.

Vast, wrinkly-hided synthetic dinosaurs tower over visitors— underground. Triceratops glowers against the clamminess of Dutch marlstone, while other red-eyed saurians, extinct animals and Neanderthals coexist in anachronistic harmony.

12 km east of Maastricht

TOWN CAVE
(Gemeentegrot)

Entrance is at Cauberg 4, off Wilhelminalaan, west of the center of town. Open November–June, daily, 10:30am–4pm;

July–August, daily, 10am–5pm; September–October, daily, 10:30am–4:30pm. Admission: 5.25 Fl; children, 3.75 Fl. Phone: (043) 601 2271.

Frescoes, bas-reliefs and graffiti transform the walls of this labyrinth which snakes under the streets of town. Romans extracting marl from the earth 2,000 years ago started the cave, and subsequent generations have enlarged and embellished it. Fossil shells and underground waterways offer a natural counterpoint to emerald-green pool-party lighting. Statues of dragons lurk in niches, and 19th-century sketches depict the royal family in loving detail across the lard-colored stone.

Volendam

20 km northeast of Amsterdam

THE CIGAR-BAND HOUSE
(Het Sigarenbandjes-Huisje)

In the Volendam Museum, Zeestraat 37. Open mid-March–mid-October, daily, 10am–5pm. Admission: 3.50 Fl; children, 2 Fl. Phone: (0299) 369 258.

In 1947, a local man named Molenaar started using his cast-off cigar-bands to make metallic "mosaics" on panels affixed to the walls of his home. Liking the effect, he made more cigar-band art depicting windmills, abstract patterns, crosses, fantasy figures, the Statue of Liberty and Big Ben. By the time Mr. Molenaar died in 1964, the surfaces of his house were entirely covered in designs that involved over 7 million bands. At this point a neighbor took over the enterprise and enlarged it by yet another 4 million bands. Today the local history museum displays Molenaar's transplanted walls, floors and ceiling—not to mention mosaicked lamps, jugs and furniture.

Waalwijk

15 km north of Tilburg

DUTCH LEATHER AND SHOE MUSEUM
(Nederlands Leder en Schoenen Museum)

Elzenweg 25, at Bachlaan, just south of the center. Open Tuesday–Friday, 10am–5pm; Saturday–Sunday, noon–4pm. Admission: 5 Fl; children, 3.50 Fl. Phone: (0416) 33 27 38.

Leather freaks are invited to fondle skin samples in this museum's "leather corner," while an on-site café serves cookies baked to resemble shoe soles. Lodged in a former factory, the collection spans the globe and includes some of the most murderously pointed toes you'll ever see. Juxtaposed with Japanese *geta*, platform shoes reveal their Asian roots, while rich embroidery on Russian aristocrats' boots proves that the Bolsheviks were right. Alligator shoes prompt homage for the beasts who died so that your forebears could be shod.

Wieuwerd

15 km southwest of Leeuwarden

MUMMIES

 In the crypt of the village's sole church (N.H. Kerk). Open April–September. Monday–Saturday, 9:30–11:30am and 1–4:30pm. Phone: (058) 250 12 26.

Little did these four citizens of the early 17th century ever dream that after they died, natural gases would seep into the crypt where they were placed and then proceed to mummify them. Now they're on display, side by side, their black coffins topped with glass for easy viewing.

NORWAY

Don't miss:

Bergen

LEPROSY MUSEUM

*In St. George's Hospital, 59
Kong Oscarsgate. Open late
May–August, daily, 11am–3pm.
Admission: NOK 20; children,
NOK 10. Phone: 55 31 66 00
(tourist office).*

The Vikings brought captive
slaves home from abroad, and
unwittingly they also brought leprosy. Thought to be God's curse, it
was an epidemic by the mid-19th
century, by which time a startling
percentage of Norwegians had claw-
like hands, dripping eyes and gory
lesions. This hospital was built as a
leprosarium in 1702, and here a
Norwegian doctor isolated the leprosy bacillus in 1873. Today it is the
world's only museum devoted to the
condition now named—after that
doctor—Hansen's disease. Tour the
old lab, the ward and the lepers'
church, as well as photo exhibits
detailing the disease's effects on the
human body.

Bødø

THE MIDNIGHT SUN
(Midnattsol)

*Visible from May 30 to July 12.
From June 3 to July 8, the entire
sun is continuously visible; before and after those dates only its
upper edge is visible. Phone: 75
52 44 06 or 75 52 60 00 (tourist
office).*

Here above the Arctic Circle,
summer nights are bathed in
sunshine and all the vampires have to
go hungry. Locals stay up until the
wee hours, when even shades can't
hide the glare.

Bødø

SALTSTRAUMEN
MAELSTROM AND
ADVENTURE CENTER

*33 kilometers southeast of Bødø
on the RV17 highway; buses also
carry visitors several times daily
from Bødø. Maelstrom occurs
every six hours according to the
tide; check local timetables; Saltstraumen Adventure Center is
open May and August, daily,
11am–6pm; June–July, daily,
11am–8pm; September, Saturday–Sunday, noon–6 pm. Admission to Saltstraumen Adventure
Center: NOK 50; children, NOK
30. Phone 75 56 06 55.*

It was Edgar Allan Poe who introduced the Norwegian word *maelstrom* into the English language. This stunning tidal phenomenon, in which billions of gallons of seawater roar and whirl as they fight to squeeze through narrow fjord entrances, is stronger here than anywhere in the world, especially during new and full moons. Near the whirlpool itself, the adventure center offers a multimedia program about the treacherous maelstrom and the myths it has inspired.

On Bømlo island, 90 km south of Bergen

WORLD'S LARGEST UFO RING

Next to the fishing village of Espevaer, southwest of Bømlo, on a small islet off the southern tip of the island; but ask directions to the ring once you get there. Always visible. Admission: free. For more information, call the Bømlo tourist office at 53 42 80 68.

They say this huge circular imprint is the ring left by an extraterrestrial craft when it landed here on Bømlo. What caused the ring? Heat from the exhaust, mysterious rays, or simply the sheer weight of the thing pressing down on the soil? Perhaps a local contactee can speculate with you. UFO aficionados have identified UFO rings in several places around the globe, but this one is the world's—dare we say *galaxy's?*—largest.

HUNDERFOSSEN FAMILY PARK
(Hunderfossen Familiepark)

13 kilometers north of Lillehammer on the Fv319 road. Open late May–early June, Saturday–Sunday, 10am–5 pm; early June–mid-August, daily, 10am–8 pm; mid-August–early September, Saturday-Sunday, 10am–5 pm. Admission: NOK 140; children, NOK 120; under 3, free. Phone: 61 27 72 22.

A thirty-foot-tall concrete troll—the biggest troll in the world—guards the park. Six more trolls, with furry overalls and noses like lingams, support a restaurant ceiling in the Fairy Tale Cave, where blonde dolls in dioramas illustrate scenes from the land of make-believe. Don't miss the world's largest caramel, on display here, or a speedway where four-year-olds learn to drive Volvo trucks. Norway's only wax museum houses Charlie Chaplin, Michael Jackson, Norway's former prime minister and, of course, Jane Wyman.

75 km northeast of Oslo

BYRUD GÅRD EMERALD MINES
(Smaragdgruvene Byrud Gård)

3 kilometers northwest of Minnesund, off road 33. Open mid-April–November, daily, 8am–8pm. Admission: NOK 60; children, NOK 30; guided tours

cost extra and must be arranged in advance. Phone: 63 96 86 11.

They say an emerald plucked from this mine is now among the British crown jewels. Discovered late last century and situated at the forest's edge on the shores of a lake, northern Europe's only emerald mine is now outfitted with a snack bar and playground. Would-be prospectors can mine all they like and keep all the emerald stones they find.

Mo i Rana

30 km south of the Arctic Circle

GRØNLI CAVE
(Grønligrotta)

25 km northeast of town, go 12 km northeast along the E6 road; turn north at Røssvoll and follow the signs to the cave. Open late June–late August, daily; tours given 10am–7 pm, on the hour. Admission: NOK 50; children, NOK 30. Phone: 75 16 23 05.

The most popular cave in a region liberally perforated with hundreds of them, this illuminated limestone cavern extends several hundred yards into a mountainside. Follow the guide along walkways, past subtly striated toast-colored walls and pitted floors. With passages and galleries forking and heading off in different directions, the cave's heart is nicknamed the "Labyrinth," and you're never far from the sound of an underground river. Another cave nearby, called *Settergrotta*, offers scarier and muddier tours for the truly adventurous.

Moskenes

In the Lofoten region, north of the Arctic Circle

THE MOSKSTRAUMEN MAELSTROM

The maelstrom is off the coast of Moskenes island, which is connected by ferry to Bodø. To arrange a visit and assess the tides, call the Tourist Information Center at 76 09 15 99, or 70 09 15 55.

On an organized boat trip, watch as up to 80,000 billion gallons of water—one of the world's fiercest and most lethal ocean currents—make a sound that Poe called "part scream, part roar," and that's louder than Niagara. The maelstrom is at its wildest during new and full moons.

Noresund

100 km northwest of Oslo

FAIRYTALE CASTLE MUSEUM
(Eventyrmuseet)

At Villa Fridheim, on the island of Bjørøya in the Krøder fjord, just northwest of Noresund. Open July, daily, 10am–6pm; mid-May–June and August–mid-September, daily, 10am–5pm. Admission: NOK 30; children, NOK 10. Phone: 32 14 94 06.

Built late last century as a merchant's vacation home, the tall angular house nicknamed "Crow Manor" was occupied by Nazis and abandoned before finding a new role as a center for Nordic folktales. Now its forty rooms are lavishly decorated with tableaux and paintings evoking fairy tales. The "fairytale forest" out back offers further excursions to once-upon-a-time.

Oslo

EMANUEL VIGELAND MUSEUM

Grimelundsveien 8: Take the underground to the Slemdal station; from there, walk west a few yards down Stasjonsveien, turn left on Frognerseterveien, then right after one block on Grimelundsveien. Open Sunday, noon–3pm. Admission: free. Phone: 22 14 93 42.

Emanuel Vigeland, the obscure younger brother of Gustav (of Vigeland Park fame) has his own little-known museum in the suburbs of Oslo. Could it be that it's way out in the middle of nowhere because it's a little *too* racy, even for Norway? Emanuel's masterwork, a fresco called *VITA,* traces all the phases of the human life cycle, and he doesn't skimp on the details. His unabashedly erotic vision of love and relationships, documented in sculptures, frescoes, and other media, is an interesting counterpoint to brother Gustav's more widely accepted output.

Oslo

THE INTERNATIONAL MUSEUM OF CHILDREN'S ART
(Det Internasjonale Barnekunstmuseet)

Lille Frøens vei 4 (Underground: Frøen). Open late January –late June, Tuesday–Thursday, 9:30am–2pm, Sunday, 11am–4pm; late June–mid-August, Tuesday–Thursday, 11am–4pm, Sunday, 11am–4pm; September–mid-December, Tuesday–Thursday, 9:30am–2pm, Sunday, 11am–4pm. Admission: NOK 30; children, NOK 15. Phone: 22 46 85 73.

Learn what goes on inside those tiny heads by perusing this collection, which numbers over 100,000 artworks by children in 180 countries. Their depictions of families, fantasies, war and friendship reveal more about kids' awareness of life, love and fear than grown-ups would like to admit. Framed pictures cover the walls, while sculptures and crafts crowd the floor. Workshops in the museum encourage young visitors to draw, paint and even make videos.

Oslo

KON-TIKI MUSEUM
(Kon-Tiki Museet)

Bygdøynesveien 36, at the tip of the Bygdøy peninsula, across the harbor from central Oslo. Open April–May and September, daily, 10:30am–5pm; June–August, daily, 9:30am–5:45pm; Octo-

ber–March, daily, 10:30am–4pm. Admission: NOK 30; children, NOK 10. Phone: 22 43 80 50.

Far from home, huge Easter Island statues glower over the balsa, reed and papyrus vessels in which 20th-century Norwegian explorer Thor Heyerdahl sailed thousands of miles across the bounding main, attempting to prove his theories about population shifts. His seaworthy *Kon-Tiki* is here, and *Ra II*, as well as relics lifted from faraway tombs and a thirty-foot model of the whale shark that nearly deep-sixed Heyerdahl.

SKI MUSEUM
(Skimuseet)

Kongeveien 5, at the Holmenkollen Ski Jump, northwest of the city center (Underground: Frognerseteren/Holmenkollen). Open October–April, Monday–Friday, 10am–4pm, Saturday–Sunday, 11am–4pm; May and September, daily, 10am–5pm; June, 9am–8pm; July–August, 9am–10pm. Admission: NOK 50; students, NOK 40; children, NOK 25. Phone: 22 92 32 00.

In the shadow of the hundred-year-old ski jump that was home to the 1952 winter Olympics, the world's oldest ski museum nestles deep in a cozy space blasted out of solid rock. Learn about the ancient Norse god and goddess of skiing. Ponder the exhilaration experienced by medieval warriors on skis,

North and South Pole explorers on skis, kings on skis and Olympic athletes on skis, and explore the finer points of ski wax. A 4,000-year-old petroglyph on display depicts a skier.

VIGELAND MUSEUM
(Vigeland-Museet)

Nobelsgate 32, off Halvdan Svartes Gate, just south of Vigeland Sculpture Park. Open May–September, Tuesday–Saturday, 10am–6pm, Sunday, noon–7pm; October–April, Tuesday–Saturday, noon–4pm, Sunday, noon–6 pm. Admission: NOK 30; students and children, NOK 15. Phone: 22 54 25 30.

If the sensuous bronze and granite statues in Vigeland Sculpture Park (which see) have left a deep impression on your mind, this museum will make it indelible. Plaster casts of the statues stand in this building, which the city erected in the '20s as a studio, home, museum and eventual mausoleum for Gustav Vigeland, whose ashes are now lodged in its tower. His 1,600 sculptures, 12,000 drawings and 400 woodcuts evoke an emotional roller-coaster ride.

VIGELAND SCULPTURE PARK
(Vigelandsparken)

Main entrance is on Kirkeveien, northwest of downtown. Open daily, 24 hours. Admission: free.

VIGELAND SCULPTURE PARK—OSLO

Expressing all the horror and glory of human relationships, hundreds of bronze and granite nudes pose along an avenue that crosses the park. Sculpted by Oslo's Gustav Vigeland between 1907 and 1942, the statues have sparked controversy for decades. It's hard to stop looking, for example, at pairs of sturdy intimate lovers, parents giving piggyback rides and a father resolutely beating the hell out of his son. A towering obelisk is composed of countless tangled bodies. Each smooth statue embodies pain and pleasure almost too lifelike to bear.

THE PULPIT ROCK
(Preikestolen)

 25 kilometers east of town, on the Lyse fjord. Buses carry visitors to and from the Tau Quay in Stavanger several times daily, June–September; private companies also offer tours. Either way, it's a 120-minute walk to the top. Admission: free; round-trip bus fare from Stavanger is NOK 41. For more information, call the Stavanger tourist office at 55 51 66 00, or the Fjord Centre at 51 70 31 23.

A two-hour walk up a trail from the Pulpit Rock Cabin (*Preikestolhytta*) stokes up the acrophobia and brings you onto a flat rock shelf whose edges plunge nearly 2,000 feet straight down into the waters of the fjord. Norwegians lounge blithely on the verge, and not a hint of guardrail mars the dazzling view of sea and open sky. A favorite activity of young and old alike is to lie flat and wriggle head and shoulders out over the sheer cliff edge, or to have a picnic inches from certain death.

Just south of Oslo

VIKINGLAND
(Vikinglandet)

 Direct shuttles run to the park from Oslo South railway station. Open May and late August–late September, Saturday–Sunday, noon–6pm; June, Monday–Fri-

day, 10:30am–3pm, Saturday–
Sunday, noon–6pm; July–Au-
gust, daily, noon–6 pm. Admis-
sion: NOK 95; children, NOK
65. Phone: 64 94 63 63.

Roam around a mock Viking sea-
port complete with turf houses,
lively market squares, workshops,
farms, rough-and-tumble tournaments, costumed villagers and other
shades of the last millennium—
including gangs of howling Norsemen bearing weapons. Voyage on a
Viking ship alongside Leif Eriksson
and his helmeted minions; explore a
mountain cave; and scarf down
Viking cuisine with your bare hands.

POLAND

Don't miss:

★★★★ Czermna: Chapel of
Skulls   258

★★★★ Wieliczka:
Wieliczka
Salt Mine   260

Czermna

100 km southwest of Wroclaw, on the Czech border

CHAPEL OF SKULLS
(Kaplica Czaszek)

Czermna is just 3 kilometers northeast of Kudowa Zdroj; from Kudowa Zdroj, take ul. Moniuszki, a street that eventually becomes the main drag of Czermna, on which you will find the chapel in the center of the village. Open daily 10am–1pm and 2–5pm. Admission: free. For more information call 074/66 12 66 or 074/66 11 62.

If you're a fan of pirate flags or labels on bottles of poison, you'll *love* this place, where the skull-and-crossbones concept is taken to extremes. The ceiling of this chapel of death, built in 1776, is thickly blanketed with hundreds of human skulls, each positioned above two crossed leg bones. Though the bones don't really move, they look like a swarm of hideous monsters descending upon you as you enter the room. The 3,000 additional skulls and dismembered

skeletons lining all the walls don't offer much reassurance. Not enough bones for you? Then ask the attendant to open the door to the crypt, where 21,000 more skulls await.

Kielce

115 km northeast of Krakow

RAJ CAVE
(Jaskinia Raj)

11 kilometers southwest of Kielce, 1 kilometer west of the main highway (Road E77) leading to Krakow. Buses running from Kielce to the nearby town of Checiny will drop you off near the cave entrance. Open April–October, Tuesday–Sunday, 9am–6pm. Phone: 66-74-18.

This compact cave, popular with local Poles, has more stalactites than you can count, all crammed into a smallish space—as many as 200 in a one-square-yard area. Creative lighting shows the rich colors deeply embedded in some of the swooping curtains of stone. Neanderthals moved in long ago, and some of their prehistoric garbage is on display.

Kudowa Zdroj

100 km southwest of Wroclaw, on the Czech border

GORY STOLOWE ROCK FORMATIONS

In Gory Stolowe National Park, northeast of Kudowa Zdroj. The most unusual formations can be

*found in two areas: Bledne Skaly
Reserve, 5 kilometers northeast
of Kudowa Zdroj, directly on the
Czech border; and Szczeliniec
Wielki Reserve, 4 kilometers east
of Bledne Skaly. A hiking trail
leaving from road 387 at the
eastern end of Kudowa Zdroj
leads to the rocks and connects
the two areas; the village of Kar-
low is only 1 kilometer south of
Szczeliniec Wielki. Visible at any
time. For more information, call
the Kudowa Zdroj tourist office
at 074/66 12 66 or 074/66 11 62.*

The geology of the entire Gory
Stolowe (Table Mountains)
National Park is impressive, but
nowhere more so than in the convoluted stone plateaus of Bledne Skaly
(Erratic Rocks) and Szczeliniec
Wielki (Great Cracks). Many of the
eroded, towering pillars and protru-
sions have been given picturesque
names such as the "Sitting Hen," the
"Devil's Kitchen," the "Camel," the
"TV Set," the "Sphinx," and (getting
very creative) the "Textile Shop." It's
easy to let your imagination run
wild. Walking trails at both sites lead
through bizarre stone labyrinths of
freakish formations; here and there
you'll squeeze through a foot-wide
fissure in the rocks, only to be
presented with a staggering vista of
teetering, bulbous, geometric mon-
trosities. Bring a camera.

Oświęcim

60 km west of Krakow

AUSCHWITZ-BIRKENAU
CONCENTRATION CAMP
(Muzeum Oświęcim)

*Ul. Wiezniow Oświęcimia 20.
From the Oświęcim train station,
take a local bus heading toward
"Muzeum Oświęcim," or on foot
follow the signs 1.5 kilometers to
the entrance gate; shuttle buses
run throughout the day between
Auschwitz and Birkenau, or you
can walk the 3 kilometers between the two. Open daily, January and February, 8am–3pm;
March, November and December,
8am–4pm; April and October,
8am–5pm, May and September,
8am–6pm; June–August,
8am–7pm. Admission: free, but
there is a small charge if you want
an English-language guide to the
site or to see the film. Phone: 33
43 20 22, or 33 43 20 77.*

As the scene of the worst crime in
history, this is a vivid testament
to the evil of which humans are
capable. At least 2 million people—
and probably many more—were
killed here between 1940 and 1945.
The site is actually two camps in
one: Auschwitz, with its chilling
entry sign reading "Work Brings
Freedom" (*Arbeit Macht Frei*), was
a forced-labor camp for dissidents
and "undesirables" of every race
and nationality; while Birkenau,
three kilometers away, was a specially built extermination center for
Jews, where at least 1.5 million victims were unceremoniously gassed
to death. In the barracks remaining
at Auschwitz are exhibits and photo
displays: victims' personal effects,

mounds of human hair, images of skeletal prisoners, cans of Zyklon B. A film explains the history of the camp. Birkenau is stark in comparison. Everything has been left intact, exactly as the Nazis left it—after attempting to destoy as much evidence as possible. At the crematoria and ash-filled pond near the back of the camp, the smell of death remains.

Wieliczka

14 km southeast of Krakow

WIELICZKA SALT MINE
(Kopalnia Soli Wieliczka)

Ul. Daniłowicza 10. Trains run frequently from Krakow to Wieliczka: Get off at the Wieliczka Rynek stop at the end of the line; from the station, follow the signs to the mine, a five-minute walk. Open mid-April–mid-October, Wednesday–Monday, 7:30am–6:30pm; mid-October–mid-April, Wednesday–Monday, 8am–4pm. Admission: 17 ł; students, 8.50 ł; permission to take pictures, 5 ł. Phone: (12) 278 73 02 or (12) 278 73 66.

UNESCO deemed this mine one of the greatest treasures ever created by the human race. It's an entire empire carved from one of the biggest salt veins on the planet. The highlight of the two-and-a-half-hour compulsory guided tour is the Chapel of St. Kinga, a mind-blowing underground cathedral carved out of the salt. Everything—but *everything*— in the cathedral is made of salt: walls, ceiling, floor, crosses, chandeliers, stairs, columns, arches, decorations, candle holders. Notice the salt Mary-and-baby-Jesus riding on a donkey, and the incredibly detailed salt filigree decorations around the niches holding the salt statues. Throughout the subterranean labyrinth you will come upon many touching and amusing scenes and statues, all pure salt. Along the way you'll encounter lakes, more chapels, long narrow tunnels, chambers, Communist-era monuments and much more. Level III holds a museum of the mine's history with a section on decorative saltcellars (check out the elegant bowl carved from pink quartz, and the colonial-era faience topless black women), as well as a café—make a big show out of sprinkling salt in your soup.

Zalipie

30 km northwest of Tarnow

THE PAINTED TOWN

Take road 73 north from Tarnow to Dabrowa Tarnowska, then a local road heading northwest. Always visible. Admission: free. For more information, call the town's cultural center at 912, or the Regional Museum in Tarnow, 22-06-25.

Zalipie is famous as one of the most colorful villages in Europe; a constant stream of native folk artists have kept their hometown thickly covered in cheery floral murals. Massive bouquets of red, yellow, pink, white, purple and blue blossoms flanked with foliage and birds sprawl across wells, utility buildings, doghouses, farms, the church and the walls of houses, inside and out. Each artist—most of them are women—tries to develop her own unique style to set her apart from her neighbors. Felicja Curylowa (1904–1974) was so prolific that her adorned home is now a museum. An annual "painted cottage" competition held every year in early June assesses the new designs created each spring, and encourages new generations of painters. A somber jury inspects each of the widely scattered houses and farms and proclaims one as the most interesting and attractive. Zalipie's artistic tradition, however, seems to be slowly dying out, so if you don't go soon you may never see the spectacle.

PORTUGAL

Don't miss:

Arouca

45 km southeast of Porto

QUEEN MAFALDA'S MUMMY

In the Convent/Monastery/Sacred Art Museum de Arouca, Largo de Santa Mafalda, off Avenida 25 de Abril. Open Tuesday–Sunday, 9:30am–noon and 2–5pm. Admission: 350$00. Phone: (056) 94 33 21.

Mafalda, the daughter of Portugal's medieval King Sancho I, was betrothed to a prince, but when he died prematurely she took the veil. The presence of such a significant nun lent her Cistercian convent a great deal of power and influence. In 1616, 360 years after Mafalda died, someone thought of peeking in on her corpse and—lo and behold!—it hadn't, allegedly, putrefied. Declared a saint in 1793, Mafalda lies here mummified amid baroque extravagance. Behind glass in an ebony casket surmounted with silver foliage and a massive golden crown, the figure is draped in embroidered black robes, her little hand clutching an artificial pink rose.

Braga

THE STAIRWAY TO BOM JESUS

At the Sanctuary of Bom Jesus do Monte, 3 kilometers east of town. Visible at all times. Admission: free. Phone (053) 225 50 (tourist office).

This granite stairway ascends a mountain with the pomposity that only 18th century masonry

THE STAIRWAY TO BOM
JESUS—BRAGA

can offer, and is as broad as the cathedral to which it leads. It zigs and zags for nearly a kilometer, as seemingly countless built-in chapels recount the Passion. Colorful life-size scenes of the Passion populate the Chapel of Christ's Agony in the Garden, the Chapel of the Last Supper, the Chapel of the Kiss of Judas, the Chapel of the Flagellation, the Chapel of the Crown of Thorns, the Chapel of the Road to Calvary, the Chapel of Jesus before Pilate, and so on. Refresh yourself at the Fountain of the Five Wounds of Christ and the Staircase of the Five Senses, where crystalline jets spurt menacingly from statues' eyes and ears. Be a real pilgrim and make the climb on foot, or lame out and take the funicular up, then walk down, seeing the Passion in reverse.

Cabo da Roca

25 km west of Lisbon, on the coast just west of Sintra

EUROPE'S WESTERNMOST POINT

 Buses run to the cape from Sintra and Cascais. Visible at any time. Admission: free. Phone: (01) 928 0081 (tourist office).

It's a 7,000-mile overland trek from the Bering Strait to this cliff topped with a lighthouse. From here you just can't go any further westward without drowning. On the cliff, a monolith bears a line from the 16th-century Portuguese poet Camões calling this the place "where land ends and the sea begins." Here continental Europe ends. In the tourist office you can buy an elegant certificate with your name on it to prove you've reached the most westerly point of the Eurasian landmass.

Cabo de São Vicente

6 km northwest of Sagres, at the southwestern corner of Portugal

THE END OF THE WORLD
(O Fim do Mundo)

 On the very tip of the peninsula. Open daily until sunset. Admission: free. For more information, call the Algarve Regional Tourist Office at (089) 80 04 00.

The Romans hailed it as *Promontorium Sacrum* ("Sacred Promontory"). Throughout the Middle Ages this rocky and weather-beaten cliff at continental Europe's most southwesterly point was considered the actual end of the world, the very hem of human habitation. Fifteenth-century Portuguese navigators learned their chops at a nearby school and thenceforth sailed out from here to "discover" half the planet. Thus for hundreds of years this cape was a key landmark on routes linking Europe to Asia, America and Africa. Today the blindingly white lighthouse, its tower tipped in red, clings to the clifftop while wild surf and winds roar below.

Evora

CHAPEL OF BONES
(Capela dos Ossos)

 In the church of São Francisco, on Praça 28 de Maio. Open Monday–Saturday, 8:30am–1pm

and 2:30–5pm; Sunday, 10am–1pm and 2:30–6pm. Admission: 100$00; extra 50$00 to take photos. Phone: 066 26910.

"We bones who are here await your bones," reads a sign poised among the skeletal remains of 5,000 long-dead Franciscan monks. Created 300 years ago, the chapel is neatly paneled with ribs, ulnas, femurs and all your favorites. Exuding a good solid sense of mortality, meticulous patterns of bones completely cover the walls and pillars.

Faro

CHAPEL OF BONES
(Capela dos Ossos)

Behind the Church of Carmo (Igreja do Carmo), on Largo do Carmo in the town center. Open Monday–Saturday, 10am–1pm and 3–5pm. Admission: 120$00. Phone: (089) 82 44 90.

When the churchyard got full to bursting with the remains of expired monks, it was decided to unearth the bones and make room for more. But what to do with the disinterred bunch? Decorate a chapel with them. Completed in 1816, the chamber's walls and steeply domed ceiling are thoroughly "tiled" in skulls and thousands of yellowed bones, industriously arranged with geometric symmetry. Hollow eye sockets stare out at you from every angle so sepulchrally that the crucifix standing in a niche looks whimsical by comparison.

Faro

ST. ANTHONY MUSEUM OF FARO
(Museu Antonino de Faro)

Rua de Berlim 9, in an annex of the Church of St. Anthony on High (Santo António do Alto) in the eastern part of the town center. Open Monday–Friday, 10am–12:30pm and 2–5pm. Admission: 110$00. Phone: (089) 87 08 70.

This large and not unrepetitive assortment is not to be confused with the St. Anthony Museum in Lisbon. Examine artworks in many media devoted to the image of the Portuguese-born preacher who tried to reach Morocco but wound up in Padua. Mildly cradling the Baby Jesus and/or gripping a lily, Anthony's dark-clad image is replicated here in several centuries' worth of paintings, engravings, sculptures, ceramic tiles and other homages.

Lisbon (Lisboa)

ST. ANTHONY MUSEUM
(Museu Antoniano)

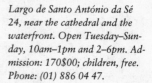

Largo de Santo António da Sé 24, near the cathedral and the waterfront. Open Tuesday–Sunday, 10am–1pm and 2–6pm. Admission: 170$00; children, free. Phone: (01) 886 04 47.

Though he ran off with a head full of ideas and died in Italy, Lisbon-born Anthony is still hailed as the city's patron saint. Right near the spot where he was born in 1195, the

museum displays documents, artifacts and effigies relentlessly honoring the gentle soul whose articulate
sermons, it is said, charmed even the
fish. Be prepared to view images of
his slender figure, complete with
brown robe and tonsured head, over
and over until you feel like you've
known him forever.

Monte

*On the island of Madeira, just north of
Funchal*

TOBOGGAN RIDES

*Rides begin on the belvedere at
or near Largo dos Babosas in
Monte, or in Terreiro da Luta
(the town above Monte), and*

Cave Country

Three spectacular cave systems lie hidden in the mountains of a national park 110 kilometers north of Lisbon, southeast of Porto de Mós.

The **Grutas de Alvados** are almost a perfect vision of hell: Tunnels and chambers thickly plastered with sharp stalactites and seemingly melting stalagmites extend as far as the eye can see into the heart of the earth, while orange, yellow and red backlighting conjures images of flames tormenting sinners just out of sight. The piped-in music of **Grutas de San António** gives a lighthearted counterpoint to the otherwise supremely grotesque yawning chambers, with misshapen concretions of every description that are said to grow by just one inch every hundred years. The largest and most commercialized of the caves are the **Grutas Mira de Aire**, a little further down the road. Pass a series of weirdly shaped formations with names like the "Martian," the "Chinese Hat" and the "Jellyfish" on your way down to an underground lake, where the tour ends with a phantasmagorical water show with music, colored lights and spurting fountains.

The **Grutas de Alvados** are 15 kilometers southeast of Porto de Mós, just outside the village of Alvados, on Road 555. The **Grutas de San António** are about 4 kilometers southeast of Alvados, on Road 1349. They share the same hours and phone: April–May, 9:30am–6pm; June and September, 9:30am–7pm; July–August, 9:30am–8:30pm; October–March, 9:30am–5:30pm. Phone: (044) 440787.

The **Grutas de Mira de Aire** are 20 kilometers southwest of Porto de Mos on Road 243, 15 kilometers south of Fatima. Open daily January–March and October–December, 9:30am–6pm; April–June and September, daily, 9am–7pm; July and August, 9am–8pm. Phone: (044) 440322.

Admission to each of the three caves is 600$00; children 6–12, 350$00.

head downhill. Admission: from Monte to Livramento, 1,700$00; from Monte to Funchal, 2,500$00. For more information, call the Madeira Regional Tourist Information Office at (091) 22 90 57.

In the mid-19th century, the island's farmers used to transport their goods up and down the steep hill with the help of wicker sleds mounted on wooden runners. Since the advent here of roads and cars, the sleds have lost their crucial role in local agriculture. But now they carry human cargo. Two passengers at a time can fit into one of the handmade wicker toboggans; two straw-hatted, white-garbed "drivers" run along on rubber-soled boots guiding the vehicle's downhill hurtle.

São Mamede

5 km west of Fátima

COIN CAVES
(Grutas da Moeda)

 Just east of town, off the 1268 road. Open April–June, daily, 9am–6pm; July–September, daily, 9am–7pm; October–March, daily, 9am–5pm. Admission: 500$00. Phone: (044) 903 02.

Discovered by a pair of fox hunters in 1971, the cave offers a fairyland of brightly illuminated chambers. Rich clusters of stalactites and humpbacked pillars glisten in the yellow and mouthwash-green lights as you descend into the mountainside. Nearly 150 feet underground, halls and limestone formations are winsomely nicknamed the "Virgin," the

"Wedding Cake," the "Spring of Tears," the "Lake of Felicity," the "Red Cupola" and the "Unfinished Chapel." Don't miss your chance to raise a glass in the cave's underground bar.

Tomar

36 km southeast of Leiria

MATCHSTICK MUSEUM
(Museo dos Fósforos)

 In the Convent of St. Francis, Largo 5 de Outubro, at the southern edge of the Old Town, near the train station on Váreza Grande square. Open Sunday–Friday, 2–5pm. Admission: free. Phone: (049) 31 66 54.

This flammable panoply includes a collection of over 43,000 matchboxes in all shapes, from 110 countries around the world. Begun by the man whose daughter now directs the museum, it opens the door to an otherwise-ignored realm that blends art, function and advertisement. Propagandistic matchboxes mark the ascent of various dictators, including Fidel Castro, and the success of certain revolutions. Don't miss the little French specimen that comes with its own tiny candle. Squint at the world's smallest; gawk at the world's largest.

Vilamoura

15 km west of Faro

ROMA GOLF PARK

Rua dos Marmeleiros, in the center of town. Open in summer, noon–1am; in winter, noon–7pm. Admission: 1800$00; children under 10, free. Phone: (089) 30 08 00.

Contemplate your big putts along the "Via Appia" at this miniature golf park, where broken columns stand bleaching in the sun. Fake Roman ruins and replicas of ancient monuments adorn the curving green fairways. Choose between two 18-hole courses surrounded by lakes, greenery, and more Roman architecture than you'll see anywhere this side of the Forum.

SLOVENIA

Don't miss:

Cerknica

35 km southwest of Ljubljana

DORMOUSE MUSEUM

Next to Snežnik Castle, 20 kilometers southeast of Cerknica, just 500 meters southwest of the village of Kozarisce. Open mid-April–mid-November, Wednesday–Friday, 10am–1pm and 3–6pm; Saturday and Sunday, 10am–6pm. Admission: 250 SIT. Phone: (061) 707-814.

The dormouse is not just an imaginary creature that Lewis Carroll made up for *Alice in Wonderland*. Dormice are real animals. Hefty rodents nearly as big as cats, they sport big furry tails, cute snub noses and glistening black eyes. They're still pretty common in these parts, which is surprising when you consider the many ways the Slovenians have devised to hunt and kill them. Dormousetraps of every description fill this museum: decapitation traps, crossbow traps, arboreal rat-trap-style traps, nooses—anything to snare these elusive tree-dwellers. Dormouse meat is considered a delicacy here, but the fur is also a hot commodity, so dormouse fur hats and capes are exhibited also. If you're (un)lucky enough to visit during hunting season at the end of September, you can watch some actual dormouse hunters on the prowl.

Cerknica

35 km southwest of Ljubljana

KRIŽNA CAVE

(Križna Jama)

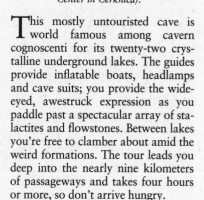

10 kilometers southeast of Cerknica, near the village of Bloska Polica. Open by prior arrangement only; call for reservation. Admission: 500 SIT (the guides prefer at least five people for each tour, so see if you can hook up with others). Phone 61 798-149 (ask for Alojz Troha, at House 7 in Bloska Polica), or 61 793 779 (the Notranjski Ecology Center in Cerknica).

This mostly untouristed cave is world famous among cavern cognoscenti for its twenty-two crystalline underground lakes. The guides provide inflatable boats, headlamps and cave suits; you provide the wide-eyed, awestruck expression as you paddle past a spectacular array of stalactites and flowstones. Between lakes you're free to clamber about amid the weird formations. The tour leads you deep into the nearly nine kilometers of passageways and takes four hours or more, so don't arrive hungry.

33 km southwest of Postojna

ŠKOCJAN CAVES
(Škocjanske Jame)

The caves are adjacent to the village of Matavun, 6 kilometers southeast of Divaca; take the main road south from Divaca toward Koper, then follow the signs leading to the caves heading eastward from this main road. Tours leave June–September, daily, at 10am, 11:30am, 1, 2, 3, 4 and 5pm; April–May and October, daily, at 10am, 1 and 3:30pm; November–March, Monday–Saturday at 10am, Sunday at 10am and 3pm. Admission: 1500 SIT; children under 13, 1200 SIT; children under 6, free. Phone: 67 60 122 or 67 60 169.

Enter one of the most spectacular subterranean scenes anywhere in the world. The ninety-minute tour starts in the Silent Cave (*Tiha Jama*), a long, twisting tripartite hall clothed in a veritable thicket of stalactites and stalagmites. This initial section alone is worth the price of admission, but it's just the beginning. Soon you enter towering Müller Hall, the start of a roaring subterranean canyon. Cross the impossibly acrophobic Hanke's Bridge, hundreds of feet above the Reka River at the bottom of the cave. Creep along the slippery path etched into the cliff face until you come to the exotic Hall of Pans or Bowl Hall (*Ponvice*), with layer upon layer of interconnected natural hollow terraces formed by cascading water. Continue through more tunnels to the massive waterfall in the Big Valley (*Velika Dolina*), with a spooky lake at the bottom of a deep hole in the earth. Then admire the natural stone bridge before ascending to the surface again on a funicular.

33 km southwest of Postojna

VILENICA CAVE
(Vilenica Jama)

8 kilometers west of Divaca: Take the road heading due west toward Lipica and the border crossing at Trieste; before you get to Lipica look for signs pointing north to the cave. Tours leave Sunday and holidays only at 3pm. Phone: 067 73 128 (ask for Viktor Saksida).

Vilenica Cave was once the most famous cave in Europe, as it was the first one ever opened to the public for organized tours, starting in the 17th century. Back then, of course, they used torches instead of flashlights, and you can still see the sooty marks left by the flames. Orange pointy stalactites menace you from above like giant vicious carrots. Delicate, wavy-striped "curtains" of stone look like muslin billowing in the breeze. Grotesque misshapen flowstone columns reach from floor to ceiling, where stalagmites and stalactites merged after thousands of years. Keep an eye peeled for intriguing helictites—tiny curlicue calcium deposits that seem to ignore gravity. The locals occasionally hold literary salons in the biggest chamber.

53 km southwest of Ljubljana

CAVE UNDER PREDJAMA CASTLE
(Jama pod Predjamskim Gradom)

 Just northwest of Bukovje, which is 9 kilometers northwest of Postojna. Tours given May–September, daily, at 11am and 1, 3 and 5pm. Admission: 600 SIT; children, 300 SIT. Phone: 67/59 260.

Perched like a big white bird in the middle of a 300-foot cliff, this tall, stark medieval castle stands atop a cave. The natural subterranean system measures some 1,800 feet and spans five different levels, connected by staircases cut into the stone. Among passages lined with slippery rock formations, including pillars and graceful rippling stone curtains, a tunnel called "Erazem's Passage" is said to have sheltered a 15th-century nobleman who fled here when his castle was besieged by the emperor's army.

53 km southwest of Ljubljana

POSTOJNA CAVE
(Postojnska Jama)

 On Jamska ceska, 1.5 kilometers northwest of town. Tours are given May, June and September, daily, at 9am, then every hour on the hour to 6pm inclusive; July–August, daily, at 9am, then every hour on the hour to 7pm inclusive; April, daily, at 10am, noon, and 2, 4 and 5pm; March and

October, daily, at 10am, noon, and 2 and 4pm; January–February and November–December, daily, at 10am and 2pm. During winter months there are extra tours on the weekends. Admission: 1,900 SIT; children, 950 SIT. Phone: 67/25 041 or 24 241.

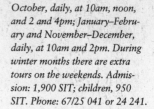

This stunning twenty-kilometer cave system, first explored in medieval times and now known as one of the world's largest, is home to *Proteus anguinus*, the so-called "human fish"—a species of white salamander so well adapted to its subterranean milieu that it has no eyes. This rare blind creature is now a mascot around these parts, and hopefully you'll see one. A colorful electric train carries passengers through galleries, passages and shafts lavishly adorned with illuminated formations, including delicate translucent curtains, stalagmites and sheaves of amazingly slender stalactites called, for obvious reasons, "spaghetti."

In eastern Slovenia, 25 km southeast of Maribor

KURENTI PROCESSION

 Processions are held during Shrovetide, on the days around Carnival (Shrove Tuesday); their exact timing and routes vary from year to year; call ahead (in February) for current dates. Phone: 62 77 15 69 (Ptuj information), or 62 21 12 62 (the Maribor area Tourist Information Center)

The villages near Ptuj celebrate one of the most primitive pagan festivals to survive Europe's Christianization. Along the mountain paths from the town of Markovci into Ptuj itself dance the *Kurenti*, costumed figures intent on ensuring fertility, banishing winter and somehow fending off death for another year. The *Kurent* costume is an all-body fur suit made of rabbit and sheepskin. A red leather tongue hangs down like a limp silk tie. The costume also boasts a mustache made of twigs, a protuberant beak/nose, horns and a huge headdress made of feathers and multicolored strips of crepe paper. Cowbells hang around the waist, and a mean looking club is encased in prickly hedgehog skin. As they hop from house to house, the *Kurenti* collect handkerchiefs offered to them by local girls, while housewives occasionally break pots on the ground.

This museum's unusual specialty is the Slovenian beehive panel, a folk-art genre unique to this region. Local beehives made in the 18th and 19th centuries had a series of removable front panels, which the beekeepers invariably ended up painting in vivid colors. The topics range from spiritual to outrageous. Many show scenes from Slovenian legends, illustrations of humorous folktales, the Virgin Mary and family, satirical images of local bigwigs, images of laughing fish, sinister foxes and unidentifiable animals murdering hapless Slovenians. The museum has the world's largest and most varied collection of these panels, as well as other offbeat beekeeping paraphernalia, including bee-feeding troughs, cages for queen bees and (in summer) close-up views of live bees dancing and mating.

Radovljica

6 km southeast of Bled

BEEHIVE PANEL COLLECTION

In the Radovljica Beekeeping Museum (Čebelarski Muzej), Linhartov trg 1, in Thurn Castle on the main square in the center of town. Open May–August, Tuesday–Sunday, 10am–1pm and 4–6pm; September–October, Tuesday–Sunday, 10am–noon and 3–5pm; March–April and November–December, Wednesday, Saturday and Sunday, 10am–noon and 3–5pm. Phone: 64 71 51 88.

SPAIN

Don't miss:

peninsula may seem like ancient history to outsiders, but the monumental consequences of the *reconquista* still reverberate powerfully in the national psyche. Nowhere is this more evident than in the Moors-and-Christians festivals that are held around the country. The most spectacular are in Alicante province, especially in the city of Alcoy. Thousands of elaborately costumed actors ritually reenact a medieval battle between the Christian Spaniards and the Moslem Moors. The Christians have St. George on their side, but the Moors usually have the edge in fashion: All of Africa and the medieval Moslem world parades through the streets, including central African tribesmen in full war regalia (bone spears, face paint), color-coordinated scimitar squads and more. In centuries past, the Moors were invariably the villains, but nowadays things are more egalitarian and both sides score points. On other days throughout the year, other cities in the region have their own *Moros y Cristianos*, especially Alicante itself.

Alcoy

53 km north of Alicante

MOORS-AND-CHRISTIANS FESTIVAL
(Fiesta de Moros y Cristianos)

The festival is held on April 23, with additional celebrations in the days before and after; the parades are held throughout the town—you wouldn't be able to miss them even if you tried. Admission: free. For more information, call the Alicante tourist office at 521 22 58.

The Moorish occupation and Spanish reconquest of the Iberian

Barcelona

AUTOMATON MUSEUM
(Museu d'Autòmats del Tibidabo)

In the Tibidabo Amusement Park (Parc d'Attraccions del Tibidabo), Plaça del Tibidabo 3-4, on Tibidabo Hill, northwest of the city center: Take the Metro to the Av. Tibidabo stop, then the "Tramvia Blau" tram to the end of the line, then the Funicular del Tibidabo all the way up to the top of the hill. Open the same hours as the park: April

*and late September, Saturday
and Sunday, noon–8pm; May,
Wednesday–Sunday, noon–8pm;
June and early September, Tuesday–Sunday, noon–8pm; July
and August, Tuesday–Sunday,
noon–10pm; October–March,
Saturday and Sunday,
noon–7pm. Admission: 200 Ptas
(once you're already inside the
park). Phone: 211 79 42.*

Early 20th-century coin-operated funfair automata laugh and wink and jerk about creepily. One of the world's best collections of antique robots is kept in pristine condition, down to the slightest detail: luscious costumes, lifelike faces, real hair and—most important—humanoid movements. Complicated scenarios are acted out on command, exactly as they have been for almost a century. Just being in the room with these mechanical golems will give you the chills . . . and then they clank into action.

BULLFIGHT MUSEUM
(Museu Taurí)

*In the bullring at Gran Vía de les
Corts Catalanes 749, northeast
of the center (Metro: Monumental, Gloriès). Open April–August, daily, 10:30am–2pm and
4–7pm. Admission: 350 Ptas.
Phone: 245 58 03.*

The bulls remembered here were famous fighters in their time, and just look at the thanks they get. Now their taxidermed heads line the wall, ears lopped off long ago for trophies. Amid a panoply of bullfighting memorabilia, man-nequins model matadors' skintight, sequin-studded costumes, complete with pompommed slippers—just right for a long, drawn-out slaughter.

EROTIC MUSEUM
(Museu de l'Erotica)

*Bergara 3, off Plaça Catalunya,
near Las Ramblas. Open daily,
10am–10pm. Admission: 975
Ptas. Phone: 318 98 65.*

All this museum's scholarly pre-tensions regarding world anthro-pology and art history can't conceal what this is: a collection of artworks and gadgets whose focus, whose the-sis, whose *raison d'etre* is getting it on—with oneself and with others. Sexy postcards from the 1920s depict big-butted models. Ancient Greek and Roman artifacts are deco-rated with those ubiquitously uncir-cumcised erections. A section on Asian erotica might inspire some vis-itors to go home and read the *Kama Sutra* after investing in a hefty set of ben-wa balls and a nice big bag of cucumbers.

HEARSE MUSEUM
(Museu de Carrosses Fúnebres)

*Sancho d'Ávila 2, in the Poble
Nou district east of the center
(Metro: Marina). Open Monday–Friday, 9am–2pm. Admission: free. Phone: 484 17 20.*

Take a vicarious ride down memory lane to the melancholy pageantry of Barcelona funerals. Horse-drawn carriages and other kinds of hearses tell one side of the city's history over the past hundred years, with each vehicle providing clues about the age, class and status of its former passengers. From little kids to aristocrats, these bygone corpses' final journeys are easy to imagine after you've seen this collection, assembled by the municipal hearse service.

Barcelona

ILLUMINATED FOUNTAIN SHOW

The Font Monjuïc, Plaça de Buïgas, just below the National Palace on Montjuïc, west of the center. Held Saturday and Sunday nights in summer. Admission: free. For more information, call the Tourist Information Office at (93) 301 74 43 or 317 22 46.

Candy-colored jets of water leap dozens of feet into the air from a circular fountain the size of several swimming pools. Designed as a set of concentric circles by Gaieta

Barcelona
The Buildings of Antoni Gaudí

Antoni Gaudí (1852-1926) was an adventurous architect, an innovative artist, a religious extremist and—most important—an obsessive eccentric whose bizarre personal visions still astound visitors a hundred years after they were built. Few architects have ever let their imaginations run so wild and yet met with such success. Gaudí's style is a genre unto itself, and almost every building he ever designed is in Barcelona. All buildings listed here are visible anytime, except where noted.

Casa Mila (*La Pedrera*) (92 Passeig de Gràcia, at the corner of Carrer Provença. Patios and terrace open Tuesday–Saturday, 10am–8pm. Phone: (93) 484 59 80. Metro: Diagonal) is a good starting point. The world-famous undulating façade is just the beginning: Inside you'll be swept up in aquatic blues and greens and a redefinition of space. If you enter the building on the Carrer Provença side, you can buy a ticket to see the newly restored arched attic and the legendary roof with its twisting Martian chimneys and ventilation ducts.

Casa Batlló (43 Passeig de Gràcia. Phone: (93) 488 06 66. Metro: Passeig de Gràcia), just down the street from Casa Mila, has sparkling colored tiles across its front and a heaving roof line meant to suggest a reptilian dragon. Guadí didn't de-

274   Spain

sign this one from scratch, but overhauled an existing building. Many of the most luxuriant and visually stunning elements are inside and on the roof, unfortunately hidden from view.

Sagrada Familia Cathedral (401 Carrer Mallorca. Open March and September–October, daily, 9am–7pm; April–August, daily, 9am–8pm; November–February, daily, 9am–6pm. Phone: (93) 455 02 47. Metro: Sagrada Familia) is Gaudí's unfinished masterwork. He spent the last 43 years of his life slowly going mad as this project completely consumed him. This allegorical Christian temple is less a building and more a living, organic creature made of stone. The soaring Sagrada Familia doesn't *have* details—it is *composed* of details which somehow all blend into a unified concept.

Park Güell (On Carrer Olot, in the hills to the northwest of the city center. Open March and October, daily, 10am–7pm; April and September, daily, 10am–8pm; May–August, daily, 10am–9pm; November–February, daily, 10am–6pm. Phone: (93) 219 38 11. Metro: Lesseps) was originally intended as sort of an upscale arty housing development, but became by default a park when practically no one wanted to move in. Now it's a surrealist fantasia bursting with a tremendous profusion of vivid, swirling mosaics; a pavilion comprising eighty-four Doric columns holding up a ceiling of dimpled arches; the world's best bench; and colonnades, towers and Gaudíana everywhere you go. Also here is the Casa-Museu Gaudí (in the park at Carretera del Carmel 23. Open April and May, daily, 10am–7pm; June–August, daily, 10am–8pm; September–March, daily, 10am–6pm), containing many personal artifacts in the house where Gaudí lived for twenty years.

Casa Vicens (22 Carrer Carolines. Metro: Lesseps or Fontana), one of Gaudí's first buildings, is notably different from his later work: A neo-Moorish mansion featuring checkerboard designs in blues and yellows, there is nary a curved line or bulging wall in sight.

Lampposts (On Plaça Reial, one block east of La Rambla. Metro: Liceu) were Gaudí's very first commission. The six you see in this plaza appear somewhat conventional at first glance, until you notice the nightmarish winged dragons perched on top, their spiraling tails wrapped around the posts.

Palau Güell (3-5 Carrer Nou de la Rambla. Metro: Drassanes or Liceu) is best appreciated from the inside: hyperbolic and parabolic arches, exotic woods, squat mushroom columns in the basement, and as always a roof populated with individualistic chimneys. The opening times allowing visitors inside were not fixed when this was written, but the city plans to turn the building into a showcase, accessible to all inside and out.

Casa Calvet (48 Carrer de Casp. Phone: 412 40 12. Metro:

Urquinaona), like Palau Güell, is more remarkable inside than out. Luckily, the building houses a restaurant so you get to poke around, though only on the bottom floor.

Pavellons de la Finca Güell (Avinguda de Pedralbes 7. Metro: Palau Reial) are the domed, Orientalesque entrance gates to a factory. Contemplate Gaudí's wrought-iron gates, which sport a ferocious but beautiful dragon.

Bellesguard Villa (Casa Figueres) (Carrer Bellesguard 46. Metro: La Bonanova) looks like a Gothic church designed by Willie Wonka; because it's a private residence, you can't get too close.

GAUDÍ'S CASA BATTLO—
BARCELONA

St. Theresa's School *(Col•legi de les Teresianes)* (Carrer Ganduxer at the intersection of Ronda del Mig. Metro: La Bonanova) is spiky and lofty and rather somber, made purposely so by Gaudí since this is a convent school—no place for wild flights of fancy.

Colònia Güell (in Santa Coloma de Cervelló, 8 kilometers west of Barcelona, on the road heading to Sant Vincenç dels Horts; Open Friday–Wednesday, 10am–1:15pm and 4–6pm; Thursday, 10am–1:15pm. Phone: (93) 640 29 36) is an unfinished workers' commune on the outskirts of Barcelona that rarely sees tourists, which is a pity. The basement crypt of the never-built church is considered an architectural miracle, with angled columns, unusual arches and a structural support system so advanced that engineers only began to understand their avant-garde significance half a century after Gaudí built them.

Buïgas, the fountain commands a place of honor on this hill. To the amplified sounds of live music, brilliant red, orange, yellow, green and blue spumes play against each other and against the blackness of a night sky and the pale domes of the National Palace. All the angst of a long summer day in the city dissolves as huge cool jets of turquoise and lemon rise and throb to the beat of a drum.

PERFUME MUSEUM
(Museu del Perfum)

In the Regia perfume store at Passeig de Gràcia 39 (Metro: Passeig de Gràcia), in the center. Open Monday–Friday, 10:30am–1:30pm and 4:30–8pm; Saturday, 10am–2pm. Admission: free. Phone: 216 01 46.

A bottle designed by Salvador Dalí and crowned with a surrealistic sun is among 5,000 choice perfume vessels spanning thousands of years. Begun by a perfumer and now one of the world's largest of its kind, the collection includes hundreds of glass and ceramic flasks from ancient Greece, Rome and Egypt. Trace the histories of famous brands like Dior and Guerlain through their bottles and labels. Inspect flacons once owned by Marie Antoinette, and hark back to the times when water was rare in Europe and bathing rarer, and perfume was the way to keep one's lovers from gagging.

SHOE MUSEUM
(Museu del Calçat)

Plaça Sant Felip Neri (no number), in the Old Town (Ciutat Vella), between La Rambla and the cathedral (Metro: Liceu, Jaume I). Open Tuesday–Sunday, 11am–2pm. Admission: 200 Ptas. Phone: 301 45 33.

Hundreds of years' worth of shoes, and boots to boot, are lodged in the medieval headquarters of the Old Master Shoemakers' Guild. Genuine antique footwear dates back to the 16th century, with reproductions filling in around the edges. The shoes of Pablo Casals are among pairs formerly worn by famous performers. Outsizing the rest by far is the gigantic metal shoe made for a statue of Christopher Columbus, which only begs the question of whether it's true what they say about men with big feet.

35 km southwest of Valencia

TOMATO FIGHT
(La Tomatina)

Held every year on the last Wednesday in August. For more information, call the Valencia Office of Tourism at (96) 394 22 22.

Tens of thousands of half-naked men pelt each other violently with overripe tomatoes, wallowing thigh-deep in pulpy red fruit as the juice streams down their bare backs like blood. Since medieval times the town has marked its patron saint's feast day with a typical fiesta, but it's not as if St. Louis liked V8. This part of the festivities began half a century ago when local tomato harvests exceeded anyone's expectations. Today the townspeople pummel each other with tomatoes to their hearts' content without recrimination, joined by thousands of out-of-towners.

SANCTI PETRI GHOST TOWN

 25 kilometers south of Cadiz: From the city, go south through Chiclana de la Frontera and turn west toward the ocean; when you get to the Nature Reserve, turn right and go to the end of the road (make sure to avoid the new resort zone called Novo Sancti Petri, a few kilometers down the coast); the ruins are in the marsh at the mouth of the flood channel. Visible at any time. Admission: free. For more information, call the Bay of Cadiz Nature Reserve at (956) 59 09 71, or the Cadiz Tourist Office at (956) 24 10 01.

Deserted, decrepit buildings from three completely distinct phases of history, all in one little area—what more could you ask for? This abandoned fish-processing town is safely within the confines of the Bay of Cadiz Nature Reserve, where it no doubt will disintegrate gracefully amid the flamingoes and crabs. Most of the buildings here were industrial—facilities for salting, canning, and processing tuna and other sea life harvested by Cadiz's fisherfolk—making it a rarity among ghost towns. Now the entire community is surrounded by silent marshland; the only distraction is the nearby Sancti Petri yacht club, a new facility that has taken the same name. At low tide you can also see the foundations of what is purported to be an extremely ancient Phoenician temple, while just a few hundred feet off the coast on its own little island are the ruins of the 18th-century Sancti Petri Castle.

25 km southwest of Santiago de Compostela

VIKING PILGRIMAGE
(Romería Vikinga)

 Held every year on the first Sunday in August. For more information, call the Pontevedra Office of Tourism at (986) 85 08 1.

The crowds of Spaniards who dress up in Viking garb and sail around in replicas of Viking ships to stage their own version of Norse revelry once a year aren't pathetic wannabes besotted with longings for Thor. A thousand years ago, actual Vikings sailed this far south, impelled by their trademark greed and rapacious lust. Let's say they found a bit of satisfaction in this corner of northern Spain, where many residents still have red hair and blue eyes. The region remembers its Nordic roots with this rite.

Cuenca

160 km east of Madrid

THE ENCHANTED CITY ROCK FORMATIONS
(La Ciudad Encantada)

25 kilometers northeast of the city: Head north from town on Hoz del Jucar, the road that runs along the Jucar River; keep bearing to the right as you cross the river and pass through the town of Villalba de la Sierra; follow the signs that point to the Ciudad Encantada; an access road dead-ends at the formations. Visible at any time. Admission: free. Phone: (969) 23 21 19 (tourist office).

Covering several square miles of a grassy plain, this is a geological fantasyland of bulbous stone monstrosities that seem to be lumbering about the countryside. What makes the Enchanted City's rock formations unique is their strange inverted orientation: Almost all of them are huge and swollen on top, and become narrower and more delicate as they reach the ground. As a result many look like giant stone mushrooms, or fat-bodied prehistoric animals with skinny legs. Centuries of wind and rain have eroded away a layer of soft stone that lies *underneath* a much harder layer, resulting in a labyrinth of submarine-sized boulders balanced precariously ten or twenty feet off the ground. The nicknames applied to some of them—the "Ships," the "Roman Bridge"—just inspire you to make up your own.

Elda

30 km northwest of Alicante

SHOE MUSEUM
(Museo del Calzado)

Calle Pico Veleta (no number). Open Tuesday–Saturday, 10am–2pm and 5–8pm; Sunday, 10am–1pm. Admission: 400 Ptas; students and children 200 Ptas. Phone: (96) 538 30 21.

In the heart of a town whose shoe-making industry goes back 250 years, this collection includes antique and modern shoes. It also uses fine art, photographs, books, machinery and more to illuminate life in the shoe factory and the cobbler's shop. Wooden, medieval platform slippers hark back to a day when the streets streamed with substances too horrible to step in. Rustic, vintage foot-measuring tools will make you grateful to live in a time when size nine means size nine and that's that.

SHOE MUSEUM—ELDA

40 km north of Girona

DALÍ THEATER/MUSEUM
(Teatre-Museu Dalí)

Plaça Gala-Salvador Dalí 5, west of the train station. Open July– September, daily, 9am– 7:15pm; October–June, daily, 10:30am– 5:15pm. Admission: 1000 Ptas; students and children, 800 Ptas. Phone: (972) 51 18 00 or 50 56 97.

Lodged inside a former theater in the artist's hometown, this museum offers surreal surprises at every turn. Under a geodesic dome, surrounded by stone arches and other architectural novelties, a sofa takes on the shape of Mae West's lips. Here and there, life-size sculptures blow on trumpets and show off their butts. Meanwhile, Dalí's self-portrait rears up everywhere, even over your head. His paintings, drawings, statues and even jewelry fill various rooms, spanning the decades of his long career and the years of his relationship with Gala, whose dark-eyed image also lurks about this place.

ENCARNACIÓN MONASTERY
(Monasterio de la Encarnación)

Plaza de la Encarnación 1, south of Gran Vía, near Calle de la Bola (Metro: Santo Domingo). Open Wednesday and Saturday, 10:30am–12:30pm and

4–5:30pm; Sunday, 11am–1:30pm. Admission: 425 Ptas. Phone: (91) 547 05 10.

Over 1,000 reliquaries containing bits of saints' bodies are lodged here side by side under the monks' care. Skulls, bones, powdered blood and bits of dessicated flesh comprise a holy motel, all the relics fastidiously labeled with the saints' names. The reliquaries are shiny boxes shaped like churches, houses, hearts, hands, heads, pillboxes, columns and crosses. Peek through crystal windows to see the remains, though the boxes' cumulative golden sheen will make you squint. In one small jar resides the dried blood of St. Pantaleon, said to miraculously liquefy on the martyr's feast day every July 27.

MONUMENT TO THE FALLEN ANGEL
(Angel Caído)

In Retiro Park (Parque del Retiro), *which is east of downtown; the statue is at the southern end of the park, at the intersection of Paseo del Uruguay and Paseo del Ecuador, west of the Rosaleda. (Metro: Atocha). Visible during daylight hours. Admission: free.*

Lucifer wasn't always such a bad guy. He once had a pretty cushy place in heaven as one of Mr. Big's favorites. But then he took a tumble and ended up down in hell as Satan. If you think Lucifer's an odd figure to merit a major monument, you're not alone: this is apparently the world's only public statue in his

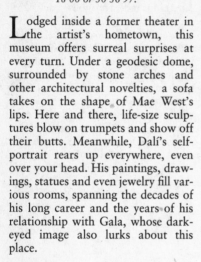

honor. He's portrayed as a handsome young devil, wrestling with a nasty-looking snake. Grinning monstrous demons await him below, clutching alligators in their claws.

Ribadesella

90 km west of Santander, on the north coast

CHAMBER OF VULVAS

In Tito Bustillo Cave (Cueva de Tito Bustillo), south of town; entrance is on Carretera a la Piconera, through a manmade tunnel alongside the Sella river. Open July–August, Monday–Saturday, 10am–1pm and 3:30–5:15pm; September–June, daily, 10am–1pm and 3:30–5:15pm. Admission: 400 Ptas; free on Tuesdays. Phone: 98/586 1118 or 98/586 1120.

Sealed for thousands of years until it was rediscovered in 1968, the cave was home to Paleolithic painters. They left behind art like that which decorates Spain's Altamira and France's Lascaux caves. Jewelry, utensils and carvings have been found in the cave's depths, and today you can admire a wall liberally adorned over 10,000 years ago with painted horses. Another gallery boasts a wall on which a menagerie of painted horses and deer roam across a red background. And a natural grotto called "La Cuevona" awaits just outside. But the part of Tito Bustillo that will invade your dreams is its Chamber of Vulvas, a small subterranean cavity vividly painted with images you just can't help but recognize. (Only the first 400 visitors are admitted each day, so arrive early in the summer.)

Ronda

60 km west of Málaga

BANDIT MUSEUM
(Museo del Bandolero)

Calle Armiñan 65, in the Old Town. Open in summer, daily, 10am–8pm; winter, daily, 10:15am–6pm. Admission: 300 Ptas; students, 175 Ptas. Phone: 287 77 85.

Walk past the Bandit Bar to explore the rest of this museum. Life-size tableaux include mannequins who stare soulfully out from under furry brows to re-create historic scenes from the world of Andalusian banditry. Learn the stories of famous highwaymen who once terrified the local populace. In one tableau, Juan Gallardo waits out his final days in a cave with only a gun and a gourd for company, while in another a kidnapping is under way. Baptism and death certificates along with clothing and other relics trace the lives, legends and often violent deaths of famous bandits. Homage is dutifully paid—in the form of uniforms and weapons—to the emergence of Spain's still-scary Guardia Civil.

Mayoresses' Festivals
(Fiestas de las Alcaldesas)

Spain's macho social structure is turned topsy-turvy every year on February 5, when in towns all over the country women seize the reins of political power. The festival's ancient origins are unknown, but now the *Fiestas de las Alcaldesas* are dedicated to Saint Agatha (*Santa Agueda*), an early Christian martyr who was tortured to death when she rejected a lecherous suitor. In **Zamarramala** (a suburb of Segovia), two town matrons don traditional red-and-black folk costumes and take control of city hall for one day, ruling with an iron fist over the temporarily emasculated men, who have been sent home to do chores. The women strut about the town, rewriting laws to give them a proto-feminist bent. Come evening, a straw man is burnt in effigy, while his mock will is read aloud to the derisive crowd. In **Miranda del Castañar** (60 km south of Salamanca), the churchwardens' wives take over and perform the curious ritual of waving a gigantic flag over the heads of the womenfolk gathered around them. **Escatrón** (60 km southeast of Zaragoza) honors St. Agatha with a procession in which young girls carry rounded bread loaves in trays on their heads—reminiscent of St. Agatha, who is said to have carried her breasts on a plate after they were sliced off by her tormentors. Despite the unsavory overtones and the sad reality that come the dawn, men will again reign supreme, all the celebrations are accompanied by much public merriment and jesting.

Salou

10 km southwest of Tarragona

PORT AVENTURA

 The park has its own train station on the Barcelona-Valencia line; buses also travel regularly to the park from Barcelona and Valencia. Open late June–September, daily, 10am–midnight; April–late June and October, daily, 10am–8pm. Admission: 4,100 Ptas; children, 3,100 Ptas. Phone: 902 22 22 20.

What are a giant Olmec head and Mayan pyramids doing here in northern Spain? The conquered tribes haven't staged a takeover—they're doing the same thing at this 300-acre international theme park as the volcano, teepees and tikis, the buffalo, the rodeo and the Great Wall of China. Five different "worlds" re-creating China, Polynesia, Mexico, the Mediterranean and the American West mix authentic images and landmarks with splash rides and roller coasters (including Europe's largest). The dancers and acrobats are all the real thing, while the lakes and jungles are persuasive.

San Pedro Manrique

35 km northeast of Soria

FIREWALKING
(Paso del Fuego)

 Held every year on the night of June 23. For more information, call the Soria Tourist Information Office at (975) 21 20 52.

Testing their faith, the men of San Pedro Manrique traipse barefoot across a sprawling carpet of live coals and emerge without being burned. Marking St. John's feast day—celebrated on June 24 with bonfire festivals throughout Europe—the rite draws crowds who marvel as the determined walkers offer piggyback rides in order to deepen their own contact with the hot coals.

SANTA MARÍA DEL SAR LEANING CHURCH—SANTIAGO DE COMPOSTELA, SPAIN

Santiago de Compostela

LEANING CHURCH

 The Colegiata de Santa María del Sar, off Rúa do Ponte do Sar, in the Sar district above the Sar river southeast of the center, 1 kilometer below Avenida de Lugo which rings the town. Visible from the outside at any time. Admission: free, though there is a charge to enter the museum. Phone: (981) 56 28 91.

Built on unstable ground in the 12th century, this church has struggled to stay upright; the result resembles an ecclesiastical funhouse. Columns lean this way and that, floors tilt, archways look stretched and squished. The church has served as a convent and a leper colony. But-

tresses were added in the 18th century to keep it upright. Maybe the saints give it a helping hand every now and then as well.

Tabernas

28 km north of Almería

MINI HOLLYWOOD

 Off the N340 road, in the desert just outside of town. Open July–September, daily, 10am–9pm; October–June, daily, 10am–7pm. Admission: 950 Ptas; children, 500 Ptas.

How many times have you watched *A Fistful of Dollars* and thought, That desert landscape looks exactly like southern Spain?

Sí. Sergio Leone erected sets here in paella country to make his spaghetti Westerns, probably figuring that if you've seen one dry gulch, you've seen 'em all. Now the leftover sets have been fortified to create a tourist attraction, complete with costumed cowboys and mock bank robberies on summer weekends.

Valencia

BONFIRE FESTIVAL
(Las Fallas)

Held every year throughout the city on March 12–19, culminating at midnight on March 19, which is technically March 20. Phone: (96) 398 64 21 or 394 22 22 (tourist office).

As this festival approaches, monumental artworks reaching fifty feet high take shape all over Valencia, depicting bodybuilders, nudes, genies, pirates, rock stars, sinister angels, fat men in G-strings, giant fruit and tangled menages of fantastic figures. Detailed down to the last bucktooth, erect nipple and bulging pectoral, the figures' skin is smooth and glossy, their postures and faces lifelike. Each of the complex structures is a visual joke, rife with symbols and clues and upfront jabs at public figures and current events. Artists and neighborhood groups spend all year designing, planning and then erecting the tableaux, known in local dialect as *ninots*. Throughout a week of festivities, thousands gather around and savor the ninots, which are torched on the final night and go up in flames—a dizzying spectacle that symbolizes winter's end and life's fragility.

Valencia

BULLFIGHT MUSEUM
(Museo Taurino)

Pasaje Dr. Serra 18, on the east side of the bullring, between Calle Jativa and Calle General San Martín, south of the center.

Open Monday–Friday, 10am–1pm and 4:30–8:30pm; Sundays, 10am–1pm. Admission: free. Phone: (96) 351 18 50.

The world's first museum of its kind, now imitated all over Spain, houses rare souvenirs from the ring. Gory photographs and even bits of bone and other physical relics commemorate mortal battles that the bulls won, only to be hacked up into steaks later anyway. Mounted bulls' heads stare with glassy forebearance. Famous matadors tell their stories through clippings and posters. Bullfighters' snug shiny costumes look very feminine when examined up close. Paintings, engravings and other elegant artworks date back to the 18th century, proving that Spain cherishes the blood sport as a thing of beauty.

FALLAS MUSEUM
(Museo Fallero)

Plaza Monteolivete 4, near Avenida de la Plata in the Mont-Olivet district southwest of the center. Open Tuesday–Friday, 10am–2pm and 4–7pm; Saturday–Sunday, 10am–2pm. Admission: free. Phone: (96) 3552 54 78.

Every year, after months of preparation, all of the elaborate satirical sculptures known as *ninots* go up in flames during Valencia's Fallas festival—except one. According to a tradition begun in 1934, by popular vote a single best-loved ninot, simply too good to burn, is "pardoned" from the fire. These *ninots indultats* are on display here, housed, ironically, in a former military prison. Contemplate the evasion of fate while examining countless exquisite details intended for a fiery demise: nostrils and shirt buttons, expressive eyes, poised fingers and ringlets.

THE HOLY GRAIL

In the cathedral, on Plaza de la Reina in the center of town. Open Monday–Saturday, 7:30am–1pm and 4:30–8:30pm; Sunday, 7:30am–1pm; the foregoing hours are for the Holy Grail Chapel (Capilla del Santo Cáliz); the cathedral itself is also open Sunday afternoon. Admission: free. Phone: (96) 391 81 27.

Parsifal should have taken a right turn at Birmingham, continued straight through Saint-Tropez and kept on till he reached Valencia, because a big hefty cup on display here is surrounded with legends and lore indentifying it as the grail. Historians trace the jewel-studded gold and agate confection, with its graceful double handles, back at least to the 3rd century, and they agree that it might be even older. In that case it could have belonged to any Esau, Isaac or Abraham who happened to live in biblical times and only ever took it off the shelf for Mothers' Day and Rosh Hashanah. But then again . . .

MUSEUM OF THE FALLAS ARTISANS' GUILD
(Museo del Gremio Artistas Fallero)

Calle del Ninot 24. Open Monday–Friday, 10am–2pm and 4–7pm; Saturday, 10am–2pm. Admission: 300 Ptas; children, 100 Ptas. Phone: (96) 347 65 85.

It takes a bit of skill to erect an eight-ton, fifty-foot sculpture—even if it's destined to go up in flames. These *ninots* which star in Valencia's Fallas festival are not only works of art and handicraft but also of engineering. Learn what goes inside a ninot and the whole painstaking, year-long process that makes these structures what they are. Models, pictures and even some "pardoned" ninots are displayed here by the guild that oversees their creation, and which comprises hundreds of fine artists, industrial artists and engineers.

Verges

20 km northeast of Girona, inland from the Costa Brava

DANCE OF DEATH
(Baile del Muerte)

 Held every year on Holy Thursday (Jueves Santo). For more information, call the Girona Tourist Information Office at (972) 22 65 75.

Flaming torches punctuate the dark of a winter's night as dancers clad in scary skeleton costumes make their way through the town. Crowds line the streets to watch prancing skeletons of all sizes, topped with gleaming skulls and clutching big sickles. A unique variation on Spain's morose Eastertide festivities, this lively *danse macabre* harks back to medieval plagues that swept through here striking down the population.

Vilanova i la Geltrú

45 km south of Barcelona

MUSEUM OF NAUTICAL CURIOSITIES
(Museu de Curiositats Marineres)

 Carrer d'Alexandre de Cabanyes 2, near the waterfront. Open Monday–Friday, 5–8pm. Admission: 200 Ptas; children, free. Phone: (93) 815 42 63.

Juanita is a goldfish who swims to the surface of her large basin and drinks water from a tiny dropper held in the proprietor's hand. TV crews from all over the world have come to film the fish, which lives outdoors amid decommissioned prows. The rest of the museum is crammed with figureheads, seashells and enough novelties to sink a you-know-what. Giant clams poise, ajar, alongside huge rusted anchors, ships-in-bottles, broken masts, flags, ropes, torpedoes, knotwork, foghorns, ships' wheels, taxidermed shark heads and other sailor souvenirs all jumbled together in manic profusion. Over 300 model ships made by the indefatigable owner jut out from everywhere and dangle from the ceiling, while portraits of seamen stare out from the walls. A diorama, cleverly assembled inside a porthole, illustrates the *Titanic*'s descent.

Zamora

55 km north of Salamanca

HOLY WEEK
(Semana Santa)

 Held every year throughout the week preceding Easter; processions depart from churches all over town. For more information, call the Tourist Information Office at (980) 53 18 45 or the Holy Week Museum at (980) 53 22 95.

The KKK didn't invent the robe and pointed hood with tiny eyeholes. Spain's penitential brotherhoods have been wearing this costume since at least the 14th century, when Zamora's Holy Week processions began. Throughout the week, day and night, the mournful cry of trumpets and the ominous snap of flaming torches accompany dozens of somber parades, whose shuffling masses of robed figures carry prized artworks evoking the gore of the Passion. Crowds gather to watch the Brotherhood of Most Holy Christ of the Good Death, the Brotherhood of Silence and other fraternities as they wind through the streets, anonymous in their costumes and creating a sustained air of misery.

Zamora

HOLY WEEK MUSEUM
(Museo de Semana Santa)

Plaza de Santa María Nueva (no number), in the town center. Open in summer, Monday–Saturday, 10am–2pm and 5–8pm,

Sunday, 10am–2pm; winter, Monday–Saturday, 10am–2pm and 4–7pm, Sunday, 10am–2pm. Admission, 300 Ptas; children, 150 Ptas. Phone: (980) 53 22 95.

If you've arrived in town at the wrong time of year to enjoy its processions of hooded penitents, this museum will help assuage that yen. Holy Week memorabilia on display here includes the colorful, life-size wooden tableaux depicting scenes from the Passion, which are carried through the streets during the seven-day festival. Lovingly carved to emphasize every last grimace and thorn, and painted in appropriate shades of blood red, ashen white and funereal black, they are mighty educational.

SWEDEN

Don't miss:

Ängelholm

25 km north of Helsingborg

THE UFO GLADE
(*UFO-Gläntan*)

In the southern part of the Kro-noskogen forest, near the water-front south of the center Visible at any time. Admission: free. Phone: 0431-821 30 (tourist office).

A flying saucer is said to have landed here on May 18, 1946. That's a whole year before the American UFO sightings that launched a worldwide craze. The young man who saw the alleged craft and communed with its crew is an old man today, having lived on to develop pharmaceutical products whose formulas he claimed to have received from his extraterrestrial visitors. Today the UFO's landing prints are preserved in the woods, along with a large cement sculpture of the mysterious, lentil-shaped, high-masted vessel. It's a monument to the event that goes on record as Sweden's most famous UFO experience. The tourist office leads guided tours to the site every summer, with a special UFO drink included in the price.

Dala Husby

200 km northwest of Stockholm, in the Dalarna region

NATIVE AMERICAN MUSEUM
(*Djusa Indianmuseum*)

House 7, in Djusa, a town just outside Dala Husby, which is 8 kilometers west of Lånangshyt-tan, southeast of Falun. Open June and August, Wednesday–Sunday, noon–6pm; July, Tuesday–Sunday, noon–6pm. Admission: 25 kr. Phone: 225-41121.

In the land of Swedish meatballs and midnight sunshine, Aztec dancers whirl upside down in the midst of a traditional dance, their feathers streaming. A Swedish couple, diehard members of the Wish-I-Was tribe, operate northern Europe's only Native American museum in a big old barn. They've stocked it with an impressively authentic collection of bows and arrows, beaded moccasins, buckskin robes, tomahawks, peace pipes, pine cones, headdresses, hanks of white sage and hundreds of vintage photographs. Taxidermed animals evoking the American West—including the ubiquitous jackalope—jut out in aggressive poses all over the place; actual Indians perform on the grounds outside.

Göteborg

MEDICAL HISTORY MUSEUM
(Medicinhistoriska Museet)

Oterdahlska Huset, Östra Hamngatan 11, near the Göteborg Maritime Center at the harbor. Open Tuesday, Wednesday and Friday, 11am–4pm and Thursday, 11am–8pm. Admission: 20 kr. Phone: 031-711 23 31 or 031-711 23 88.

In this historic building, take a trip down medical memory lane as you examine instruments once used for blood transfusion, amputation, dental surgery, tuberculosis treatments and more. See primitive X-rays that probably caused more cancer than they cured. Statuary and photographs illustrate this parade of infirmity yet further. Göteborg's first ambulance is here too—not much more than a wicker basket on wheels. The linens atop old gurneys still bear suspicious dark stains, and doleful mannequins avoid looking at the metal bowls on the nightstands beside their beds. A rather sexy statue of a woman symbolizing health and fertility watches over it all.

Helsingborg

MEDICAL HISTORY MUSEUM
(Medicinhistoriska Museet)

Bergaliden 20, five blocks inland from the waterfront, just northeast of the city center. Open Tuesday–Thursday, 11am–3pm; Saturday, 1–3pm. Admission: 10 kr. Phone: 042-10 12 79.

A former children's hospital dating back to 1888 has been painstakingly restored so that visitors can relive the thrills, chills and spills of childhood sickness and accidents. Infantile paralysis, anyone? As you tour the ward and respirator room, envision these silent chambers peopled with small, unhappy creatures.

Hillerstorp

60 km south of Jönköping

HIGH CHAPARRAL

6 kilometers southwest of town on road 152, 20 kilometers northwest of Värnamo. Open July, daily, 10am–7pm; June and August, daily, 10am–6pm. Admission: in July, 110 kr; June and August, 100 kr; children under 1 meter tall, free. Phone: 0370-827 00.

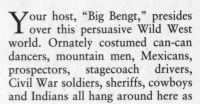

Your host, "Big Bengt," presides over this persuasive Wild West world. Ornately costumed can-can dancers, mountain men, Mexicans, prospectors, stagecoach drivers, Civil War soldiers, sheriffs, cowboys and Indians all hang around here as if they weren't practically in the Arctic Circle. Bison, horses and cattle add an authentic fragrance to a sprawling landscape dotted with teepees, a Mexican village, cabins, waterways, lots of Wild West architecture, stuntmen and windmills. Pan for gold, ride the "Oregon Express," watch the Indian Show, the Mexican Show, the Saloon Show or the Lucky Luke Show—or chuck the old West completely and jump on the waterslide.

Höör

35 km northeast of Lund
STONE-AGE VILLAGE
(Stenåldersbyn)

In the Scania Deer Park (Skånes Djurpark) camping complex, in Jularp, 3 kilometers north of Höör on road 13; Stone Age Village is at the southern end of the park. Open for tours in summer, daily, variable hours; on-site youth hostel is open year-round. Admission: 25 kr. Phone: for current schedule, call 413-532 70.

Wolves howl in the darkness while diners sit around a campfire on animal skins, eating pickled boar and drinking mead. For a real taste of how their slackjawed ancestors lived 4,000 years ago, groups can stay overnight in the village's troglodyte lodgings. Shorter visits include a guided tour of the low-slung houses and verdant grounds, all constructed with the help of Swedish university scientists. Examine ongoing Stone Age activities and get tips on skills such as weaving, primitive cooking and herb lore.

Jukkasjärvi

In Lapland, north of the Arctic Circle, 15 km east of Kiruna
ICE HOTEL
(Ishotellet)

Location may vary year to year, but the town is so small you won't miss the hotel, wherever it is. Open daily every year, late winter–early spring, often December–March. Admission: free to look around; prices vary for hotel rooms. Phone: 0980-66 800 (tourist office).

The snow comes early and deep to Swedish Lapland, and in winter the mercury rarely—if ever—goes above freezing. The Jukkasjärvians put all that white stuff to good use by building a giant hotel complex out of pure snow. No mere igloo this: Aside from several hotel rooms fitted out with traditional Lapp bedding (furs, thick wool blankets, etc.), you'll find a concert hall in use almost daily, a movie theater, a church, a "golf room" for practicing your swing, an art gallery, a sauna (!) and a bar sponsored by a vodka company. The entire structure is made of snow—windows, arches, tables, floor and ceiling. You wouldn't think it was possible until you see it in person. The temperature in the hotel stays at -3° centigrade (27°F) to maintain structural soundness, so don't expect a fireplace in your room. A rival snow hotel in Kemi, Finland (a must-see) competes for the burgeoning snow-tourism business.

MEDICAL HISTORY AND PSYCHIATRIC HOSPITAL MUSEUMS

Both museums share the same entrance, in Pavilion 7 of St. Lars' Hospital in St. Larsparken, south of the town center. Open Tuesday–Friday, 11am–4pm, Sunday, 1–4pm; June–August and December, closed Sundays. Admission: 20 kr; children under 16, free. Phone: 046-15 17 39.

When it opened as a mental hospital in 1879, St. Lars' began the radically new practice of keeping its patients out of straitjackets and encouraging them to do constructive, self-esteem-building activities such as working in the garden, helping with hospital chores and making clothes, shoes and other staples. Secretly hoarding materials, the patients started creating artworks—paintings and drawings, but especially embroidery as writing utensils were scarce while yarn was plentiful. Today these works are on display along with a reconstructed ward room and isolation room. The medical history collection ranges from bloodletting to dialysis to ultrasound.

NOSE COLLECTION

Inside the Museum of Student Life (Studentmuseet Arkivet), at Sandgatan 2, across from the university, a few blocks north of the center of town. Open by ap-

pointment only; call the museum during opening hours to schedule a visit: September–May, Tuesday, 4–8pm, Wednesday, 4–6pm. Admission: free. Phone: 046 13 79 92.

Inside a museum documenting the antics of Scandinavian college life through the centuries is the world's only collection of noses. Over 100 plaster casts of noses are arranged tactfully in a special display area. And not just any noses, either—to be considered worthy of inclusion in "The Nose Academy" you must be a Lund luminary willing to press your face into a bucket of quick-drying goop. Yet not every nose in the collection is from Lund, nor even human: A cast of 16th-century Danish astronomer Tycho Brahe's legendary silver nose is here, as is that of an eel fished out of a river nearby—eels being a culinary favorite in these parts. The noses of a few 19th-century notables were cast from statues. The Unknown Nose serves as a memorial to all those who didn't qualify for nasal immortality.

35 km north of Lund

DINO-LAND

In the Adventureland (Äventyrslandet) amusement park, Blinkarpsvägen. Open June–mid-August, daily, 10am–6pm. Admission: 90 kr. Phone: 0435-911 01.

Besides live pettable pigs, giant toadstools, a castle, boat rides and fairytale tableaux retelling *Snow*

White, *Puss in Boots* and *Little Red Riding Hood*, this park also offers a wooded area populated with dinosaur replicas. Fifty large faux lizards rear and glower despite their homespun misfit quality. A towering Tyrannosaurus Rex, complete with gaping jaws and sharp white teeth, is fitted with overly small forelegs resembling fingers. Triceratops, meanwhile, has an oversize head and looks like a bear wearing a Halloween mask.

Stockholm

ASTRID LINDGREN THEME PARK
(Junibacken)

 On the western shore of Djurgården (the island on which Skansen is located), off Djurgårdsvägen. Open June–August, daily, 9am–6pm; September–May, Wednesday–Sunday, 10am–5pm. Admission: June–August, 85 kr; September–May, 75 kr; children, 55 kr. Phone: 08-660-06-00.

You can peruse a replica of Pippi Longstocking's house here, but she was hardly Astrid Lindgren's only outrageous brainchild. At this park you'll meet the wily overalls-clad cat and many other characters that have inspired mischievous Swedish kids for generations. Live actors in costume portray the characters, and large reconstructions of scenes from the author's books await as visitors ride a miniature train through Lindgren's wacky universe.

Stockholm

MEDICAL HISTORY MUSEUM
(Medicinhistoriska Museet)

 Eugenia T-3, in the Karolinska Hospital (Sjukhuset) complex, northwest of the center. Open Tuesday, Thursday and Friday, 11am–4pm; Wednesday, 11am–7pm; Sunday, noon–4pm. Admission: 40 kr; seniors and students, 30 kr; children, 10 kr. Phone: 8/34 86 20.

A large mural whose colors were chosen to evoke blood, phlegm and gall greets you. Then move on to inspect a mummified head and the bones of a Swedish royal who died in the 13th century. Learn about medical newsmakers like Florence Nightingale and Joseph Lister, then ponder the musical enema machine and a stone removed from King Gustav V's bladder. The reconstructed operating theater should evoke nostalgia; other rooms are devoted to childbirth and orthopedics. Arts and crafts created by mental patients are displayed in the psychiatry room, where an exhibit traces the history of Swedish lobotomies right up to the present.

POSTAL MUSEUM
(Postmuseum)

Lilla Nygatan 6, in the Old City (Metro: Gamla Stan). Open May–August, Tuesday–Sunday, 11am–4pm; September–April, Tuesday and Thursday–Sunday, 11am–4pm, Wednesday, 11am–7pm. Admission: free. Phone: 08-781 17 55.

Changing exhibitions explore the meaning and wonder of mail—from the actual missives of famous artists and writers to love letters culled from a national competition. Stamps and postcards reveal the art that often goes ignored from mailbox to mailbox, while no-longer-private notes give this museum a voyeuristic edge. Temporary exhibits focus on wacky stamp art, from Elvis to Mickey Mouse.

10 km north of Göteborg

THE ORIGINAL COKE BOTTLE

In the Surte Glass Works Museum, Highway 45. Open May–August, Monday–Friday, 10am–5pm; Saturday–Sunday, 10am–3pm; September–March, Tuesday–Friday, noon–3pm, Sunday, 11am–3pm. Phone: 303-33 01 06.

Who knew that the incomparable Coke bottle, so easy to hold, was actually invented by a Swedish guy from Surte? Local glassworker Alexander Samuelsson, after emigrating to America, used his expertise to land a job as design head at a U.S. firm. A beverage manufacturer contracted his company to create a totally unique vessel for its "healthy" new drink. Samuelsson went to work, and the rest is history. Over the past hundred years, countless hapless people around the world have owed their addiction, at least in part, to his talents. The museum displays Samuelsson's original *Coca-Colaflask* alongside other vintage Coke bottles. Over 1,000 other kinds of bottles in all shapes and colors fill out the collection.

TEMPLE OF ECHOES

Just south of town in the Teleborg suburb; go down Teleborgsvägen past the housing tract until you see a large water tower on your left. Visible at any time. Admission: free. Phone: 0470-414 10 (tourist office).

Though it was erected to serve a dull but necessary function, locals love this huge concrete water tower for a whole different reason. Completely by happenstance, the tank's underside is a perfect parabolic curve whose focal point is the ground directly underneath, so any sound you make while standing below the tank gets multiplied multiplied multiplied over and over and over for what feels like forever. For instant applause, clap once.

Vetlanda

70 km southeast of Jönköping

KLEVA MINE
(Kleva Gruva)

 10 kilometers northeast of town; go along 20 road 127, and turn left at Holsbybrunn. Open May–late August, daily, 10am–6pm; late April and late August–September, Saturday–Sunday, 10am–6pm. Admission: 50 kr; children, 30 kr. Phone: 0383-540 33.

A green lake glitters in the depths of this once-flourishing copper mine, which two centuries ago yielded five tons of copper every year but is now the lair only of bats and day-trippers. Electric lights, wooden catwalks and handrails ease the journey through several hundred yards of chilly winding passages cut from solid bedrock. Clad in the helmet that is included in your ticket price, climb and descend the stairs that go from level to level. And consider the local parish clerk who discovered copper here in 1691 but then, legend tells, went insane for disturbing a rock-sprite.

Vimmerby

100 km east of Jönköping

ASTRID LINDGREN'S WORLD
(Astrid Lindgrens Värld)

 Off Lundgatan, at the northern end of town; mini-trains from the center of town take you to the park, or you can walk there

in about 15 minutes. Open June–mid-August, daily, 10am–6pm; May and late August, daily, 10am–5pm. Admission: in high season, 155 kr, children, 90 kr; low season, 90 kr, children, 65 kr. Phone: 0492 159 50 or 0492 798 00.

This theme park based on the anarchist adventures of Pippilotta Viktualla Krysmunte Rullgardina Efraimsdotter Longstocking is located in the author's hometown. Settings from twelve stories by Sweden's most popular author are reconstructed one-third normal size, while actors portraying Pippi and other characters roam around performing scenes from the tales and encouraging visitor participation. The expansive sylvan parkland—where Lindgren herself played as a child—hides cutesy surprises throughout, like hollow trees big enough to climb inside. Those who crave yet more of those bright orange pigtails can visit a cinema on the premises screening film versions of Lindgren's books.

Visby

On the west coast of Gotland

MEDIEVAL WEEK
(Medeltidsveckan)

  Held every year in mid-August on Strandgatan and throughout the Old Town. Admission: free. Phone: 0498-21 99 27 or 0498-21 93 10 (tourist office).

Remembering 1361, when Denmark's King Valdemar arrived in Visby, the festival finds thousands of participants eagerly raising their banners and donning chain-mail, snoods, crowns and helmets. All week, jousting tournaments and pageants fill the streets with evocative grunts, huzzahs and clatter, while creepy mystery plays pitting good against evil are staged in a nearby ruin. Theater troupes, musicians, merchants, jesters and artisans ply their trade, and a week's worth of courses are offered throughout the town in Gregorian chant, juggling and rune reading.

SWITZ-ERLAND

Don't miss:

Aigle

30 km southeast of Lausanne

WINE-LABEL MUSEUM

In the attic of the Maison de la Dîme, adjoining Chateau d'Aigle, straight uphill from the train station. Open April–June and September–October, Tuesday–Sunday, 10am–12:30pm and 2–6pm; July–August, daily, 10am–6pm. Admission: 4 SFr; students

and children, 2 SFr. Phone: (024) 466 21 30.

When you rush to uncork a bottle and guzzle its contents, perhaps you pay little attention to the decorative and informative bits of paper adhering to its glassy flanks. Yet this collection reveals the importance of the wine label. Colorful illustrations of pastoral splendor and deities bespeak vintners' fantasies while the text gives crucial details for drinkers who want to know. Some 1,000 of the museum's 300,000 labels are on display at any one time; the entire collection covers 200 years and fifty-two countries. One exposition area is dedicated to Mediterranean labels, another to Swiss and a third to labels from the rest of the world, lumping together the vintages of California, Australia and China.

Ascona

On Lake Maggiore, across the River Maggia from Locarno

THE CASA ANATTA MUSEUM ON MONTE VERITÀ

Off Via Monte Verità, on Monte Verità hill just northwest of the town center; take bus 33 from the post office, or walk. Open: April–June and September–October, Tuesday–Sunday, 2:30–6pm; July–August, 3–7pm. Admission: 6 SFr; students and children, 4 SFr. Phone: (091) 791 01 81 or 791 03 27.

This seemingly modest commune on a hill overlooking lovely Lake Maggiore is the original source of the 20th century's counterculture movement. Monte Verità was a haven for utopian visionaries and intellectual outcasts, and the ideas they developed here—cooperative living, bodily purification, vegetarianism, benign anarchy, sexual freedom, absolute rebellion against governmental authority—changed the world when they finally found full expression in the '60s. Many luminaries of the avant-garde spent time here, including Isidora Duncan, Kropotkin, key feminist Ida Hofmann, Master Templar Theodor Reuss and a parade of dadaists, nudists, dancers, surrealists, artists and romantic idealists. The buildings of the long-gone commune have been restored and now house exhibits about the revolutionary philosophies, lifestyles and art of Monte Verità's residents. All beats and beatniks, hippies, anarchists, vegetarians, naturists, flower children and free-love advocates should make this pilgrimage at least once.

slices with Swiss precision, the slices arranged side by side as in a grocery store. You'll never eat cold cuts again! Severed faces stare masklike through fluid, while skinned hands, fetal skeletons and severed vulvas fringed with silky hair await inspection. You'll be amazed at how large a tongue is after it's been torn out. On the rear wall are Siamese twins. Also here are a double-skulled skeleton and feet with six and seven toes. The body of a baby strangled by its umbilical cord is displayed, womb and all. Note the similarity between placentas and Portuguese men-o-war.

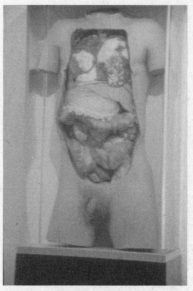

ANATOMY MUSEUM—BASEL

ANATOMY MUSEUM
(Anatomisches Museum)

Pestalozzistrasse 20, northwest of the center; take tram 11 to the St. Johanns-Tor stop. Open Thursday, 2–7pm; Sunday, 10am–2pm. Admission: 4 SFr; students and children, 2 SFr. Phone: (061) 267 35 35.

A human bone tied in a knot and several disembodied patches of tattooed skin are among the first exhibits welcoming visitors to this collection of organs, bones, heads and whole bodies. The specialty here is corpses and heads cut into thin

CARICATURE AND CARTOON MUSEUM
(Karikatur und Cartoon Museum)

St. Alban-Vorstadt 28, near the Münster and the Wettsteinbrücke, just south of the Rhine. Open Wednesday and Saturday, 2–5:30pm; Sunday, 10am–5:30pm. Admission: 6 SFr; students and children, 3 SFr. Phone: (061) 271 13 36.

Spoofing politics and Picasso and everything in between, these sophisticated cartoons from all over the world might make you shudder before they make you laugh. Changing exhibitions focus on individual artists, countries, eras and other themes. You are not likely to escape witnessing that irrepressible European tendency to draw hideous beleaguered characters whose noses take up half their body weight. Casper the Friendly Ghost it ain't.

WINTER'S END CELEBRATION
(Vogel Gryff)

Held every year on the morning of January 13, 20 or 27, alternately; event culminates at noon on the Mittlere Brücke over the Rhine. For more information, call the Tourist Information Office at 268 68 68.

In the frosty morning, crowds gather to watch as a raft glides down the Rhine bearing a pair of drummers, a blasting cannon and the *Wilde Mann*. Garbed in foliage and gripping an uprooted pine, this figure dances slowly, careful to keep his face toward the Kleinbasel district which the river separates from Grossbasel on his left. Under the Mittlere Brücke, a costumed lion joins him, as does the *Vogel Gryff*, a gryphon with dangling red tongue and stiff green wings. The trio dances on the bridge precisely at noon, scrupulously keeping their eyes off Grossbasel as drums beat. The 600-year-old rite anticipates the end of winter, and echoes age-old neighborhood rivalries.

ADOLF WÖLFLI COLLECTION

In the Museum of Fine Arts (Kunstmuseum), Hodlerstrsse 8-12, four blocks north of Bahnhofplatz. Open Tuesday, 10am–9pm; Wednesday–Sunday, 10am–5pm. Admission: 6 SFr; students, 4 SFr. Phone: (031) 311 09 44.

This world-class art museum boasts rooms full of Klee, Matisse, Chagall and Kandinsky. Yawn. What excites *us* is its unique collection of works by legendary schizophrenic doodler Adolf Wölfli. A mentally disturbed child molester, Wölfli took to art in 1899 after he was locked away for life in the nearby Waldau Asylum. The museum's Wölfli exhibit changes every three months, so you never know which of his detailed, hyperbolic explosions of psychosis you might encounter. But you're guaranteed a disturbing glimpse into the inner workings of a very twisted soul.

THE BEARS OF BERN

The bear pits (Bärengraben) *are east of the center, across Nydeggbrücke at Muristalden. Open April–September, daily, 8am–6pm; October–March, daily, 9am–4pm. Admission: free. Phone: (031) 311 66 11 (tourist office).*

The city of Bern is named after bears, a bear appears on its coat of arms and bears adorned Bernese coins and flags for centuries. Some say it's because a long-ago duke vowed to name the town after whatever he killed on his next hunt. But archaeologists say ancient Celts worshiped a bear-goddess here. For whatever reason, Bern has housed live bears since the 1400s. The pits were recently renovated to give the bears more pleasant surroundings (a natural floor, places to clamber around), and their population was reduced to eliminate overcrowding— mostly in response to Swiss animal rights activists. Though captive, the living civic symbols seem content enough. They are not above doing tricks in exchange for snacks flung by fans.

CHILD-EATER FOUNTAIN
(Kindlifresserbrunnen)

On Kornhausplatz, near Marktgasse. Always visible. Admission: free.

The Swiss calmly sit around the stone basin munching snacks and enjoying the flowers in the square, while high on his pedestal a giant in a pointed red hat devours a baby. More infants struggle to escape from his arms, but their fate seems sealed. Also called the Ogre Fountain, the structure dates back to 1544.

CHILD-EATER FOUNTAIN—BERN

Bern

MUSEUM OF PSYCHIATRY
(Psychiatrie-Museum Bern)

Bolligenstrasse 111/117, in the Ostermundigen district northeast of the city center, on the Waldau University campus: From the train station, take bus 15 to "Waldeck," then RBS bus B to the "Klinik." Open Wednesday, 2–4pm, or by appointment. Admission: free. Phone: (031) 930 91 11.

This museum traces Switzerland's attitudes toward mental illness from prehistory straight up to the present. Treatments of all sorts are examined, starting in the good old days when we used to drill holes in people's heads to let out the demons. Then it moves through the shackles-and-straitjackets phase to the beginnings of psychiatry, then to a variety of shock treatments including insulin shock therapy and electroshock. This hospital is where the legendary mentally ill artist Adolf Wölfli spent much of his adult life. The museum has four armoires he decorated, and—the best reason to visit—a collection of amazing artwork created by Wölfli and other Swiss mental patients over the last century.

Bex

45 km southeast of Lausanne

SALT MINE
(Mine de Sel)

Tours of the mine begin in the adjacent village of Le Bouillet; follow the brown signs from Bex. Open April 15–November, daily, 9am–4pm; reservations are mandatory. Admission: 14 SFr. Phone: (024) 463 24 62, or (204) 463 03 30.

This is no mere relic peopled only by mannequins. It's a working mine whose subterranean complex comprises nearly thirty miles. Ride the sleek narrow-gauge train and follow your helmeted guide through three chilly miles of passageways. Navigate stairways cut neatly into the rock and chambers rich in sodium. Visit an underground reservoir, salt springs and a museum while viewing evidence of the mine's 300-year history. Don't lick the walls; it will just make you thirsty.

Bürglen

30 km southeast of Luzern

WILLIAM TELL MUSEUM

In the Wattigwilerturm (Wattigwyler Tower). Open late April–June and September–October, daily, 10–11:30 a.m. and 1:30–5pm; July–August, daily, 9:30am–5:30pm. Admission: 4 SFr; students, 3 SFr; children, 1 SFr. Phone: (041) 870 41 55.

Born in Bürglen, William Tell ignored the hat that a pompous Austrian official had hung from a pole and asked all the locals to revere. The irate Austrian forced Tell to shoot an arrow at an apple balanced on his son's head. The rest is history, but what you probably didn't know is that Tell killed the Austrian with his subsequent arrow. Nor did you know that Tell's son was named Walter. The museum uses paintings, crossbows, lithographs, books, coins, engravings and marksmanship badges to laud the 13th-century archer who has inspired his share of patriotism and cartoons. See the apple-piercing drama replicated over and over and, when you get your second wind, visit the town's Tell Chapel and Tell Fountain.

Cantine de Gandria

On the southern shore of Lake Lugano, across from Gandria

SWISS CUSTOMS MUSEUM
(Museo Doganale Svizzero)

Open Palm Sunday–mid-October, daily, 2:30–5:30pm. Museum is accessible by boat only; departures daily at 1pm from Lugano Giardino. Admission: free. Phone: (091) 910 48 11 or (01) 218 65 11; for information on boats to the museum, call (091) 971 52 23.

Try sneaking into Switzerland with a fake passport. Then you can add your humiliating saga to the others memorialized at this interactive museum, which highlights contraband and the irrepressible human urge to transport it. Life-size models impersonate customs officers interrogating suspects and cooking lonely meals, while actual artifacts include smugglers' boats that were confiscated on Lake Lugano. Mourn slain customs officers in the Memorial Room, admire the drug-sniffing dog and inspect counterfeit designer goods. Roam several floors full of exhibits, then wander a garden whose vintage Swiss boundary stones look like gravemarkers. Then test your skills by playing the museum's "McCustom" computer game: A top score could win you a knife.

Caslano-Lugano

On the western arm of Lake Lugano, just southwest of Lugano

CHOCOLATE MUSEUM
(Museo del Cioccolato)

At the Chocolat Alprose factory, Via Rompada 36. Open Monday–Friday, 9am–6pm; Saturday–Sunday, 9am–5pm. Admission: 3 SFr; children, 1 SFr. Phone: (091) 606 61 43 or 611 88 56.

America wasn't all Columbus discovered, if this museum's proprietors are to be believed. And it's hard to argue with them after they've given you a free sample from the chocolate fountain that spouts thick languid jets near the door. Stand on a catwalk and watch the hypnotic precision of Swiss chocolate manufacture, and peruse exhibits that trace the valiant liberation of cocoa butter from hard little beans. Silver chocolate-serving utensils and automated figures help tell the story of how Western civilization tamed this wild and bitter fruit.

Estavayer-le-Lac

On the eastern shore of Lake Neuchâ-tel

FROG MUSEUM
(Musée des Grenouilles)

In the Musée Communal, 13 rue du Musée. Open March–June and September–October, Tuesday–Sunday, 9–11am and 2–5pm; July–August, daily, 9–11am and 2–5pm; November–February, Saturday–Sunday, 2–5pm. Admission: 4 SFr; students, 3 SFr; children, 2 SFr. Phone: (037) 63 1237.

Taxidermed and accessorized, 108 bloated frogs replicate scenes from 19th-century human life: a schoolroom, a card game, an election, domestic chores and more. Seated on miniature chairs and outfitted with tiny spoons, pointers and knapsacks, the little dead things attend class, cheat at poker, cook meals and march off to war.

Interlaken

JUNGFRAUJOCH ICE PALACE
(Eispalast)

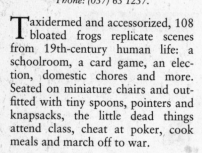

The Ice Palace is at the station on Jungfrau peak. From Interlaken East train station, buy a special combined ticket to Jungfraujoch station (see below for prices). A series of trains on private lines will take you through Lauterbrunnen, Wengen and Kleine Scheidegg and then finally through the mountain up to the peak. Once you're at the station, take the elevator behind the post office to a corridor that leads to the Ice Palace; signs point the way. Open daily from the arrival of the first train until 4pm. Admission to the Ice Palace is free, but to reach it you must buy a round-trip ticket on the Jungfraubahn for 158.20 SFr. Phone: (036) 26 41 11, or (033) 828 72 33.

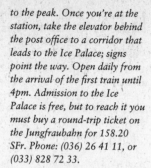

Just getting here is a hair-raising (and hair-raisingly expensive) adventure in itself. After the vertiginous views and oxygen deprivation of the world's highest railway station, a glacier full of wacky ice kitsch may be the last thing on your mind—which only serves to make the experience even weirder. Walk down tunnels deep into the heart of the Alps' longest glacier to a world of permanent ice sculptures. Everything here is carved straight out of the glacier. The technique for making ice art is similar to that for making marble sculpture. To make an ice sumo wrestler, for example, simply remove all the parts of the glacier that *aren't* sumo-shaped. Which is exactly what they did here. They also removed all the ice that wasn't a piano, a car, a room full of furniture, Sherlock Holmes, a cafe and an ever-changing selection of incongruous creations. Cold? You bet it's cold. Very cold.

Interlaken

ST. BEATUS CAVES
(St. Beatus-Höhlen)

8 kilometers west of Interlaken, off the road running along the shore of the Thuner See, just west

of the town of Sundlauenen; signs clearly indicate the caves' entrance. Open Palm Sunday –October, daily, 10:30am–5pm. Admission: 14 SFr; students 12 SFr; children, 6 SFr. Phone: (033) 841 16 43.

The Irish holy man St. Beatus banished a dragon that dwelt in this cliffside cavern. Then he installed himself in the dragon's lair to Christianize the ungodly Swiss. After his death the cave became a pilgrimage site, though it was not until centuries later that speleologists discovered a labyrinth of spooky passages behind the shrine. Now this kooky attraction houses a waxwork depicting a topless prehistoric cave family, and another showing a bedraggled St. Beatus reading the Bible in his rudimentary troglodytic hermitage. Passageways lead past underground pools, waterfalls, stalagmites and formations with names like the "Witches' Cauldron." A large green dragon roars beside the entrance; kids can slide down his sinuous tail to the picnic area. Next door, a speleology museum glorifies the adventurers who plunge into the earth for the hell of it.

La Chaux-de-Fonds

50 km northwest of Bern, on the French border

INTERNATIONAL CLOCK MUSEUM
(Musée International d'Horlogerie)

29 rue des Musées. Open June–September, Tuesday–Sunday, 10am–5pm; October–May, Tuesday–Sunday, 10am–noon and 2–5pm. Admission: 8 SFr.

Phone: (032) 967 6861 or 967 6889.

Who else but the Swiss could create such an exhaustive homage to humankind's long struggle to master time? Pompously exhibited against postmodern concrete and curved glass, the collection's thousands of timepieces date back to intricately engraved but inaccurate Renaissance watches, and progress through centuries of jeweled and enameled models to our own era's digital meanderings. Many are displayed partially dissected with their workings on view, but hey—does anybody really know what time it is?

La Tour-de-Peilz

20 km southeast of Lausanne

SWISS MUSEUM OF GAMES
(Musée Suisse du Jeu)

In the Château de La Tour-de-Peilz, rue du Château 11, near the waterfront just east of Vevey. Open Tuesday–Sunday, 2–6pm. Admission: 6 SFr; students, 3 SFr; children, free. Phone: (021) 944 40 50.

Competitive types who get off on crushing their opponents in contrived ritual battles will feel right at home here. In this medieval castle, a historic collection covers games of strategy, games of chance, games of skill and role-playing games, not to mention educational games. Cards, darts and colorful clowns that ask you to assault them are only the beginning. Visitors are encouraged to indulge their bloodthirsty urges by playing games right then and there, including chess in the castle garden with knee-high plastic chessmen.

Lausanne

COLLECTION OF "ART BRUT"

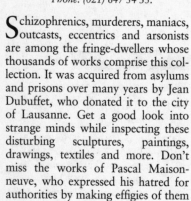

Chateau de Beaulieu, Avenue des Bergières 11, near Avenue de Beaulieu, northwest of the city center; take bus 3. Open Tuesday-Sunday, 11am–1pm and 2–6pm. Admission: 6 SFr; students, 4 SFr; under 16, free. Phone: (021) 647 54 35.

Schizophrenics, murderers, maniacs, outcasts, eccentrics and arsonists are among the fringe-dwellers whose thousands of works comprise this collection. It was acquired from asylums and prisons over many years by Jean Dubuffet, who donated it to the city of Lausanne. Get a good look into strange minds while inspecting these disturbing sculptures, paintings, drawings, textiles and more. Don't miss the works of Pascal Maisonneuve, who expressed his hatred for authorities by making effigies of them from seashells.

Lausanne

MUSEUM OF THE HUMAN HAND
(Musée de la Main de l'Homme)

At the Fondation Claude Verdan, rue du Bugnon 21, north of the train station and the lake. Open Tuesday–Wednesday and Friday–Sunday, 1–7pm; Thursday, 1–8pm. Admission: 6 SFr;

students and children, 3 SFr. Phone: (021) 314 49 55.

In his work as a surgeon who reconstructed damaged hands, Dr. Claude Verdan came to believe that prehension is the key to our species' success. The fact that we have hands and not hooves or paws and can easily lift pitchers of Kool-Aid and operate tweezers is why we're more productive than, say, zebras. Changing exhibitions use objects of art, science and medicine to celebrate the human hand in its power and diversity. X-rays, sculptures, rubber models and dissected specimens spotlight the hand's role in world domination.

Locarno

ELISARION MUSEUM
(Museo Elisarion)

Via R. Simen 3, in the northeastern suburb of Minusio. Open Monday–Tuesday, 2–5pm. Admission: free. Phone: (091) 751 03 33.

Occupying one room in a cultural and conference center, this museum celebrates the art of Elisar von Kupffer. The Estonian-born painter and poet, who died here in 1942, launched a more-or-less anti-Christian ideology. It focused on the relationship between clarity and chaos (he called it *clarismo*), and it inspired the paintings on display here. Mythical figures, wryly smiling ample-buttocked nudes, flowers, and helmets in tropical hues—stylistically the work has a definite touch of Gauguin, though one Roman soldier looks a great deal like John Lennon. If you long to jump on the *clarismo* bandwagon, an on-site library offers volumes on the topic.

45 km south of Luzern

SHERLOCK HOLMES MUSEUM

Conan Doyle Platz, near the train station. Open January–April, Wednesday–Sunday, 3–6pm; May–September, daily, 10am–6pm. Admission: 3.80 SFr; children, 2.80 SFr. Phone: (033) 971 42 21.

Arthur Conan Doyle was a frequent guest in these mountains. He chose to kill off the great detective at the Reichenbach falls, which bears a commemorative plaque and which you can visit on a funicular. The museum boasts a replica of Holmes' messy living room, as well as Conan Doyle lore and trivia. On display are two bullets resembling those with which Watson was once wounded, and a Swiss walking stick resembling the one Holmes *might* have used en route to his meeting with Moriarty. An Afghan War medal resembles one to which Watson, as a veteran, was entitled. A deerstalker hat appears alongside a black top hat and a homburg with the revelation that Holmes wears the homburg in as many as twenty-two illustrations and the top hat in nine, but the deerstalker in only eight. Also here are Valentines futilely sent to Holmes.

Lucerne (Luzern)

GLACIER GARDEN AND HALL OF MIRRORS
(Gletscheregarten und Spiegellabyrinth)

Denkmalstrasse 4, a few blocks north of the Vierwaldstattersee. Open April–October, daily, 9am–6pm; November–February, Tuesday–Sunday, 10am–5pm; March, daily, 10am–5pm. Admission: 8 SFr; students, 6 SFr; children, 4.50 SFr. Phone: (041) 410 43 40.

Lucerne was a palm-fringed paradise for dinosaurs. But that was 20 million years ago, and then the Ice Age came and spoiled the fun. Detailed dioramas depict what Lucerne must have looked like at various points in the earth's history, with glaciers and tropical plants deuling it out for eternity. Today this covered "garden," discovered in 1872, whose smooth stone is all cratered and sculpted by millennia of ice and water, makes you realize that human life lasts but an instant. In this lighthearted spirit, move on to the Hall of Mirrors, built for a world's fair in 1896. Patterned after the Alhambra, it's replete with impossible twists and turns—try not to walk face first into its walls of glass too many times in a row.

Melide

5 km south of Lugano

MINIATURE SWITZERLAND
(Swiss Miniatur)

 On the lakefront (no address), south side of Melide: follow the signs: It's hard to miss, as it's the only attraction in town; trains run frequently from Lugano to Melide. Open mid-March–October, daily, 9am–6pm. Admission: 11 SFr; children, 6 SFr. Phone: (091) 640 10 60.

This lakeside park is littered with precision-engineered miniature reproductions of what seems like every single structure and vehicle in Switzerland—not just castles and churches, but farmhouses, factories, restaurants, schools, lakes, steamships, trains, bridges, mountains, harbors, country estates, plazas, towers, airports, even shopping centers. As the management proudly points out, the only authentic features *Swiss Miniatur* lacks are tiny tax collectors, striking workers and mean policemen. Instead, dinky folk dancers twirl merrily and contented peasants parade down Main Street with their diminutive cows. We could learn a thing or two from them.

St-Léonard

5 km southeast of Sion

SUBTERRANEAN LAKE
(Lac Souterrain)

 Just outside the village of St-Léonard; signs point the way. Open June–September, daily, 9am–5pm; March 15–October, daily, 9am–5pm. Admission: 6 SFr; teenagers, 4 SFr; children, 2 SFr. Phone: (027) 203 22 66.

Extending a sinuous 300 meters, blessed with a sandy beach and overhung with natural rock archways, the waters of Europe's largest underground lake lie mirror-smooth in their windless realm. Once used by local vintners to cool bottles of wine, the lake was first navigated in the '40s and now glints with green and blue tints as visitors glide around in simple wooden rowboats. Marble and calcite form ominous chambers, all under the protection of *Notre Dame des Gouffres* (Our Lady of the Abysses), whose statue the cave's first proprietors promptly installed in an underground shrine.

SUBTERRANEAN LAKE—ST.-LÉONARD

Schönenwerd

40 km southeast of Basel

BALLY SHOE MUSEUM
(Bally Schuhmuseum)

 Haus zum Felsgarten, Gösgerstr. 15, just south of the train station. Open January–mid-July and mid-August–mid-December, the last Friday of the month; guided tours at 2:30 and 4pm. Admission: free, but for a price it is possible to arrange tours on evenings and Saturdays. Phone: (062) 858 26 41.

Pharaonic sandals, an English archbishop's boots and Goethe's slip-ons are here. Over 5,000 years' worth of specimens step out in this collection, begun by the shoemaking Bally family 100 years ago. Teaching world history, sociology, anthropology and psychology from the ground up, the shoes reveal more than you'd ever suspect about medieval castles or the French Revolution. Learn how Louis XIV launched a fad for red leather high heels, how the women of bygone Baghdad increased their height with platform slippers and how the rich ladies of 18th-century Europe—dressed in useless satin mules—weren't meant to leave their homes at all. Contemplate the oppressiveness of *Cinderella*. Accompanying the footwear are utensils and other artifacts in shoe shapes.

Valais Canton

Southwestern corner of the country

COW BATTLES
(Combats de Reines)

 The battles take place in several towns throughout the canton, including Aproz, Sembrancher, Turtmann, and others; buses run from Sion, the capital of the region, to the battle towns. The staged contests are usually held on Sundays in March, April and May, as well as a few in early October. Admission: Each battle has its own price, though generally the tickets are not very expensive. Phone: (027) 322 31 61 (Valais Tourist Office), or (027) 324 61 11 (Banque Cantonale du Valais, the sponsor).

The genetically aggressive cattle in this part of Switzerland battle among themselves for the title of Queen of the Mountains and the right to lead the herds up to the spring grazing grounds. What makes this naturally occurring annual ritual unique is that only the females of the species fight for supremacy, while the nerdy bulls sit around and watch. Not content to leave nature alone, the Swiss have turned the instinctual struggle into a tightly orchestrated professional cow-battle season, with a knockout format leading to the climactic championship fight, usually held in Aproz in mid-May. Tremendous crowds show up to watch the combats and place bets. The battles themselves are fierce but bloodless, a little like bovine sumo: The massive black cows lunge at each other, lock horns and bash heads, each attempting to force the other off the field.

They push mightily amidst the clangor of cowbells, until one cries uncle (aunt?) and flees for the sidelines. The grand champion is garlanded, declared queen and gets to lead the pack on the yearly migration to greener pastures.

Vevey

17 km southeast of Lausanne

ALIMENTARIUM

Rue du Léman at Quai Perdonnet, near the shore of Lac Léman. Open in summer, Tuesday–Sunday, 10am–5pm; winter, 10am–noon and 2–5pm. Admission: 6 SFr; students, and children, 4 SFr; children under 12, free. Phone: (021) 924 41 11.

Cinnamon rolls might lose their playful appeal after you've seen the subject of food exhaustively deconstructed at this museum. Dozens of exhibits explore the history, science and sociology of what we eat, why we eat it and what it does to us. Reconstructed dwellings from around the world illustrate how diners of various cultures acquire, prepare and devour their chow—and even its role in religion. Learn why humans use ketchup and animals don't, and examine the beady stare of a composite chicken-fish-pig-sheep-steer sculpture that might make you give up meat altogether.

Wiler

30 km northwest of Brig, in the Lötschental valley.

UGLY MASK PARADE

Held every year on the Saturday before Shrove Tuesday (Mardi Gras). Phone: (028) 49 13 88 (tourist office).

It's not Halloween, but hideous masks are popping up all over Valais Canton's Lötschental Valley, including the villages of Ferden, Kippel, Wiler, Ried, Blatten and Fafleralp. Intended for the ubiquitous purpose of scaring away evil spirits, the grotesque wooden masks are augmented with animal fur and animal teeth to create distended, grimacing, goggle-eyed countenances. Groups of masked youths rampage around looking frightful during the days before Shrove Tuesday—a tradition that in the past drew recriminations from the Church. At the Saturday parade, wearers compete to see whose mask is the ugliest.

Winterthur

TECHNORAMA

Technoramastrasse 1; from Zurich Hauptbahnhof take suburban line 12 to Oberwinterthur. Open Tuesday–Sunday, 10am–5pm. Admission: 15 SFr; students, 10 SFr; children 8 SFr. Phone: (052) 243 05 05.

Over 400 intriguing hands-on displays give you a whole new lease on light, sound, mathematics and more. At this interactive science wonderland, watch your hair jump when you touch the half-million-volt generator. Then conduct an electromagnetically sensitive Theremin for that "Good Vibrations" sound. Play with electrons in the Plasma Ball, see yourself float in the Anti-gravity Mirror, match wits with a robot, spark a sandstorm, explore M.C. Escher's impossible staircase and touch a tornado. Then ride the kiddie train.

28 km north of Lausanne

HOUSE OF ELSEWHERE (MUSEUM OF SCIENCE FICTION, UTOPIAS AND EXTRAORDINARY VOYAGES)
(Maison d'Ailleurs)

 Place Pestalozzi 14, near the castle. Open Tuesday–Sunday, 2–6pm. Admission: 8 SFr; students and children, 5 SFr. Phone: (024) 425 64 38.

Big-breasted hitchhikers from outer space are *de rigueur* here, where changing exhibitions feature various artists, writers and other themes. On permanent display is the lifetime collection of a Swiss sci-fi fan whose toys, records, posters and artworks recount the diversity of droids and death planets. Among over 30,000 books in the collection are some that offer rare glimpses of protofantasy dating back as far as the 17th century.

27 km south of Zurich

HELL GROTTOES
(Höllgrotten)

 Just southeast of Baar, which is 3 kilometers north of Zug; walk from Baar's train station, or take a bus from Baar's Lorzentobelbrücke stop. Open April–October, 9am–noon and 1–5:30pm. Admission: 7 SFr; students and children, 3.50 SFr. Phone: (041) 761 83 70.

Limestone formations that look like clusters of lymph nodes and festoons of disembodied lungs are evidence that this might in fact be hell. But the cave's proprietors have slyly named these features "Grapes" and the "Magic Castle." Also here is the "Nymph's Grotto," with what is obviously a giant petrified human brain ascending from its still waters—but which, the proprietors insist, is called the "Beehive." As you walk along guided paths to see the depths, appropriately lit in yellow hues, no tour guides are here to lead the way. You're on your own in hell.

THE BEYER WATCH MUSEUM
(Museum der Zeitmessung Beyer)

 Bahnhofstrasse 31. Open Monday–Friday, 2–6pm. Admission: free. Phone: (01) 221 10 80.

Sundials, sand- and water-clocks are part of Switzerland's largest privately owned clock collection, which was assembled by a watchmaker. It all inspires daydreams of what you'd buy if your dollars were worth anything in this country. Primitive timepieces dating back to 1400 B.C.E stand in contrast to jewel-studded creations like the soaring pagoda clock and amazingly intricate specimens like an all-ivory pocket-watch and the curious eyeball watch.

BURNING THE "BÖÖGG"
(Sechseläuten)

Held every year on the third Monday in April; Böögg is lit at 6pm on the Sechseläutenplatz, between Theaterstrasse and Utoquai on the shore of the Zurichsee. For more information, call (01) 853 17 77.

Come late April, Zurichers say "Enough is enough" and burn winter in effigy. In this 650-year-old ritual, a huge cotton-wool snowman called the Böögg is stuffed with fireworks, mounted on a pole and set into a towering pile of brushwood. After an elaborate parade, at the stroke of six (which is what *Sechseläuten* means) the wood is torched and riders gallop around the pyre. Thousands gather to watch flames leap toward the Böögg, who stands calmly, smoking a pipe and wearing a hat. When the snowman is blown to bits in a storm of fireworks, spring begins.

JOHANN JACOBS MUSEUM OF COFFEE

Seefeldquai 17, at Feldeggstrasse, on the shore of the Zurichsee. Open Friday–Saturday, 2–5pm; Sunday, 10am–5pm. Admission: free. Phone: (01) 388 61 51.

There's more to your cup of joe than mere beans. This museum dedicated to the cultural history of the drink displays porcelain and silver coffeepots, coffee cups, coffee spoons and other utensils as well as drawings, paintings and sculpture depicting humankind's long, happy java jive. Interesting historical facts, such as how coffee's popularity led to the development of porcelain and modern ceramics, are revealed through artifacts. The new cafés of the 18th century led to a mixing of social classes, explored in an impressive collection of contemporaneous artworks. European attitudes toward colonial natives is another theme in the artworks.

MEDICAL HISTORY MUSEUM
(Medizinhistorisches Museum)

Rämistr. 71, in Zurich University's main building. Open Tuesday–Friday, 1–6pm; Saturday–Sunday, 11am–5pm. Admission: free. Phone: (01) 257 22 98.

A replica of an 18th-century pharmacy is outfitted with everything the doctor ordered, including an alligator, a starfish, a blowfish and eels. Landmarks and low points of European medicine dating back to prehistoric times all have their place in this collection: leprosy, the plague, syphilis, smallpox, TB and AIDS. Implements and equipment offer glimpses into surgery's murky heritage. Other exhibits focus on anesthesia, X-rays and more topics you would rather not learn about firsthand.

Zurich

MUSEUM OF SWISS HOTELS AND TOURISM
(Museum Schweizer Hotellerie und Tourismus)

Trittligasse 8, in the Old Town; museum is in the basement. Open Wednesday and Friday, 2–5pm; Saturday, 11am–5pm; Sunday, 11am–1pm. Admission: free. Phone: 391 82 78.

Countless honeymoon dreams have unfurled or unraveled in Swiss hotels. Their vigilantly engineered rustic charm and pristine glamor are irresistible, and everyone knows how much Diana and Fergie loved those Alpine resorts. Changing exhibitions at this museum, snug in medieval lodgings, focus on different regions, cities, mountains and trends in Swiss tourism. Hotel china and silverware feature prominently, along with furniture and dioramas showing what awaits those who have nothing to fear from yodeling, fondue and alpenhorns.

Zurich

WAX-MODEL COLLECTION
(Moulagensammlung)

Haldenbachstr. 14, north of the center. Open Wednesday, 2–8pm. Admission: free. Phone: 252 46 47.

Say you've got a big paper to write on tertiary syphilis. It's due tomorrow but try as you might, you can't find a single tertiary-syphilis patient who will hold still while you examine his or her disfigured flesh. Or, hey, say you've just got to study smallpox lesions, right now. What to do? Foresightfully guarding against such crises, this wax-model collection was begun in 1917. The lifelike handcrafted models replicate faces, hands and other parts of bodies afflicted with skin diseases and other afflictions. Sleekly mounted, their cheeks tinted with a realistic pink blush offset by the brighter colors of inflammation, necrosis and simulated pus, they invite hours of inspection.

Zurich

ZIC-ZAC ROCK-HOTEL

Marktgasse 17, near Rathausbrucke, several blocks south of the central train station. Rooms range from 65 SFr to 240 SFr. Phone: 01-261 21 81.

After a lifetime of obsessing about your favorite band, Heart, you can finally take the dream one step further. Each of the thirty-six rooms in this pair of restored medieval townhouses is decorated with a different rock act in mind—including Heart. Pay homage to Led Zeppelin, the Stones, Bryan Addams and many more, without even having to wake up.

VATICAN CITY

Don't miss:

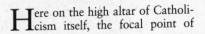

Vatican City

X-RATED HIGH ALTAR

In St. Peter's Basilica (on Piazza San Pietro), directly beneath the dome in the center of the church, under the Baldacchino, a bronze canopy with spiraling columns. Open April–September, daily, 7am–7pm; October–March, daily, 7am–6pm. Admission: free. Phone: (06) 698.84466 (Vatican Information Office).

Here on the high altar of Catholicism itself, the focal point of worldwide Christianity, you will find eight carvings of a woman's genitals. Yes, the whole works in surprising anatomic detail. This papal altar was commissioned by Urban VIII as a sign of gratitude for his niece having survived a troubled pregnancy. Bernini, the sculptor commissioned to do the job, decided to tell the story of the difficult birth through carvings on the column bases around the altar. Each of eight panels shows the niece's face, belly and genitals. Three large bees from the Pope's coat of arms substitute for the woman's breasts and navel. As the pregnancy progresses, her face grows more and more pained, her stomach swells, and her labia start to open up. Near the end, a strange foliate head seems to emerge from her vagina as she screams in agony, but in the final scene all is well. A baby's face replaces hers and everything returns to normal "down there." Over the centuries, many have speculated as to the occult significance of such overt feminine sexuality on the Pope's private altar, but its true meaning may never be known. As a counterpoint, numerous pudgy angels and Cupids throughout the basilica sport life-size penises, to ensure equal exposure for both genders.

Calendar of Weird Festivals

ANNUAL DATE	FESTIVAL	LOCATION
January 8	Women's Domination Days (*Gynaecocratia*)	Northern Greece
January 13, 20 or 27	Winter's End Celebration (*Vogel Gryff*)	Basel, Switzerland
February 5	Mayoresses Festivals	Towns throughout Spain
March 9	Traffic Blessing	Rome, Italy
March 12–19	Las Fallas Bonfire Festival	Valencia, Spain
Sundays in March, April and May	Cow Battles (main season)	Valais Canton, Switzerland
Sunday seven weeks before Easter 'til Shrove Tuesday	Busójárás Procession	Mohács, Hungary
Thursday before Shrove Tuesday	Battle of the Oranges	Ivrea, Italy
Saturday before Shrove Tuesday	Ugly Mask Parade	Wiler, Switzerland
Shrove Tuesday	Carnival of the Gilles	Binche, Belgium
Shrove Tuesday	Pancake Race	Lichfield, Great Britain
Shrove Tuesday	Free-for-all Football	Sedgefield, Great Britain
Shrovetide, around Shrove Tuesday	Kurenti Procession	Ptuj, Slovenia
The week preceding Easter	Holy Week	Zamora, Spain
Holy Thursday	Dance of Death	Verges, Spain
Third Monday in April	Burning the Böögg (*Sechseläuten*)	Zurich, Switzerland
April 23	Moors and Christians Festival	Alcoy, Spain
April 30	Witches' Festival (*Walpurgisfeier*)	Bad Harzburg, Germany
April 30	*Walpurgisnacht*	Thale, Germany
May 1	Hobby Horse	Minehead, Great Britain
May 1	'Obby 'Oss	Padstow, Great Britain
Saturday before the first Sunday in May	Liquefaction of San Gennaro's Blood (first event)	Naples, Italy
2nd Sunday in May	Cat Parade and Festival	Ieper, Belgium

ANNUAL DATE	FESTIVAL	LOCATION
Sundays, mid-May–mid-September	Pied Piper Play	Hameln (Hamelin), Germany
May 15	Corsa dei Ceri	Gubbio, Italy
May 21	Firewalking Rituals *(Anastenaria)*	Northern Greece
Late May	Sexhibition Erotic Fair	Helsinki, Finland
Ascension Day (late May)	Procession of the Holy Blood	Brugge, Belgium
Trinity Sunday (late May or early June)	Battle of the Lumeçon	Mons, Belgium
The Tuesday following Whitsunday (late May or early June)	Hopping Procession of St. Willibrord	Echternach, Luxembourg
First Sunday after Pentecost (late May or early June)	Holy Blood Procession	Voormezele, Belgium
Late May or early June	Cotswold Olimpick Games	Chipping Campden, Great Britain
Corpus Christi (a Sunday in June)	Infioratas	Lazio region, Italy
June 16	Bloomsday	Dublin, Ireland
June 23	Firewalking	San Pedro Manrique, Spain
June 27	Witches' Sabbat	Ellezelles, Belgium
Last weekend in June	Shrimp Pageant	Osstduinkerke, Belgium
Last Sunday in June	Tarasque Parade	Tarascon, France
Last Sunday in June	*Gioco del Ponte*	Pisa, Italy
Summer, every four years	Nemean Games	Nemea, Greece
July 2	Palio of Siena (first race)	Siena, Italy
First week in July	*Ommegang*	Brussels, Belgium
July 20	Witches' Sabbath	
July 23–24	The Mysteries of St. Cristina	Vielsalm, Belgium Bolsena, Italy
Last Sunday in July	Croagh Patrick Mountain-Climbing Pilgrimage	Murrisk, Ireland
Last Sunday in July (every other year)	Witches' Parade	Beselare, Belgium
Late July or early August	Medieval Market	Turku, Finland
First Sunday in August	Viking Pilgrimage	Catoira, Spain

ANNUAL DATE	FESTIVAL	LOCATION
A Friday in early August	The Burry Man	South Queensferry, Great Britain
August 10, 11 and 12	Puck Fair	Killorglin, Ireland
Mid-August	Slaying-the-Dragon	Furth im Wald, Germany
Mid-August	Medieval Week	Visby, Sweden
August 15	Snake-Handling Festival	Markopoulo, Greece
August 16	Palio of Siena (second race)	Siena, Italy
Last week in August	Beatle Week	Liverpool, Great Britain
Last Wednesday in August	La Tomatina Tomato Fight	Buñol, Spain
Last Friday and Saturday in August	European Middle Ages Festival	Horsens, Denmark
Last weekend in August	Medieval Festival	Eastbourne, Great Britain
September 3	Santa Rosa's Tower Procession	Viterbo, Italy
The Monday after the first Sunday after September 4	Abbots Bromley Horn Dance	Abbots Bromley, Great Britain
Second weekend in September on even-numbered years	Living Chess Game	Marostica, Italy
Second and third Sundays in September	*Giostra della Quintana*	Foligno, Italy
Third Saturday in September	Crab Fair	Egremont, Great Britain
September 19	Liquefaction of San Gennaro's Blood (second event)	Naples, Italy
First Sunday in October	Donkey Palio	Alba, Italy
Sundays in early October	Cow Battles (late season)	Valais Canton, Switzerland
November 3	Hunters' Mass	Saint-Hubert, Belgium
November 5	Guy Fawkes Night (Bonfire Night)	Lewes, Great Britain

Category Indexes

NATURAL WONDERS

RELIGIOUS CURIOSITIES

REMNANTS OF OPPRESSION

STRANGE TOWNS

General Index